No Cheering
in the
Press Box

Newly Revised and Expanded

Recorded and Edited by
Jerome Holtzman

Henry Holt and Company
New York

Henry Holt and Company, Inc.
Publishers since 1866
115 West 18th Street
New York, New York 10011

Henry Holt® is a registered trademark
of Henry Holt and Company, Inc.

Published in Canada by Fitzhenry & Whiteside Ltd.,
195 Allstate Parkway, Markham, Ontario L3R 4T8.

Library of Congress Cataloging-in-Publication Data
No cheering in the press box / [edited by]
Jerome Holtzman.—Newly rev. and expanded, 1st rev. ed.
p.   cm.
First-person accounts by sportswriters, recorded 1971–1973.
1. Sportswriters—United States—Biography.
I. Holtzman, Jerome.
GV742.4.N6   1995   95-13335
070.4'49'7960922—dc20   CIP

ISBN 0-8050-3824-8
ISBN 0-8050-3823-X (An Owl Book: pbk.)

Henry Holt books are available for special promotions
and premiums. For details contact: Director, Special Markets.

First published in hardcover in 1973 by
Holt, Rinehart and Winston.

First Revised Edition—1995

Designed by Sandra Kandrac

Printed in the United States of America
All first editions are printed on acid-free paper.∞

1   2   3   4   5   6   7   8   9   10
1   2   3   4   5   6   7   8   9   10
(pbk.)

Several chapters of this book first appeared in *California Living,*
The Chicagoan, Midwest Magazine, New York, and *The Philadelphian.*

To Marilyn, my once and future queen

"There is no remembrance of former things; neither shall there be any remembrance of things that are to come with those that shall come after."

Ecclesiastes

Contents

Editor's Note

This is the second edition of *No Cheering in the Press Box*, twenty-two years after the original, and it includes six new chapters: Al Abrams of Pittsburgh; Fred Russell, Nashville; Wendell Smith, Pittsburgh and Chicago; Gene Kessler, Chicago; Ray Gillespie, St. Louis; Jim Schlemmer, Akron.

All of these interviews were done in the same period as the others, from 1971 through 1973. I thought of the possibility of starting anew, collecting the memoirs of some of the sportswriters who had been overlooked. I decided leaping two decades forward would affect the integrity of the book.

When the first edition was approaching completion, my editor, the late Donald Hutter, who was very good, insisted that we go to press after eighteen chapters. Otherwise, we would have missed the deadline. I was disappointed but nonetheless satisfied that the most interesting interviews were included.

Two years ago, for the first time since publication, I exhumed some of the material. To my surprise, I discovered the quality of the six additional chapters is equal to those previously offered. With this edition, twenty-four of the forty-four interviews are now in print.

The only men considered were of the two generations prior to mine, men who had devoted a major portion of their working lives—if not their entire working lives—to sportswriting. None of the interviewees was given the opportunity to edit or alter his remarks. Nor did I take editorial liberty in regard to interpretation or the insertion of any words or comments.

Once again I want to acknowledge my debt to the forty-four sportswriters, almost all of whom are deceased. In alphabetical order:

Al Abrams, Jesse Abramson, Les Biederman, Ned Brown, Warren Brown, Jimmy Cannon, John Carmichael, Joe Cashman, Bob Considine, Dan Daniel, Allison Danzig, John Drebinger, Braven Dyer, Nat Fleischer, Stanley Frank, Ford Frick, Paul Gallico, Ray Gillespie, Tommy Holmes, Al Horwits, Marshall Hunt, Abe Kemp, Gene Kessler, John Kieran, Joe King, Al Laney, Fred Lieb, Lloyd McGowan, Edgar Munzel, Harold Parrott, Cy Peterman, Shirley Povich, Ed Prell, Fred Russell, Jim Schlemmer, Gary Schumacher, Chet Smith, Ken Smith, Walter (Red) Smith, Wendell Smith, Wilfrid Smith, George Strickler, John R. Tunis, and Richards Vidmer.

Jerome Holtzman
Evanston, Illinois
May 1995

No Cheering
in the
Press Box

No Cheering
in the
Press Box

Dan Daniel

Dan Daniel was once described, and accurately so, as the Arnold Toynbee of baseball. He wrote baseball for more than sixty years, covering for a variety of New York papers, and was also the national correspondent for The Sporting News, *a weekly now embracing all sports but in Mr. Daniel's time devoted exclusively to baseball. By his own estimate, Mr. Daniel wrote five thousand words a week for* The Sporting News. *He was baseball's high priest, alternately reporting and editorializing, and constantly issuing encyclicals for present and future conduct.*

After retiring from newspaper work, but still vigorous at eighty, he put in a half day as an associate editor at Ring *magazine, a boxing monthly. It was in the* Ring *office that I found him, bright and alert, strong of voice. He expressed pleasure that he hadn't severed his connection with baseball. "Believe it or not," he said, "I do stories for Little League. I keep up. I just wrote a story for their World Series program on the use of aluminum bats."*

At the end of the interview, as if by instinct, Mr. Daniel had a message for baseball, which had been losing ground to football. "I will never stop loving baseball," he said, his voice rising with authority. "It's the national pastime, no matter what. But I do wish baseball would put on a stronger front. Please! Please! A stronger front." Mr. Daniel was elected to the baseball Hall of Fame in Cooperstown, New York, in 1973. He died in 1981 at the age of ninety-one in Pompano Beach, Florida.

I was one of the fastest writers who ever covered baseball. If it didn't go fast, it was no good. I quit. It had to be fast. If the ideas didn't come quickly, if the response wasn't immediate and I dragged, then it meant my inward conscience was not with the idea. I just quit, that's all. I had a knack of writing fast and, mostly, I did things the first time out of the box. It had to be good the first time. I couldn't afford the time to dillydally too much. I worked best in the morning, starting at nine o'clock. It never mattered where I was—home, at the ball park, in the hotel, on the trains. I could write anywhere. There were times when I got tired of writing, but I enjoyed the fun of baseball and everything about it until that damn night ball came in. That ruined the whole business.

Forty years on the road with a ball club. But I have no regrets. You see, the conditions were so different. After the game you came back to the hotel, had your dinner, went up to your room and batted out your game story. Then you went down to the lobby, and who was in the lobby? The manager, the coaches, and a few players. I was not a gourmet. I ate in the hotel, usually. I didn't chase around. I didn't go to movies. I was pretty much addicted to the hard and fast lines of the job. I had very few diversions. I decided when I left home it was business. I had all the diversions I needed when I got back home to my family.

It was tough on my family. I spent thousands of nights on the road, but I didn't regret it because in those days baseball writing was the number-one assignment on any paper. Now, it's number one hundred. This thing of night baseball, this dashing down to the clubhouse after the game to interview the manager and dashing back to the press box. By that time the guy who runs the elevator has gone home. You have to run up five or six flights, sit down and bat out your story, and you're batting it out against time. Or if it's a getaway day, you're batting it out against the manager's idea of when the plane should leave. Or if it isn't the plane, you have trouble getting a taxi after the ball game. Some places it's impossible.

Scoops? Oh, I had a hundred of 'em. My last big story was on the *World-Telegram*, when Dan Topping was chief of the works with the Yankees. He gave me a story, in privacy, but it wasn't off the record. I could do what I wanted. I printed. The other men covering the Yankees hollered murder. Somebody big had signed a contract, I can't recollect who it was. But it was a big story. The other fellows went to Topping, and he denied the story. Insisted he didn't say it. The man running the *World-Telegram* was delighted with my dilemma. He wanted me out.

About two weeks later the Yankees had a press conference. Topping did something no other baseball executive ever did in the past or has done since. In front of two hundred newspapermen and the television people, he admitted he had lied and that the story was right the way I had written it. He explained he was sorry that the conditions at the time prevented his giving it out to other people and he was ready to make amends. I took his apology in good faith. I understood the conditions which forced him into that strange position, which I believe was the only time in baseball history that a club president had to eat crow. And he seemed to more or less relish the idea of getting it off his chest.

I started my sportswriting career on the New York *Herald* in 1909. I was writing in the office one night, sitting around and waiting for things to happen. The man who usually covered the Dodgers in spring training had a serious altercation with the sports editor. He sent in brief accounts daily and had been getting three dollars a day. He demanded five dollars. The sports editor got angry about it and told him, "Rather than give you five dollars a day, I'll send a boy from this office," and out walked the incumbent and I was called to the desk. I was in college at the time, moving between City College and Columbia. Where I was exactly I don't recollect.

I asked Mr. Al Stimer, the sports editor, "What's up?"

He said, "Do you want to go to Macon, Georgia?"

"To do what?"

"I want you to go down there to cover the Dodgers and show this guy Cutiair we can do without him."

Cutiair was a Western Union telegrapher who took his vacation when the Dodgers were in spring training. He had that arrangement with Western Union. Every day he would send in a few paragraphs to the *Herald*. Not very much. The *Herald* was very thrifty, so thrifty we didn't have electricity and they didn't turn on the gas until one o'clock in the afternoon. If you wanted to work before that, you did it at home.

I landed in Macon, Georgia, and found the Dodgers training next door to Spark's Circus, which was also training for the coming season. At times it was difficult to say which was the Brooklyn ball club. It was a joke. Old-timers will recollect that the Brooklyn club in those days did not resemble the Dodgers in later years who were fighting the Yankees in the World Series. That was in 1909, more than sixty years ago.

I was at Macon for two weeks and then asked to be relieved because my parents were raising the devil. They didn't want me to be a full-time sportswriter. I was supposed to be a doctor. I broke a line of doctors in the family that went as far back as we could trace. I even served a short recess with the College of Physicians and Surgeons in New York. That's the big regret of my life. I would have been a helluva doctor, a helluva doctor for kids. I am medically inclined, but I couldn't take the cadavers. I just couldn't do it—the dissection. I couldn't stand the atmosphere. They tell me it's different now. But I don't know. You still have to fool around with cadavers.

But it wasn't destined to be, and I continued as a part-time sportswriter, going to college in the daytime and sitting around the office of the *Herald* at night. I made about twenty dollars a week, which was a lot of money, to me anyway. In time I got an offer, oddly enough, from Mr. Fleischer, who is in there right now, still working for *Ring* magazine, which he started fifty years ago, and who has become a big man in boxing the world over. He was the sports editor of the New York *Press* and offered me the astonishing sum of thirty-five dollars a week, which was really the Comstock Lode. This was when Frank Munsey had just taken over the *Press*. Munsey wanted to be United States ambassador to Great Britain, and he bought the *Press* and was about to buy the *Globe*, the *Mail*, the *Herald*, and everything else and kill almost everything that he bought. He had a strange New England philosophy that a paper had to make money or it had to get out. From then on I became a professional sportswriter. I think that was around 1911.

I became a member of the Baseball Writers Association of America in 1913, and I remember I was one of the first users of the typewriter in a New York newspaper office. When I was on the *Herald* we wrote with pen and ink. I had a chance to buy an old Oliver for twelve dollars. I conceived the notion that being a very poor man with a pen, I could produce things faster and better on a typewriter, and so it worked out. You couldn't carry an Oliver. It was too heavy. The first machines that sportswriters began to carry were the old Coronas, which were tiny and light but very wearing on the writer. You produced all the power. The springs were primeval. I carried a Corona around the circuit, and later I changed to a Remington and it became a badge of servitude.

The *Press* flourished. We had four sports pages every morning and eight on Sunday. If there was any baseball around the United States, it got into the *Press*. Munsey combined the *Press* with the *Sun* and later he combined the *Sun* with the *Herald* and then sold the *Herald* to the *Tribune*. All these evolutions and convolutions are of no great interest now, but as I went along, I'll say this: at no time in a career of more than fifty years was I fired. I went along with all of Munsey's changes. If he stepped up, I stepped up with him. The only thing that put an end to my sportswriting career was the total demise—the mess created by combining the *Journal*, the *Herald Tribune*, and the *World-Telegram*, which I call the murder of New York journalism. They should not have died. It was a matter of terrible management, terrible management.

Baseball writing started out in a very elementary way. The men who wrote baseball in the early days were far from the real experts who came later—like Ring Lardner and Grantland Rice. A lot of the early baseball writers spent too much time by the wayside, and by "the wayside" I mean with too close an association with John Barleycorn. The finest examples of that deterioration lie in the memories of the old-time baseball writers in Chicago. I don't want to name any names, but they had the worst situation in America. Watching what happened to many of these men, I said to myself, "This will never happen to me."

Even to this day my total consumption of liquor is a quart a year, and it was a whole lot less when I was hitting the circuit. I would have nothing to do with booze and—oh, well, I don't want to praise myself for a whole lot of things. What they were I'll leave to your imagination. The years went along and the quality of baseball writing improved and improved. Better men, more college men. In the old days we had a whole lot of office boys who graduated into the sports departments and began to write baseball and racing and whatnot. As we got more college men, the style of baseball writing became more fluent, more accurate. Baseball thrived with it.

The baseball writer of my heyday had something to tell. He had opinions. He was a critic as well as a historian. Now you go into the clubhouse after a game and you find baseball writers wandering around, at times even putting words into the mouths of some of the boys. That's one of the big beefs of the players—that they are made to say a lot of things either they didn't want quoted or that they didn't say in the first place. I think today's baseball writers could improve their job vastly and should offer more of their opinion, and not simply stand and quote the manager. In my time I went out myself, on my own. I was known as a digger for scoops.

I signed Babe Ruth for eighty thousand dollars. I made the deal with him. He was holding out, in St. Petersburg, Florida. This was in 1930. He wanted a two-year contract for eighty-five thousand a year. In those days this was unheard of, not like it is today with so many players getting more than a hundred thousand. The Yankee players were on the practice field, working out every day, getting in shape for the season. But the Babe was out at a place called The Jungle, playing golf and taking it easy. Mrs. Ruth was with him. Without the Babe there wasn't an awful lot to write about. You couldn't write the story of his holdout every day. It got monotonous. I could see that without the Babe we were going to have an awful lot of trouble in the stadium, and so I got hold of Ruth and had a talk with him.

I said, "What's the matter with you? Did you know that this afternoon in Union Square in New York there was a riot? A lot of people were rioting for bread."

"What did you say?" he said.

"A lot of people in New York are rioting for bread. They're broke. There's a depression. And you're holding out for eighty-five thousand a year while they're starving. It's making a very bad impression and hurting baseball."

He told me, "Why don't people tell me these things?"

I said, "Don't you ever see a newspaper?"

Nobody told him about any depression or a riot. He asked me what he should do. I told him Jake Ruppert—the owner of the Yankees—would agree to give him eighty thousand and that he should end his holdout.

Babe said, "Bring him around. I'll sign for eighty thousand before noon tomorrow—and if I don't I'll turn my uniform in and go home."

I went to tell Ruppert—but first I wrote the story. I remember it was a rainy Friday night. It was raining cats and dogs. We had just seen a movie around the corner in the Florida Theatre in St. Petersburg. Dennis King was the star of the movie. Then I wrote the story for page one of the *Telegram*. I said exactly what had happened, how I had talked to the Babe and how I had talked to Ruppert.

I had no idea that I had the story alone. I thought I had the story in company with another writer whose name I don't want to mention because he has had a very important connection with baseball and his story and my story don't coincide. In any event, I wired the story in for page one. I wrote about eight pages, a lot of stuff to go over the wire. About half-past eight the next morning I was awakened. The managing editor of the *Telegram* was on the phone, congratulating me on a beat.

Suddenly it hit me that something was wrong. The other writer with whom I believed I was in partnership on the story had quit on it during the night. He didn't send it to his paper. I had seen him writing it. I had looked into the Western Union office after midnight, and there he was batting it out under one light. When I realized his story didn't run, I said, "There's something bad about this. This is a beat I don't want because there's something going on."

So I called up Ruth. I said, "You told me yesterday you would sign for eighty thousand or turn in your uniform and go home."

"That's what I told you yesterday," the Babe said. "But remember, yesterday it was raining. Today the sun is out and the birds are twirping. I've changed my mind."

I told him, "Babe, you sign for eighty thousand or you turn in your uniform. You're not going to do this to me."

"Be reasonable," he said.

"I'm as reasonable as I can be. You're going to sign before twelve o'clock."

He told me he'd be at the hotel in a half-hour. I went out looking for Ruppert. He was taking a walk around the lake. I grabbed him in great excitement and said, "Colonel, I've got the Babe down at the hotel, waiting to sign for eighty thousand."

"Oh, well," the colonel said. "I'm in no hurry."

"Colonel, I'm in a heck of a hurry. I wrote this story and I'm stuck with it if you don't back me up."

We went back to the hotel, and as soon as the Babe got there I took him up to the top floor of the Princess Martha, to the colonel's suite. They shook hands, and that was how Ruth signed for eighty thousand.

The other writer involved was Ruth's ghost. Later, I realized what probably happened is, after I had my talk with the Babe they had met for dinner and the Babe had filled him in. But the other writer, even though he wrote the story, lost confidence in it. He couldn't believe the Babe was going to turn in his uniform and go home. He figured the holdout would last at least a few more days and that I'd be left holding the bag. I had to be very sharp with Mr. Ruth because I didn't like the idea of being made a sucker of. And as it turned out the result was happy. The Babe put on his uniform, went to work, and began to hit home runs.

Another man I handled for the ball club was Red Ruffing, a great pitcher for the Yankees. He had been acquired from Boston and was holding out. He lived in Chicago and was working out at the University of Chicago field house. The Associated Press sent out a story which was printed in every newspaper in America quoting Ruffing as saying, "If I don't get an extra five thousand dollars for my pinch hitting, I won't sign."

The Yankees were going west to Grand Rapids, Michigan, with a stop in Chicago. I got off the train at Chicago, in the morning, while the club and the other writers changed for Grand Rapids. I went up to the Auditorium Hotel, had my breakfast, and called Mr. Ruffing at his home. I told him I wanted to see him. Ruffing came down to the hotel, and I said, "What do you want? Without you the Yankees are going nowhere."

The season had started—this was, I would say, in 1932 or '33.

He said, "This is a fake. I'm in a terrible fix."

"What fake?" I asked.

"I never told that guy I wanted five thousand dollars to be a pinch hitter. I'm tickled to death to grab a bat any old time they want me. He put that into my mouth. I never said it."

I said, "Okay, will you say that to Ruppert?"

He said, "Sure."

I called Ruppert at the brewery in New York. I told him I had Ruffing with me and that the story about the extra five thousand dollars for pinch hitting was a fake.

"He's ready to go to work, Colonel. What do you want to give him? Twenty-five thousand?"

The colonel said yes. I turned to Ruffing. "Will you take twenty-five thousand?"

"Fine," Ruffing said. "I'll join the club tomorrow."

That was the end of Ruffing's holdout. Those things don't happen anymore.

Nobody was ever afraid of me. Nobody who ever ran a ball club, general manager, president, no player. I have the most remarkable association with old-time ball players extant. I played everybody on the level. I wasn't going around derogating people, or looking for bugs. If I saw something good I played it. I played every man for what he was worth. I wasn't looking to run baseball down. I was eager to run baseball up.

I don't recollect that I ever had any arguments with managers. I was a close friend of Miller Huggins. I was an honorary pallbearer and I was sent by the paper to Cincinnati for his funeral. I was on fine terms with Joe McCarthy. In fact, a certain newspaper in New York filed an official complaint that Joe was talking to me and nobody else. I had no complaints about Joe McCarthy. He and I were the closest of friends.

One day the Yankees were off and I went up to the Croydon Hotel where Joe lived. Mrs. McCarthy was there. I was on friendly

terms with the family, and she said, "Joe is in the newsreel theater."
Joe was a nut about newsreels.

"Oh," I said, "I'll see him tomorrow at the stadium."

She said, "No, sit down. I want to talk to you."

She asked me why the baseball writers didn't like Joe McCarthy.

I said, "Who said they don't like Joe McCarthy?"

"Now stop the blarney," she told me. "I know a lot of the boys at the stadium don't like Joe."

"Well, Babe, I'll talk to you about this, but if you ever tell Joe about it I'll be very sore."

She says, "What is it?"

"You reach out for Joe and you think you've got him for a friend, and then your head hits plate glass. So far you can go and no further. Joe was very badly injured by his experience in Chicago where Hornsby was put in his place. A lot of baseball writers who Joe felt to be his close friends didn't stand up. He's never forgotten, or forgiven. It changed his entire viewpoint toward the press. Babe, nobody knows Joe McCarthy. I think I know him, but there are times I'm forced to admit I don't know him."

The following winter the McCarthys were coming from Buffalo to Washington to pick up the main line into St. Petersburg. I got off the train and I saw the McCarthys coming down the platform. Joe was feeling very jovial. He grabbed me by the shoulders and said, "Do you know who I am? I'm the man noooooobody knows."

I learned more about the mechanics and the winning system of baseball from Miller Huggins than from anybody else. Huggins was not in very good health. He wasn't a very strong man. On the road, after a game, he'd go up to his room and get into his long drawers and lie there exhausted. Then, he'd begin to discuss the game, inning by inning, move by move. Why he did this, why he did that, and it registered with me because I heard so many of his lectures and dispositions and analyses. He knew an awful lot about baseball.

John McGraw needs a book. McGraw was the greatest manager in baseball history, the most independent man who ever ran a ball club. He ran everything. He organized the club, signed the ball players, watched over the farm system, such as it was in those early days. There was only one thing wrong with McGraw, and that was an occasional overindulgence. But as a leader, as a manager, nobody was near him. He was very arrogant in his attitude. If McGraw said, "I did this because I did this," he expected you to agree with him one hundred percent. He called the pitches. He called everything. A lot of players couldn't take that kind of managing, not today. He wouldn't last two weeks with all of his genius, because the players wouldn't take it.

I had an argument with McGraw once but not about anything that happened in a ball game. I was at the Giant office one day, and in the elevator I passed Judge Emil Fuchs, who owned the Boston Braves, an ownership that wasn't very prosperous. McGraw was in the office and said, "I'm going to tip you on something. Tris Speaker is the new manager of the Braves."

I wrote the story and it was ridiculed by the other writers. Tris Speaker never did become manager of the Braves. Later, I went to McGraw and told him he had made me look like an awful boob. I appreciated his desire to keep me posted on inside stuff, but I told him, "You certainly didn't do me a big favor."

He said, "I did you a helluva favor. When I talked to you in this office, Tris Speaker was the manager of the Braves."

"What happened?"

"I can't tell you what happened."

That was my only argument with McGraw.

I had a lot to do with Ralph Houk becoming what he is today with the Yankee organization. Houk was sitting around in the Serena Hotel in St. Petersburg during spring training, refusing to join the Kansas City club. George Weiss, who was then running the Yankees, had optioned Houk out and was very adamant about it. He told Houk, "You go to Kansas City and you'll be back."

Houk told me he was returning to his home in Lawrence, Kansas, and going to work for his father in the contracting business. He was very disconsolate. I told him, "Ralph, don't be a fool. Do you like baseball? Do you like to play baseball? Would you like a career in baseball?"

He said, "Yes."

"Then stay with it. Go to Kansas City. You'll be back. I'll wager you a hundred dollars to ten you'll be back before the season's out. Don't sit here sulking. I know you are unhappy, but get out of here and go to work."

He took my advice. He was back that year. If he had gone to work for his father, Mr. Houk would not be managing the Yankees today.

When Casey Stengel got the Yankee managing job, we thought he was a stopgap. We thought he was in there to tell jokes and while away a season or two until the club could get tightened up and reorganized. To everybody's amazement he made it the first crack out of the box. As a manager he was whimsical. He made a lot of fast decisions. McCarthy, for example, watched the smallest detail on the field and made it work for him. McGraw overdid strategy, and Huggins played the game by rote, percentages. Casey wasn't that thorough. He made a lot of spur-of-the-moment decisions, and he paid the highest regard of any Yankee manager to the opinions of his coaches. I got along beautifully with Casey. I had no complaints. He never told me anything that wasn't true. And he told me just about everything I wanted to know. But getting too close to the manager wasn't always good for your social life with the other fellows in the press box. They resented it. In spite of that, I was chairman of the New York chapter for five years in a row, which is the record. I am proud of that.

Almost every argument I had with a player was a result of being the official scorer and making a call someone didn't like. I scored about twenty-one games during DiMaggio's streak. Once in a while, during the streak, I got a very deep scowl from DiMaggio, but he never, not once, complained. Scoring during his streak was a precarious life. His fans would gather behind the press box in the stadium, and they raised Cain. They felt every time he hit the ball it should be a hit. You got something like fifteen dollars a game, and it wasn't worth the trouble. The responsibility was heavy. I wouldn't have done it over again for five thousand dollars. Now Joe will tell you that my strict adherence to my notion as to what was a hit was wonderful because there wasn't a hit he wasn't entitled to. I never favored him one iota and made him get his hits as I saw them.

For thirty-two years I moonlighted for *The Sporting News* in St. Louis. I wrote far more, about five thousand words a week, for

The Sporting News than most baseball writers wrote for their own paper. My association with Taylor Spink was warm in spite of the fact that he fired me twice a week. I was his big man, not only in New York, but all over. We had a very close association, and he went a whole lot by advice. He was a strange character.

Taylor would call you at six o'clock in the morning and get you out of bed. Since he was up, everybody else had to be up. And he'd call at the stadium in the second or third inning and expect you to have the final score. That you didn't have the final score was your fault. But I got along great with him.

One of the things I did for the *World-Telegram* was a question-answer column. It was called "Ask Daniel" and ran for more than twenty years. It was the brainchild of Joe Williams, who was the sports editor and columnist for the *Telegram*. One particular time something happened of universal interest in baseball, and I got a lot of letters on the subject and Williams said, "Publish 'em and answer 'em." That was the inception of "Ask Daniel."

One question came in day after day. It never died. Did anybody ever hit a home run or, in effect, hit a fair ball out of Yankee Stadium? Of course, nobody ever did. But one man gave me an awful lot of trouble. Actually, two men. When they tore down the wooden center field bleachers, the lumber lay right there, deep in the outfield where it had been wrecked. One afternoon George Selkirk hit a line drive that eluded the center fielder and the right fielder and bounced into the lumber pile. Selkirk got a home run and laid claim to the feat of having hit a fair ball out of Yankee Stadium. But the ball didn't go out. It was in the lumber, hidden away somewhere. Lefty Gomez—the famous pitcher who went around the country appearing at banquets and telling stories—backed up Selkirk. And these two men, Gomez and Selkirk, gave me Hail Columbia!

I wrote lots and lots of stories. Thousands and thousands of 'em. One I'll never forget was in 1925, the last game of the World Series. Walter Johnson lost the game, and when it was over he stood out there on the mound, in the rain. The rain kept pouring down the visor of his cap. He looked like he was crying his head off.

I wrote that story and got a watch from the Baseball Writers Association which I prize very much and which I have to this day. The

Baseball Writers used to give a watch for the best story of the year. Grantland Rice and Ring Lardner and one other judge picked it. It went on for two years. Buck O'Neill won it the first year. I won it the second year, and then they decided to stop. I don't know why. I think it should be revived.

Marshall Hunt

Marshall Hunt's newspaper career was in two parts—twenty-one years as a New York sportswriter specializing in baseball, and then, back in his native locale, twenty-seven years as the managing editor and editorial writer for the Daily Olympian *(Washington). There he attacked left-wing Democrats, with constant pleas against the growth of government and welfare programs. "I wrote sharply," he said. "I didn't pull any punches."*

Additionally, Mr. Hunt was able to do a service for the late Westbrook Pegler, his lifelong comrade. In the final years, when Pegler's syndicated columns were in disfavor and often trimmed and hidden in the back of most papers, the Daily Olympian *published them in their entirety. If not for Mr. Hunt, the library of Pegler columns would have been incomplete.*

Mr. Hunt, who like Pegler was the son of a newspaperman, attended the University of Washington, majoring in journalism. He enlisted in the service several days after World War I was declared. He was an air cadet and spent six months in France, in the midst of the Bordeaux vineyards where he acquired a knowledge of wines and a remarkable palate.

After retirement Mr. Hunt wrote a weekly column for the Olympian, *and lived with his wife in a three-room log cabin overlooking a secluded oyster bed on Puget Sound. While in his home I saw no mementos of Babe Ruth, no autographed pictures, no autographed baseballs. The only remnant from his sportswriting days was a hard-backed photograph of himself as a young man, an overblown head shot, the kind usually hung on the side of circulation trucks. During the interview he several times lamented that the closest good restaurant was a thousand miles away. Mr. Hunt died in 1974 at the age of seventy-nine.*

Lots of people say I've known the Babe better than any other writer. Well, that's probably true. Many of them say, "Why don't you do a book on him?" I think I just have to wait awhile and let nature do a few things before I'd write that book, because I might run into a suit. Several things happened up in the Babe's farmhouse, outside of Boston, that are worth a couple of thousand words. That's never been touched, never been used. But I want to wait till that female is out of the way. Oh, she's a—well, I wouldn't trust her.

When I came to the Northwest, not very many people knew I had been with the Babe so long, although there were quite a few magazine stories. Nevertheless, they didn't quite get my connection and I said nothing. I didn't bring this to the front, but gradually some of the service clubs asked me to talk about the Babe and major league baseball. So I tried it once. I worked several days on that speech. I hate stage waits. I don't like hesitations on the part of a speaker. I practically memorized it so I could rip it off fast, and in that first attempt I realized that they had no idea of what major league baseball was like, what the players were like, how they lived.

I think they thought they traveled around in day coaches whereas they traveled in the best of trains, ate and lived in the best of hotels. I couldn't seem to explain to them what Babe was like, what the other players were like with the Yankees. They couldn't quite understand why we lived so well, enjoyed ourselves. They had no idea what the whole setup was about, so I never, never made another talk because I was not getting the point over. They couldn't grasp what it was all about. It was too much for them. My God, major league baseball was such a big thing then, occupying a third of the front page of the final editions of the New York, Boston, Philadelphia, and Chicago papers. Politics, everything else, was pushed aside. They didn't realize that Ruth was getting daily perhaps twice as much publicity as President Coolidge.

Somebody pointed that out to Babe one time, and Babe said, "Yes, I deserve it."

That was true. He did deserve it.

The Yankees got Babe in a trade with the Red Sox, and when he came down from Boston we knew a lot about him. He'd been an amazing pitcher up there, a great hitter, really a good fielder. The general manager of the Yankees then, Ed Barrow, had been his field manager in Boston. We knew the Babe. When we were in Boston we always went down to the clubhouse. It's not like now. You were welcome. The players would sometimes come over and shake your hand, even though you had kidded them badly the day before.

Captain Joe Patterson—he was the founder of the New York *Daily News*—was always looking around for some outstanding people in tennis, football, baseball, or something, that we could latch onto and sort of cultivate and make our own and have exclusive stuff on. We would go up to his apartment at night, take him fishing, hunting, anything. We recognized the Babe as a guy we could really do business with. And right away he started to hit home runs, and right away I was always around him, never toadying, nothing. He hit the baseballs. I did the writing, sometimes kidding. We tried not to be too serious. So the Babe became sort of a *Daily News* man because we covered him more—more pictures, more stories. We covered him twelve months of the year. I don't think he was ever aware of his role as a circulation builder. We got along fine.

I never had a cross word with the big baboon. He was no intellectual, you know, but an agreeable guy. He really liked baseball and he liked people. And he tried to be agreeable. I never tried to exploit him or take him to this benefit or that, at all. Once in a while another sportswriter or the AP would grab him off and take him somewhere, kind of boring for him but that was okay.

In the springtime he would go down to Hot Springs, Arkansas, to boil out and take the baths there for three, four weeks, maybe five weeks. It all depended on how he felt and whether Barrow looked at him and said, "My God, you slob. Off to Hot Springs."

Barrow would call me and the Babe, and I would take off. The Babe and I would play a lot of golf and take a lot of hikes. Other people would come through there, and they thought I was Babe's manager. Many prominent people in Hot Springs would come over and ask if I could introduce them. I usually did just that. You got an awful lot of Midwest businessmen and industrialists down there to boil out, too. We played golf every morning, and then we'd get tired of the food in the hotel and I'd hire a car and we'd go out in the country looking for farmhouses that said "Chicken Dinners." What Babe really wanted was a good chicken dinner and the daughter combination, and it worked that way more often than you would think. After maybe about a month of that we would join the main team in Florida or New Orleans, wherever it was. We did this every year, all the time he was in New York.

I was boiling out one time, and Jake Ruppert, the owner of the Yankees, came to the baths there and signed Babe to his contract. And I was giving good-natured advice to both sides. He signed naked in the bathtubs. Then, when we'd get down to Florida, the Babe would be in big demand, charity shows at Palm Beach. We'd perform on the stage, and I'd throw a few cotton balls at him and he'd bat 'em out, all in the interest of charity. The way they worked it, the net take would be up in the hundreds of thousands of dollars with all those winter people down in Palm Beach. In Florida we did a lot of fishing together at night, just to get away. Babe loved to fish as much as I did. I was a born fisherman. So was he. We'd sneak away, night after night. I had a boat tied up four or five miles from the hotel. We'd hang a lantern and fish until midnight.

The Yankees trained for five or six years in New Orleans. Socially, I think it's a rather cold town. The old-timers sort of hang together down there. But Babe somehow broke the crust, and after we'd been down there a couple of times he got invited out to some of those fine old Southern homes—mansions, plenty of help. Frequently I'd get invited with him and we'd be treated to long, long real old Southern meals. Excellent cooking. Finest kind of ingredients, treated right in the kitchen. The host, coming from an old-time family, would put on an act. He'd have Negroes in hose, dressed just as they were at the end of or before the Civil War. And a big show in the kitchen, waiters, all sorts of attendants, sometimes a small orchestra. So we'd sit there and get a sample of food that very, very few people really ever get a chance to eat.

The Babe was a good trencherman. So he enjoyed this. He conducted himself very well. Usually when the host told a story, it'd be a simple thing, and the Babe could understand the point, so he would laugh at the right time. We had opportunities down there to see that life that very few outsiders ever had. I thought it was wonderful. If more families would have meals, not elaborate things like that, but good meals and a laugh or two at the table, we'd be a whole lot better off in this country. The families are falling apart, bad. That's really serious.

Babe came from awful surroundings, as did Jack Dempsey. To me, it's really marvelous that having no formal education and coming from awful neighborhoods, they acquired at least quite a fine veneer as gentlemen. It got so you could take either of them anywhere with greater safety than a lot of businessmen around town and a lot of others. They could even hold out their little pinkie, you know, and they knew the right answers. They'd bow, "Charmed to meet you," and so on. They could carry on a real conversation, and the people they were talking to always enjoyed it. It was clean and they were civil, polite, even gallant at times.

After spring training we'd break camp and head north, playing exhibitions on the way home. The writers always used to wonder how large crowds would assemble as the Yankee train went through. Well, undoubtedly the telegraph operators would hear from New York that Ruth was on Number Four coming through at four-eighteen, and the telegraph operators would call all their relatives, spread the word around, and there'd be five hundred people down there. Maybe the train wouldn't stop. They wouldn't even see Babe. But if it did stop, Babe would be playing cards and they'd all wave and he'd wave, and he might come back and talk to them.

One time we were on our way to Hot Springs. The first real stop was St. Louis, the end of the line. Then you changed over to the Missouri Pacific and went down to Hot Springs. And there was one whale of a crowd in St. Louis. Maybe the year before, Babe had set a record or something. Anyway, he was in high esteem with the fans there. I mean, there was a big crowd.

We fought our way through and got to the taxi stand. One of the drivers had been assigned to take care of the Babe because we were just stopping to eat before taking the nine o'clock train to Hot Springs. We were standing by the taxi and Babe was autographing any old thing, ladies' sweaters, anything that would take ink. Finally the noise died down and the taxi driver said, "Where to, Babe?"

And the Babe said, "To the House of the Good Shepherd."

Well, this taxi driver, a rather chunky fellow, shouted at the top of his voice, "To the House of the Good Shepherd."

That was for the benefit of the starter to know where we were going. Of course that was St. Louis' leading hook shop. And everyone in the audience knew it. And they thought the Babe deserved a hand on that one, and he got it, too. And they followed the cab as it drew out with us in it. Young ones ran, following along, and yelling, "To the House of the Good Shepherd."

The House of the Good Shepherd served the best steaks ever served in this world. The best meals. That madam, I've forgotten her name, a very nice woman. That night we had dinner there and Babe accommodated a couple of them. Then I think he got one free. I think he got one on the house that night. Then we went down and got on the train.

Lots of times on the road—in Detroit, St. Louis, and other places, Babe had connections in rural places, really choice. I mean, if you liked a steak they just ripened it. And everything else was excellent. Some big mommy would do the cooking, and she also took care of the rooms, of course, after each accomplishment. But the food was excellent. Just the type that Babe loved. I'll say I never tasted riper meat. The meat had been enzymed to death, until it looked like currant jelly. Not a cell left in it. Beautiful stuff. So sometimes the Babe would call me up and say, "I got it fixed tonight. Don't eat in the hotel, and I'll meet you about six-thirty." I'd meet the Babe and off we'd go. It was a little additional touch to the trips.

Speaking of gourmet stuff, St. Louis was a spot to pick up spareribs out in some special butcher shop or out in some farm where they had them already prepared. And frogs' legs. Babe loved them. So did I. We knew where we could drive out for a fine mess of frogs' legs. We didn't do much eating in the hotel in St. Louis.

Babe wanted to go somewhere one night out there in St. Louis, and he called up Barrow and I think he fibbed a little to Ed and Ed said, "Okay, but how are you going to get back?"

Babe said, "I'm going to fly."

Nobody flew then but me. So Barrow called me. He said, "What the hell have you done out there?"

"I didn't do this one," I told Ed. "This is his own and he's invited me."

We stayed over in St. Louis, after the club had left for New York on the train. We stayed over so we could go to a party. Then we would take the eleven o'clock plane and be in New York ahead of them. That was the deal. We went out to this place, and it was a whole lot of near-beer and everybody had a great time.

Then this big heavyset woman kisses the Babe a couple of times and said, "I've got a gift for you."

And she gave the Babe about thirty or thirty-five pounds of the choicest spareribs. Great big. The Babe looked at me. I said, "Take 'em, Babe, what the hell."

They rode us out to the airport, spareribs and all, and we got in the plane, an old TWA shaker, and took off for New York. We'd already eaten ourselves silly out at that place, choicest beef, cold cuts, salad. Pretty soon I hear noises, and Babe has opened the big bundle and is chomping away on the spareribs. There was just a pilot and Babe and me in that plane. And half the time to New York the pilot was in the back with us, sawing away. We ate them all. I've often wondered what the janitor thought when he cleaned up that plane. Piles and piles of sparerib bones. They were delicious.

Another time Babe was on a vaudeville trip. I didn't accompany him everywhere, but I caught up with him in some small town in Minnesota. It was in the wintertime. We were in a two-story brick hotel, which was no bargain, standing in his room looking at that dismal little public square. It was hailing and snowing. Terrible. So Babe said, "I don't think we can hack it today."

Then the village band showed up, and this hail was coming down so hard you could hear it through the window, hitting the metal instruments. But the thing that Babe and I loved was this tuba player, absolutely bald, blowing his guts out with this hail just popping. A devoted musician.

So I said, "Babe, just pause for a minute and think of your position in this country, in society, and every other thing. Here you are. Reverence is being paid by this poor band out there in that hail. The mayor has already welcomed you. We don't know what will happen the rest of the day, but it sort of gives you another chance to gauge your position in the United States of America. Look at that tuba player down there. It's a sight I'll never forget. And Babe, you shouldn't forget this welcome here."

The Babe just turned around and said, "Okay, kid, let's eat."

The Babe made two movies. I went out to Hollywood on one of them. The Babe insisted that I be installed as some sort of technical adviser. The movie was called *Headin' Home,* with Anna Q. Nilsson. She was one of the stars of the day. This was in 1928 or '29, right when Hollywood was at its absolute peak. Lord, he was big out there.

It was a budget film and had to be completed at a certain time, and Babe saw all this stuff around town. So Barrow sent Artie McGovern out to be his keeper. Artie had a couple of fancy gymnasiums in New York, a fine physical director. He put the Babe to bed every night, usually at nine o'clock. Broke the Babe's heart. He was never in the midst of so much at one time and could get so little.

One night the Babe and Artie were invited out. They had permission to go. The Babe had promised to autograph a couple of hundred baseballs. So he came down to my room and asked me to do him a favor.

"What is it, Babe?" I asked him.

"Well, there's a bunch of baseballs on my bed. Will you autograph 'em as fast as you can? And then just leave 'em on the bed?"

I autographed about 250, and the Babe came back with Artie and knocked on my door. I was reading. He said, "I saw the baseballs and they're good. Thank you a lot."

The next morning I was having breakfast and Babe came over to my table and said, "Say, kid, don't get too good with that pen."

When it came time to go back to New York, we got on the Union Pacific. I was walking through the cars and who do I run into but Joe Patterson, publisher of the *News.* I didn't know he was out there. He said, "Hey, what are you doing here?"

I told him and he said, "Is the Babe actually on this train?"

I said, "Well, yes, sure. We're going back to New York."

So here was Patterson on the same train. He was a great newspaperman. He realized by us latching onto the Babe we had done a good thing. It was Patterson, from the beginning, who saw we could increase circulation by developing a strong sports department. He always wanted us to write in kind of a bouncy way. Very biff, bang, boom stuff.

I could see he was awed when he realized we were on the same train, and he asked me if I could get the Babe back into his drawing room for a little chat.

I said, "Oh, I think so. I'll talk to him."

So Patterson said, "I'm awfully tired. But if you can bring the Babe back to the drawing room, I'll talk to him for a while. And when I signal like this"—he brushed his fingers against his coat—"just say, 'We've got to go, Babe. We've got to go.' " That was sort of the brush-off sign, the sign for us to leave.

I brought the Babe in and I thought we'd be talking for about ten minutes. I kept waiting for the sign. This went on for about two hours. The Babe enjoyed it. Patterson had played some baseball at Yale, and even after he became publisher, he would occasionally come out to the ball park. Patterson went out to see things for himself. That's what set him aside from most publishers. Finally, I got the signal and I said, "Okay, Babe," and we left. I never saw Patterson on the train again. I ducked him. I thought we had done a pretty good job, as it was.

Only once did I have an awkward time with the Babe. There was the question of the paternity of a daughter in 1923. And Payne —he was the city editor in New York, really a busybody—called me up in New Orleans and asked me to go up to the Babe and find out, because the story was breaking in New York. Hints came out.

I went up there and I said, "Babe, I've never asked you any of these personal questions before, but the heat's on from the office and I'm going to have to ask you some questions."

He said, "Go ahead."

But when I started he began to hedge. He was a little bit mad. He stalled his way through, lying like hell. I knew that. So I called Payne back and said, "Listen, we've got along fine with the Babe and he's done a lot of things for us. You try to get somebody else to worm this thing out in New York and not through the Babe, because we don't want to go on this personal bend that some of the other papers had tried to do."

Long before the Babe was through as a player, the columnists in New York were always trying to find out if some owner would be wise enough to grab him off and make a manager of him. You could never get any reaction. If you asked the owners why they didn't grab the Babe, they had evasive answers. They didn't think he was qualified to handle others. He was a great star and all that, but, oh, they didn't think they could trust his judgments and so forth. The truth of the matter is that it really hurt the Babe. You couldn't expect him to act otherwise. My God, he was entitled to something more than he finally got.

Right after World War I, New York attracted writers, many of them very skilled, from all parts of the country. There were more than twenty papers in New York then, you see, there was opportunity, and the competition was fierce. But once somebody stabbed you good, you paid no attention, and then proceeded to stab him. You were all very friendly and yet you're out trying, well, to sabotage every other writer. For the fun of it. There was great enthusiasm, something you don't find anymore. And the number of people traveling. Ring Lardner showed up. Grant Rice sprung up, Westbrook Pegler and Paul Gallico, and all of that.

Gallico married the daughter of Burt Leston Taylor, the famous columnist of the Chicago *Tribune*. Before Taylor died he asked Patterson to take care of the girl. The girl, Alva Taylor, wound up on the *News* doing clothes or some sort of column. Gallico got a job there doing movies. Patterson didn't like the way he did the movies and told Payne, the city editor, to get rid of him. But Payne saw something in Gallico. He kept him. They wanted to make me sort of a director of the sports department, but I wanted to stay outside. I had seen enough of that rim business and makeup, and all of that. I was brought up in the newspaper business. I had no fancy for that stuff.

So they put Gallico in sports. I stayed out on baseball, on my own, picking my assignments. Then Paul started writing. Anything where there would be a story, we'd be there. Especially if there was a story that would attract Patterson's attention. He would read it. Sometimes he liked it, sometimes he didn't. But he saw we were in there digging and producing stuff in off-season which others weren't touching. And again the circulation was going up, so Gallico took over a column that I'd been doing on the side, not every day. He developed it into a two-column width and it caught on.

Paul had been an oarsman at Columbia and he knew sports pretty well. He knew quite a few native New Yorkers, people around town. He had a good background in many things. One of them was music. His father was a well-known piano teacher in New York, Paolo Gallico. Paul was brought up with a musical background. Being a native New Yorker, he saw a lot of the Met from the time he was a kid until he left. He could write a good review on music.

His sports column really grabbed New York. He'd flub awful once in a while, fall down terribly because he wasn't quite familiar with a subject or went at it the wrong way. But, you see, Patterson liked that because he was in there stabbing. So if he had two good ones a week and of the others one was a joke, and the others weren't much good, he was still being read, and Patterson wanted to put out a readable newspaper. Paul had one terrible habit. I'd be up at Yankee Stadium going along fine with the game. If the Yankees were ahead I'd have my story written, polished up, nicely rewritten, waiting for a lead, and then that telegraph operator next to me would say, "Gallico wants to talk to you." I knew what that meant. He wanted me to produce a column during that game and have it ready. Paul became sports editor because I wanted to stay out on the road. Sure, I'd do the column for him. You got so you had a spare one in your pocket, or you had thought out an idea and had made some notes for a column. Then when the pinch came, you just sat down and batted one out. This happened about once a month.

In the twenties and thirties the sportswriters were a very versatile lot. They were, surprising as it may seem, great readers of ancient literature, modern literature, the magazines, the newspapers. They were critical. Sometimes they'd pick up a phrase, nurse it for six months, and then use it themselves. Most of these fellows on a trip would start out with three or four good magazines, then they would have a volume of Thomas Hardy. John Kieran always had three or four volumes of very hefty poets. He went just a little bit too deep into that for me. But he really was a student of literature, as was proved when he was on "Information Please."

So versatile were the sportswriters that every once in a while there would be a good story in court, maybe crime or an investigation that needed some color. The witnesses were colorful, the judge was colorful. So they'd yank a baseball writer and send him down to court for six weeks until the case was over because the sportswriters did a better job of describing. They were a little shaky on law, maybe, but that could be taken care of very easily by going to the prosecuting attorney, or any attorney, and getting straightened out on the terminology. They could do this after the day's hearing. The sportswriters were absolutely the best writers on the papers in those days, and baseball writing was the best of all the jobs on a newspaper. You'd think that of the drama reviewers, but that was a different deal. You were dealing with a strange bunch of people there. Some papers had excellent drama critics. They wrote very, very well —about drama. Sometimes a publisher or a managing editor would send the drama critic to the ball park to cover a World Series game and he'd fall flat on his face. Write some of the most ludicrous stuff in the world. Some of it so preposterous that the managing editor, in reading it when it came over the wire, would throw it in the garbage can.

In the twenties and earlier, the publishers wanted long stories. The reporters were paid by space, by the inch. I think they got ten dollars a column, about twenty inches to the column. The one thing these fellows wanted to avoid was having their stories cut. So they became very practiced and could weave a story like a cable, or a chain. They wrote with pencil, sometimes very swiftly.

Take the case of Jack Kieran. He'd be assigned to a Yale-Harvard game at New Haven, and he would have with him a program from the year before and he would write how the band struck up and played so-and-so and so-and-so. Then the chorus sang so-and-so. Then they marched around the field and then Yale sang this and Harvard sang that. Then Jack would describe the crowd, how it was a little slow getting into the stadium. He would write all of this in longhand, on the train, going up to New Haven, page after page. He would even quote the song, three verses. Then he'd put that in his pocket, get off the train, have lunch, and go out to Yale Bowl. He'd make copious notes. At the end of the game, in the cold weather, Kieran would attack the typewriter and write and write. Sometimes Yale wouldn't sing the full three verses of a song. Jack would edit the copy he had written in advance so it would be accurate and, of course, it made a great impression around town. How could a man write so much and so fast? They didn't know the trick.

Dan Daniel was another one who did that very successfully. Dan, who was a prolific writer, anyway, would go up to New London to cover a Yale-Harvard regatta. Dan, at the time, was working for Munsey, a notorious penny pincher. The first thing Dan would do after he got off the train in New London would be to go up to the Mohican Hotel, copy off most of the names on the register, then write down the names of others he saw in the lobby. Dan would interview quite a few old-time Yale-Harvard fellows he spotted in the lobby. Then he wrote about the regatta and the old grads at the hotel, because his boss, Munsey, owned it. And, of course, he'd throw in a few words about the superb cuisine and the excellent service that everybody enjoyed there and he would mention Munsey once or twice. That pleased old Munsey a great deal. Others would wonder how Dan could write so much, so fast. He did it in takes. Dan knew most of the angles about writing, covering things minutely.

I always got a kick out of Will Wedge, who worked for the New York *Sun* for a long time. Will covered nothing but baseball, really. He had a few assignments in the wintertime, and of course, traveling along with Wedge was Ford Frick, who was born in a small town in Indiana, went to DePauw University, then got out in Colorado somehow or other. Arthur Brisbane, old double dome, picked him up in Colorado and sent him into New York. There was quite a bit of country about Ford, really. Apparently while at DePauw, Ford had earned a few dollars by doing stenographic work. He was very fast with the typewriter. Wedge was a poet and he tried to have everything sound like literature and was an awfully slow writer. At the end of a game, Frick, with his lightning touch, could bat out an overnight story in eight minutes flat, right there at the ball park, put it on the wire, and he was through for the day. Wedge, before the game, had probably interviewed a rookie, at great length. He knew the size of the guy's underwear and everything else. But whereas Ford would be finished in eight minutes, Wedge would still be working at midnight.

Frick was one of the many ghost writers for Babe Ruth. He dashed those things off in a few minutes, too. Frick was a rather impatient writer. He wrote breezy stuff, very readable. He never put much effort or thought into it, but maybe the editor of the *Journal* didn't want too much thought. It was a different type of newspaper.

Frick was a highly likable, well-read, decent fellow and that's one of the reasons why he finally got to be baseball commissioner. You always liked Ford. Very pleasant. He'd go along with almost any conversation. He was never a drag.

Ring Lardner was part of the baseball crowd in New York for quite a while. He was a quiet fellow, very sour at times. He didn't have very many friends on account of his—well, he was never obnoxious or anything like that. He just didn't mingle too well. He got a little bit sour toward the end when he realized his style of writing was passé. I think he came into town less and less. When you read his stuff now it's very dated. I liked him fine, but if you went out with him for an evening you just didn't find much in common to talk about.

Damon Runyon was another baseball writer who was frequently yanked out of sports to do a sensational trial. He wrote that stuff in court in longhand, and you never had to change a word. He would describe a woman on the stand as being a "frosty blonde." He used fine terms, and quick. A fellow had to be very much disinterested in everything not to read those stories from start to finish. He presented the case. You understood what it was about. He always checked with attorneys on the few little technicalities so he would be all right.

I knew Runyon better than any of the others. He would seclude himself and I think kind of feel sorry for himself. But I got acquainted with him. He sometimes would come down to Hot Springs, when the Babe was tubbing. He'd come down to write a few things about the Babe but mainly to get away from New York, to hole up in a hotel room and write short stories. And when he was writing these he was quite touchy. Well, I didn't care whether he was touchy or not. I used to kid him and try to get him out to play golf, for dinner, and finally one morning at one of the better hotels—we were eating on the veranda, having baked scrod. Lots of people wouldn't eat that fish for breakfast, but we did. He looked up at me and grinned and for the first time he seemed to mean that grin, and from then on we hit it off. We talked a lot about newspaper work, writing, baseball, books—everything—wherever we met, in New York or any place. He had been in the Spanish-American War, a drummer or something. He began picking up expressions, and he was one of the few fellows who could take the words of the mob and get them into print and make them sound right. He had a good ear for dialogue and that's how he wrote those short stories. Much of it is dialogue. He didn't invent those names. He just changed them. They all had screwy names. He had cancer at the end. He was in terrible shape. I didn't see him then, but Bill Corum and a few others went up to see him. He couldn't talk. You'd write questions and he'd write the answers below it. He was in agony.

Heywood Broun got a pretty good knowledge of things at Harvard, and he wrote quite a bit of baseball and then he wrote a column. But he got off too left-wingy to suit me and he certainly got off too left-wingy to suit Pegler. Of course, Pegler was always jumping on him. They were good friends at one time. Broun had a house up in Connecticut, near Pegler's house. They visited up there and the Brouns got into the habit of walking down the lane stark naked. Peg didn't think that was quite right. Broun married Ruth Hale, a writer. They must have owned that place because they named that pond Hale Lake. Broun was a likable guy, really. He wanted to act, so he got into a couple of shows there, did a monologue, leaned up against the proscenium, and wasn't any too hot. Some of his columns were well written and well thought out. He was a good spot reporter. He wasn't a regular on baseball, but he liked baseball and he'd be up at the stadium or at the Polo Grounds quite often.

One of the things I can't understand is why Grant Rice is considered the patron saint of sportswriters. He wrote a lot of poetry and had it published, but I always regarded it as pretty flossy stuff. I didn't like Grant for that reason. I used to kid about his style, in print, and found that lots of people really liked it, so that it boomed back on me a little. But I never cared.

If you ever get a chance, I suppose he has lots of works in an omnibus or something that you can get your hands on. I wouldn't waste my time doing it, but you'd see for yourself. He used fancy phrases, like the "Four Horsemen." I always thought the "Four Horsemen" type of writing was just a wee bit above our readers over in Williamsburg in Brooklyn, to say nothing of the Bronx. I wanted something more solid. There were many controversial issues of our time, stories that were hot and full of meat. But Grant never got involved. He never bit into anything.

I used to tell the other writers that I didn't like his stuff, that it was all floss. And a few of them would say, "Oh, why, the idea of you criticizing Grantland Rice." So I'd start all over again just for the fun of it. The only pal, the only supporter I ever had in any of this was Pegler. That was down his alley, too.

Peg and Grant were great friends. The last time I saw them together was in that Clover Club in Los Angeles, quite some years ago. We had a big dinner and Grant had lost quite a bit of money on the tables there. Then we went back to Grant's suite in the Ambassador. We were always friendly. This particular time Peg said to him, "What the hell! Why do you keep writing that pantywaist stuff all the time?"

Grant just smiled and said, "Deal the cards."

I like to see a guy improve on something and then whammit! Peg was like that. He had a tremendous influence on the writing of sports and other things. He had a sharp mind. He saw things in a baseball or a football game the other writers didn't see, or didn't choose to write about. His leads and descriptions of a game were so sharp. He had greater ability than they had, and there was sort of an envy, I suppose, not among all writers but some, and as Peg went on and you sometimes brought up something he wrote with other newspapermen, they just snickered and got angry. If you tried to defend Peg, they'd still try to tear him apart. It was simply because he was better. He had a sense of humor that they never seemed to realize he had. But he did. Some of his best stuff was rich with humor.

Peg lived near me in New York. We saw a great deal of each other. I just took the fellow in stride and sometimes I kidded him in print and discovered he was quite thin-skinned. He loved to dish it out but couldn't take it, really. Peg did fine stuff for such a long period of time. He was, as you say, knocking. He was knocking because he genuinely despised four-flushers and con artists, mountebanks, any phony. He despised that, especially from politicians.

The head of his syndicate began receiving quite a few letters calling Peg various names and asking why he couldn't see the bright side. Why couldn't he write something constructive? Why couldn't he once in a while praise a fellow? Some of these letters landed on the desk of the head of the syndicate, and that man went to Pegler and said, "Listen, Peg, old boy, as far as I'm concerned you're doing fine, but some of the readers are beginning to complain of your one-sidedness. They call you nasty and a lot of other things. Why don't you just for a while say something real nice about somebody?"

So Peg had an occasion to write something about Knute Rockne, the Notre Dame football coach. He filled his yarn on Rockne with all of the clichés and corn that other writers, admirers of Rockne, had used for years, and it was printed in many newspapers. Then came the explosion. The readers saw such a change in Peg they wrote in, calling him all sorts of names, asking if he had been bought out by Rockne and others. They said he ridiculed Rockne.

And that was Peg's first attempt to really write this type of stuff, kind of slush, that others had been writing about many sports figures, and it backfired on him. Naturally he never tried it again. The readers thought this was a big put-on and they resented it. I looked up that story years later and I could see exactly how they felt. It was awful. It wasn't in Peg, ever, to write that kind of stuff. He had no Pollyanna phrases in his vocabulary.

I sometimes think that Peg's boyhood was responsible. His father was a newspaperman and a good writer, but he was sort of a no-goodnik. Peg never liked him. I think Peg felt he had been brought up on the wrong side of the tracks by this fellow, and by God, he was going to get even with somebody—everybody. Well, I can't blame him for going after phonies, politicians, and some of the so-called businessmen. They were so palpable. Peg had a great influence on baseball and sportswriting because others, though they were envious, realized he had a vocabulary and they didn't. Peg was a little bit special. I think that it caused a lot of sportswriters to read more, to observe more, to polish up their prose. They would never admit that, never. But I was there. I could see what was going on. And I always liked Peg's stuff. I liked anybody who could knock 'em out with a fine lead, funny, or good description of something, something that told the story quickly. It's a real art to do that, and Peg was an artist.

I remember one time Peg covered a dog show in Madison Square Garden, and he started out saying there were all these thousands and thousands of dogs but he discovered not one of them was named Rover or Troy, not one of them out of three or four thousand dogs. He developed that theme right on through beautifully. He didn't even know who won, but it was easier to read his story than the one in the *Times* that ran two columns, listing all those long names those beasts have.

Toward the end of Peg's connection with the Hearst outfit his stuff was buried in the back of the paper—in the classified ads, among the rupture pads and patent medicine ads, electric belts and all that. It drove Peg furious. Newspapers across the country owe quite a debt to Peg. His writing inspired young reporters to improve their product, to put more punch into it, to assemble a greater vocabulary, to be more careful with the structure of sentences.

I heard Peg say one time, "My God, if you're going to spend a couple of hours writing, why not do some good? Why not entertain people, or annoy people? Just don't turn out a bunch of dull tripe."

I don't know who ordered Peg's stuff into the back of the paper, but I suppose it must have been the same young Hearst that Bill Slocum of the New York *American* and I used to lead out to the ball park, by his hand. Slocum, working for a Hearst newspaper, had the duty of picking the kid up and bringing him to the ball park. Sometimes I'd take my car and we'd pick him up somewhere. He'd sit through the game, very well behaved.

I still hear from Mrs. Pegler once in a while. She likes oysters. She calls up and I go over to the oyster plant and have them send out a good fat order. They arrive there in very good shape. She's a good cook. They have a nice place down there, in Tucson. He bought it when he was married to Julia Hartman. He bought forty acres, then later, I think, he took over forty more—adobe house, big swimming pool, a very comfortable place. And a Union Pacific caboose out in front which he wanted to use as an office. But he didn't live long enough.

I don't know how the modern baseball writers feel about the

players and the owners, but I think that the relations are not the same as in the twenties. Most of us looked at the whole thing practically as a business. The owners, we noticed, wore Brooks Brothers suits and had rather round stomachs. They got into the barber shop every day. Their shoes were shined. They lived in nice houses. They drove in good cars. Well, that was okay with us. We never toadied to them. Every once in a while they'd throw a dinner. We'd go. Then the baseball writers, in turn, would throw a real fine dinner and invite the owners. The writers' relations with the owners and players were good.

I only had one argument with a manager—with John McGraw. He was a feisty little devil. He got into lots of fights. Never won a single one of them, I think. Started in fighting when he was a third baseman for the Baltimore Orioles years ago. One night, on a station platform in Pittsburgh, he came at me and said he was going to knock the Jesus out of me. And I said, "Go ahead. Try it."

He had been drinking a lot and was objecting to a story I had written a day or two before about a couple of his Giant players being fined twenty dollars apiece for not obeying a signal and for not being alert. I rode down to the station in a taxicab with the two players, rookies. Didn't even know them, hardly at all. They were talking about these fines. McGraw never announced fines. They spilled everything. So when we got to the station I wrote about fifty words right there, handed it to Western Union and it was in the New York *News* that night. A day or two later McGraw heard about it, probably from a phone call from the New York office. So he went after me on that platform, but some player sort of grabbed McGraw and he cooled off instantly. I never liked him particularly. He was ill up in his home in Westchester County, and as I say, he was the least of my favorite managers. But he asked if I would come up and shake his hand before he died. I went up. I couldn't hardly see any sense in not going.

John Kieran

The erudite John Kieran, a sportswriter for twenty-five years, lived in Rockport, Massachusetts, near Boston, in a frame house on the edge of the Atlantic Ocean. When I wrote asking for an interview, he replied: "I spend my mornings doing fieldwork in natural history but am at home writing almost every afternoon, so if you want to come down and put me on the grill I am ready to give up my body to science. I usually go to my desk about 1:30 or 2 P.M. and have reached the stage where I love an excuse to stop writing and just talk."

Mr. Kieran started at The New York Times *in 1916, where he remained until 1922. After brief stretches with the* Herald Tribune *and the* American, *he returned to the* Times *on January 1, 1927, and began writing the* Times's *first signed daily column, "Sports of the Times." A heart attack forced him into semiretirement in 1942, and for two years he wrote a general column, "One Small Voice," for the*

Sun, also continuing as a panelist on "Information Please," a radio quiz show which had made him a national figure.

He began devoting all of his time to nature studies in 1944 and has edited an anthology of verse and written books on wild flowers, trees, and birds. Other books include The American Sports Scene, Footnotes on Nature, The Natural History of New York City, *which won him the Burroughs Medal, and* Not Under Oath, *an autobiography. He does his writing in an upstairs bedroom. On the wall hangs a Blackburnian Warbler, one of his four original Audubon prints.*

On the day I saw him he had spent the morning in the field, and he expressed excitement with his discovery of an orchid bed. While I was with him I had to write and telephone an early-edition story to my paper. I was in Boston covering the Chicago White Sox and had carried my typewriter with me, but asked if I could sit at his desk and use his. Later, when he escorted me to my car he pointed to his second-floor study and said, "If I could look far enough, I would see Spain from my window." He died in 1981 at the age of eighty-nine.

"Information Please" started in 1938. They got Franklin P. Adams first and then they hired Kip Fadiman—he was the moderator. They hired a few other fellows. One was a high school teacher of science, and one was an editorial writer on the New York *Herald Tribune*. They were good men but they just didn't fit the director's idea. They didn't go over big enough, I guess. So the director was looking for other regulars. He wanted four regulars and discovered he needed someone to answer sports. He had to have some sports in there for the younger people. And the older people, too. They didn't want all geology and chemistry and history and literature.

So Frank Adams said, "Get John Kieran!"

And the fellow said, "Who's he?"

"He's writing the sports column for *The New York Times*."

"Sports column?"

"Yes."

"Well," he said, "will he answer anything but sports?"

And Adams said, "He'll answer everything."

So he called me on the phone.

I didn't know him, either. Dan Golenpaul his name was, a bright fellow. He'd had other radio shows before that. But this time he just had this idea. They had those quiz shows where people in the audience were asked questions. You know, "Fifteen dollars to the lady in the gray hat!" "Ten dollars to anyone. . . . You, sir, can you answer this?"

These shows were horrible because the poor people, well, you know, pick out anybody, and they were so unlettered, let us say. It was embarrassing.

But Golenpaul got the idea of putting the shoe on the other foot. He wanted to get a panel of experts, people who were supposed to know something, and see how much they knew.

So he called me and said he had a radio show and would I go on. I said, "No."

"Why not?"

I had been on these radio shows. It was just a waste of my time. You got no money, which was the case in those days. The more I said I didn't want to go on, the more determined he was to get me on.

"Look," he said, "I can get lots more famous sportswriters than you."

"Fine," I said. "I know you can. Go get 'em."

But he wouldn't give up and asked if I would try it just once. I wanted to get rid of him more than anything else. I said, "All right. Where and when?"

"Tomorrow morning at NBC at ten o'clock."

I thought that would be the end of that.

Ten o'clock the next morning I was there, seated beside Frank Adams and two other people. I can't remember who they were. Anyhow, they threw a lot of questions, about everything. Poetry, history, automobile mechanisms, banking statements, one thing and another, including a few sports.

So I answered. I had no trouble. Didn't bother me at all.

After it was over, Golenpaul says, "Listen, how about coming on regularly with us?"

I asked when, and he said, "Friday night, nine o'clock."

I said, "Okay, they're fun."

Then he told me, "I can only offer you forty dollars a night, now. Once a week."

"Forty dollars!" That was a lot of money—just for a few questions. I said, "I'll be there. Even without the forty dollars."

So I went on, and after that I was there for about eleven years until it finally went off the air.

Naturally, I answered all of the questions on natural history. There were some very good arguments. For instance, one question— it had five different parts—asked the various ages that animals lived to. Kip Fadiman, of course, had the questions and answers on his card. He called me wrong on every answer.

One of the questions was "How long does a downy woodpecker live?"

I said about two and a half years, on the average.

"Wrong," he ruled. "On my card it says twenty-one years."

I said, "How many downy woodpeckers twenty-one years old do you know?"

I spent the following week calling up all the naturalists I knew, at the Museum of Natural History, the Bronx Zoo, the St. Louis Zoo, places like that. Then I got back to Kip Fadiman and said, "Where did you get your information?"

He told me they had checked the *World Almanac* and, of course, the *Almanac* was wrong. The life span of a downy wood-pecker is about two and a half years. An ordinary small bird lives about that. The longest, the record for longevity, known longevity, is about sixty years for some of the Royal Swans on the Thames River which are counted every year and tagged. But, of course, an animal lives in captivity a great deal longer than it lives in the wild because they're protected.

I was the Nature Boy at the *Times* for years. It happened in an odd way. I was always interested in natural history—that's what I've been doing for the last twenty-five years, as a matter of fact. I was in the sports department at the *Times* and one day read a story about trees in the *Times*'s Sunday magazine. It was illustrated with etch-ings, very beautiful. The story started fine. I thought, "Gee, it's a good story. I'm enjoying that."

Suddenly, I began realizing I had read this somewhere before. I went on and on and I said, "I know where this came from, an old book written by a woman by the name of Huntington." I looked up at the head of the column to see who had written the story. It was by a man, a stranger.

I went to one of my editor friends and I said, "Look, what goes on here at the respectable *New York Times?*"

So they sent a boy over to the public library, got the old book out, and compared it with the story, and it had been taken word for word.

Well, a little later the editor of the Sunday magazine got some nature photographs he wanted to use and he said, "Well, if that fellow in the sports department knew about trees, maybe he knows about something else. Maybe he could write the text for this article."

That's how I started. For the next fifteen years I wrote about a half-dozen nature stories each year for the Sunday magazine.

When I would travel on sports, I used to look for trees, flowers, birds, snakes, turtles, and everything else. Bill Cunningham, who was a famous sportswriter here in Boston, used to write in his column about finding me wandering from a golf championship into the woods, searching for a yellow-throated whistledicker or something like that. You know, kidding stories.

My nature stuff was separate. I didn't weave it into sports. But everywhere I went I kept my eyes open. I remember covering a Harvard-Yale football game in the dusk. It was late in the season and my telegrapher and I were the last fellows in the stadium. Everyone had gone. I remember a flock of Canada geese flying right over us, going south, they were.

I recall leaving a football game at Princeton once. I walked down to the Yard, near the stadium where the railroad trains were parked. I was walking out to get this special train and there was an owl, a screech owl sitting right over my head. I remember that, and it must have been over forty years ago. I can still see that little owl sitting in the dusk right over my head.

It was wonderful, the education I got going from town to town with a baseball club. The rest of the fellows played cards at night, so they were tired in the morning, but I'd have an early breakfast, as early as the dining room would open. Then I was off. I used to go to all the art galleries, all the libraries. I could tell you where all the good pictures are in this country, just by traveling the old baseball circuit.

I never traveled with a ball club—to Boston, Chicago, St. Louis, Philadelphia, Detroit, Washington—that I didn't go to the art museums. I read French and I could get Proust in the library at St. Louis when they wouldn't allow him on the shelves of the New York Public Library.

And I went to all the parks. Schenley Park, in Pittsburgh, was wonderful. We stayed at the old Schenley Hotel. The art museum was down the street and the university is across the square, and beyond the ball park was a golf course where you could not only play golf but you could observe the migration of birds. Every golf course is a bird refuge. Full of birds. Pittsburgh was wonderful. From the press box in Forbes Field you could see Schenley Park over the outfield fence.

I knew Dierheller, the director of the famous St. Louis Zoo. He was a great baseball rooter and a friend of Sam Breadon, who owned the Cardinal ball club. If Dierheller happened to be in New York, going to Europe or somewhere to get some animals, he'd always come into the *Times* sports department and see me there. He was a great baseball nut, and he and I and Sam Breadon used to put on baseball uniforms in the morning down in St. Petersburg when the Cardinals were training there. We'd work out and have a lot of fun and then go out to the beach and have soup and bread for lunch and go back to the ball park in the afternoon.

I always worked out in spring training. I had played baseball in college, at City College in New York. Played other sports, too. Fancy diver, slightly. Competed against Yale once. Didn't win, naturally.

When I was writing baseball I got along fine with all of the managers and the players. I was good friends with all of them. They used to think, you know, a baseball writer from New York wants New York to win. I didn't care. They were all friends of mine. Another thing they liked me for was they knew I could play ball.

Once, when the Yankees were training in New Orleans, I suited up during batting practice. It wasn't anything unusual. Anybody could go out there. At this particular time there was a golf tournament going on in New Orleans, or about to go on, and the golf pros, a lot of them being baseball rooters, came out to watch the Yankees practice.

A fellow by the name of Chick Fewster, who later played with the Dodgers, fine boy, was playing third base. I was playing short-stop. I was a good fielder but I couldn't hit. I think Aaron Ward was playing second base. I've forgotten who was at first.

Along comes a friend of mine, Ray McCarthy, who was just starting to be a manager for golf tournaments. He was a New Yorker. I knew him well. He was standing around first base with Leo Diegel, the great golfer. They were watching the practice.

There was a fellow batting called Camp Skinner. He was a rookie trying for the team, but they expected a lot from him. Not much of an outfielder but a whale of a hitter, all line drives. While Ray McCarthy and Leo Diegel were looking, this Camp Skinner hit the fastest thing I ever saw in my life—a line drive right at me. I got my glove up just in time and caught it right on my leg, at the ankle. If I hadn't caught it, I think it would have torn my ankle off.

Diegel was amazed. He says, "Who's that kid at short?"

McCarthy looks and says, "That's John Kieran. He's a baseball writer."

"Baseball writer!" Diegel says in surprise, and afterwards when I met him at the golf tournament he went around telling the other pros that I made the best baseball catch he ever saw.

Miller Huggins kept trying to get me out of there. He said, "You'll be killed." Finally, I did take myself out. It was in Sarasota, with the Red Sox. The Red Sox regulars had gone to Orlando, or somewhere, and left some of the rookies at home, and also Jimmy Foxx. Something was wrong with Jimmy. Or he wanted to rest. I was playing third base. Jimmy hit a ball back to the pitcher, who was trying out for the team, and this kid pitcher put his hand up to stop it and he broke part of his hand. That's when I said to myself, "Look, you better get out of here." By that time I was getting on to-ward forty.

I never told any manager how to manage or any ball player how to play. The most stupid ball player knows more, really, about the game than any baseball writer I ever knew. A lot of them play base-ball the way a beagle runs a rabbit. They do it instinctively.

Now, Babe Ruth was not a smart fellow. He was smart in a way, but he played baseball instinctively. I never saw him make a bad play. There was a fight in the Yankee dugout one day, when we were in St. Louis, between the Babe and Wally Pipp, a college fellow. Wally was tagged out on the bases and fouled up a rally. When he got into the dugout, the Babe started to ride him.

Wally went over—he was a pretty good boxer—and gave the Babe a couple of good wallops and, of course, everybody jumped in. Wally was a quiet fellow, one of the nicest fellows who ever played baseball. But he was so mad for the rest of that trip that they couldn't get him out. I think he hit .650 the rest of the trip and was knocking down the fences.

Lou Gehrig was, of course, one of the great Yankee players and among my favorites. When he was stricken they had a special Lou Gehrig Day at the stadium. The players chipped in and presented him with a big silver bowl. There was some verse written on it. I contributed the verse. I have a plaque of it upstairs. It reads:

> We've been to the wars together;
> We took our foes as they came;
> And always you were the leader,
> And ever you played the game,
>
> Idol of cheering millions,
> Records are yours by the sheaves;
> Iron of frame they hailed you;
> Decked with laurel leaves.
>
> But higher than that we hold you,
> We who have known you best;
> Knowing the way you came through
> Every human test.
>
> Let this be a silent token
> Of lasting Friendship's gleam
> And all that we've left unspoken;
> Your pals of the Yankee Team.

I was among the last in sports to see Gehrig. In fact, I was at Clarkson College getting an honorary degree, doctor of science, and when I came home they told me I was to call the Gehrig home. I figured what it was because he had been getting weaker all the time.

I called, and Mrs. Gehrig came to the phone and she told me he had died. She wanted me to give out the news and make up a list of honorary pallbearers. So I did. I called the *Times*, the AP, the INS, and whatever else.

I liked them all. What I think is the mistake of a baseball writer, or a sportswriter in general, is to become a fan of his own team. That warps your judgment. We're all full of prejudices, and if you're prejudiced in favor of your team it's going to warp your judgment no matter how hard you try to be fair. I had as many friends on the Cardinals and the White Sox—on all the teams—as I had on the New York clubs.

During World War II, I was on several tours. We would travel about, speaking to the boys in the service. Once our show appeared for the Red Cross at a hospital in Atlanta. The boys were asking questions, and one of them said to me, "Was Luke Appling a good shortstop?"

Well, you have to be careful when people ask you questions. I was in another hospital ward somewhere else and a boy said to me, "Was so and so a good heavyweight?"

I said, "No, he was lousy."

"Thanks," the fellow said. "He was my brother."

So I thought to myself, "Luke Appling a good ball player?" But luckily I said, "Luke Appling was a shortstop who twice led the American League in hitting. I'll say he was a good ball player!"

Then everybody began to laugh.

Finally, I said, "Is Luke Appling in the house?"

Sure enough, he was. He was stationed there, taking rehabilitation patients and getting them back into physical shape. I was glad to see Luke. I hadn't seen him in years.

You know, I didn't expect to be a sportswriter. I expected to be on the city staff. I would say I got on the *Times* through pure merit except for the fact that the assistant managing editor was a family friend and couldn't turn me down. I went in to see him—it was in June 1916—and he said, "Come back in the fall and I'll put you on the city staff."

I mentioned that since it was summer, maybe some of the sports staff was on vacation and suggested perhaps I could fill in. He thought that was a good idea and took me to the sports editor. Since all of the writers on the *Times* were on space then, salary was no object. You got paid for the stories that were used. I worked all summer and I made thirty-five cents, or something like that.

But in the meantime I played golf. I was a pretty good golfer. I wrote three or four stories about golf links and they weren't printed. But one day it rained all through the East and everything was off except horse racing. There was no tennis, no golf, no baseball. The sports editor had about fourteen columns to fill and nothing to put in them. So, in self-defense, he used one of my stories about a golf course—who had played there, and a history of some of the characters around the place.

The city editor at that time, a man named Ralph Graves, was a golf nut and had been trying to sell the idea that the *Times* should lean on golf—that the people who were buying the things that were being advertised, the carriage trade, were *Times* readers. He thought the *Times* should have its own golf writer.

He read my golf story, after that rainy day, and ran right around to the sports editor and said, "Who wrote that?"

The sports editor told him it was some young kid, and he said, "Well, make him your golf editor. That's the man! Don't let him go."

So they made me golf editor. I went out and had cards printed, "John Kieran, golf editor, *The New York Times*."

I showed them to the sports editor and he said, "Fine," and that's how I began as a sportswriter. I stayed writing golf until World War I came along and then I volunteered. I was overseas about three months after war was declared. Then, after I came home, Grant Rice hired me as a baseball writer for the *Trib*. A few years later, Damon Runyon was told to reorganize the sports department of the *American*, the morning Hearst paper. So Damon sent for me. What's-his-name was the managing editor, Gene Fowler. A famous writer of the time.

I walked in, and Gene asked what I wanted.

Well, I was getting a hundred dollars a week, big money for a young writer in those days. I said, "Well, how about a hundred fifty?"

He said, "Okay, do you want a contract for one, two, or three years?"

At the *American* I had more freedom. For instance, they sent me to Saratoga for the meeting. I wrote a column while I was up there called "Wild Oats and Chaff." I wrote verse, too, and I traveled with the baseball clubs. And they used me on fights and on hockey, and when I wasn't covering I was doing a column.

By then the *Times* decided they wanted a sports column. They had no sports column and no signed stories. They had a few feature and news writers, or political experts who would sign their stuff occasionally. When I wrote that golf story I was John W. Anonymous along with everyone else on the *Times*. Mr. Adolph Ochs was pretty sensible that way. He thought, why build up a man, give him a signed by-line, and then when he gets a name on the *Times* he sells the prestige of the *Times* and goes elsewhere. There's something to that.

I returned to the *Times,* taking a drop in salary, and on January 1, 1927, started what not only was the first signed sports column they had but their first signed daily column of any kind. Called it "Sports of the Times." What else?

In those days the promotion department of the *Times* had a few of us going around speaking at swanky prep schools. The *Times* was trying to catch them young, realizing they were all potential subscribers. The only way they could work me in was to have me participate in a course of lectures scheduled for every Sunday night. I did one at Yale later. But at this prep school I was talking to boys.

The professor who ran the course was apologetic about having a sportswriter on the program. He implied that sportswriters usually didn't know much and wouldn't be allowed to give one of these lectures. He was very condescending and explained that I was different from most sportswriters.

I got my back up right away. Naturally, I'm sore because I'm very fond of a lot of sportswriters. You've got ignorant sportswriters, same as you have ignorant lawyers and judges, and even doctors. Anyhow, I was sore and then this professor, this supercilious ass, pretended to know more than he did. He quoted some Latin and made a mistake.

So I got up and the first thing I did was correct his Latin for him. Then I hit him over the head with a half-dozen more Latin quotations and left him for dead. You never saw a bunch of kids so hilarious in all your life.

Walter Winchell—he was then the top columnist—heard the story and thought it was good. He added something to it, and the next fellow who repeated it added a little more. You know how these things grow. Each columnist added another personal touch.

Finally it was the senior class at Yale, and the story now is that I gave a baccalaureate address, and that I gave the whole speech in Latin. But that's a myth. It was nothing but a handful of Latin quotations, and all because of that pompous ass of a professor. It wouldn't be fair to mention the name of the school.

Fred Lieb

Fred Lieb, a familiar and authoritative sports byline for more than half a century, was still at the typewriter at the age of eighty-six, doing a weekly hot-stove baseball column for the St. Petersburg (Florida) Times. With an eye and ear for history, he authored an entire shelf of baseball books: Connie Mack, The World Series, The Baseball Story, Judge Landis, *and* 25 Years of Baseball *(ghosted for J. G. Taylor Spink), a volume on baseball humor, and team histories of the Detroit Tigers, St. Louis Cardinals, Boston Red Sox, Baltimore Orioles, Philadelphia Phillies, and Pittsburgh Pirates.*

One of four children of George and Teresa Lieb, Mr. Lieb was born on March 5, 1888, in Philadelphia. He made his first sale while still in high school, winning a five-dollar gold piece for a short story about "some bad men in Western Pennsylvania" who robbed a bank and who were caught and hung. "In those days," said Mr. Lieb, "you strived for a happy ending."

Mr. Lieb worked on a succession of New York newspapers and, as he says, was in the "foremost freshman class that ever broke into the New York press box." This was in 1911. Other New York rookies that season were Grantland Rice, Damon Runyon, and Heywood Broun. All four are enshrined in baseball's Hall of Fame in Cooperstown, New York. Mr. Lieb's induction came in 1973. "I'm only sorry," he said, "that my wife didn't live long enough to see some of these honors that have come to me in recent years." The Mr. Chips of the baseball writers, Mr. Lieb covered forty-eight consecutive World Series, from 1911 through 1958. He died in 1980 in Houston, Texas, at the age of ninety-two.

Lou Gehrig and I always hit it off very well. I suppose it started because of Mom Gehrig. Lou usually would talk German to his mother, and the fact that I could talk German to Mom Gehrig brought a sort of kinship. Lou thought the world of his mother. There was a mother-son complex there that was as bad one way as the other. I remember when we were over in Japan, on one of those postseason exhibition tours, Lou spent something like seven thousand dollars on gifts for his mother—silks and ivory animals, expensive jades and jewels, all kinds of Japanese stuff.

We often went over to her house for dinner. I remember one time she had turkey *and* roast pig. Mom Gehrig was proud of her cooking. It was her way of exhibiting her ego with this thing that she did best, especially when Lou was going with some girl and brought her home for dinner. Mom could be very intimidating.

Mom Gehrig did everything to prevent Lou from getting married. But Mom finally lost. Eleanor won.

On the morning of the wedding—actually it turned out to be just a reception—Lou Gehrig came up to me and said, "Fred, I want you to do me a favor. It's a very important favor, and I don't know anybody but you who could do it. I want you to get Mom to come to the wedding."

"Gosh," I said, "you mean she's not going to the wedding?"

"No, she won't go. But I'm hoping that you and Mary"—that was my wife, Mary—"can talk her into going."

Mom Gehrig was at the ball game that day. She always sat in the same seat, near the Yankee dugout. I went down to see her during the game.

I said, "Mom, Lou just gave me an assignment. It's something he wants me to do."

"What is it?"

"To bring you to the wedding on Long Island tonight."

"I won't go, I won't go!" she said. "I've no intention of going."

I told her, "Now, Mom, that's no way to talk. Nobody knows better than I how close you and Lou have been during the years. If you want that closeness to last, this is a time you have to stand by. Your son is marrying another woman and that other woman is coming between him and his mother, and you now have that choice, whether he's to be married under good circumstances or bad. This could lead to a complete break, which it does sometimes."

Then she said some things about Eleanor, which I won't repeat. And she said, "I'm not going because I'd only raise hell."

I told her, "Mom, I'm going to be by your house at half-past five so we can make the six o'clock ferry. I'm going to honk and I want you to be ready. Mary will be with me."

She said, "It's no use because I won't go."

Anyway, I did go and honked once, and she was there. Everything went off all right. Actually, it was just a reception. Lou was so afraid of Mom's reaction that he and Eleanor had been secretly married the day before by the mayor of New Rochelle.

The only baseball people at the reception were Bill Dickey and his wife, Vi, and myself and my wife and daughter. I had a little more champagne than I usually drink, and on the way home, while we're on the Long Island ferry, I feel someone tugging at my shoulder. I didn't know who it was. I turned around and it was Mom Gehrig and she whispered, "Wasn't I a good girl? I didn't raise any hell."

We retained our friendship with the Gehrigs from the time they were married, and with Mom and Pop, too. There was always friction between them. Mom and Pop had a nine-room house in New Rochelle, that Lou had been buying on time. But after he was married he didn't keep up the payments and they had to let that house go back to the bank. Mom and Pop had to go into a comparatively cheap apartment in Mount Vernon, something like Archie Bunker has in "All in the Family."

One of the reasons for Lou's self-effacement and inner timidity was because of his parents. It wasn't that he was ashamed of them. Really, he was quite proud of them, but he was irritated that Mom and Pop were not more appreciated and that they hadn't made more progress in this country until he, their only surviving child, made it big. Also Lou felt sort of sorry that he was the only one of four Gehrig children who lived past infancy. Once Mom, in explaining her affection for Lou, said, "He's the only big egg I have in my basket. He's the only one of four who lived, so I want him to have the best."

My wife and Eleanor got along pretty good. After we moved to Florida the women kept in touch. Early in the winter of 1939, Eleanor wrote my wife that Lou hadn't been feeling too well. A New Rochelle doctor had diagnosed Lou's trouble as gallbladder and was giving him treatments, or medicine. Lou had been pretty well tied up with some things, and Eleanor thought if he came down here to St. Petersburg about a month early, before the Yankees started spring training, he could put that time into fishing and just lolling around in the sun. She asked if we could get them a house somewhere near us, near the old ball park which is where the Mets practice now, on Thirteenth Avenue and Fourth Street. We got them a place. Shortly, they came around.

The Gehrigs had a ouija board, and one night they brought it over to our house. We were living on Seventh Avenue, that's four blocks north of here. We used to get a contact on this board that called itself "Mark Antony"—without the H. And we really got some amazing stuff which I have in another book, not a baseball book. It's called *Sight Unseen*. Harper put it out in 1939.

We began this session, and almost the first thing was "ELEANOR YOU WILL MEET THE MOST DIFFICULT PROBLEM OF YOUR LIFE."

That may not be the exact words, but that's how I recall it. And "Mark Antony" reiterated that. "Mark Antony" would talk back and forth to us like I'm talking back and forth to you. I can't explain it. It's somehow the subconscious mind. Whether it was my wife's subconscious mind or not, I don't know. This wasn't an actual voice. The message would be spelled out on the board.

"Mark Antony" spelled this out, repeatedly, and we'd talk back.

I would say, "Now, Mark, you're not being fair." Or "That isn't fair. You're telling these people how Eleanor's got this problem, but you don't give us any inkling of what it's about."

"WELL SHE'LL KNOW ABOUT IT SOON ENOUGH."

So then we began asking different questions. I don't recall whether it was Lou or Eleanor who asked if it was about the adopted child.

"Mark Antony" said, "NO."

Lou and Eleanor were married in '33 and this was '39, six years later, and they didn't have any children. She was supposed to be two years younger than Lou. Mom Gehrig always insisted she was two years older. They didn't think they could have any children and had given thought to adopting a child.

As soon as Mom Gehrig heard about that she flew up to the ceiling. If there was going to be a grandchild, and if it wasn't a Gehrig, she wouldn't be interested. They never did adopt a child.

They were both concerned when they left our house, and so were my wife and I. And then the exhibition season opened and Lou got off to quite a bad start. You could tell he was sluggish. He kept saying, "I'm not getting enough work. I'm not in shape."

And I told him, "Hell, Lou, that's stupid. Everybody knows you can hit a ball. Why worry about it if you don't hit down here? It's only spring training."

Lou would come out to the ball park earlier than anybody else and be the last guy to leave. But trying to work out and play ball, with this disease already in his system, only exaggerated the condition. There was one game, a high-scoring game with the Braves. Lou was the clean-up hitter and came up four times and didn't get the ball out of the infield. Finally he came up in the ninth inning with the bases filled and two outs, and the Yankees behind, 7-6, and he popped up to the second baseman.

Lou was very low that night. He kept saying, "What in the hell is the matter with me? What in the hell is the matter with me?"

I said, "You'll snap out of it, Lou. Don't worry."

Eleanor, at that time, had no idea anything was seriously wrong. Later she said she had noticed that when he stepped off a curb, one foot would kind of plop down.

The Yankees left Florida, heading north, and played an exhibition game in Norfolk, and Lou had three home runs. I thought, "Well, he's finally snapped into it." Both my wife and I were overjoyed.

Then the season started and in his first seven games, maybe it was the first nine games, he hit about .145 or something like that. These were the last seven or nine games of that long, Iron Man record.

Later, Lou said the thing that really made him decide to take himself out of the lineup was when he had made a play which any high school first baseman could have made. It was an ordinary ground ball, and he threw the ball underhanded to Johnny Murphy, who was covering first base. Murphy had gone into the game as a relief pitcher. Murphy and Tony Lazzeri put their arms around him and slapped him on the back. "Good play, Lou! Good play, Lou!"

"That hurt me more than anything they could have done," Lou said. "If I'm so bad that when I field an ordinary little grounder I could have eaten up when I went to high school and they say, 'Great play! Great play!' then I know I'm hurting the club."

The Yankees were to open a western trip, and Lou went to Joe McCarthy, the manager, and told McCarthy to play Babe Dahlgren at first base. That's when his streak was broken.

I went up to New York earlier that year than I usually do. We stayed in Mount Vernon because my daughter lived nearby. When we got there I called Eleanor and I said, "We're coming over this afternoon!"

At first she said, "No, Fred, you better not come today." Then she said, "On second thought, I want you to come. I've got a very important phone message coming from Lou, and I'd like to have you with me when I get it."

Lou had called earlier in the day. He was up at the Mayo Clinic, having tests. I was there when he called the second time. Eleanor took the call in another room. And when she came back she said, "I need a drink. I need a drink." She took a stiff hooker of liquor and said, "You know what that Dutchman just told me? 'Don't worry, Eleanor. I have a fifty-fifty chance to live.'"

But soon I found out it wasn't a fifty-fifty chance. It was one out of a hundred. Eleanor found out, too. It was some kind of disease of the spinal column, or the cord. The kind of disease that makes the spinal column turn into chalk. On July 4 of that year, at Yankee Stadium, the people of New York paid Lou Gehrig the finest tribute a ball player has ever received. It was Gehrig Appreciation Day, Lou's farewell. That's when he said that, despite everything, he still felt he was the luckiest man in the world.

The Babe and Lou had been good friends, for about the first eight years that they played together. Quite often the Babe would be a guest at the Gehrig house. He and Mom Gehrig would have a lot of fun. It was there that I first knew that Babe could talk German, really, surprisingly well. Eleanor objected to this very much. She always thought they were talking about her.

Gehrig and Ruth were complete opposites. You couldn't find two more different personalities. Lou was a fellow with quite an inferiority complex that followed him into professional baseball. He once told me about the time when his coach at the High School of Commerce asked him to come out to practice for the baseball team. Lou walked around the outside of the field three times, without going in, and then he walked home.

The next day the coach said to him, "Why didn't you show up?"

And Lou said, "I was doing something else."

Lou was sort of ashamed that his father was a janitor in a tenement. He told me one time, when we were on the road, "You know, when some of the writers come up to me and ask me questions, they think that I'm rude because I don't answer right. But I'm so scared I'm almost shitting in my pants."

Lou had a real admiration for the Babe and was content to be in the Babe's shadow. You know, of course, about the Babe's "called shot" homer, the one off Charlie Root in Chicago, in the '32 World Series. There was never any question that Ruth called the shot. I had dinner with Lou the night of that game. Lou hit two home runs himself, but all he could talk about was "What do you think of the nerve of that big monkey calling his shot and taking those two strikes and then hitting the ball exactly where he pointed?" That was how Lou was. He was content to push himself backward and push the Babe forward.

Mom Gehrig thought well of the Babe, too. I don't think she spurred Lou on to exceed the Babe as much as Eleanor did. Once Eleanor told me, "I've got to start a campaign on this Dutchman. He's got this inferiority complex that he's second to Ruth. Now, we know that Ruth is the big man of baseball, but he isn't going to last too much longer and the one who must take his place must, necessarily, be Lou. And I'm trying to build him up to the point where he knows he's good. Babe takes it for granted that he's good. Lou has never had that kind of confidence."

The Gehrigs and the Ruths took part in that Japanese tour of 1934. Something happened on that trip. I think it started with the two ladies, Claire and Eleanor. Whether that had anything to do with the cooling off of their relationship I don't know. But it was about five years before they spoke to each other again, and that was when they met at Lou's farewell at Yankee Stadium.

I still see Eleanor occasionally, usually at the Hall of Fame inductions in Cooperstown. But the old intimacy is gone. We had a falling out after Lou died. I found out that Lou's grave—he's buried in Westchester County—was very much neglected, a lot of weeds, birdshit all over it, and so on. I wrote a letter to a third party about this, to Christy Walsh, the agent. I wrote to him because he was doing some things for Eleanor, following up some deals that Lou had been in, and I said if he didn't do anything about this, about the neglected grave, that I would complain to the commissioner, who was then Chandler.

I thought he would approach Eleanor in a nice way. But he went directly to her with my letter. She called me up, oh, it was about three o'clock in the morning, St. Louis time, and accused me of being a false friend. She said she could sue me, but because of our former relationship she wouldn't. Then she asked to talk to Mary, my wife. Mary objected to Eleanor calling us at that time in the morning. They talked for about a half an hour and finally Mary said, "I don't want to talk anymore."

I've seen the Lou Gehrig movie—*Pride of the Yankees*—several times. They still play it on television. Walter Brennan plays the part of a sportswriter who is Lou's personal friend. I suppose you could say he played my part, though my name isn't mentioned.

I'm mentioned in *The Babe Ruth Story*, which is supposedly based on the book by Bob Considine. The book is under Considine's name, but I gave him most of his information. I dictated that book for about a week prior to the 1947 World Series. I told everything I could recall. Not everything, but everything that could be printed. Considine gave me a copy of the book and inscribed on the title page, "To my good friend Fred Lieb—Without whom this book would not have been possible."

I didn't get in on the royalties, but my name is mentioned in the movie. They said that Fred Lieb measured the six-hundred-foot homer that Ruth hit at Tampa, Florida, during a Red Sox–New York Giant exhibition game in the spring of 1919. Many people believe it was Ruth's longest homer, and he hit it well before he became the nation's home run idol. Actually, the homer was measured by two Boston writers, one of them Mel Webb. I believe I am the only one alive of the New York and Boston writers who covered that game.

I've been somewhat amused this past summer reading about the trouble Hank Aaron was running into when he was chasing Ruth's record. Aaron said—and it came out in the papers—that the fans were writing him abusive letters, calling him "nigger," and he said that Babe Ruth was never confronted with anything like that.

What Aaron doesn't know, and I suppose what most people don't know, is that some of Babe's teammates on the Red Sox were convinced he had Negro blood. There was quite a bit of talk about that. Many of the players, when they wanted to badger him, called him "nigger." Ruth had Negroid features, Negroid nose, mouth, lips. But when you saw him naked, from the neck down, he was white, a good deal whiter than most men.

Ty Cobb once refused to share a cabin with Ruth. I'm sure of the authenticity of this. They were assigned to the same cabin, but Cobb objected and said, "I've never bedded down with a nigger and I'm not going to start now." This was when they were down at Dover Hall, a hunting lodge near Brunswick, Georgia. A lot of baseball men would go down there in the off-season.

Cobb and Ruth never did get along. Cobb disliked most people, and particularly someone like Ruth who would take any of the glamour off himself. They had a fight once. It was in Detroit. They almost wrecked the place. I've forgotten now why it happened, but they had to call off the game the next day because the fans tore the seats loose and threw them on the field. There must have been five thousand dollars' worth of damage.

The Yankees were at bat and Detroit was in the field. Cobb was the playing manager, and when the fight started he came running in from center field. Ruth got off the bench and ran out to meet him. They met like two football linemen, each trying to put the other out of the play. One shot out in one direction and the other in the other. I have that in my Detroit book. I could look it up if you want me to.

Ruth didn't talk much about Cobb. One time, when I was doing a story on the Babe, I called on him about four in the afternoon and stayed with him until midnight. Despite the fact that Ruth had a sore throat—this was just before he died—we talked for more than eight hours, straight through. He said he thought Cobb was a great ball player but a no-good, mean sonofabitch. Babe wasn't alone on that. Ninety percent of the players felt the same way. Cobb was very much hated. The players hated his guts.

Cobb was a mean, cruel man. I didn't witness this myself, but was told about it by another newspaperman who would have no reason to distort the incident. Cobb was sitting on the porch at Dover Hall with some other baseball men, including some baseball writers. Someone had petted a hunting dog, and the dog came up a few steps on the porch. Cobb got up, almost leaped at this dog, and kicked him about fifteen yards. It wasn't just kicking. He kicked the dog like a football would be kicked, and shouted, very angrily, "That's a hunting dog, not a pet dog. He knows better than this, to come up on the porch." To me, that shows the latent cruelty within Cobb.

Cobb once threatened to punch me in the nose. It was when he was managing Detroit. He was always late sending his lineup to the press box. We had a rather stupid, almost illiterate guy who was the field announcer at Yankee Stadium. He would go on the field before each game and bring the lineups to us. We bawled him out because whenever Detroit was playing he was always late, though I suppose it wasn't all his fault. One time he tried to hurry Cobb into giving him the Detroit lineup. Cobb gave him hell and said, "Why should I worry about those twenty-five and fifty-dollar-a-week sons of bitches?"

I wrote a column the next day blasting Cobb. I headed it with his ridiculing us twenty-five and fifty-dollar-a-week sons of bitches. I said without us there wouldn't be anybody to record his .400 batting average, things like that.

Cobb sent word he wanted to see me. He said, "I didn't like that column you wrote."

I told him, "Well, I only wrote what Jack Lenz told me."

"Who in the hell do you believe? Do you believe that stupid son-ofabitch? Or do you believe me?"

I said Lenz had no reason to lie. I believed him.

So Cobb said, "We're going to have this out man-to-man."

I said, "Well, I guess you outweigh me by a few pounds."

Then Cobb relaxed. He smiled and said, "Anyway, you had the guts to come down here. A lot of you sons of bitches wouldn't come down here. I admire you for that."

After that experience Cobb became one of my best friends. It was about this time that we started writing preseason stories on each team, on the prospects of each club and how they figured to do during the season ahead. One spring I couldn't get to see the Tigers. I wrote to Cobb, asking him about his club. And surprisingly enough, he sent me a nine-page handwritten letter telling me who his best new prospects were, things like that. So here the guy is supposed to be so tough, and yet he stayed in his room long enough to write me a long personal letter.

I always thought Cobb was embittered, as a young man, because of the shooting of his father—the way he was killed. His mother shot his father. Supposedly it was an accident, a case of mistaken identity. I know Cobb had a great admiration for his father. He spoke of him often. I never heard him mention his mother.

His father was superintendent of schools for the county they lived in in Georgia. The story was given out that the father was on a trip in one of the more remote parts of the county. He came home unexpectedly and his wife, according to the story, thought he was an intruder and shot and killed him.

This happened right about the time Cobb won his first batting championship. That would be 1907. His father very much opposed his going into baseball. He wanted him to be a doctor and get an education. An older newspaperman told me that Cobb's father told him, "Well, all right, go ahead and play baseball. But don't come back unless you've made it." Eventually his father was reconciled to his playing baseball.

In his later years, long after he was out of baseball, Cobb tried to change his image. I saw him only a few times in the last years of his life. He was hungry for companionship. He'd want you to have lunch with him, and then he insisted you stay for dinner. It'd be midnight before he let you go. He would talk incessantly. He admitted he didn't have too many friends among the ball players, and he kept repeating he wasn't as mean as people made him out to be. I always had the feeling that if he had had another chance he might have done things differently.

I was in the middle of a famous scoring controversy that involved Cobb. It was in 1922, the last year the Yankees played in the Polo Grounds. The game was being played in the rain, and the other writers, including Jack Kieran, the official scorer, left the press box and scrambled into the top rows of the grandstand for cover.

I stayed in the press stand because I was handling the play-by-play wire for my paper, the New York *Press,* and because I was doing the box score for the Associated Press. Cobb hit a grounder to Everett Scott, the Yankee shortstop. Scott kicked it, fumbled it a bit. The field was wet, and ground balls were difficult to pick up. I figured with Cobb's speed he would have beaten it out for a hit.

If Jack Kieran had been in the press stand, I would have turned to him and asked how he scored it. But he wasn't there. I credited Cobb with a hit in the AP box score and thought no more about it. But Jack, in the official box score which he sent to the league statistician in Chicago, didn't give Cobb a hit. He charged Scott with an error.

This was in August, and nobody noticed until the end of the season when the official averages were tabulated. The AP had been sending out weekly averages which were used by all the newspapers but, of course, were not official. At the end of the season the AP had Cobb hitting .401, but Irwin Howe, in Chicago, the league's official statistician, had Cobb hitting .399.

Howe checked and found this game in August and then made a bad, bad mistake. He decided that since I was the more experienced scorer, my judgment, my decision, should be made official. But there was more to it than that. Howe was working for the president of the league, Ban Johnson, and Johnson wanted the American League to have a .400 hitter, more or less as evidence that the American League was superior to the National League.

I objected to this, but Howe and Johnson insisted they were going to honor my judgment ahead of Kieran's. It so happened that I was the national president of the baseball writers that year, and in the winter I presided at one of the stormiest meetings in our history. We had eleven chapters then—one in each major league city. As I recall, two chapters were not voting, or perhaps they weren't present.

I was really rooting for Cobb's .399. We voted by chapters and the vote was 5-4 in favor of Cobb's .399 and, of course, in favor of Kieran's decision. But Johnson and Howe continued to insist on the .401, and we said if they listed Cobb's .401 in the record books and in the baseball guides, then they should have an asterisk after it, saying, "Not recognized by the Baseball Writers Association." But they never did use an asterisk. That's how Cobb hit .400 for the third time.

I was the official scorer in the first American League game that I attended as a writer because the New York *Press* had befriended the Yankees—they were the Highlanders then—in their early years. So whoever wrote baseball for the *Press* was the official scorer at all Yankee home games.

In the middle of my first year as a scorer, Frank Farrell called me up one day and bawled me out. He owned the Yankees then. He was a politician, a Tammany man. He had been a gambling house owner and collector of a lot of bawdy houses.

Anyway, Farrell called me and said, "You know what I'm paying Jack Knight?"

I didn't know.

"I'm paying him four thousand dollars for playing short, a lot of money for an infielder. He made two errors yesterday, and I pick up my morning paper and I don't see any errors for him."

I explained it was a matter of the judgment of the scorer, that they were difficult chances. But Farrell wasn't interested. The conversation ended with him saying, "Whenever anybody on my club makes an error, I want you to give it to him."

I always had confidence in my ability as an official scorer. I had played a lot of baseball in my early years. That's how I got started in the business. I was a baseball nut, but I was a mediocre player. I played for our church team—the Prince of Peace. We were all Princes of Peace. I had a pretty good left arm, but I was a sucker at the plate and struck out frequently, so the next best thing was to write baseball.

I got started rather early, after high school. I worked in a railroad office in Philadelphia—that's my home town—and I began writing on the side. I contacted *Baseball Magazine,* which was then a new publication. I think it started around 1908 or 1909. In the fall of 1909 they took two of my stories, biographies of Hans Wagner and Ty Cobb, and from there I went to Fred Clarke and Hugh Jennings, the managers of the two World Series clubs of 1909. They liked them and had me do a monthly biography of the great players.

Eddie Collins was the first player I ever talked with. Eddie was pretty nice, but Christy Mathewson was quite reticent, and John McGraw was hard to reach. McGraw would bawl the hell out of you at something that you wrote that displeased him. He would say, "Why don't you come to me when you want some information on this? Why do you just write it?" He bawled me out once for a story about how he let Heinie Wagner go. Heinie was a shortstop for the Red Sox in the 1912 World Series, and McGraw let him get away. It wasn't even an important story, just a fill-in, but McGraw bawled hell out of me anyway.

I also had the good fortune in 1910 to sell two baseball fiction stories to a magazine called *Short Stories.* That was one of the pulps at that time, and later they became an ace in the hole. If I couldn't sell a story to *Top Notch,* or *Popular,* or *Railroad Man's Magazine,* I'd send it to *Short Stories* and invariably they took it.

Then I was briefly with the Philadelphia News Bureau, which was the Philadelphia outlet for the *Wall Street Journal.* My former railroad boss got me acquainted with Clarence Barron, the big boss of Dow-Jones and *Barron's Weekly.* A meeting was arranged for me and Barron, a job interview, at the old Waldorf-Astoria in New York. I met him there, in his room, and the first assignment I had from him was "Draw me a bath."

Barron had one of those big stomachs, and when he lay in the tub this big stomach looked like a big turtle up there. He said, "So you want to write, do you?"

I told him I had visions or ambitions to be a sportswriter, and he says, "Oh, bah, sportswriter! Sportswriters make pennies. Why don't you become a financial writer? That's where all the money is."

Barron was a lineal descendant of Priscilla Alden—you know the Priscilla Alden story—"Speak for yourself, John." I worked for Barron for about four months and then I went to the New York *Press,* which wasn't a great newspaper, but it had two distinctions. At that time it was the only Republican newspaper in New York City, and it gave more space to baseball than any other paper in the country.

That was in 1911. But actually my start as a baseball writer was two years before that, because of those *Baseball Magazine* biographies. That was when Al Spink of *The Sporting News* got out a book on baseball, a *Who's Who, People Worth Knowing in Baseball,* and had me in there as "baseball's foremost biographer." Of course, I was only a kid, twenty-two or twenty-three years old, but it made me think I was a pretty important person.

Armed with these biographies, I got the job at the New York *Press.* I stayed there until 1916, and then I went to the *Morning Sun.* Later I moved to the *Telegram,* then to the *Post.* In 1934 I came down here to St. Petersburg and began free-lancing full-time, writing books and magazine articles. In the summer I usually went up to *The Sporting News* in St. Louis, as an extra man to help out when others went on vacation. Sometimes I'd spend almost half the year there. Eventually I worked for *The Sporting News* full-time.

This is the sixty-second year that I have a card in the Baseball Writers Association. Only John Wheeler has been a member longer. Wheeler was out of New York City and went into the syndicate business. I believe he's worth several million now. There's nothing else I would have rather done. When I walked into the New York press box for the first time, I couldn't have been happier, not if I'd made the Oval Office in the White House.

○ ○ ○ ○
○ ○ ○ ○
○ ○ ○ ○

Paul Gallico

Paul Gallico was a sportswriter for thirteen years, from 1923 to 1936, all with the New York Daily News. *He then turned to fiction. The Gallico library fills an entire shelf: twenty-seven books. His first book,* Farewell to Sport, *is one of the few true sports classics.* Snow Goose, *a story of crushing tenderness, was converted into an award-winning television film, and* The Poseidon Adventure *was made into a movie which in the first nine months of 1973, stimulated sales of the book's paperback edition to over 800,000 copies.*

Mr. Gallico was born on July 26, 1897, in New York City, the only child of Paolo Gallico, a pianist with the New York Philharmonic Orchestra, and the former Hortense Erlich, both immigrants from Europe. He spoke fluent French and German, made six successive summer trips abroad, beginning at the age of ten, and in his middle years was drawn to Europe. He bought a home in South Devon, England, in 1936 but didn't move abroad permanently until

1950. He has lived at various times in a village on Lake Como in northern Italy, on a mountaintop in Liechtenstein, at Ashford Castle, Ireland, in Lucerne, Switzerland, and in the south of France.

A private person who didn't like to be irritated by neighbors ("nor do I irritate them") the aristocratic Mr. Gallico met me at the door in a green velvet smoking robe. He was living in secluded splendor, in a 450-year-old, five-story brick house in Antibes, surrounded by thousands of books, with servants and a secretary, and his fourth wife, the former Virginia Curtis-Bennett of London who managed his business affairs. As I was leaving he said, "Tell everyone I'm still full of piss and ginger." He died in 1976 a week before his eightieth birthday.

On the afternoon of the fight, when I came to Jack Dempsey's camp, Hype Igoe was sitting at his typewriter doing some preliminary stuff. He was the boxing writer for the New York *Journal,* one of the famous sportswriters of the time. He looked up and he said, "Say, you're Gallico, ain't you?"

I said, "Yes, Mr. Igoe." Very respectful.

And he said, "I understand you're going to go in the ring with the champ."

"That's right, Mr. Igoe. But, you know, we're just going to sort of fool around and take it easy."

Hype looked at me over his glasses and said, "Son, don't you know that that man can't take it easy?"

I was twenty-four, just a few years out of college, in very good shape. I'd been on the crew for four years at Columbia, so I looked like an athlete—six three and a half and a hundred ninety-two pounds. I'd been in the sports department for about a year, hidden really, out of sight. Just a copyreader and paste-up man. When they did send me out on an assignment, it was always as an extra man to do color and crowd stuff for the early editions. No by-line. I simply didn't exist.

I had attended fights here and there and seen guys hit on the chin and go wobbly. I wondered what this was all about. I thought if I found out and wrote a first-person story, it would be a good feature. It would be exclusive. Nobody else had done it.

I went to Dempsey. I'd been covering his camp—this was for the Firpo fight—for about a week and had been sending stories back every day, little side pieces, about sparring partners, about Saratoga Springs, the crowds and the color. Jack Farrell was our boxing writer. He was doing the main camp.

Dempsey knew me by sight, that I was one of the reporters. But he didn't know my name. I was a young kid. Nobody had ever heard of me.

Anyway, I was smart enough to say this was not my idea. I said my editor had sent me up and had suggested I go in the ring with him and write a story of what it was like. I remember his answer: "What's the matter, son, don't your editor like you no more?"

I talked him into it. Jack Kearns, his manager, was away at the time, scouting Firpo in Atlantic City. Kearns wouldn't have allowed it. I'm fairly sure of that because he gave Dempsey hell when he came back. He said, "Listen, you don't know this kid. He might be a ringer."

Dempsey said, "Well, I promised the kid and I don't break a promise."

Kearns told him, "All right, but don't be a fool. Don't take any chances. Get him quick."

I had about five days of suffering before the so-called bout. I was scared stiff and felt like a fool. I had never boxed before. To get into the ring with the champion of the world didn't seem like a very sensible thing to do.

The fight took place on a Sunday. It was to be part of Dempsey's show, part of the regular training. Three thousand people were there at a dollar apiece, a lot of money in those days. I had to wait at ringside. I had headgear and was in trunks and an undershirt, a rowing shirt from college. He had about five sparring partners, little ones for speed, big ones for heavy hitting. Three of them were on the program ahead of me, and each one was carried out. I said, "Okay, Gallico, you're next!"

Kearns was the referee and made the introductions, very formal. He said, "In this corner, the heavyweight champion of the world, Jack Dempsey," and everyone said, "Hooray!" Cheers. Applause.

"And in the opposite corner, his opponent from the *Daily News* of New York, Paul Gallico."

There was a dead silence.

Kearns called us to the center of the ring and we got instructions. All I knew about boxing was to keep my left arm out. I knew the position. Dempsey came in, bobbing and weaving. As he came in he walked into my left. It wasn't a hard punch, more of a jab. He looked like a very angry tiger. I retreated and he chased me. I stabbed him again and I thought, "I'm doing all right."

There is one photograph in the *News*—pictures were taken all through this—of which I haven't the slightest recollection. But there I am bent over and Dempsey's left hook is whistling over my head. I have no recollection of ducking that one. But I didn't duck the next one. I found myself on the floor. Everything went sort of black. The ring made one complete revolution clockwise and then went back, counterclockwise.

Kearns was saying, "Six, seven, eight." Like a God damn fool I got up.

Dempsey pulled me in, next to him. By then he knew I was a bum. He knew he had me, that I was no fighter. He whispered to me in the clinch, "Hang on, kid, until your head clears."

But he couldn't stop. That was the nature of the beast. He hit me with six straight rabbit punches on the neck, all perfectly legal, and the next thing I knew Kearns was saying, "Thirty-eight, thirty-nine, forty."

It was as if a building had fallen on me. The whole thing lasted a minute and thirty-seven seconds. I came out with resin on my pants, a cut lip, and a headache.

A half-hour later, I was writing my story. I wrote exactly what had happened, from beginning to end. I've always written fairly fast. When we had to make an edition and I was covering a fight, I mean no sooner had the body been dragged from the ring than I was saying, "Lead all, Gallico," and was dictating to the operator.

Captain Patterson, the publisher of the *News*, laughed his head off. He thought it was very, very funny, and the next day I had a by-line on that story. Two months later Patterson appointed me sports editor. He had been fed up with his sports editor anyway.

It was my initiative on the Dempsey stunt, and Patterson, you know, was a very rugged guy. He admired physical courage—not knowing that I didn't have physical courage but purely curiosity, and was willing to endure something for my curiosity. In fact, Patterson was a man who would sometimes go out and pick fights just for the fun of it—fist fights, anybody in a bar. He was a big man and a soldier, don't forget, a captain of artillery in World War I. He was rough and tough, and he liked people who had ideas. So he made me sports editor, and a year later he gave me a column.

I wasn't a stranger to Patterson. He had originally hired me as a motion picture critic. I got that job because of my first wife. I had married the daughter of Burton Leston Taylor—BLT, does that name mean anything to you? BLT was the poet and columnist for the Chicago *Tribune,* our sister paper owned by Patterson's cousin, Colonel McCormick. BLT wrote a literary column that ran on the *Tribune* editorial page, with poetry and epigrams. To make BLT's column was an accolade. He was as famous in his day as Winchell was in his.

BLT's daughter, Alva, had studied piano with my father in New York. She was a Radcliffe girl. When we were married she moved to New York and Patterson was going to give her the job as movie critic on the *Daily News.* He wound up giving me the job instead. The year before I had spent about eight months on the National Board of Review, censoring movies. That was a volunteer organization. At that time there was only state censorship, so the picture producers, to protect themselves and get a decent censorship on their pictures, paid this national board. It was sort of a charity organization. They paid them six dollars a reel to review pictures. We had about two hundred people and we would screen pictures all morning, all afternoon. I worked as review secretary with these committees. The idea was for the review secretary to control the meeting and see that nothing really smutty got by, but at the same time to keep the do-gooders and wowsers from taking out pieces of the picture which would gut it. I was just out of college and that was my first job.

I liked being a movie critic, but Patterson didn't like my reviews. I was young, a smart aleck, thought I knew it all. I was constantly criticizing. Patterson came to me one day and said, "Listen, Gallico, people like movies or they wouldn't go to them. Take it easy."

I didn't believe him and kept criticizing everything, and finally Patterson said, "Gallico, you don't enjoy movies. We're going to get another movie critic." Patterson sort of fired me, but there was an editor, Phil Payne, and Phil liked me and hid me out of sight, in the sports department.

I didn't come to Patterson's attention again until many months later when I was doing the predate. Our circulation had gotten so big that we couldn't get the papers out to the Pacific coast on time, so Patterson started what probably was the first predate. It was a misbegotten edition, made up and published two Sundays ahead. The new boy always got it. Actually, there could be no hard news in the predate. It was mainly feature stories, but we'd also write ahead, about events and games that were going to occur. I designed it. Wrote it. Edited it. Everything.

I worked the predate to my own fancy and cooked up a number of articles which attracted Patterson's attention. One of them was the perfect athlete. It was an article and photo montage. I took Babe Ruth's eyes, Dempsey's body and fists, somebody else's wrists, somebody's legs—about six or seven great athletes. I took a part of each and made a man out of them. It ran the whole length of the page, with a long piece I wrote to go with it.

Patterson liked that. And of course he liked the Dempsey stunt, so well that he got me to follow it up. I caught passes from Benny Friedman, and I went on the baseball field and caught Dazzy Vance, or was it Herb Pennock? It was Pennock. He had that great curve, all sorts of stuff on the ball. I caught him to actually see what the batter saw. It gave me an idea of the exquisite timing of these guys. I rode with Gar Wood, the speedboat driver, and I rode with Cliff Berege at the Indianapolis Speedway, about ten times around the track, just for the sensation. I played tennis with Helen Wills, golf with Bobby Jones. I always picked champions. I even went up with Al Williams, a famous flyer. Did acrobatics with him.

In recent years George Plimpton has done some of these things, but George did give me credit for being the first one, and that's one reason I'm completely at peace with George. He's a very good writer and a square guy. That book he wrote, *Paper Lion,* was very well realized. I would never say a word against George. He was smart enough to commercialize on it, just as Billy Rose was smart enough to commercialize on my water circus.

My water circus was a reply to the utter dullness of swimming races. Patterson wanted girls in tight bathing suits, those one-piece black swimsuits. They made very sexy pictures. So we ran swimming races as a promotion, but they are insufferably dull. The only thing interesting is the high diving. So I got an idea to combine the races with a water circus. I went out to Jones Beach. Bob Moses was then the Commissioner of Parks, and we got together and put on a show with elephant and clown acts, acrobats, fire divers from the high platform—interspersed with swimming races. Of course, it was for free. We drew seventy, eighty thousand people.

I always had a star for my show. Eleanor Holm was my star one year. Billy Rose came out because he was in love with her, married her. He saw this production and took the idea of combining acts and swimming down to Texas, where they were having one of these centennials. Then he brought it back to New York and made a couple of million dollars on it. He made his fortune on that water show. And this again never worried me. Fine. If anybody has the brains to commercialize something, go to it.

I started a football contest called the Ninety-eight-Percent Wrong Club Football Contest. We published a coupon of ten games every Monday, the ten games coming up on Saturday, and challenged the reader to pick the results of these ten games against me. The reader who came closest to predicting ten games would get two tickets for the big game the following week. The dunces, the losers, got a pin, a lapel pin, a football with two donkeys' ears attached to it.

I was a bad picker. I was a real nonexpert, and this club which I started in my column said that the way to make money was to bet against Gallico, who was ninety-eight-percent wrong. Murray Lewin, the boxing writer of the *Daily Mirror,* the Hearst tabloid that was our big rival—they used to advertise that his boxing picks were ninety-six-percent right. As a burlesque of that I said mine were ninety-eight-percent wrong.

It had the most curious effect. In the newspaper business, as you've found out, you never know what results something will have. The *News* had always been suffering from lack of male advertising. It was known as the cooks' delight. Only a female readership. And whenever our advertising agent tried to get men's advertising, they said, "Who reads the *News*?" Why should Hickok Belts or this shaving cream advertise in the *News*? So the third week of the Ninety-eight-Percent Wrong Football Contest the advertising agent went around to a couple of advertising agencies, and when they said, "Men don't read the *News*," two kids came in carrying waste baskets and dumped two-hundred-fifty thousand letters on the desk of the guy and said, "These people read the *News*. These are men." And from then on we had male advertising and I got a raise. You couldn't figure that.

As sports editor I chose my assignments and went where I thought the story lay. I did some crazy things, like trying to cover— actually I did cover—five major sports championships in one day. I did it flying in my own plane. That kind of thing gave me a kick. I learned to fly because Patterson learned to fly. I was vain myself. It was something different and it gave my publisher a kick. He liked it.

I flew up to Boston for a golf tournament and did nine holes, following Bobby Jones. By that time he was so far in front the story was over. On the way back I flew over the America's Cup yacht race, off Newport. My plane at the time was an amphibian, so I landed and filed a story. Next I flew over the Belmont racetrack, wrote a story on a futurity. I didn't know what horse won, but I wrote a story anyway. Then I landed at Meadowbrook and covered a polo match late in the afternoon. Then to Long Island Stadium to cover a lightweight title match. Barney Ross was fighting somebody.

Patterson was wonderful to work for, a marvelous man. He was known as God around the *News*. Somebody would say, "God's in the building." He was an absolute autocrat. What he said went. His word was law. But he didn't say it that way. He was a benevolent God. He had one of the sweetest smiles of any man I've ever known, and he was fair and just. He was always at my side and in my mind, looking over my shoulder, so to speak, whether he was there or not.

I'll give you a story on Patterson's kind of justice. I had been sports editor for quite a while. The predate was still going, but somebody else was doing it. Patterson came into the sports department one day and the predate was on my desk. The top headline said, "YALE MEETS HARVARD." It was two weeks ahead, just up from the press room for me to look over and see if there were any mistakes, if it would be necessary to replate.

Patterson must have been distracted; I mean, his thoughts were wandering. He looked at the predate and said, "That's a stupid thing to do. What do you mean by that? Yale isn't playing Harvard this week."

He gave me hell in front of my staff, really bawled me out. "You're supposed to be sports editor," he yelled, and stalked out, leaving me pale and shaking and thinking, "Well, there goes my career."

I took another look at this paper and said, "Oh my God, this is the predate." I hadn't realized it. When you're being bawled out like that, you figure you've pulled one. God speaks and the thunder rolls. You sort of fall apart. But I was more worried about his being wrong than that I was right, and I went to Frank Hause, the managing editor, and said, "Look, Frank, I'm in a hell of a jam."

Hause said, "What's the jam?"

"The jam is that Patterson is wrong and I'm right, and I don't want to be right where God is concerned. I'm really in trouble because he bawled me out in front of my entire staff. Everybody will know he was wrong."

He said, "Well, okay. Go back and forget about it. There's nothing you can do. He just got mixed up."

Well, we had a house organ for the employees, called *News-Pix,* which came out once a month, on smooth paper. You know, "Joe Doakes, the linotyper, is to be married next week," that sort of thing. And in it was a two-page apology from Patterson to me. He wrote it out and said exactly what had happened, that he had come into my office, how he made this awful mistake. He apologized in this house organ to the entire paper.

Patterson was really idolized. I don't think he had ever been a reporter, but I'm sure he could write. He wrote a novel, I think, in his early days. I never saw any stories he wrote, but I saw him edit and I saw his ideas. He got close to the people, which his cousin, Colonel McCormick, never did. To me, the Chicago *Tribune* always reflected the colonel and his stuffiness, while the *News* reflected Patterson, his toughness and closeness to people, his understanding of his audience. Patterson built our circulation because he understood readers.

He instituted what we called circulation tours. We had to get up at four o'clock in the morning and go around with him on the circulation trucks, to see where the papers were dumped. Then we'd hang about and see who bought these papers and get an idea of our audience. We did that about once every three months.

Also, once a month we had an evening drunk at an Italian restaurant called Minetta, downtown in the Italian section. All of the department heads would be there. Patterson would buy dinner and a lot of vino, and the barriers went down. We all got sloshed. Then he'd start to talk about the paper. Well, after drinking with him some of the awe went, which was his purpose. When he asked a question he got an answer. Nobody was afraid to talk.

The Golden Gloves was born down at Minetta's when Patterson asked me about amateur boxing. I told him how disgusted I was with the way the AAU ran its boxing tournaments at the Garden, how they were taking advantage of these boys. What they were doing, they'd have an amateur tournament and sixty or seventy-five boys would show up and they would draw enough for, say, sixteen bouts. That meant thirty-two boys, and they'd send the rest home. They wouldn't get a bout. And then a kid who had had five bouts might find himself in the ring with a veteran of fifty or sixty amateur bouts. Some of these kids were pros, you know. So we started the Golden Gloves to give all these kids a chance.

These were exciting times, but nonetheless I began tiring of sports. I'd always wanted to be a short story writer, and I had begun to sell stories to the *Saturday Evening Post*. Above all, I was beginning to find I was repeating myself in my column. I was scared stiff of becoming an old sportswriter, a veteran sportswriter. I could already read and hear, "Gallico, that veteran sportswriter."

An episode occurred, in 1933, in the Garden on fight night. We sportswriters were very elite. We just walked in. "Hiya, Joe. Hiya, Bill." At the ringside we had our bronze nameplates. I came in early. I always did. If the first prelim was at eight-thirty, I was in my seat at eight-thirty. My paper was paying me to cover an evening of fights and I felt it was my duty to be there. And you could never tell when something would happen in a prelim. I saw a fighter killed in a prelim.

Anyway, I was there in my seat. It was a big fight, a lightweight championship. Just before the main event, during that buzz and hum before the fighters come in, a sportswriter who shall be nameless arrived. I can still see him. He was wearing a coat with a fur astrakhan collar. He plunked his typewriter over everybody's head and climbed over us to his seat. Then he stood up, counting the house, to make sure everybody had seen his arrival, and from about the fourth row a voice shouted, "Sit down! You're only a sportswriter."

Something went *bo-ing*. There, but for the grace of God, are you, Mr. Gallico. There is the estimate from the man in the street. You're only a sportswriter. From that moment on I ceased being a sportswriter. It took me three years to get organized, but I got out in 1936. I remember Bill Cunningham of Boston wrote a very nasty column about me, saying who does Gallico think he is quitting sportswriting? He was furious. How dare I leave for something better? Then I wrote *Farewell to Sport*.

I always knew that eventually I would write fiction. That was always at the back of my head. I wasn't using sports as a go-between, but the thing about sportswriting which is so marvelous is that it's constant drama—and drama is the basis of fiction.

I belonged to the gee-whiz group of sportswriters. Pegler was the aw-nuts. I was impressed by athletes, by what I was seeing and also what I was trying to do. I thought I ought to impress my public, impress the people who were reading, because if I didn't make a game that I saw, and which excited me, if I didn't make that exciting to the reader, I was a lousy sportswriter.

We had an overwhelming innocence in those days. We were so naïve. Not only we sportswriters but the whole country. We had fought a world war, and supposedly won, and thought that we'd saved the world for democracy. Everybody was happy. There was a big boom. There were no problems. You could let yourself go on sports. A heavyweight championship fight, the build-up, was tremendous. It was like the Israeli-Arab war, the way one approached it. Your side and their side. The goodies and the baddies. Whether it was a ball game, or a boxing title, or a tennis or golf match, there was this built-in conflict and struggle, and we were witnesses to these struggles. When the Detroit Tigers came to town we hated them. Ty Cobb was a dirty word in New York. When Helen Wills played Suzanne Lenglen, when they met for the first time, you would have thought the world was coming to an end if our fine American girl got licked by this dreadful frog, this awful Frenchwoman. That's stupid, when you look at it now, but in those days it was all played that way, for high drama. You try that today and you'd be laughed out of the newspaper office.

I contributed to this innocence, this naïveté. Tremendously. I believed in it and was impressed by athletes and by what I was seeing. And while the title of your book is *No Cheering in the Press Box*, I've seen and heard plenty of cheering in press boxes when we sportswriters got excited about something. I remember young Jimmy Cannon, I think it was at a Billy Conn fight, getting up and yelling, "Lay down, you dirty son of a bitch of a dog! Lay down!"

I was getting a hell of a big salary from the *News* at that time, between forty and fifty thousand dollars a year. At the time I quit, a syndicate offered me seventy-five thousand a year and a three-year contract as a sports columnist. I turned it down. It wasn't what I wanted to do anymore. I was fed up with sports and wanted to be a fiction writer.

After I quit the *News,* George Horace Lorimer, the famous editor, sent for me. By this time I had been selling the *Post* regularly. He knew who I was, my reputation, but he wanted to look at this new writer. At our first meeting he told me, "We're very glad to have you with us on the *Post*. We very badly need a man who can give us good sports stories."

I said, "Thank you, Mr. Lorimer, but I want to play Hamlet."

"Oh? What form does your Hamlet take, young man?"

I said, "I don't want to write sports stories. I don't want to be typed. At the moment I want to write newspaper stories, about newspaper people."

Lorimer looked me over and said, "All right, young man, I'll tell you what. I don't care what your background is for your stories, as long as you tell me a story. If you tell me a story, we'll buy it."

And I went home very happy.

One of my phobias was getting typed. Damon Runyon made a fortune out of being a Johnny One Note. He wrote about these gangsters, Broadway characters. He never wrote about another subject. And of course, he became a classic. Fine. I didn't want to do that. I wrote a series of golf stories, about a golf salesman. I had my debutantes—two debutantes from Chicago—and ran them through about eight stories. And I had my newspaper stories. I've always tried to keep throwing switches, so they wouldn't say, "Gallico can only write this kind of story."

I moved to England and bought a house in Salcombe, a little fishing village on the Devon coast. I'll tell you why I bought a house in Devon. It was because of my first trip to Europe, when I was ten years old. That must have been 1907, and the steamers didn't go to Southampton then. They stopped at Plymouth, in Plymouth harbor, and discharged their passengers by tug. I remember waking up and the ship wasn't moving anymore, and I looked out the porthole—it was the end of the trip—and the first thing I saw were those green Devon hills sort of sloping down to the cliffs, and the cliffs down to the sea. Then we landed and I saw more of this countryside, and something in me—I was only ten then—said, "Someday I'm going to come back here." I can't tell you why. There's nothing mystical about it. It was just my first glimpse of Europe. Later on, when I was a sportswriter—when I was age thirty-three, thirty-four—and people talked about what they really wanted to do—you know, somebody wanted to retire to Florida and somebody else wanted to have a hunting lodge in Wisconsin—my story was that some day I was going to have a cottage with a thatched roof on the green hills of Devon. I heard myself say this so often that I finally said, "For Christ sake, Gallico, you're becoming the town bore. Either do it or shut up. If you want a cottage in Devon, go get it." And so I did.

That was my first stop in Europe. I was able to live cheaply, and of course, I was able to get out of that squirrel cage I was in in New York, where I had to run twice as fast to stay in one place. New York was too expensive. If I failed to sell a story I was in a hell of a fix, and the *Post* didn't buy them all. I could do a stinker occasionally.

I stayed in South Devon for four months, doing these newspaper stories, first about Perry Brown, reporter, and then Hiram Holliday, copyreader. Eventually, I ran them through eight, maybe ten stories. But I had the mistaken idea that all I knew was about sports and that I needed more experience, more rounding out. So I went back to the *News* as a cityside reporter at forty dollars a week, minimum guild.

Patterson took me back. He said, "Okay, Paul, if that's what you want."

This time I stayed eight months, got a couple of beats, and was raised to seventy-five dollars a week. I was becoming a fairly good writer, and what happened then was that the *News* began using me as a feature writer. They wanted a feature from me every Sunday. Well, hell, the *Post* was paying me two thousand dollars for a feature. This was bad economics. So I left again and went back to England, wrote short stories, and in the fall—this was '38, just before the war —I went to work for the Hearst syndicate as a special writer. The Hearst people paid me well, four hundred a week, but kept me on the move. They sent me wherever they had a paper. Three weeks in Seattle. Three weeks in Los Angeles.

I was still free-lancing, writing short stories on trains, in hotel rooms at night. Then it suddenly dawned on me I was being stupid. I didn't need to be a reporter. I could use my imagination. After all, fiction is fiction. I finished my Hearst contract, which was for one year. I never went back.

I've been writing fiction ever since, so I've been at it a long time. I've sold a lot of stories, I'd say easily eighty to ninety to the *Post* alone.

I was ten years old when I wrote my first story. I was in Europe with my parents, in Brussels. They were out on the town and I was alone in the hotel room.

I wrote a story about a little boy who was walking along the street and came to a construction site. They were putting up a building. There was a pile of pebbles there. They made their own concrete in those days, in the street, shoveled the stones and mixed them up. These are pretty colored pebbles and I wanted to take a pocketful of these pebbles, and the Italian worker said, "Go on, get out of here, you little bastard." He chased me away and I didn't get my pocketful of stones.

Later this Italian worker is sent up to the top of the building to work on a girder, riveting, and he slips and he's hanging onto a beam and they shout, "Hang on, Pietro! Rescue is coming!"

But—and here was the kicker—his strength gives out and he thinks to himself, "If only I had let that little boy have that shovelful of stones, I wouldn't have had to shovel that shovelful of stones. My strength would have held out." And that's what he's thinking as his grip gives way and he falls to his well-deserved death, the son of a bitch, for not letting me take that shovelful of stones. This was my first short story. I published it in my book, *Confessions of a Story Writer*.

I've often thought that my father helped make a story writer out of me. His name was Paolo—that's the Italian for Paul. I was an only child and was named after him. He was a concert pianist, composer, and piano teacher. He had his studio on Fifty-ninth Street. He didn't teach in his own home. We lived separately. He would come home from his studio around six or seven o'clock every night and shave. He shaved with a straight razor. I would sit down on the edge of the bathtub, and while he shaved he would tell me a story and the story would continue each night. I'd say, "Oh, Father. Tell me more."

"Nope, continued tomorrow."

Father was a nineteenth-century man. He was born in 1868, in Italy, and studied music in Vienna, where he met my mother, at the conservatory. My mother was then studying singing, but she never kept it up.

I had none of these problems of hating my father and all that psychological complication. He was a very kind father, very loving. He had a wild Italian temper and there would be outbursts, from time to time. But he always got over them immediately.

He loved me greatly. He was a soloist with the New York Philharmonic. I would go to his concerts and I'd sit up in a box and see my father down there on the platform. I'd be very, very proud of him and very excited. There was something I've never forgotten. One night, at Carnegie Hall, he sat down at the piano when he was about to play and looked up. He caught my eye and winked at me, and I felt marvelous, that this artist had singled me out for a wink.

Our home was always full of European musicians. The conductor of the Philharmonic was always around. Artur Schnabel, a great pianist. Stransky, Bodansky, conductors. Singers from the Metropolitan. This was the atmosphere in which I grew up. Father did make one attempt to make a musician out of me. But I got St. Vitus's dance and that was the end of that. He had the good sense to give it up. I simply had no talent for playing.

As I grew up father gave up concertizing and concentrated on his teaching. At that time, he was the best-known piano teacher in the country. His students came from all over, and not only students but professional pianists, concert pianists, who came to him for final coaching. I can't say that my boyhood was ever troubled by financial worries. My father may have had them, I'm sure he did, especially during the Depression, but he didn't transfer them to his family or to me.

I had an absolute New York education. I started at Public School 6, then shifted to P.S. 70, in a very tough neighborhood, Third Avenue and Seventieth Street, on the East Side. You had to fight, you know. You had to carry your own. Then I went to De Witt Clinton High School. I'm wearing Clinton colors tonight—red and black.

I was something of a puzzle to my family. My parents were very small and when I was, say, eighteen years old and stretched my arms out, like so, horizontally, they could stand under them. My father couldn't figure out where this giant came from. Well, of course, I was first-generation American. I was born in a country where there was proper food for kids and proper supervision.

I grew up completely as an American boy. It was important for me to do things that American boys did. The only real breach that I ever had with my father was over football. I made the high school team, in my junior year, and was due to play on the varsity and win my Clinton C, which I craved more than the crown jewels.

My father was baffled by my great desire to play football, just as he was baffled when I was on the Columbia crew. Football, rowing. This is foreign to a European. He couldn't understand why I was so proud to have a big C on my chest, especially with a crossed oar, which is the highest letter you could get at Columbia. I rowed six at Columbia, won my freshman numerals and three letters.

But my father did stop me from playing football in my senior year in high school. He insisted football was too dangerous and I never did win my Clinton C. I never forgave him for that, so to speak.

I was very angry, and when I went to Columbia I made up my mind I would work my way through and do exactly what I pleased. I was going to pay my own tuition, and nobody was going to tell me what to play and what not to play. And I did. I did translations, from German and French to English. I tutored kids. For a while I was a longshoreman, working on the docks. I did anything that came along. We had an employment office, to get jobs for students, and about once a month I'd go in looking for jobs.

It was while I was at Columbia that I first became aware of fencing. In the wintertime we used to be on the rowing machines, indoors. There were eight machines lined up, with tension and the sliding seats. It was like being in a shell, with oars, except there was no water. We were on those machines every night for crew practice, and after the workout Coach Jim Rice would say, "All right, you fellows, twenty times around the track."

So we'd all go trundling around the floor, and as we'd run around we'd pass the wrestling room, the boxing room, handball courts, the fencing room, the various minor sports. I would stop at the fencing room and watch Jim Murray, the fencing coach. He was about ninety years old, but he was amazing, like a flea on a hot stove. Nobody could touch him.

I said, "Someday I'm going to do this, but I can't now." Crew takes up all your time. But I never forgot those fencing sessions, and it wasn't until 1932, when I was in Rome, that I began fencing. I started with the Nadi brothers, Aldo and Neddo. Aldo was the world champion at the time. I continued fencing when I came back to New York, with a teacher named Joseph Vince. Later I took lessons from Santelli. And then I joined the Fencers Club of New York.

I've been fencing ever since. It gives me enormous pleasure at my age, at seventy-six, to diddle somebody twenty-three, confuse them. They see me and they say, "Here's an old man. I can take him." And then they find out that they can't take the old man. It's a kind of vanity, I suppose, but it's also good exercise and keeps me fit. My legs, my arms. It gives me a complete workout in an hour, and complete mental relaxation. It's physical chess. You've got to use your nut. I'm soaking wet when I finish. I always feel and look well after fencing. It's like a week in the country.

You can fence a stranger and in five minutes you will know all about him. I don't mean to say that you're going to know if he beats his wife. But you'll learn about his character. Is he honest, meaning does he mean his attacks? Or is he bluffing? Has he got some dog in him? Is he scared? Does he retreat all the time? At the end of an épée you've learned an awful lot about your opponent.

It's a sport that you can do well up to any age, if your heart stands up. I don't go in for competition anymore. That would be stupid. I can't go into competition for the same reason that prize fighters can't fight after a certain age. Your legs go. I'm fine for the first six, seven minutes. I can hold my own with anybody, amateur or pro. It's something I can do in my tempo. I fence a bout and sit down and rest. Somebody says, "Would you like five touches?" "Sure." If you feel that you're getting a bit tired, you bluff a bit and fiddle and take a rest. You can pace yourself to the point where it's thoroughly enjoyable.

When I'm in London—that's where I go to play—I fence four times a week, at the Lansdowne Club. I'm in London three months of the year, on holiday. I don't do any writing there. Now, I fence twice a week. We have a little club at Fort Carré, across the bay. The concentration required is so intense that it's the only way I can forget my work. Otherwise, I'm working all the time.

I've lived here, in Antibes, for the last twelve years, in this house, doing my work, not bothering anybody, not being bothered by anybody. We're sort of locals. We live a very quiet life. Early to bed, get up early, do my work, don't see many people. In that way I am a private person. I don't like to spread myself. I did my stunts when I was young. I prefer to live a life where I can concentrate on my work. You have to concentrate to write. You can't be disturbed. You can't do a lot of running around. You can't stay up late at night. You can't drink too much. I have my two drinks a night and that's it.

Antibes is a working town, not like Cannes and Nice. There's no casino here, no nightclubs. One of the things I find so pleasant here is that I don't have to compete. I don't have to drive a Cadillac or a Rolls-Royce. I drive the same French car that everybody else drives. And the French don't pry. They don't interfere. They don't get around your neck, and they don't give a damn what you do as long as you mind your own business and don't bother them.

For many, many years my books were not translated into French. I don't know why. Yes, I do. I'm too much of a fantasist and the French are realists. They're tough, and I write fairy tales. But *The Poseidon Adventure* changed all that. It hit hard, really hard, and I now discover I've become *le grand écrivain américain*—the big American writer.

The Poseidon Adventure was serialized down here in the *Nice Matin,* the big local paper. It ran for three months. I thought it would never end. It made me better known here in France, and now they're going to translate some of my other books. But don't emphasize this so-called sudden fame. The people here don't take off their hats, and meat isn't cheaper. It's a subtle thing. They've known I was a writer, but suddenly they have a different concept because they've been able to read a book I've written.

I cut my ties with the United States, as a home, in 1950 and have been in Europe, in one place or another, ever since. That's twenty-three years. I've lived in England, in Switzerland, and in Italy, on Lake Como in a little town called Bellaggio. I lived in Ireland, at Ashford Castle, where I wrote the life of St. Patrick, and I've lived on a mountaintop in Liechtenstein. I've sort of been around, you know.

You can call me an expatriate, but that doesn't bother me. I'm not an expatriate. I'm an American who likes to live in Europe. But I've kept my American citizenship and pay full American taxes. I have no tax haven. If the United States needed me, I'd say, "Yes, sir," and report.

I fought for the United States in World War I and did my job as a war correspondent in World War II. One of the wonderful things about being a United States citizen is that you can do as you God damn please. If you want to live in Europe, you can.

The important thing, to me, is that I'm a writer, a storyteller. If I lived two thousand years ago I'd be going around to caves and I'd say, "Can I come in? I'm hungry. I'd like some supper. In exchange, I'll tell you a story. Once upon a time there were two apes," and I'd tell them a story about two cavemen. I'm a modern version of a *jongleur,* that's the troubadour who went through France in the thirteenth or fourteenth century and sang his songs and told his tales for a night's lodging.

In a modern sense this is me. I'm a storyteller. I'm a rotten novelist. I'm not even literary. I like to tell stories and all my books tell stories, a great many of them fairy stories. And before I fold up I hope to write stories that are better than the stories I've written. You're always trying to improve, but people are like children. What a child likes best is to hear the same fairy tale told over and over and over again. And when Mommy leaves out something, the kid says, "Oh, but Mommy, you forgot where the dwarf said so-and-so."

Grown-ups are like that. When they get something that they like, which appeals to them, they want another one. People sometimes say to me, "When are you going to write another *Snow Goose*? When are you going to make me feel as I felt when I read that story?" But *Snow Goose* is gone, thirty years ago. I don't feel that way anymore. I see things differently. There's been no Dunkirk. There's been Vietnam, a horror from beginning to end, and the Korean War, another horror. What am I to do? Romanticize Watergate?

I'll tell you a story. Hemingway was one of my heroes. When I was a young man he was, so to speak, ahead of me, ten years. I'd read Hemingway and I'd say, "Gee, I wish I could write like that."

One night I had a meeting with some people in the Stork Club. They were late and I sat up at the bar and Hemingway was sitting next to me. We introduced ourselves. "Have a drink." "Have a drink." And Hemingway said, "You know, Gallico, *Snow Goose*—I wish I'd written that." And that forever ended any jealousy I ever had of any other writer. I can't write Hemingway, but Hemingway couldn't write *Snow Goose*.

I'm seventy-six, but I don't feel old. I can't sit around with a long puss and say, "Ooooh, my joints are creaking." The hell with that! At any moment they can pat me on the face with a spade, but until they do I'm still ambitious. I'm working on two books now, and I will continue writing until they shovel dirt on me. I'll write as long as my brain is able to put together two sentences. I'll die with a half-finished book in my typewriter.

○ ○ ○ ○
○ ○ ○ ○
○ ○ ○ ○

Al Laney

Al Laney, when interviewed in the early 1970s, had a foot in the best of both worlds. In the winter he lived in New York City, in Upper Manhattan, with his wife, Irene, a pianist, and their son who is a cellist. Then, in the early spring, Mr. Laney returned to his two cottages thirty yards apart on a two-acre plot off a side road near Redding Ridge, Connecticut. He remained there until Thanksgiving, in almost total seclusion (his wife visited on weekends), enjoying the solitude and the freedom from the social ramble. "Oh, heavens, I've had all I want of that," he said. He cooked his meals, did his wash, walked in the woods, and often was at his typewriter long after midnight. Told he appeared to be living in the manner of Thoreau, Mr. Laney smiled and replied: "Maybe so. But I've no pond."

The son of an attorney and one of six children, Mr. Laney was born on January 11, 1896, in Pensacola, Florida. He was self-educated and working, full-time, at the Pensacola Journal *at the age of fourteen. He was an infantry officer during World War I and was wounded in the Argonne Forest. His newspaper career spanned fifty years and was essentially as a sportswriter, but he was also a general reporter and worked in Europe for eleven years, mainly at the Paris* Herald *where he was night city editor. His books include* Paris Herald, Golfing America, Prep School Report, *and* Covering the Court. *Death came in 1988 at the age of eighty-two when he was working on a biography of the late Percy MacKaye, a prolific American poet-dramatist.*

There is no such thing as a born reporter. You have to learn, just like you learn to play the piano. And if you're no different, then what's the use? You exist as a reporter by being capable but at the same time being different from other writers, having and developing something of your own. I learned by trial and error, by doing it, and having somebody throw it back and say, "Get this down from four pages to one." Or, "Look, here's your lead. Put that in front."

One of the reasons sportswriting tends to decline is that the writers, particularly the younger ones just beginning, don't have enough supervision, like you find on the city desk. A sportswriter begins to cover things and the first thing he does is to sit down at the typewriter and write his own name.

I read the papers, read everything I could, and every time I read a good piece I would say, "Gee, I wish I'd written that." And then I'd look at it closer and say, "And if he had done it this way it would have been even better."

Some people are very good writers without going through all that. But they aren't good reporters. You have to learn to report, to get the essentials in there and do it well and do it with some charm. I see baseball stories today, and they're too long. The essentials are spread out. Many of the stories I read now, especially the wire service reports, are flowery as hell.

Bernard Darwin was the best sportswriter of all. He was the grandson of Charles Darwin, of the *Voyage of the Beagle.* He wrote for the *Times* of London, without a by-line, from 1910 to 1950. He covered golf. He himself was a tournament golfer, played in many tournaments, always as an amateur.

In 1922 he replaced a stricken member of Britain's first Walker

Cup team. He would carefully avoid mentioning himself in his stories, unless, of course, he won a tournament. Then he had to, but it wasn't of consequence because the *Times* had no by-lines, none at all. Darwin didn't write exclusively about golf. He wrote about anything he encountered. I clipped everything he wrote and studied it.

I can recall the precise moment I became aware of him. I was sitting on a cafe terrace in Paris, in 1925. I had gone to the American Express office to get a full week of newspapers. You could do that in those days. It was a miserable, bleak day and I sat for several hours and read Darwin's daily accounts. He was reporting a tournament in Rye, called the President's Putter, put on by the Oxford and Cambridge Society.

I thought it was the damnedest way for a golf reporter to write. I thought, "Gee, I'd never do it this way." But when I read them a second and third time, it occurred to me that this fellow had a lot of pleasure in writing these stories and they were giving me pleasure just to read them.

They were full of stuff. One of the things I learned from those pieces was that the men still curse and swear in the Spanish tongue in the harbor of Rye. I learned that William James had a house there and that Joseph Conrad was living in Hythe, just up the Sussex coast from Rye, when he wrote *Nostromo,* his most famous novel. All of this was included in Darwin's golf pieces.

As it happened, Darwin was the defending champion in this tournament. But he never mentioned his name. He had this marvelous style. He would say, "Well, at this point it was tea time, so I left him at the tenth hole and didn't pick him up again until the fifteenth." He'd put that in his piece. Nonetheless, they were straightforward reports. He was an extraordinary reporter.

Darwin had a great influence on my writing, so much so that I was afraid for a time I was trying to imitate him. Even to this day it embarrasses me when someone says, "I like your stuff, it reminds me of Darwin." In a literary way, all influences are bad, if you imitate. It's natural for a young writer to try and follow someone he admires, but it's bad. You can't write the other fellow's stuff. Really, you are never able to match anybody's style.

Darwin was just one of two sports essayists in all of England. It's difficult to indicate what a big figure he was, not only in golf but in letters. He had gone to Cambridge to read the law, as they say, but he found the law dull and started writing golf. And, of course, Darwin was upper class. He knew his position and didn't mingle much with the other sportswriters. Newspapermen didn't have any status in those days. Darwin was a good talker, if he had listeners, but you didn't do much talking when you were in his company. He could be very rude.

I met him for the first time in 1926. He was around fifty and by this time had written many books and many magazine articles. It was in Sunningdale, outside of London, on a famous golf occasion when Bobby Jones had the most perfect round of golf ever played in England. That's what they called it over there. Jones had a 33-33—66. He had 33 putts, 33 other strokes, no fives or twos on his card. The next week Jones won his first British Open championship, at Lytham-St. Anne's.

On the first day at Sunningdale I was introduced to Darwin by Bob Harlow. Harlow had been a golf writer and was Walter Hagen's manager. He knew I was an admirer of Darwin. The *Times* was always sticking out of my back pocket. I stood in such awe of Darwin that I said, "No, don't introduce me. I don't want to meet him."

Harlow insisted. He said, "C'mon, he won't bite."

He took me over and presented me. But Darwin did bite. I stuck out my hand to shake with him, and he didn't take my hand. Instead he started to talk to Archie Compston, a famous golf pro at that time. I was crushed. Oh, gee, I turned away, crying.

I was away at Ascot the next day, on a different assignment, and Harlow read Darwin a lecture. Harlow wasn't afraid of anybody. He bawled hell out of him and told him, "You shouldn't insult him. You should encourage him. He's a great admirer of yours."

The next week, at the British Open at Lytham, Darwin hooked his arm in mine at the first tee and walked me down the fairway. He showed himself very friendly, just talking in generalizations. I knew I was in the presence of a master. I was kind of bewildered. Lytham opens with a par three, so it wasn't much of a walk, and he dismissed me gently. At any rate it was obvious he had done what he intended to do, sort of make amends. From then on until the war I saw Darwin at every tournament I covered. He was always civil enough. But he didn't communicate. No one was ever close to Darwin.

You can't say Darwin's style was so-and-so. The words aren't there. Style is something you can't describe, much less teach or imitate. It's elusive. But when you read Darwin you knew the style immediately. You couldn't read a piece of his without knowing it was his.

Darwin was an essayist, and we don't have that anymore. We have columnists. The columnist tells us how we should think. The essayist tells us what he thinks. Our journalists, though trenchant writers, some of them, never seem to have found the proper mood and relish for rambling, a mood essential to the essayist.

"They write of what they presently find or meet without much choice." This is what Ben Jonson wrote describing essayists, and particularly referring to Montaigne who, I may add, would himself not have been unhappy in the company of Darwin and Neville Cardus.

Neville Cardus was the equal of Darwin. Cardus wrote cricket and was the music critic for the Manchester *Guardian*. Of course, cricket was something I was less familiar with but I never missed any of Cardus's pieces. I read his music criticism, too, both for the musical judgment and for the style. Cardus was active as a writer until the war and I suppose for a few years after. He's an old man now. He's living, but barely, in Australia.

Unlike Darwin, Cardus had a by-line. I compared the two of them many times. I would read them side by side. There was a difference in style. I recognized it immediately. These two men were my school of journalism, the only one I had. I never graduated from high school.

You may know of Joseph Szigeti. He was a great fiddler. Not one of the greatest technicians but one of the most beautiful violinists of our time. I was once going to Hot Springs to join the Giants— they were going down to boil out—and I stopped off in Louisville, where my oldest friend, Dwight Anderson, was head of the conservatory. He was sort of the musical dictator of Louisville. Szigeti was playing a Beethoven concerto with a local orchestra, and I went with Dwight and his wife to a rehearsal. In the intermission Szigeti came down and I was presented to him.

He said, "You a musician?"

I said, "No, I'm a sportswriter."

"Oh, well," he said, "I'm not surprised to see you here because the finest sportswriter in the world is also the finest music critic in the world."

I said, "You mean Neville Cardus, don't you?"

And Szigeti was absolutely delighted that an American knew who he was talking about.

Darwin was a great admirer of Cardus. Darwin once wrote of him, "Cricket is his daily bread, but he spreads it with all matter of most delicious jam."

I have a distinct feeling that every sport ought to have a style of writing all its own. The pace, the mood is different. You write golf in a particular way because it applies to golf. You can't be very specific on this. You can't quote chapter and verse. But a golf story has a certain general style. A baseball story has quite another style.

Simply consider that the game of golf takes an entire day before the story is developed. They tee off at seven A.M. and are still on the course at six P.M. You have a story that is constantly growing. The winner of a golf tournament may be playing miles from his challenger, who, in fact, may not challenge him until hours later. I was looking through some clips of mine from the 1926 U.S. Open. It was Jones's first major tournament. He finished an hour and a half before Hagen came in on the last hole with a chance to beat him. And Jones was standing there, holding his club and going crazy.

Baseball has that marvelous climactic action, something that doesn't exist in any other game. It's no easy job, if you're a baseball writer. The baseball writer must always be looking for a strong angle, but still he must say who won the game. He must take all these threads and weave them into a coherent story. He's writing about past action. That's one of the differences between him and the broadcaster. The broadcaster talks about something taking place that instant. But a morning paper reporter is always writing about what's done, what's over with.

Joe Durso of *The New York Times*, who had his training on the city desk, writes a damn good report, and it's only a straightforward report of what went on. But it's also well done from the standpoint of literature, from the use of words and images. He can take a World Series game and weave it into a damn interesting narrative. I've often wondered if Durso went to the files and studied Drebinger's stuff. You can be completely factual and still write well.

You used to find that in Dick Young's stuff, too. Always Young wrote his story around what happened. A reporter can be interpretative, but it has to be wound around an adequate report. Ordinarily, I don't believe in a punchy style. That was the thing I abhorred in Runyon. He always used the present tense and was very punchy. I'm a believer in smoothness. Young has a punchy, breezy style but he writes for a tabloid, where it's permissible.

Reporters can get into trouble when they think of what they're going to write before the event. We once had a young reporter on the *Herald Tribune* who was sent to cover a motorboat race from Albany to New York City, in the winter, in very bad weather. Before he left the office to go up there he showed us a lead for the story he was going to write.

The lead said, "A lot of people wanted to get from Albany to New York yesterday in the worst way." And he did use that lead, although it had nothing to do with the event. This is a good example of what I think is bad reporting. The lead should always come out of what happens, not be thought up ahead of time. Every time the lead is written before the event it is obvious in the story. And worse yet, it usually distorts the report. The report is then mulled around to fit the preconceived lead.

Of all sports, golf lends itself to writing, to literature. I think it has the best literature. It has attracted many, many fine writers. It is also the last sport where there is still a distinction between the professional and amateur. Yet golf writing isn't as good today because of this new tendency to get quotes all the time. It's becoming terrible in golf, really astonishing. Only the people who really love golf write good reports anymore.

Everybody else just sits and waits until things are brought to their typewriters. Nothing can happen that isn't brought to you. When you're covering a golf tournament you've seen the man play, you've seen the essential strokes. The only reason to quote anybody is if somebody draws a penalty, or makes a mistake, or violates a rule. Then, of course, you want to speak to the guy.

Good heavens, you've got 150 guys playing in those big tournaments, and you're only to be concerned with those few at the top who have a chance to win. A mere handful. But do you know what they do? Every time a guy scores anywhere near par he's escorted into the press tent and must go through this question-answer routine.

And these people aren't articulate to begin with. Very few. Palmer, yes, but not many others. Some writers open their lead with a quote and just plod on, stringing the quotes together, and of course, most of the quotes are dull, wooden statements. They clutter up the story, terribly. They blur the event. If my paper wants quotes they should send a second man. I think this applies to all sports.

Golf is a simple game. The ball is stationary. There's only one rule in hitting a golf ball. You bring the club square into the ball and the ball square to the target. That's all there is to it. There's an awful lot of bunk written about golf. In the preface of this golf book I have, *How to Play Golf*, the author says, "I question whether I ought to impose another golf book on the public. There have been so many." This book was published in 1896, and since then there have been five thousand books on how to play golf and how to hit the ball. They make so much to-do about it.

With tennis, of course, you're hitting a moving ball. There are two men playing with the same ball, and that's very different. What one player does to the ball affects the other player's response. I don't say it's more difficult to play tennis at the very top level, but it is more difficult, technically speaking.

I can offer this example. We all have, on occasion, had golf shots of professional perfection. We've come out of the sand stiff. We've holed fifty-foot putts, or made great recovery shots. Or once in a while we hit one a mile. I can play golf with Ben Hogan, if he gives me a handicap. Golf is unique in that way. But what good club or district tennis player would have a chance of getting a game from Pancho Gonzales or Rodney Laver? The club player would do nothing but pick up balls all afternoon.

The same is true in baseball. You couldn't pitch to Mickey Mantle, could you? Of course not. He'd hit the ball five hundred feet every time. And the least pitcher in the league would strike you out, pop you up, unless, of course, you are a good player yourself. The ordinary person can't do that. Baseball, at the professional level, is a game of immense skill.

In boxing there is a certain skill. I can understand how people like boxing above the brutality of it. When you see Sugar Ray Robinson, and I saw a great deal of him, it's immensely clever what this fellow does. I worked in Minneapolis briefly and would go to the gymnasium there and watch Mike Gibbons. He was the middle-weight champion for many years. He would stand with his hands on his hips, and his sparring partners would try to hit him. They'd never touch him. He would duck and he would shift. This sort of cleverness is appealing, to spar and wait, to watch, to get your man.

This plateau of skill isn't required in football. What does it take to play football? You have to be quick and big and strong and like to knock people down. But otherwise, what is there to it? Every year there are so many thousand-yard rushers in football. But how long does it take to get a DiMaggio or a Hornsby or a Willie Mays? A generation, usually. Hitting a thrown baseball by a fine pitcher is the hardest thing in sports. Hitting it safely. Outstanding baseball players are rare.

But outstanding football players keep coming, year after year. My God, there is simply no comparison. How many football players are there right this minute that you never heard of who are going to be celebrities by this time next year, when the season's over? The parade of football stars seems to be endless. They come and go by the dozens.

What distresses me, really, about football, professional football, the way it is now, is that if you come through and knock down the quarterback and he doesn't get up, goes off on a stretcher, everybody cheers. The idea is to maim the quarterback. That disturbs me, ter-ribly, that people should succumb to this sort of thing. What does this do to people? The whole of football has come to this.

It's primitive. It's the same thing that drew old Rome to the am-phitheater, when the gladiators fought to the death with swords. It's the violence of the game that appeals. Football may rate as a sport, in the minds of some, but I think it has become a spectacle. A brutal spectacle. The way they dress, the colorful costumes. It's show busi-ness.

I was an idealist, you could say, and I had the good fortune dur-ing most of my career to work for Stanley Woodward, a man of im-mense integrity. He practiced it in his own writing. There was the time when he got word that Dixie Walker and several other malcontents on the Brooklyn Dodgers were going to walk out if they had to play on the same team with Jackie Robinson. This was when Robinson was breaking the so-called color line.

Woodward got the story confirmed and knew what to do. Talk to nobody! Don't call up Ford Frick! And Stanley wrote the piece, and this was more effective than if he had run around telling people how bad it was. This was how Stanley worked. He simply wrote what was happening, with no flourishes and interpretations. He didn't have to say it, but, of course, the implication was there, that this was a terrible thing. You simply give the facts, and if you do it well, people will interpret for themselves.

That same day, maybe it was the very next day, Frick had these players on the carpet and said to them, "If you don't want to play with Robinson then you're out of baseball." They played.

Woodward was very exacting. One time Harold Rosenthal wrote a piece and in it said, "The game saw the Yankees win" by such and such a score. Stanley was ill in the hospital at the time but immediately sent him a note, saying, "The game can't see."

This was the sort of thing Woodward was looking for all the time. Clichés. Misuse of words. He was more severe on himself than anybody else. If something like that ever slipped into a piece of his, he was furious. You could hardly live with him.

"What in God's name is the matter with you?" I would ask.

"Did you read my piece?"

"Yes, I read it."

"Oh, well," he would say, "then you don't need to ask what's the matter with me."

Stanley knew better than anybody I have ever been associated with what reporter, what man to choose to do a story. And he was remarkably resourceful. I have to credit him for giving me the idea, and the opportunity, to do the Sam Langford story. Of course, that's my most famous story, what I'm best known for, and while it has had all of this circulation I have never told how it came about.

It happened this way. Woodward and I had been reporters together before he became sports editor. Soon after he took the job I was covering hockey at the Garden. I didn't really care for hockey, but there wasn't much else to do in the winter. At least it kept me busy. One day Woodward said to me, "Look, the hell with hockey. Take a few weeks off and see if you can scare up something." And then he had this idea of finding forgotten people. He sent me out to see who I could find.

Over the next three winters I found fifty or sixty of them. I did about one piece a week. Woodward left me absolutely free. The first one I did was not Langford, but Johnny Hayes, who had won the Olympic marathon, way back in London, a famous occasion at that time. I found him operating a tea and coffee shop in Lower Manhattan. Another I did was Larry Doyle, the great second baseman for the Giants. I did Ernie Shore. Even found Dick Rudolph, the old pitcher from George Stallings's Miracle Braves. He was an undertaker.

I think the Langford piece came about midway of the first year. I think he was my idea, but for the longest time I couldn't find him. Oh, I had a long list of people to ask, and a lot of them tried to help me. I remember Tommy Holmes, our baseball writer, giving me two leads. One was an old fighter who was known as "The Ghost of the Ghetto." I can't remember his name now, but he was a very famous fighter. It wasn't Joe Jeannette. I did Joe Jeannette later. Sam fixed me up with that.

I went all over Harlem searching for Sam Langford. Nobody even knew the name. Nobody had heard of him. Finally, it was Stanley who said, "You know, when I was at Amherst I played against Fritz Pollard, a Negro from Brown. Find him. Maybe he can help."

I went back to 125th Street and asked for Pollard and was told, "Oh, sure, he's a booking agent. He books Negro acts into all the Negro theaters."

I found Pollard and said, "Look, I want to find Sam Langford. Do you know anything about him?"

He didn't. But I figured he could still help me. I wrote a piece about him, as a matter of fact, to butter him up. It wasn't really one of the series because there wasn't much to write about him. Anyhow, one day he said, "Let's go to the ration office." This was during the war and he meant the place where you got your ration books to buy a pound of meat and so on. We went down there. They had never heard of Langford.

"Well," Pollard said, "let's go over to the welfare office."

At welfare, they said, "Yes, Langford used to come in. He used to be on welfare."

That was the first lead I had, after almost a month. So we knew Langford was somewhere in the area. We left, and as I was walking with Pollard down Lenox Avenue, he said, "Let's go in here." It was a butcher shop. Pollard said, "I know this fellow. He's a great sports fan."

The butcher was a white man. Pollard asked him if he had ever heard of Sam Langford. The man said, "Sure, he comes in here every day. I give him pig's feet. He lives around the corner."

That's where we found him, in a terrible, terrible old room. He was blind, of course. I knocked on his door, this rickety old door, and I said, "Sam?"

And this voice says, "Yes, c'mon in."

We went in. I could see by the light through the door that he was reaching for a string to turn on the light above him. He was sitting on this bed, the only thing in the room. There was a tiny little window facing onto the courtyard.

I sat and talked with him. The stench in the place was awful. He was so cheerful, laughing all the time. Of course, he didn't know me from Adam. I told him who I was. He asked if I knew Runyon, if I knew all the old people he used to know. We talked and talked. He told me he had been on and off of welfare so much the welfare office had lost track of him.

I went back to the office and wrote a piece that night. It ran the next morning. It was quite a short piece, no more than a thousand words. When I saw it in the paper I said to myself, "My God, what a terrible job I've done."

But then I was deluged with money. Every day came dozens and dozens of letters with postage stamps and dollar bills and two-dollar bills, and quarters wrapped in bits of paper. The piece had been picked up by the Associated Press and put on the wire. So this stuff was coming in from all over the country.

This was early in December, and at Christmas I went back to see him again and do another piece. I neglected my family to go up there. By this time we had all this money, and I bought him a guitar, a box of cigars, a bottle of gin, all that stuff. He loved to take a slug of gin. He never took much.

Sam was wonderful, and there was this one wonderful touch.

He was blind, remember, but he said, "I got a little money now. Buy me a couple of candles, will you?"

He fished into his pocket and gave me a quarter. "I want you to light the candles. I can't see them. But I want the candles lit for Christmas."

The Christmas story turned out better than the other. In the anthologies they put the two stories together because they supplement one another. They put a title on it, "A Dark Man Laughs." It's in a dozen or so anthologies.

I wrote five pieces on Sam altogether, and we raised twelve thousand dollars. Woodward got a lot of pleasure out of the Langford story and took a great part in the organization of the fund. He wrote many letters. And I'll tell you who else took a great part. The fellow who wrote that Negro play, Marc Connelly, the playwright. He helped organize the committee.

Sam was such a wonderful person. There was no evil in him. Nothing but sweetness. He had no grudge against anybody. The only person he didn't like was Harry Wills. He kept telling me, "Don't you accept nothing from Harry Wills. I don't want anything from Harry Wills."

Sam had fought Wills nineteen times and beat him every time. But of course he couldn't fight for the title. No Negroes were fighting for the title back then. By the time Jack Johnson was champion and Negroes were beginning to be accepted for the big bouts, Sam was practically blind. He got that lime stuff in one eye, and the eye was gone. But he still fought on. He fought at 160 pounds. Fought the heavyweights, too.

Sam and I were friends until he died. We got about a hundred dollars a month for him, which was plenty at that time. He got more and more feeble and then he got diabetes very badly. He kept telling me, "I'm going back to Boston." He had a friend up there, a fellow who ran a pub. He finally came down and got Sam and put him in a nursing home. There was enough money to pay his way up there. That's where Sam died. I think it was 1942.

I guess the Langford story is a good example of what can be done by publicity. I'm not sure how outstanding it is as an example of newspapering. I think it's good, that's all. People regard it very highly, but maybe just because it was so successful. If the response had not been so great, would people think it was a great story?

I know I wrote that first story too quickly, that I ought to have waited a day. The extra day would have given me a closer feeling to Sam. There was one thing I forgot. Sam is noted for calling everybody "Chief," and I forgot to put that in the story. The first thing I heard him say was "C'mon in, Chief."

When I realized I had forgotten it, it disturbed me terribly. Damon Runyon picked it up and I'll never forgive him for writing it in a column. He said the story was faulty because I didn't quote Sam properly, because I didn't use the word Chief. But I was conscious of it long before Runyon wrote that. Runyon was ill by this time. He had cancer of the throat and couldn't speak, and he just had to write a column every day.

The Langford story was not a straight job of reporting. It was interpretative, in a sense editorializing. For the facts about Sam, you could say, "There he is. He's forgotten. He's blind. He hasn't got any money. And he's very cheerful about it." That's all there is to it, that would be the whole story, if you were just using facts. But this kind of feature reporting is different, where you are trying to be vivid, to write in a beautiful way, and you use figures of speech you would not use in the report of a baseball game, or something of that kind.

I've been fortunate. I never had a job in my life except on a newspaper. I was born in Pensacola, Florida. I never finished high school. I was working on a newspaper when I was twelve, thirteen years old. I bounced around, Dallas, Minneapolis, Atlanta, and I was in the war. I went into the army in 1917. I was a lieutenant and was in the fighting in the Argonne Forest. I commanded an infantry platoon. I got a small shrapnel wound in the foot, that's all.

I came back to the States, eventually went to New York and found a job on the *Evening Mail*. My God, there were fifteen papers in New York at that time. Munsey bought the *Mail* and knocked it on the head, and I went to Europe. I think this was in '24. They gave us two weeks' pay and I had another five hundred dollars accumulated. That was enough to keep me for a while. Everybody was going to Europe at that time.

After I spent the five hundred dollars, I caught on with the Paris

Herald. That was what everybody called it, although it was actually the New York *Herald,* Paris edition. I worked there on and off for ten years, and at the same time was covering for the New York *Tribune.* Golf and tennis were very important, especially with Bobby Jones playing over there all the time. I would file as much as two or three columns on some of the matches. In the summer I shuttled back and forth, from Paris to England, covering Wimbledon, the Davis Cup, the British tournaments, that sort of thing.

I got to know Ernest Hemingway and Gertrude Stein. This was Paris in the early twenties. You can say I knew Hemingway before he got famous. He was one of the most charming young men I have ever known. But of course this was before he got imbued with his role of the importance of being Ernest. I didn't know Gertrude Stein as well. Hell, who knew Gertrude Stein? I'd been to some of her salons, that's all. She had these lilies, these at-homes. Anybody could go. They were sort of tea parties, although it was mostly liquor that was served. I tried to write a novel. All of us were busy writing novels. But I never wrote one that I wanted to submit. Eventually I did four books. *Paris Herald* was the first, just an account of the paper itself.

After I had this connection with the New York *Tribune,* I would come home every year. I'd sit on the desk for a month or so, to get a little money, then I'd go back to Europe. In the mid-thirties I came back for good and was assigned to the sports staff. I still would go to Europe, annually, usually in May. I was on the *Herald Tribune* to the end, until it folded. Then I had to retire. Nobody would hire an old goat like me.

I always had the feeling, in my early years, it would be ideal to have a column, that this was the height of sportswriting. After years of serving in the ranks, it seemed that a column would sort of top everything off. Woodward gave me the chance. But six months later I was looking to get rid of it. It was odd. There was more money in it, yes, but not enough to compensate for having to come up with something good five or six days a week.

A columnist is confronted with the fact that he must editorialize. He must take a position. I just preferred being a reporter. As a reporter, you see, I could work my style around an event. But it was irksome to have to come up with something of my own every day, especially if I didn't feel it was good enough. Maybe I had put the standards too high. I don't know. I wrote some good columns and I wrote some bad ones.

The best sports columnist this country ever had was W. O. McGeehan. He was the grandaddy and the best of the lot. I still remember many of the columns he wrote. He could take the hide off phonies. He wasn't exactly a reformer, but he delighted in deflating the inflated stuffed shirts. McGeehan was quite different from Darwin and Cardus. He wasn't a stylist. I would characterize his style as enlightened skepticism.

I remember a typical column of his. He was writing about some argument that Babe Ruth had had with his manager, Miller Huggins. He quoted Babe as saying, "Where does that Huggins, a .210 lifetime hitter, get off knocking me?" And McGeehan took this and said, "This is the same cry that has been heard through the ages, the cry of the creative artist against the critic."

McGeehan was the only one who predicted—he did more than predict—he insisted that Gene Tunney would beat Jack Dempsey. McGeehan and Tunney had been quite friendly. They used to go to Europe together. But they had a falling out. McGeehan finally got fed up with Tunney's pretenses of erudition, of being a Shakespearean scholar and all of that. Tunney once wrote a book about his fighting experiences. McGeehan destroyed him with one stroke of the pen. He wrote: "Gene Tunney, who has written one book and read several others . . ."

McGeehan got one hundred dollars a column, a terrific lot of money in those days, nothing now. Copyboys get that much. And he wrote 365 columns a year until he died in 1933 or 1934. I was very fond of him and his wife, Sophie. She was a playwright and had two or three successful plays. He ran poor Sophie crazy. One time he had come into Grand Central Station from an out-of-town trip. He got off the train and had his suitcases, preparing to go home, when he noticed a crowd of athletes boarding a train. He discovered it was the Giants. They were going to spring training. He found Eddie Brannick, the road secretary, and said, "Where are you going?" Brannick told him they were going to Los Angeles.

"Wait, I'll go with you," McGeehan said. Then he shouted for a porter and said, "Get my bags on that train."

And just as surely as McGeehan was the best sports columnist, I'm equally convinced that Stanley Woodward was the best sports editor, certainly the best I encountered. I said I was an idealist. Stanley was, too. The *Herald Tribune*, under his direction, had an absolutely wonderful sports page. He had such marvelous newspaper instinct and tried to hire the best writers. He always said he didn't want anyone on his staff who couldn't outwrite him.

Stanley has a sister, Hildegard Woodward. She lives over in Brookfield, nearby. She was a painter, a wonderful woman. She's gone blind. I go over there and visit with her once, sometimes twice a week. I read to her, generally the *New York Times* book reviews. I just watch the papers for things that would interest her.

○ ○ ○ ○
○ ○ ○ ○
○ ○ ○ ○

Richards Vidmer

Richards Vidmer was not the garden variety sportswriter. Unlike many of his colleagues, he was an outstanding athlete: He played baseball at the minor league level (under the name Widmeyer, to protect his college eligibility), and football at George Washington College; and he later coached football at St. John's University in Washington, D.C. He was also an accomplished equestrian and a scratch golfer. During his second marriage, to the daughter of a Borneo rajah, he broke the boredom of a life of ease by working as a golf pro. Not surprisingly, he was closer to the athletes than most of his peers and admitted, "I didn't hang around with the writers. The ball players were my friends."

Mr. Vidmer was the inspiration for the book Young Man of Manhattan, *a romantic novel about a playboy sportswriter. He more or less stumbled into newspaper work, starting on the Washington*

(D.C.) Herald, *and is best remembered for his work in New York, first as a baseball writer for the* Times *and then at the* Herald Tribune, *where he succeeded the famous Bill McGeehan and wrote a column titled "Down in Front." "The thing that saved my life in the newspaper business," explained Mr. Vidmer, "was that I never had any desire to have a drink until five o'clock, until after my work was done. Then, I could catch up with anybody."*

The son of a highly decorated brigadier general who fought at San Juan Hill, Mr. Vidmer lived on army posts on four continents. For several years he was a mascot of the football teams at West Point, when Eisenhower, Patton, and Mark Clark were cadets. Mr. Vidmer survived an air collision during World War I, as a pilot, and during World War II was in intelligence, principally under assignment to General Eisenhower's headquarters. He died in 1978.

Hell, I should have been dead twenty years ago. If I'd known I was going to live so long I would have taken better care of myself. I was careless, reckless. I've done things—well, I must have been crazy. Like one time in Philadelphia. I was on the twelfth floor in a hotel, in a corner room, and there was somebody I wanted to see in the next room—another guy. I'd been drinking. Instead of going around the corner and walking in through the door, I climbed out my window and crawled from one ledge to the other. Now, how stupid can you be?

I was what you might call either a playboy or a rounder. I suppose I was more of a playboy. I wasn't much of a rounder. I mean, I didn't get drunk and wind up in alleys or things like that, if that's what a rounder is. A playboy is a guy who takes life as it comes, has a good time, and enjoys himself. I've certainly enjoyed my life.

I was raised in the army. People ask me where I come from. Hell, I don't come from anywhere. I didn't have a home town. I've lived all over the world—Japan, Philippines, Iowa, Vermont, Texas, My father was a career officer. He wound up a general—in the cavalry. He was a captain during the time I was growing up. Whenever he went out on maneuvers or something like that, why, I'd go out with the troops.

He was the adjutant at West Point in 1912-13-14, when I was a brat around twelve years old. I was the mascot of the Army football team and the bat boy for the baseball team. They took me along on their trips. I had a card, had it for years, "Admit Bearer to Army Team Wherever It May Be."

One of my favorite conversation pieces is a magazine that I've got around here which West Point puts out three or four times a year, a rather ornate thing. Someone sent me this copy which was devoted primarily to Eisenhower. Ike played on the football team, and there's a picture of him with some of the other players. My favorite thing is to say, "Now find me." They search around looking at the players. They can't find me. But I'm the little fellow standing right next to Ike.

The fellows at West Point when I was up there, the cadets at that time, were big generals in the second war. Eisenhower, Bradley, Gerhardt, Aker, Mark Clark. Hell, I knew Patton all through his life, more or less. And, of course, I served in both wars. Air force. I was in an air collision during the first war. Miracle that I came out alive.

I was a sportswriter for thirty years, between the wars. I guess I was a romantic guy in those days. Everybody who comes around asks me if it was true that I married a rajah's daughter. It's true. She was the daughter of the Rajah of Sarawak. It's the northern portion of Borneo and embraces an area larger than England, Scotland, and Wales put together. The rajah owned the whole thing, and it was a very rich country.

There was this book, *Young Man of Manhattan*. It came out in the late 1920s, '27 or '28. It was written by Katharine Brush. She wrote seven or eight books. Some of what she wrote was racy stuff in those days, but it'd be tame today. She was a girl friend of mine. She built the book on me, what she knew of my character. It was a successful book. They made a movie out of it. Preston Foster played the male lead.

But it was all fictionalized, of course. Toby McLean was the hero of the book. He's a sportswriter—a playboy, always having a good time, but never getting down to real business. He's going with this girl and she's always after him to write a book. "Write a book! Write a book!" And he procrastinates and tells her, "Okay, okay!

Someday! Someday!" It's during Prohibition, of course, and he gets some bad liquor and goes blind. Then, while he's blind, he writes a book, dictating it all to her, and when it's published she puts the book into his hands, a very tender scene. And of course the book's a great success. Kay Brush was wonderful. Oh, she could write like hell.

The other sportswriters got a big kick out of it. Some people still call me Toby to this day.

I'll tell you the kind of writer I was. One day this editor called me—this was in New York, when I was doing the sports column for the *Herald Tribune*. He was from one of those highbrow magazines. What's the name of it? *The Atlantic Weekly*? No, *The Atlantic Monthly*, that's it. He said would I write a piece about Joe Di-Maggio, and I said, "What kind of piece?"

He said, "Anything you want to do. We just want you to write a piece about Joe DiMaggio."

I said, "How much for how much?"

He said, "Well, three hundred dollars for twenty-five hundred or three thousand words."

"Sure, I'll do it. When do you want it?"

They didn't need it until the twenty-eighth of the month. This was about the third of the month. "Sure," I said. "No problem."

Of course, you know me. I could have sat down and written it then. But I just put it off. By God, the twenty-eighth arrives and he calls me up and says, "You know, we haven't gotten that piece from you yet."

"Hey, you haven't? Now wait a minute, I sent that up there yesterday by messenger. Wait! I'll see if it's gone." I let the phone hang there for a minute or two. Then I said, "No, it's still here where I left it. It hasn't gone out yet."

You know, I sat down and wrote that thing—three thousand words. Never even read copy on it. Got a messenger and sent it up there, and the next day he called me up. I thought, "Oh, oh, here comes the rewriting."

I said, "Did you get the piece all right?"

"Oh, yes, we've got it. Just exactly what we wanted. Exactly."

I remember Bill Corum—he was an old friend of mine. We'd been on the copy desk together, when we were young fellows. Bill once said, "When you sit down and write something in a hurry, it's good. But when you sit down and labor over it, it stinks."

One time—this was when I was married to my first wife—I had been in Pittsburgh and had gotten back home late. I was asleep. She woke me up about eleven o'clock and said, "We've got to be down at so-and-so's at noon because there's a buffet luncheon and cocktails."

I thought, "Oh, Jesus," but I said, "All right" and we went. It was a good party. Bankers and brokers, and everybody having a lot of drinks and a good time. I never wrote on Sundays for Monday's paper. All of a sudden, it's about five o'clock, and I said, "This isn't Sunday. It's Armistice Day. It's Monday. I've got to write a column!"

So I blew out of there, jumped on the train to the city. On the way in I thought, "What the hell can I write that won't take much time?" I decided I'd write some Armistice Day poetry. So I kind of got it in my head, and when I got up there I knocked it out on a typewriter. It didn't fill a column, but did fill this much and it was something different. Very serious. Of course, I'm drunker than hell.

Son of a bitch, if Alexander Woollcott doesn't call me the next day wanting to know if he could put it on the air.

I don't know if you feel this way, but when you get through writing a column, do you think, "Jesus, that's good"? I wasn't that way. Almost every time I did a column, I said, "Well, Jesus, I'll write a better one tomorrow. That's the best I can do today." I always said that. But every day it was the same thing. I always thought I'd do better tomorrow.

But once in a while I'd write a column and I'd say, "Jesus, there's a dinger." Yet the ones that I felt stunk, I'd get a hundred letters, sometimes, saying that was a great column, and the ones I thought were great, I'd never hear a word. I was a bad judge, I guess.

I wasn't a good reporter. I always figured you could read a box score and know what happened. I still do. When I'd write a ball game, I'd write about some particular thing, not "In the first inning Gehrig singled to right, in the second inning Meusel tripled to center, and in the third inning so-and-so grounded into a double play." The hell with that.

Oh, I'd bring it all in—who won and the important plays—but I used to start my stories with some angle—like, well, there was the day the Yankees had the bases filled with two outs in the ninth inning and they sent Mike Gazella to pinch hit. An awfully nice guy. Went to Lafayette. And he stood up there and got a base on balls to force in the winning run. So I started off, "He also serves who only stands and waits."

I played a lot of golf. I played every morning on the road. As a result, I was generally late to the ball games. I'd get to the press box in the third inning and ask someone to fill me in. One time, in St. Louis, I got there pretty late in the game, maybe the fifth or sixth inning, and I asked Will Wedge—he was the baseball man at the *Sun* —if anything special had happened.

"Oh," he says, "Babe hit another home run," which was routine in those days. But he said they had broadcast on the loudspeaker that they wanted the ball back.

I said, "What for? Was it especially long or something?"

Wedge didn't know, but he said a little Italian kid had retrieved the ball and had given it to the Babe. Wedge gave me the kid's name.

Then I remember that Babe and Claire—that was his wife—and I had been to a movie a couple of nights before, and Babe happened to say, "Well, the next one I hit will be my five hundredth."

Now you know what a big to-do there is today when a guy hits five hundred home runs. Writers and photographers follow him around for weeks. But Babe had just mentioned it casually. I was probably the only writer who knew it was his five hundredth.

So I sat down and wrote how Babe had hit this home run and this little kid in the alley, an Italian kid, had chased the ball, and how he'd been trying to get a ball all these years but he never got one because the bigger kids had always beaten him to it. Finally, he gets a ball, his big moment, and a cop comes up and says to the kid, "Come with me."

The kid's scared.

He says, "I ain't done nuthin', I ain't done nuthin'."

And the cop says, "Babe Ruth wants to see you."

Now the kid knows he's in trouble.

So they bring him into the Yankee dugout and Babe Ruth gives him five bucks and a brand new ball.

That was my story for the next day, not the fact that the Yankees won 18-4 or 9-1, or something like that. What the hell, you can see that in the box score. Hell, I'd have it moving. I'd have some drama in it, or romance, or some damn thing. Not like they do it today.

But don't get the wrong impression. I wasn't a big scoop artist. Christ, no! That's why I had so many friends. I never could see blowing the whistle on somebody just for a big headline, a one-day sensation. I'll give you an example.

The day Lou Gehrig took himself out of the lineup and went up to the Mayo Clinic, I wasn't traveling with the Yankees. I was writing a column then, and the Yankees were on the road when Lou took himself out. When the club came home I went into the clubhouse and said, "What the hell's the matter with you, Lou? When you going to get back in the lineup?" I was always kidding with him.

He said, "Wait a minute," and called this fellow over. It was his doctor. He said to the doctor, "Talk to him." And the doctor looked at Lou and Lou said, "Go ahead, tell him anything you want. He's my pal." And Lou walks away.

I asked the doctor, "What's the matter with Lou?"

The doctor told me he's got a creeping paralysis. Nobody knows what causes it. If they knew they could cure it, or at least stop it.

"What are his chances?"

"Well," the doctor says, "there has been much progress made in paralysis these last few years because of President Roosevelt. We hope we'll discover the cause and cure it in time."

"Suppose you don't?"

"Well, I'd say two years is the limit."

I'm the only writer who knows what's the matter with Lou. But I didn't write it. And why the hell should I? The public has to be informed, my ass! None of the public's damned business as long as he plays ball or doesn't play. That's the way I felt, and that's why Lou told the doctor he could level with me. Lou knew damn well I wasn't going to rush into print for the sake of a headline.

Then, maybe two weeks later, Jimmy Powers found out and he spreads it all over the *News*—saying how all of Lou's teammates are afraid to sit next to him in the dugout, and so on, which was a God damn lie. But it was sensational, all right.

I was always reticent about writing anything that was going to hurt somebody, and of course, I would never write anything told to me in confidence. I only read excerpts of the Bouton book. I thought it was damned interesting and amusing—and true. I had seen the same thing, or similar things, thirty years before. Sure, ball players are like that. All athletes are like that. For God's sake, all men are like that. But I just don't see where a public figure's private life is anybody's business.

Hell, I could have written a story every day on the Babe. But I never wrote about his personal life, not if it would hurt him. Babe couldn't say no to certain things. Hot dogs was the least of 'em. There were other things that were worse. Hell, sometimes I thought it was one long line, a procession.

I remember once we were coming north, at the end of spring training. We used to barnstorm and stop at all the little towns. We traveled on the train. Babe and some of the other ball players and myself, we'd play bridge between the exhibition games, in the morning before they had to go to the ball park, and then after the ball game until the train left, generally about eleven o'clock that night. In those days they used to start the games at one o'clock, or one-thirty. We'd be through by three and we'd go back to the hotel to Babe's room and start playing bridge, and surer than hell the phone would ring. I'd always answer it.

"Is Babe Ruth there?"

And I'd say, "No, he's not here right now. This is his secretary. Can I tell him who called?"

"This is Mildred. Tell him Mildred called."

And I'd say, "Mildred"—and the Babe would shake his head, meaning no. Get rid of her.

I'd say, "I'm sorry, he's not here right now, but I'll tell him that you called."

Well, before I could finish, Babe would be across the room, grab the phone, and say, "Hello, babe, c'mon up."

He couldn't say no.

Up she'd come and interrupt the bridge game for ten minutes or so. They'd go in the other room. Pretty soon they'd come out and the girl would leave. Babe would say, "So long, kid," or something like that. Then he'd sit down and we'd continue our bridge game. That's all. That was it. While he was absent we'd sit and talk, wait for him.

One evening in Philadelphia I was in the dining room and Babe had me paged. I went to the phone and Babe said, "What are you doing tonight?"

I said, "Nothing in particular."

And he said, "Come up about nine o'clock, will ya?"

I didn't know what he wanted, but I went up there at nine o'clock. Babe was in his dressing gown. There was some whiskey and ice, soda and whatnot on the table. Babe always had a suite. We had two or three drinks and chatted away about a lot of crap. He talked about Joe McCarthy. Babe had ambitions to be a manager and he never liked McCarthy. He always said McCarthy was a dumb Irishman who didn't know anything. After about a half-hour of this I saw a shadow at the door in the other room, the bedroom, and I said, "Say, Claire isn't down with you, is she?"

He says, "No, she didn't come down this trip."

So I says, "Have you got a doll in there?"

And he said, "Yeah."

"Jesus, Babe, why didn't you tell me? I've been sitting here chewing the fat with you, and all the time you've got a doll in there."

"No, no," he says. "That's why I wanted you to come up. I thought I'd need a rest."

Oh, sure, that sort of thing is funny, but I didn't think it would add anything to the public image of the Babe. The public already had a good picture of him.

If you weren't around in those times, I don't think you could appreciate what a figure the Babe was. He was bigger than the President. One time, coming north, we stopped at a little town in Illinois, a whistle stop. It was about ten o'clock at night and raining like hell. The train stopped for ten minutes to get water, or something. It couldn't have been a town of more than five thousand people, and by God, there were four thousand of them down there standing in the rain, just waiting to see the Babe.

Babe and I and two other guys were playing bridge. Babe was sitting next to the window. A woman with a little baby in her arms came up and started peering in at the Babe. She was rather good looking. Babe looked at her and went on playing bridge. Then he looked at her again and finally he leaned out and said, "Better get away from here, lady. I'll put one in the other arm."

My friends were the ball players. I didn't hang around with the writers much. I was close to the players for a couple of reasons. I had been an athlete. I played football, even coached football one year, and I played minor league baseball, at El Paso. Most sportswriters, I'd say a good eighty percent of them, have never competed. They haven't seen the other fellow's side to it. I understood when a guy made an error that it could happen to anybody. And I played a lot of golf with the players. I was a pretty good golfer in those days. I played off scratch for seven years. But I think the reason I got along so well with the athletes in the first place was because they trusted me. They knew I wasn't going to blow a whistle on them.

In a sense I suppose you could say I fell into sportswriting. I was going down the street one day, in Washington, D.C., and a fellow came along and said, "Hello Dick," and I said, "Hello."

Then he stopped and said, "Just get out of George Washington?" and I said, "Yeah," and he said, "What are you doing?"

I said I wasn't doing anything, and he said, "Do you want a job?"

"Sure."

"Come down to see me tomorrow. I might have a job for you."

I asked him where I could find him and he said the Herald Building.

I didn't know who the hell he was, but I didn't want to ask his name because he apparently knew who I was. So I went down to the Herald Building and spoke to the elevator operator. Fortunately, the guy I had run into was easy to describe. He was a small man with a little mustache and very light hair. The elevator man said, "Oh, you mean Mr. Garnett. He's the managing editor."

I went up and Mr. Garnett offered me a job. Twenty-five dollars a week. I did general assignments, kind of dull. One day he asked if I wanted to spend a weekend at Virginia Beach. He wanted me to drive a Marmon car down there and write about the trip, particularly how the car performed. They had a seven-column ad for the Marmon car and wanted one column of writing to go alongside of it. A promotion thing.

Then Garnett got involved in starting up the Washington *News*, a new tabloid, and began recruiting a staff. He knew I'd been active in sports, had played some football and coached, things like that, and he made me sports editor. Now, I'll tell you I didn't know a damn thing, I was ignorant as hell about editing and things like that.

After I'd been sports editor about a year and a half I went to New York for a fight, the Dempsey-Brennan fight, in the Garden. Remember, I was pretty much of a kid, didn't know anybody, didn't know where to go. I had a couple of hours before my train was going back to Washington and I thought, well, I'll go down to this almighty *New York Times*. I had always looked on it as Valhalla.

I went to the *Times* and got to the elevator and the fellow said, "What floor?"

I said, "City room."

A receptionist stopped me and said, "Who do you want to see?"

Well, I had to see somebody to get into the place. So I said, "I want to see the managing editor."

I wrote my name on a card and they took it in. And to show you my luck, it apparently was between editions and Carr Van Anda, the famous managing editor of the *Times*, was sitting there having a cup of coffee in his office, with nothing special to do. He asked me what I wanted to see him about. Well, I had to see him about something. It was just a wild, wild dream. I said, "I thought I'd come up and see if I could get a job." Hell, I didn't have any hope in hell of getting a job on the almighty *New York Times*.

We talked for a while, maybe twenty minutes, and he took me into the sports department and introduced me to Mr. Bernard Thomson, the only sports editor I ever knew who everybody called Mister. He was a man of great dignity. He didn't have an opening but said he would contact me. A week or two later I heard from him and I had a job on the *Times*. I covered various little things, Brooklyn baseball on a Sunday, things like that, and one day Mr. Thomson called me over and said, "Do you know anything about polo?"

They were starting an intercollegiate polo tournament over in Fort Hamilton the next week, and he wanted someone to cover it. I told him my father, being in the cavalry, was a pretty good polo player and that I played a little bit myself when I was a kid, on army posts.

"Why, you're an expert," he said.

That was sort of the start, and then I began covering everything —major league baseball, football, and of course, later I went to the *Morning Telegraph* and then to the *Herald Tribune*. But I got tired of covering sports. The second war did it. I was overseas three and a half years in the second war and saw quite a lot of action, and it kind of got to me. Sports was no longer glamorous to me, not in comparison to what had gone on over there.

I remember one time we were kidding Grant Rice about him making heroes out of the Four Horsemen, and whatnot, and he said, "Well, I'll tell you. When athletes are no longer heroes to you anymore, it's time to stop writing sports."

Grant—there was a guy. What a sweet guy. Everybody loved him. When I was writing a column we always traveled together. If he was going to a certain football game, I'd go. We'd go to the World Series, big fights, golf tournaments, and so on. We were together all the time.

We'd be up in the room, maybe at the golf tournament. We'd have our stories written and be sitting around having a few drinks. The phone would ring. I'd answer.

"Is Grant Rice there?"

I'd say, "Who is this? Oh, it's so-and-so. Just a minute."

I'd give the phone to Grant.

And he'd say, "Hello! Who? Oh, you old sonofabitch. How the hell are you? My God. Well, where have you been? Well, gee whiz, where are you now? Well, c'mon up. No, no, there's just three or four of us sitting up here having a few drinks. C'mon up. I want to see ya. Yeah, we'll be waiting for you!"

Grant would hang up and say, "Anybody know who Joe Mitchell is?"

Anyway, I took Grant's advice. When I came back after the war, Mrs. Reid, the owner of the *Tribune*, asked me what I wanted to do. I told her I'd like to go back to Europe, but this time as a foreign correspondent. And that's what I did.

I had been married before, in Washington, when I first went

into the newspaper business. Very beautiful girl, very social. We had three children. Then the second war came along, and the separation kind of broke it up. I guess that's what you'd blame it on. But it was another thing. Two people, you and I as young men, go into business together and, gee, we hit it off fine. We are twenty-one, twenty-two years old. But when we're thirty-five, your life has changed and my life has changed and we're not good business partners anymore. That's what happens to marriages a great many times, especially when people get married very young.

I went back to England and that's when I married my second wife, the rajah's daughter. I met her through her mother, the Ranee of Sarawak—that's the same as queen. We fell in love and I married her. We lived in England while I was on the *Tribune,* had a beautiful place in the country. That's when I played my best golf. Then we decided we'd like to go down to Barbados, and we lived there for three years. I was the best golfer there, even became sort of a golf pro.

Then I wanted to return to New York, or rather to the States, and go back to work. I hadn't really been working down there, and she didn't want me to work. There was a potful of money, of course. I came back to the States anyway. She came to see me a couple of times, but a few years later we were divorced. I'm married again, the third time, to a remarkable woman, a remarkable businesswoman.

I had a physical examination the other day and they had a questionnaire and it said "Hospitalization." It had three blanks. You know what I put down? "Many." I can fill a whole page. Hell, I've always felt I've been lucky to have lived this long. I never thought I'd hit seventy-four.

When I was a small kid—when we were in Cuba—a big, iron-grilled gate fell on top of me. Damn thing was ten feet high. I was unconscious for thirty-six hours. I had about six doctors. Five of them said I'd never regain consciousness, and the sixth said I'd regain consciousness but I'd be an idiot the rest of my life. Maybe he was right.

I was hit in the hand by a sniper, up near Cherbourg, in the second war, but it was a superficial wound. The worst time I ever had was in the first war. I was in an air collision. It happened out on

Long Island. I was in the Signal Corps, aviation section. Another plane hit me in the tail, cut it off, and killed everybody but me.

My nose was broken. I had a hole in my cheek that was so big I could put my finger through it and into my mouth. I had a bunch of teeth knocked out, and my left side was partially paralyzed. But what kept me in the hospital was my damn leg. This leg was all crushed, broken. They tried to set it and it didn't work. Then they operated two or three times. They used to come in and pour raw alcohol on the damn thing every morning. I would take hold of the bed and bend the piping. Finally, they gave up on it and said, "Well, the only thing we can do is amputate. At least you'll be able to walk."

I said okay and they told me, "All right, no dinner tonight and no breakfast tomorrow."

I got to thinking about it and I thought, "Oh, Jesus, this is a terrible thing. The rest of my life with one leg."

I got into a wheelchair and wheeled up to the recovery ward where a nurse I knew was on duty. I told her what was going to happen and she said, "What do you want to do?"

"Well, I'd like to go out and have a good dinner and a couple of drinks. One last fling with two legs."

She said, "All right, you be on the porch at the officers' ward at six o'clock, and I'll get a car."

Well, we went out to the theater, went to the Willard Hotel for a big dinner. We didn't get in until two o'clock.

They came in to amputate the next morning and I said, "Oh, no, not today. I've got a hangover."

That hangover saved the leg. They couldn't put me under an anesthetic, and then in the next week there was a change of command at the hospital. A Colonel Keller took over. He was making his rounds of the wards, and he came to my bed and said, "Why hello, Dick. What are you doing here?"

Colonel Keller had been the surgeon at West Point when I was a kid, and had performed a double hernia operation on me. I told him about the leg and how they were trying to take it away from me. Damned if he didn't save it. He made a sliding bone graft. A year and a half later I was playing football at George Washington University.

I was always meeting people I knew from West Point. Hell, I knew almost all of the generals. Early in the Second World War, I went to London for assignment with the Eighth Air Force. My second day there I got a note from General Eisenhower. Now here is the kind of guy Eisenhower was. He had seen my orders, and he could have sent word that he wanted to see Major Vidmer. But he didn't. He wrote a note. He said, "Dear Dick, I understand you are in the United Kingdom. If you are ever in London I'd appreciate it if you would drop in and we can talk about old times."

I went down to see him, and he asked where I was going. This was in the spring of 1942. I told him the Eighth Air Force, and he said, "Oh, they won't be activated until along in the fall. They won't be doing anything. You best stay here with me."

I didn't argue with the commanding general. So I was assigned to his headquarters, in intelligence, and along about September he called me and said, "We're going to have a very distinguished visitor over here, and I have to have somebody with her twenty-four hours a day. I need somebody who won't be awed, and I want you to take the job."

"With *her?*"

He said, "Mrs. Roosevelt. I want you to be her military aide."

I said, "Well, I'm trying to run an intelligence section." I didn't want any part of it.

And he said, "This is intelligence. Everything that she does, every place she goes, every reaction, is going right back to the White House, and I want you to come in here every morning at eight o'clock and brief me on what happened the day before."

I spent the next twenty-eight days and twenty-eight nights with Eleanor Roosevelt. I thought it was going to be one hell of an assignment. But to put it briefly, Mrs. Roosevelt charmed me. I thought she was delightful. We never had any conflict. We got along beautifully. Hell, I even got a commendation for it.

I never did see General Eisenhower when he became President, but I was in the White House once. I was there with the worst President we ever had—Harding. This was when I was just a kid, still going to college. I was living at the Wardman Park Hotel in Washington and I had some friends there, the Mortimers. They took me to the White House one evening.

It was after dinner. We went in about nine o'clock and stayed until about eleven-thirty. It wasn't much of a party. It was, well, I'd say an orgy, to a certain extent. Harding, at one point, went over and pissed in the fireplace. Hell, I was shocked. I never saw a President piss in a fireplace before. Haven't seen one since, either.

○ ○ ○ ○
○ ○ ○ ○
○ ○ ○ ○

Shirley Povich

"Mr. President, this is Shirley Povich. He's the best caddy in the United States and he's going to caddy for you today." The seventeen-year-old son of Nathan and Rosa Povich, immigrant Jews from northern Europe, caddied for President Warren Harding on that afternoon but, of considerably more consequence, was also given a job in the editorial department of the Washington Post. *He is still there today, more than sixty-eight years later, and is without dispute the best-known newspaperman in the nation's capital.*

Except during the war years, Mr. Povich has covered every World Series, Kentucky Derby, and approximately one hundred heavyweight championship fights since the early 1930s. His column, "This Morning," is a treasure of literary elegance, and offers textbook examples for all sportswriters. Mr. Povich has won the Grantland Rice Memorial Award, the Headliner's Award, four awards from the Washington Newspaper Guild, and was cited for distin-

guished work as war correspondent at Iwo Jima and Okinawa.

The eighth of ten children, Mr. Povich was born on July 15, 1905, in Bar Harbor, Maine, and was the sports editor of the Washington Post *at the age of twenty-one. He did six columns a week, in addition to daily stories on the Washington Senators, for more than a quarter of a century. He has written two books—a team history of the Senators and an autobiography,* All These Mornings.

Mr. Povich has been the sports editor emeritus of the Post *since 1974 and still writes two or three columns a month. Mr. Povich is the last leaf on the tree, the only survivor from the original edition of* No Cheering in the Press Box.

You will find me in *Who's Who in American Women,* 1962 edition. I am the only male listed, right between Louise Pound and Hortense Powdermaker. They had asked me to fill out some data, which I threw in the waste basket. Some gross mistake. My heavens, the book appears and the Associated Press is calling me up. I couldn't believe it. They had taken my biography out of *Who's Who in America* and reprinted it. Didn't change a word. It plainly says I am married to a woman named Ethyl Friedman and that I have three children.

It was carried all over the country. One California paper had my picture grouped with Marilyn Monroe, Elizabeth Taylor, and Eleanor Roosevelt. *Time* magazine ran a picture of me and my cigar, which I smoked especially for the occasion. All that sort of thing. The publishers quickly apologized. They were relieved to discover that I wasn't planning to sue.

As a matter of fact I was delighted and wasn't embarrassed at all. For years I've known it's no longer a man's world. I was glad to be officially listed on the winning side. But the next year they dropped me—like I'd married a stripper, or something. The snobs. They never put me back in.

I was also a member of the League of American Penwomen. Following World War II—when I returned to Washington and sportswriting—I got a letter addressed to "Miss Povich" and it says: "Dear Madam, We have seen your articles and stories and have often wondered why you have not become a member of the League of American Penwomen."

I was properly impressed with the names on the stationery—Dorothy Thompson, Mary Roberts Rinehart, Edna Ferber, all kinds of babes. So I filled out this form idly, didn't tell any lies, where I was born, and that sort of thing. They asked, for example, "Has sex been any handicap to you in the journalism profession?" and I could say, truthfully, "None at all." And they asked, "How do you get along with the men in your office?" and I simply said, "I only try to be one of the boys."

I had no idea it would take. The next thing you know I'm getting my card. They too threw me out. I'm no longer a member. Some years after I got my card I was invited to address the Washington-Virginia chapter of the League of American Penwomen. I did appear, and of course I was unmasked. I'm the only male speaker they ever had who was able to get up and say, "How do you do, fellow club members."

I have often been asked if I was bothered by the name of Shirley. Well, heavens, it was such a boy's name in Maine where I grew up. I went to school with three or four boys named Shirley. And the golf pro—he was named Shirley Liscomb. One day, in high school, there was this strange new girl named Shirley Johnson. We thought that was odd.

I was named after my grandmother, Sarah. In the Orthodox Jewish faith, a child is named after someone deceased. I was the eighth child and they were running out of boys' names. They already had used Abe, Julius, Morris, and Burt. My parents wanted something close to Sarah, and they took the Yiddish transliteration of Sarah, which is Sorella, and said, "Gee, that's close enough to Shirley."

My father came here in 1878 at twelve years of age, with his father—my grandfather. They emigrated from Lithuania. They had one small taste of city life, in Boston, and within a few weeks moved to Maine, where the climate is similar to the Baltic region. They went the traditional route and became typical Yankee peddlers.

In those days you went with a pack on your back and you peddled notions—needles, threads, small pots, pans, shoelaces—anything of this kind. They worked as a team. Typically, they graduated to a horse and wagon. And then, of course, you're no longer a poor peddler. You have a horse. They traveled all through the Maine countryside. This was at the turn of the century when Maine was more of a farm community.

When they took off on their trips they could be away for a week, stopping at farmhouses and always getting shelter. People were nice in those days. You paid nominal sums for overnight shelter, like fifty cents, and you would leave your horse at a livery stable and take a fresh horse at small extra charge. After getting rested and fed, your horse would be hired out the next day. The livery stable itself was an industry, like our gas station.

But then they graduated from horse and wagon to shops. My father opened a store in Bar Harbor. He sold furniture of all kinds, mostly to the summer residents, who were usually millionaires of the Vanderbilt, Astor, Rockefeller type. Bar Harbor, during the summer months, was a so-called millionaire's playground, the rival of Newport, Rhode Island, and Saratoga, New York.

My parents had nine children—actually ten. The first child, still an infant, crawled out on the back porch and, great tragedy, fell into the water and was drowned. Our first home, as I understand it, was built on pilings over the water, as were a great many homes.

We were very much Jewish Orthodox, Jewish oriented. There were only two or three Jewish families on Mount Desert Island, which includes Bar Harbor. There was no congregation, no synagogue, no rabbi, no Hebrew school. My father brought in the Malamuds, the circuit riding teachers who taught us Hebrew. The Malamuds came in from Boston, year after year. With five boys in the house, there was always one boy preparing for a Bar Mitzvah.

My teacher was an old Russian Jew, and he was my hero. He had escaped from the czar's army but not before getting a big saber wound across the cheek. And in this connection, let me tell you that my grandfather, whom I remember as a handsome, bearded man, had one eye deliberately put out to escape service in the czar's army. He had his eye put out by friends. This was not an uncommon occurrence.

As in every Jewish home, the emphasis was on learning. It was common, endless. Education was the highest priority, outside of the practice of the faith. We all went to the public schools and we knew

that our duty was to get an education. There was no thought of rebellion or revolt. Teachers were to be respected. We had to do our
homework, recite and memorize poems, and then the lucky ones
such as myself, we began to like it.

It was an idyllic country boyhood. There were always many
things to explore and to do—fishing, ice boating, skating, sledding,
and hunting. And in a large family you were left to your own
resources. We invented all kinds of card games and played with jacks
and jackstraws. It was a musical family. I played the piano, as did all
of my sisters. Two of my sisters also played the mandolin. One of my
brothers played the violin and another played the trumpet. My
mother loved to sing, and my father played the Jew's harp. All together, we had our own orchestra.

I liked sports and was quite athletic, but I was handicapped. I
didn't weigh more than 105 pounds in high school and couldn't
make any of the varsity teams. But I had a great interest, and
whereas the high school teams only played one game a week, I
played ball every day on the so-called sandlots. Maybe I shouldn't
blame my size because my brother Abe, two years older but no
bigger, was an all-state quarterback and all-state in basketball and
baseball.

Every boy caddied in the summer. Those millionaires lived in
forty-room manor houses and came with their gardeners and their
servants and their horses. Some of them brought as many as forty to
fifty horses, complete with coachmen and footmen. J. P. Morgan
came in his yacht. The harbor was full of yachts.

To appreciate the mores of the times you must understand these
were very wealthy people and they had their place and we had ours.
There was never anything demeaning about our relationship. We
held them in no particular reverence. Awe, but not reverence. They
simply had all this money. We didn't have it. We didn't understand
their wealth, or how they got it, and it was no great concern. And if
anybody told us we were being demeaned, in any way, we would
fight them.

One hot summer afternoon came an episode that was to influence my entire life. We all caddied at the Kebo Valley Golf Club,
one of the very oldest, if not the oldest golf club in the United
States. Each caddy had a number and waited in the caddy yard, be-

hind a chain. My number was 23; I remember because that was in the era of 23 Skidoo.

It was one of the hottest days—weather we call hot—about eighty, unbearable up there. All of a sudden me and another boy, Russ Richardson, decided we would go swimming. He was number 22. There was a swimming hole down by the fifth hole, where we could go in naked, cool off, and have fun. We didn't think we'd get out that day anyway.

But the caddy master's assistant, a new young fellow from college, saw us and gave chase. We could have outrun most of them, but not this guy. He grabbed us before we got two holes away and he said, "Either you come back, or you'll lose your number." So he dragged us back.

Well, how lucky can a kid be? It's my turn and here comes this man, a big handsome man with a small mustache. He weighs 210, 215 pounds, and I've got his golf bag. He seemed to be such a friendly, amiable person. He hit a tremendous ball, but his golf was high eighties. He came to one hole—I think it was the second hole—and hit a ball over the green. He hit it with what in those days was a spade mashie, a big heavy club. It not only cleared the green, but it cleared the road and went into the woods.

And he says to me, "Nobody will find that ball." Then he says, "What's your name?"

I told him Shirley.

"Give me another ball, Shirley. Nobody will find that ball."

Well, fine and good, except what a challenge. I knew every root and tree trunk and leaf in that woods. And when he said nobody could find that ball, I thought I'd be a wise kid. I ran into the woods, picked up the ball just where I figured it might be, and when I came back with it he exclaimed, "Shirley, I've never seen anything like it."

At the end of the round he gave me two dollars, and at the same time said to me, "Shirley, will you caddy for me tomorrow?"

Well, heavens, of course I would, and he says, "Do you know where I live?"

I didn't know. He told me and said, "Can you come to my house? I'm going to play at about eleven o'clock." I said yes, and he said, "Fine, we'll ride out together."

Then I ran home and told my mother a man had tipped me two dollars for caddying. In those days a seventy-five-cent tip was average, a dollar was considered very generous. Two dollars was unheard of.

My mother asked who had given me the two dollars. I didn't know. All I knew was that his bag had the inscription "E.B.M., Chevy Chase."

"Well, that could be Edward B. McLean," she said.

I knew where the McLean manor house was. I had also worked as a postal telegraph boy, so I knew all the houses.

I caddied for Mr. McLean all summer, and finally it came to the point where he said, "I'll pick you up, Shirley," and he would come to my house, at my front door, in his Rolls Royce with his chauffeur in the back, and Mr. McLean and I sitting up front. Everybody was very amused. But some of the old fogeys at the Kebo Golf Club didn't like it—some of the old members of the club such as the Robbins brothers, Arthur and George, who tipped you a dime. The greens committee and the hierarchy at Kebo didn't allow private caddies, or else the biggest tippers would get the best caddies. So Mr. McLean deputized me as his valet and told me with a wink, "Shirley, they can't say my valet can't caddy for me."

Mr. McLean was a man of great means. He owned two newspapers—the Washington *Post* and Cincinnati *Enquirer*—though I didn't know this until much later. Mrs. McLean was a Walsh. Their marriage was a merger of two fortunes. She wrote the book *Father Struck It Rich*. He had made his money in Montana mining—copper. The McLeans, when I knew them, owned the Hope Diamond, the so-called ill-starred Hope Diamond. It had a history of tragedy, bad luck to all who bought it. And God, as it happened, their elder son, Vincent, was killed at ten years of age in the driveway of their home in Washington by a little panel truck that was delivering flowers, adding to the grim story of the Hope Diamond.

Mr. McLean was a gay chap and a man of strong impulses. With his kind of personality, he'd say, "Gee, I like this kid," and that was that. And he thought I was an excellent caddy, which I think maybe I was. It was not a highly personal relationship. He never talked seriously about anything I can remember. But he always asked about my family. He knew my father very well. He had been in our furniture store more than a few times.

Once Mr. McLean saw a public links golfer named George Voigt win a tournament in Washington and he says, "What do you do, Voigt?" Voigt turns out to be an illiterate typewriter mechanic for the State Department. Mr. McLean took him as a plain companion for years. He also had a private golf pro, Leo Diegel, whom he hired and brought up to Bar Harbor.

Mr. McLean was a fine man, but he was a man of great extremes and excesses which unfortunately did him in. On one of his trips to Europe he had a driving platform, a tee, constructed on the *Britannica* so he could drive balls into the ocean. Another index of the impulsive tendencies and wealth of this man—he had taken up golf because President Harding, who was one of his closest pals, was a golfer, and would you believe it, right here in Washington, on Wisconsin Avenue, he built an eighteen-hole championship course for the President and himself.

The summer that I graduated from high school, Mr. McLean was late getting to Bar Harbor, so until he got there I caddied for another man named Joseph Pulitzer, Jr., the son of the founder of the New York *World*. Mr. Pulitzer was a good golfer, but he wore thick glasses and, believe me, he didn't see the ball after he hit it. I caddied for him for more than a month that summer. He, too, thought I was a fine caddy.

We got to talking one day and he said, "Shirley, when do you get through school?"

I said, "I'm through with school."

And he said, "Are you going to college?"

I told him I didn't think I'd be able to find a job and I'd probably enroll at Bowdoin College or at the University of Maine. In those days there was no trouble going to college. The people who went to Harvard thirty and forty years ago didn't have to be admitted. They simply walked in. All you needed was the money. This is why so many dunces went to Harvard.

And this man, Mr. Pulitzer, whom I knew only by name, says, "Why don't you come to New York and work on my newspaper?"

When Mr. McLean came along I caddied for him and forgot

about Pulitzer, and one day Mr. McLean asked me the same thing. He told me he wanted me to work on his newspaper in Washington and that, at the same time, I could go to Georgetown, which was his school. Here I was, just out of high school, a kid who had never seen the inside of a newspaper office, and I'm getting bids from two newspapers. Even Bill Stern couldn't come up with a story to match that.

Georgetown meant something to me because it had one of the finest college baseball teams in the country. I knew that from reading the Boston newspapers.

My mother was tearful about my leaving home and all that sort of thing, and now Mr. McLean was telling me his private train would be leaving from Mount Desert, twelve miles across the bay from Bar Harbor, on September 28 or September 30. They called them private trains, but they were private cars hitched onto trains. You know, Diamond Jim Brady. I had never been on a train in my life. This was going to be a very exciting experience.

But, nope, impossible. My mother tells me that September 28 or 29, it's going to be Rosh Hashanah and Yom Kippur and we do not ride trains. We go to synagogue, eight days of penance between holidays, and God forbid, the last thing we do is ride trains. I very painfully have to tell Mr. McLean I can't go with him. He understands and tells me to come on when I can.

An older brother and two of my sisters were living in Washington by this time, all working in government service. They met me at the railroad station and the next day put me on a streetcar and told me how to get to Mr. McLean's house.

I went into the big house and the butler and the servants recognized me. How happy they were to see me. They took me around to the back of the house, and there was the first tee. This was Mr. McLean's private golf course, the one he had built for President Harding. They were just about to start off in a foursome—Mr. McLean, President Harding, George B. Christian, who was Harding's secretary, and Leo Diegel.

When I walked out there, Mr. McLean grabbed me up, hugged me, and said, "Great, I'm sure glad you're here," and he put me down and he says, "Mr. President, this is the greatest caddy in the United States and he's going to caddy for you today."

I didn't know what the hell Mr. McLean was talking about.

When he said "President," I didn't realize it was President Harding. And so help me, Harding and the secret service men got rid of the caddy he had and I took Harding's bag.

Everybody was having a simply marvelous time on the first tee. There was a waiter with trays and whiskeys. What a grand way to play golf—your own course, your own waiter, own whiskey, your own trees. Oh, Jesus! Then after we're all through, Mr. McLean says, "Shirley, do you want to go to the college? Or do you want to go to the law school?"

I picked the law school, I haven't the faintest idea why. Mr. McLean told me to see Mr. Fahay, the bursar at Georgetown, and that I should tell him to enroll me in the law school and that Mr. McLean would be paying the tuition. And he told me I should also go to the Washington *Post* and see Mr. Marks—Arthur Marks, the business manager, and that he should give me a part-time job.

I got so excited I ran all the way to the Washington *Post*. At this point, you must understand, Mr. McLean didn't know what kind of job I was to have. He wasn't very forehanded in saying, "Put this fellow in the news department, or in the editorial department, or in the sports department."

Mr. Marks was absolutely suspicious, very skeptical, and then, in what seemed a simple effort to get rid of me, he told me to go to the city room on the third floor and see Mr. Fitzgerald. I have since realized Mr. Marks could have sent me anywhere—to the press room, or the composing room, or to the mail room—and my life would have been entirely different.

I walked into the city room and I didn't know where the hell I was, or what I was in, or who these people were. If they had told me I was in an engraving shop I wouldn't have known the difference. I said, "Is Mr. Fitzgerald here?" and I didn't have to ask because Jim Fitzgerald saw me. I had caddied for him several times in Bar Harbor, when he had come up with Mr. McLean. He was so happy to see me. He told me, "Find out your school hours and come back and we'll give you a job."

I worked in the city room as a copyboy, and soon I began to get some general assignments, until somebody decided I was too young to be out with the vice squad. But I was always hanging around the sports department, always wondering how the games came out, and

Norman Baxter, a wonderful sports editor, said he could get me five dollars more a week if I wanted to be a sportswriter. Heavens, he didn't have to offer me a raise. I leaped at the chance to get into sports.

I might say, too, that as a copyboy I began at twelve dollars a week. I recall my mother and father coming to Washington to visit me. My father said he would like to see Mr. McLean, and I went to Mr. McLean's office with him. They were very good friends, and Mr. McLean said, "Nathan, you've got a good boy here."

"I know that, Ned," my father replied. "But you're not paying him enough. Twelve dollars a week isn't enough."

My father didn't know Mr. McLean was giving me an additional twenty dollars for caddying on Sundays.

I worked in sports for two years, covering colleges, and in 1926, when I was twenty-one, there were several changes. Norman Baxter was promoted to managing editor, and I was made sports editor. This came as a great surprise to me. I was the youngest man in the department. Actually, the guys in the sports department were very happy to see me get the job.

I don't like to say this in the sense of maligning Mr. McLean. I never would. But his was a kind of absentee ownership. He didn't pay strict attention to the paper. He and Hearst would go to Europe together, with some romantic interests they had. Once when he came back from one of these trips he discovered the paper was losing money—some of it drained off by himself. I think this may have been 1928 or 1929, at the start of the Depression.

Mr. McLean walked into the office and announced, "Mr. Baxter, I've decided to cut everybody's salary by twenty-five percent. We're having such hard times."

Baxter quarreled with him and said if he had to make a salary cut, the most it could be was ten percent. Mr. McLean told him, "Well, I'm the publisher of this paper." Baxter continued to protest, whereupon Mr. McLean said, "And for your information, Mr. Baxter, I'm cutting your salary a hundred percent."

The paper was sold to satisfy unpaid bills. The sale was consummated while Mr. McLean was in an institution. He died in 1932, a year before the paper was auctioned off on the front steps of the building. Mrs. McLean had wanted to buy it. They were still a wealthy family, but this was in the depths of the Depression and she was told by her financial advisers that she didn't have enough cash. The sales price was $875,000, in addition to a $475,000 debt owed to the International Paper Company.

For two weeks the buyer remained a mystery. I was in St. Louis, covering the Senators and the Browns in Sportsman's Park, when I got a telegram from Walter Haight, the assistant sports editor. It brought thrilling news: "Whoever bought the Washington *Post* has just restored our salary cut."

The buyer turned out to be Eugene Meyer, member of a Wall Street banking family. Soon after the purchase, Mr. Meyer called me in and said, "This newspaper cannot have influence in this community unless it's a success itself. I am prepared to spend a lot of money —and I will. But I will not endow this newspaper." When Mr. Meyer bought the Washington *Post* the circulation was 52,000; it is now 700,000.

Despite the fact that I was a precocious young sports editor, I would describe myself as a late bloomer. Maturity came late to me. I was about thirty when I discovered I wasn't a clear thinker. I was a hero worshiper, a romanticist, highly sentimental, and entirely impractical. I was constantly overwriting, often attempting to make the event and the game more exciting and dramatic than it was.

I covered the Senators, traveled with them for more than fifteen years, and when I started all the players were heroes to me. Some of them were worthless bums and shouldn't have been my heroes, though they were good ball players. I simply had to keep readjusting my values. It was a slow, evolutionary process. It began, probably, when I became a father for the first time and suddenly realized there was something more important than covering baseball games; that the squeeze play and the bunt and friendship with ball players were not quite the end of the world.

I am not going to say that I was acclaiming everybody in those early years. But I was considerably less critical than I should have been. It was just that I was so excited. I simply hadn't matured. Here I was covering a big league club, and yet, in retrospect, I was somewhat the same boy I had been in Bar Harbor, the boy who had dreamed and wondered if he would ever see a big league game.

There was another thing, too, darn it! This may never have

been said before, and it may be unkind, but too many young sports-writers in my era had the wrong writing heroes. Certainly, we all ad-mired Runyon and Rice and Pegler, idolized them, but we gave up too quickly and said, "We can never write like they can." They were simply untouchable.

We made the mistake of imitating other, closer heroes—the As-sociated Press writers, Alan Gould and Jack Bell. Their copy was regarded as lively copy, and many of us, in our sheer stupidity, as-sumed that since they were the stars of the Associated Press they had to be fine writers, fine reporters. And we followed blindly.

But these wire service guys were guilty as hell. They were al-ways writing leads such as "Gene Sarazen and his blazing putter," and "Notre Dame came roaring from behind." Every pitcher had somebody "eating out of the palm of his hand"—all those horrid metaphors.

They made everything cataclysmal. They couldn't give you the short action word. They were overmoderated, the adjectives were endless and the same. A baseball or football team doesn't come "roaring from behind." Heavens, there is no sound. And so myself, and others like me, were constantly inserting these metaphors, or some slang. When I see it now I want to upchuck.

God, I must have been pandering to the public taste, or some-thing. I never asserted any individuality in those days. I had to unlearn so much over so long a period that it became an educational process. As I began detaching myself from the ball players, I gained the independence and the exhilarating confidence that no matter who they were, or what happened on the ball field, I would be able to write it as it happened. This is a significant difference. The skill-ful writer need not fret or worry in anticipation of the event. He awaits the event—and then reports it. You say to yourself, "They're the ball players. Let them play the game. I'm a reporter." It's a nec-essary separation.

I don't want to sound pedantic, but for a reporter, it's more than just a game. It's a great challenge in the sense that there it is—it has happened in front of you and now you must sit down at the typewriter. It's a task.

But it doesn't come easy. I've worked with guys who come in at two in the afternoon, sit down, and bat it out in an hour. I see them and I say, "What the hell am I doing here beating my head against the steam pipes when it's so easy for him?" I can get snow-blindness looking at that white sheet of paper. And if you don't recognize how tough it is, I'd say you're hopeless, because if you think it's easy your product isn't going to be much good. But I do enjoy the sweating and I do enjoy the working, the chore of it, the challenge, the hard part. I like to attack and write.

I'm not a rewriter, but before I commit myself I like to give it some thought. I like lucidity, and I am a firm believer in getting the key—a musical key, if you will. I know nothing of music. I am not a musician. But I must have the key in the first fifty or one hundred words. I want to know what key I'm playing in. Once you hear it, it will flow. It's when you don't have the good pitch, that's when you're in trouble.

And sportswriters, above all, must realize they should not contend with the ball players for popular favor. The ball players are the heroes, and the sportswriters better know this. You just recognize it and are not affected by it. You don't try to be popular.

George Allen, for example, has been a horrible person to deal with here in Washington, especially this year. But no sportswriter can be as popular or as well received as the guy who took the Redskins to the Super Bowl. You can't win. You lose. No matter how wrong George Allen may be, or how correct and ethical your position, George Allen is the hero.

Or take Ted Williams—after all he did to the fans in Boston. He spat on them, gave them the obscene and vulgar gesture, and, Christ, he hits a home run and they all stand up and cheer. You can't boo a home run.

A sportswriter can go to banquets, if he likes, but I don't think it's good policy. Why should we be there? Let them toast the heroes. It's the ball players who have a public, not the sportswriter. Like the baseball writer in Cleveland years ago. He was fired, and he says to the managing editor, "You can't fire me. What will my public say?" And the managing editor says, "What public? Screw your public."

You're not writing for a public, you're doing it for a newspaper, for yourself, for your pride, for your satisfaction. Never think that you're writing for the people out there. Anybody who believes this is riding for a fall. You're writing for that white sheet of paper in the typewriter, for your newspaper, and for yourself. There's nobody out there.

Ed Prell

Ed Prell, like an itinerant printer, moved from one city to another and was the sports editor of newspapers in five states—Kansas, Oklahoma, Nebraska, Texas, and Ohio—before settling down at the Chicago Tribune *where he remained for thirty-one years. He wrote all sports for the* Tribune *and spent the last eighteen years before his retirement tramping the country with the Cubs and White Sox. He had the reputation, fully deserved, of never having written a poor story.*

Mr. Prell was born on November 25, 1904, in Pittsburg, Kansas, the third of four children of George Prell, a peace officer, and the former Mamie Gallagher, who set type by hand for the old Pittsburg Headlight-Sun. *A regular contributor to some of the nation's leading magazines, Mr. Prell was also the co-author, with former Cub manager Charlie Grimm, of* Baseball I Love You. *He died in Kansas City, Missouri in 1981 at the age of seventy-six.*

The reason I became a writer was that I wanted to be a baseball player. I grew up in Pittsburg, Kansas, a small coal mining town which had been named after Pittsburgh, Pennsylvania, and I wanted to be an athlete. I think I would have been a big league baseball player because I had the height, 6-3, and my normal playing weight would have been 190 or 200. But I got polio in the summer of 1919, when I was fifteen. I had played baseball and had run the quarter-mile and high jumped and broad jumped in high school, and after this happened I couldn't go out for the team again.

I think I caught it from a dog we had called Buster. He was about ten or twelve years old, and I remember he was in our back yard one day, and I noticed he was in bad shape. He was almost collapsed and I went and helped him, maybe gave him a drink of water. He died a day or two later. A few days after that I came down with polio. I used to shag flies for the Pittsburg semipro club, and this one afternoon, I went out there and fielded a ball in the outfield, threw it back, and it went about twenty feet. The next morning I got up from bed and my right leg collapsed on me. I knew I had polio.

I hid it from my parents for two or three days. Finally I told my father, and he took me to Mayo Brothers in Rochester and we had an examination there. It was not a tough thing, but it was just enough that I couldn't be a hundred percent. I used a cane for a couple of weeks and it came back slowly. But the big thing that hurt me was that, gee, now I'm out of athletics. I couldn't go out for the team again, and in the fall, when I went back to school, I was hoping the coach would say, maybe one day on the field or in the chapel, "Well, we're not going to have Ed Prell this year. He can't play anymore. It's too bad. Old Ed, you know, had polio."

But nobody ever mentioned it. There was no acknowledgment, and maybe there shouldn't have been. But it kind of killed me. The colors of Pittsburg High School were purple and white, and I had my mother make a P letter in felt on a purple sweater. I wore it for a couple of years after I had polio.

I'm lucky that it wasn't any worse, because I was still able to get around, play a little golf once in a while. I don't know, maybe I would have never made it. I was a right-handed hitter, but at that time—now this was fifty years ago—I saw the advantage of switch hitting and had started on that. But who am I to say? I might not have made it. But I know this: I had that determination. I would have tried.

Looking back, it was a pleasant boyhood. From the start, I just seemed to like to play, all sports. I started playing softball when I was seven or eight, then went into baseball, although in those days there wasn't the opportunity of the different organizations which later sponsored teams. There was no organized sports program in Pittsburg. We made it on our own. As a freshman in high school I was lucky enough to make the school baseball team. We had a terrific schedule. We played four games.

There really wasn't much to do unless you were rich enough to join the YMCA and pay the two or three dollars a year it would cost. We didn't have radio or television then. My folks were very poor, you might say. I used to go to the grocery store and buy brisket of beef or a soup bone for ten or fifteen cents, and we'd cook that with beans for our meals. I envied some of the other boys and girls who I went to school with, because their folks were a little richer and so forth, and I used to think that, well, one of these days I'm going to get on the other side of those tracks.

I don't want to downgrade my parents. I'm so proud of my father. At the age of twelve he was digging coal in the mines, and before he died in 1951, at seventy-six, he had become one of the best-known lawmen in the Middle West. He was born in Germany in 1875 and came over with his mother and a couple of sisters and another brother. His father had preceded them to Kansas. But when my father came over by boat with his mother and sisters they were sent to Pittsburgh, Pennsylvania. They couldn't speak English and had been tagged and sent there by mistake.

They finally got to Pittsburg, Kansas, and soon afterwards my father's father died of typhoid fever. My dad was the oldest child, so now he was the head of the family, at twelve years old. He had gone to school in this country for six weeks but then he had to start digging coal, and naturally he never went back to school. After several years he injured his eye from the sulfur in the mines, and went on to some small jobs. He was a dog catcher for a while, and he worked in the shops of the Kansas City Southern Railroad, which runs from Kansas City to New Orleans.

Later, he was a policeman in Pittsburg. From there he really made it big. Here's a guy with no education at all, and he became a railroad detective. He was so interested in his work, the law work, that he became a fingerprint expert. He went up and down the line on the KC Southern and established fingerprint departments in Joplin, in Tulsa, and a lot of other towns. He was a big guy in law enforcement at that time. His territory went through Oklahoma and Arkansas. He used to chase Pretty Boy Floyd and some of those gangsters in the old Cookson Hills around McAlester, Oklahoma. Bonnie and Clyde were in his territory, too. The word would go out that these outlaws were on the rampage, and everybody would follow.

My mother was Irish—her name was Mamie Gallagher. She's still living, ninety-two years old. I had a letter from her the other day, and her handwriting looks like somebody who might be about forty. She's a charter member of the Pittsburg Typographical Union and she set type by hand on the old Pittsburg *Headlight Sun.* She set the headline type on the shooting of President McKinley. My mother, maybe, went to the seventh or eighth grade, but she was always a great speller. I think that's one of the things she handed down to me. I don't misspell too many words.

We had no books in the house, none at all. I mean, this was a poor family with no intellectual background. There's only one book I remember—*The King of the Golden River.* I can't tell you what it was about, but this was at the Pittsburg Public Library. My mother sent me to school when I was about five years old, and I did well enough. I never was a good student, although I usually passed. I was probably the worst pupil in our high school English class. In fact, when I told my old teacher, Effie Farmer, that I wanted to go out for the *Booster,* the high school newspaper, she said, "Are you sure you want to do that?" She knew what a dumbbell I was in English. I never could parse a sentence or do anything like that.

I said, "Well, I'd like to try."

My thought was that now that I couldn't play baseball, I would like to write about it. I'd like to get into the big leagues as a writer. So I started working on the high school paper, and also the hometown paper, the old Pittsburg *Headlight Sun.* This was when I was a junior. We had Sunday games and I would cover them for the *Sun.* Did it practically for nothing, maybe a few bucks a week. But that was the start. Before, when I was thirteen or fourteen, I worked for a clothing store one Saturday, got fired, and never went back. Outside of the fifty cents I made that day, I never made a dime except in newspaper work.

I got out of high school in 1922 and went on to college, Kansas State Teachers College in Pittsburg. But I was still working for the Pittsburg *Sun*. I went to college for four years and I was still a sophomore. I think I went there strictly for background. I would enroll each year and then drop out because of the newspaper work. Eventually, I became sports editor of the *Sun*.

In those days there were some pretty good fighters around Pittsburg, and the best was a guy named Billy Atkinson from Scammon, one of the nearby coal mining towns. Billy was good enough to go to the west coast, where he came under the management of a guy named Flynn. When Flynn brought Billy Atkinson back to Pittsburg to fight some real tough German kid in a place called the Mizrah Shrine Temple, it was a big event. I built it up in the paper because I thought it was a good attraction. I did it on its merits. It drew about two thousand people and ended in a decision for Billy. The day after the fight, when I came down to the little office of the *Sun,* there in my typewriter was an envelope from Flynn. Fifteen dollars! That was my payoff for the fight, the first I ever took as a sportswriter.

You hear a lot of stories about sportswriters who were on the take, and there have been a lot, though I think it's now decreasing. I was making about twenty bucks a week then, and ten dollars, or a bottle of booze was something. There was this one guy I got to know later, on the Chicago *Examiner*. He was a makeup man and an assistant sports editor. He used to measure with a ruler how much they owed him. He would charge by the inch.

I got fired from the *Sun* in 1927. We were having these weekend parties in Pittsburg, and my girl, Cal Taylor, who was soon to be my wife, was teaching school in Fort Scott. She would come down for the weekend and meet me at the *Sun* building with her weekend case, which was a hatbox. This one time, I had bought a couple of bottles of wine the night before and had stashed them in the bathroom at the newspaper. As I was taking the bottles from the water closet and putting them in Cal's hatbox, one fell on the floor and broke. We wiped up the wine and threw the paper in the wastebasket, but on Monday the publisher called me in. He was a wonderful newspaper guy, Fred Brinkerhoff, who was there fifty years. But he was proper, and he fired me. A couple of my friends on the paper left in protest, although they were not involved, and that night we had our party. I think that was the night Cal proposed to me.

The next stop was Ponca City, Oklahoma, about 120 miles south of Pittsburg. The managing editor there was a fellow named Marion Craycraft who had been with the Pittsburg paper, and he hired me as sports editor, telegraph editor, and police reporter. One of the most fabulous guys I ever met in the newspaper business was Sam Tulk, the chief of police in Ponca City. Sam was a big guy, the embodiment of the Southern sheriff that you see in the movies, and he was making a lot of money. This was during Prohibition, and Ponca City was a hustling oil town. Right in his office Sam would have all this confiscated liquor, white mule and so forth, and he would have a hose to siphon off the moonshine into bottles.

Sam had a sergeant named Art Adams in charge of the raids on the stills, and all I had to do was to tell Art, "Tomorrow night, Art, we're going to have a little party," and he would say, "What do you want?" Anytime we had a party, we just called up the police station and Art would get us whatever we needed. He would bring over the confiscated booze in a laundry bag, and of course he would be part of our deal. When Cal and I got married, our wedding present from the chief of police was this home brew outfit, consisting of a five-gallon jar, with the tubes and all that. You would put in your sugar and different stuff.

We went to Wichita in the summer of 1928, and I went to work for the Wichita *Beacon*, which was owned and operated by the Levand brothers, Max and Louis and John. These three had grown up and learned all the tricks with Bonfils and Tamman, the notorious operators of the Denver *Post*. The Levands were real crooks. There was this young kid—he had won the amateur golf championship of Kansas and his father was the head of some milling company—and this kid had just been married and was caught by the police in the balcony of a theater doing things to himself. The *Beacon* heard of this, and the Levands called up the kid's father and said, "We have this extra. We're ready to publish it. Would you like to buy it?" Well, he bought it, I think for a thousand dollars.

The biggest thing in Wichita then was the fights, and there was this big, tall kid named Babe Hunt who actually got pretty good, a real heavyweight contender, but who apparently was tied in with the Levands and never made it out of there. One night I was appointed one of the fight judges when Hunt was fighting Tiny Roebuk, an Indian from Haskell. I was nervous about how I was going to vote. Hunt knocked him out in the first round.

Whenever Hunt was to fight at the Forum, the paper would put out a one-page scorecard, round by round, over the regular edition. After one of these fights, John Levand called me up and said, "Ed, we've got seven hundred copies left, maybe ten cents apiece. Could you call Babe's manager, Dennis Magirl, and ask him to buy them?"

I told John, whom I liked well enough, to do it himself. I didn't want any part of it.

From Wichita we went to the Omaha *Bee News,* a Hearst paper. This was late in '28. It was six days a week, and the hours were from four in the afternoon until two in the morning. Sometimes I wouldn't get home until a lot later because of the nightly poker game. We would have a runner either from the editorial department or the composing room go to what we called the Peach Farm, which was about a mile away. He would get these half-pint bottles of peach brandy for fifty cents a bottle, and that would keep the game going until early morning. My wife was teaching school in the stockyards district, and sometimes I'd be getting home just when Cal was getting up to go to work.

A year later I got a call from a fellow named Charlie Clift. He was from Pittsburg and had worked with me in Wichita and was now on the Chicago *Times.* He said, "Ed, come up here and work on the desk—the news desk, not sports." So I went to Chicago and joined the *Times* on November 29, 1929. Well, I'd never done any real copyreading. I didn't know how to copyread. After a day or two the slot man—I can't think of his name. Anyway, he was almost deaf. Instead of calling me aside and telling me, he did what a lot of these slot guys do. He wrote me a note, saying, "Starting tomorrow you will come to work at three A.M.," the lobster shift.

I stood up and said to myself, "Not me." So I quit. My Chicago career is three days old and I quit.

As this time, right across the street from the *Times,* at 326 Madison, were the Chicago *American* and Chicago *Herald Examiner,* both Hearst papers. I figured before I'd go back to Omaha, or wherever, I'd go across the street to the *American.* I talked to Eddie Geiger, the sports editor. He had just fired Harold Johnson, an old-time baseball writer, for maybe the thirtieth or fortieth time. So he said, "Come to work."

He asked me where I'd been and I said, "Well, I've been working for the *Bee News* in Omaha. If you want to know any more about me, call my old boss on the *Bee News.* His name is Ralph Wagner."

Geiger said, "That doesn't make any difference. Show up in the morning."

The next morning Geiger looks at me and says, "So, you're temperamental, huh?"

"What do you mean?"

"Well, I called Ralph Wagner. He says you've got some ability but you're awful temperamental."

And then I got mad and said, "What'd he say that for?"

Geiger says, "See, that shows you're temperamental."

Geiger was a wonderful boss, but he was notorious for taking gifts from news sources, and so forth. This was around the first of December and there was no reason for me being on any Christmas lists. But Geiger got me on the lists for both the Cubs and White Sox. The Cub gift that year was a blue silk robe, with matching blue silk carpet slippers—a very, very good thing. I don't remember what the White Sox sent.

But of all the take artists in Chicago, the greatest was Ed Cochrane. After I went to work for Arch Ward on the *Tribune* in 1939, Arch told me when he heard Cochrane was coming from Kansas City to Chicago, he called his old friend Clyde McBride, who was then the sports editor of the Kansas City *Star,* and McBride told him, "Where Eddie Geiger puts his hand out, Cochrane backs up a truck."

Cochrane was a tall, distinguished-looking man who could have been a senator, looking at him. He had been sports editor of the

Kansas City *Journal-Post* for fifteen to twenty years. He had a farm in Missouri, near Rolla, and grew grain there that he claimed would make horses run faster. He sold a lot of grain to Ben Lindheimer, who had the two biggest racetracks in the Chicago area.

On top of that, Cochrane officiated football games, he refereed boxing matches, and he owned fighters. He had this one fighter named Billy Britton who was a pretty good middleweight out of southern Kansas. On certain nights when he had Britton fighting in Atchison, Kansas, Cochrane would also be there as the referee. So he managed the fighter, he was the promoter, he was the referee, and the matchmaker. And you could say he also handled all of the prefight publicity and covered the fight for his paper.

Cochrane couldn't write a lick, but he had all this going for him. He was also a well-known football official in what was then the Big Six Conference, which is now the Big Eight. The Chicago writers called him Big Six and resented him coming up here. This was in '38, after Geiger had left. The story was that King Features, which at that time was the Hearst syndicate, had this syndicate salesman, or maybe he was an executive, visit Kansas City and sell their features to the *Journal-Post*. Cochrane and this fellow became social pals. Cochrane had an engaging personality, and this fellow recommended him, not only to be the head of sports for both Hearst papers in Chicago, but the chief sports editor of all the Hearst papers, including New York and the Pacific coast.

When Cochrane came to Chicago, Warren Brown, who was probably the most brilliant writer in Chicago of that period, had the job of taking Cochrane around and introducing him to the different sports people in town. Warren had been there since the early twenties and was burned up having this guy as his boss. And it didn't help when Cochrane signed on as a head linesman in the National Football League. I've always been told, and I can well believe it, that Cochrane's fee was more than the average paid by the league at that time.

The two baseball writers when I came to the paper were Harry Neily and Harold (Speed) Johnson. Speed couldn't handle the booze too well. When he was incapacitated on the road, the other writers would cover for him. They'd file for him. There was one time when Johnson wasn't able to typewrite and three guys filed stories for him. After the third story came in, Eddie Geiger wired Johnson, "Liked your last one the best. You can quit filing now."

Harry Neily liked to dress up like Hopalong Cassidy. He was enamored of all that fancy Mexican gear. He would show up in the winter, when he didn't have anything to do, and he'd have on cowboy boots, those skinny pants, a checkered shirt, and the big hat, a sombrero. He also had a goatee.

One time, I think it was in Shreveport, Louisiana, in 1927, all the newspapermen were in Neily's room playing poker. The radio was on, and in the middle of a poker hand Neily suddenly stops the game and says, "Wait, I've got to hear this. This is really funny." The radio broadcast was in Spanish. Neily started laughing and hitting his legs, saying, "Oh, this is really funny. This is something. Too bad you guys can't understand Spanish."

He kept this thing going until the guy was through. Then an English-speaking announcer came on and said, "You have just heard the Mexican weather report."

But actually Neily was a very good writer, when he wanted to write. He did a column called "One Dozen Shorts," and as I remember there were more than a few times when he would become immobilized. So he would wire his office and say, "Please reprint 'One Dozen Shorts' by request." Of course, this meant they could pick up any previous column.

Neily had this outdoors complex. The ball clubs traveled by train, and many times Neily would go up with the engineer and ride in the open cab. There was this particular night—I think we had gone from Brooklyn or New York to Philadelphia. It was the night Hornsby was fired. Neily staggers into the hotel room in Philadelphia and Bob Lewis, the traveling secretary, tells him they've got a big announcement. Neily didn't even ask what it was. He just said, "Well, I have just driven the Iron Horse from New York."

Bob Lewis tells him that Charlie Grimm had succeeded Hornsby as manager. Neily's story the next day started out something like this: "The Cubs have a new manager. So what?"

It was different in those days. I remember hearing about the time when Speed Johnson was covering the White Sox. They were in Texas, playing exhibition games, on their way home to open the season. The Sox made a big announcement that they had purchased

Willie Kamm for something like $100,000. It may have been the biggest cash purchase up to that time. The Sox were staying in this little two-story hotel, and Speed didn't like the restaurant. So he started out his story, "In this small Texas town, where you can't get anything to eat, the White Sox today bought Willie Kamm."

It was quite a group. I was strictly a busher, a farmer. I worked on the desk for a couple of years, and then I took over as a baseball writer after Johnson had disappeared again. That was 1932. I went with the Cubs. It was a great year for me. Here I was, a kid who had been frustrated playing baseball, who had told himself he'd at least like to write about it. And here I was covering big league baseball four years after leaving Pittsburg, Kansas.

I couldn't believe it. It was just like a dream. In a sense, I was like a player who made it. I was talking to Charlie Grimm and Woody English and Hornsby and Riggs Stephenson and guys like that. I became very friendly with some of the players, especially Woody English and Lon Warneke. I think probably our closest friends in baseball were Lon Warneke and his wife, Charlene. He was from our part of the country, too, so we got along real good, just a couple of hillbillies. We used to go down to his place in Mount Ida, Arkansas, and go fishing on the Ouachita River, and in the off-season, we'd go hunting together, knock off a few quail and things like that.

Another of our great buddies was Andy Lotshaw, the Cub trainer. On our first trip into Boston that year, to play the Braves, Lotshaw came to my room, knocked on the door, and gave me a pint of bourbon which the Cubs had bought from some bootlegger. It was right out of a gunnysack, smelling of salt water. I suppose it was brought in by some boat running the gamut of the revenue boats.

I covered the Cubs through 1935 and then got tired of the traveling. Besides, I'd always had a feeling for the Southwest, and so I went to Fort Worth as the sports editor of Amon Carter's *Star Telegram* for two years, covering baseball and writing a column. But I kept moving. Then I went to Toledo with the old *News Bee,* a Scripps-Howard paper. But soon after we arrived the paper folded, and so here we were in Toledo with two kids and no job and the Depression was still on.

We loaded up our furniture and sent it to Chicago without

knowing where we were going to stay. We went back to our old apartment, and a friend of ours talked this apartment manager into letting us in though I didn't have a job. I did some work for the *American* for a couple of months, but then there was a newspaper strike. The guild was just forming. I went to see Arch Ward, who I'd known before, and he said, "Ed, you can come to work the first of the year." I joined the Chicago *Tribune* January 1, 1939. I stayed there for thirty-one years, until I retired.

I was always Arch Ward's man. Arch's column, "In the Wake of the News," was the oldest continuous sports column in the country. Ring Lardner had started it. Arch was about the fifth in line. But being a promoter—that was Arch's thing. Whenever he got around to writing, Arch could do a good story or column. But he was a promoter. He always figured he could have somebody else write the stories. "You can get a writer for a hundred dollars a week," he used to say.

He had three or four of his staff writers ghosting the column for him—Pat Patton, Howard Barry, Dave Condon, and myself. And again that goes back to the fact that Arch didn't put too much of a premium on writing, and maybe he was right. I don't know. But I do know he gave me a job when I didn't have one, when there was a strike and the Depression was still on, and I stuck by him.

I used to line up Arch with some great guys for columns, like Eddie Arcaro, top people. I remember this one time we had Stan Hack lined up. Hack had just been named manager of the Cubs, and like always, we had our meeting in the Sheraton-Chicago Hotel, in the lounge there because Arch liked their manhattans. Stan comes into the hotel and Arch and I are there and we started belting down manhattans, and after the third or fourth one I started asking questions and taking notes, because I've got to do the column.

But the manhattans came too quickly, and we wound up at Arch's home on Lake Shore Drive. We kept drinking at Arch's place, and a couple of hours later Stan and I left. When I got home that night I had all these notes, but they were so garbled I couldn't read them. So I went to the ball park a couple of hours early the next day and did another interview with Stan.

Arch was always promoting. He expanded the Golden Gloves, he started the College All-Star football game, and he started the All-

Star major league baseball game. And he had some kind of water show on the near North Side, and I did the promotion stuff for that. To be honest, I think Arch was actually self-centered, a bit on the cold side. He could simulate being the good guy, the big promoter, but basically he was a country boy. He was from Dubuque. Going into the big hotels, being a big shot, were things he took on almost unnaturally. He dressed and acted the part, but he still seemed the small-town guy who had been caught up in this thing.

The National Football League offered Arch the commissionership in the early forties. Arch turned them down, but he suggested that they hire Elmer Layden as commissioner, and they did. The *Tribune*'s pro football writer at the time was George Strickler, and he went with Layden as publicity director for the league. Arch gave me Strickler's job, and I started covering pro football in 1941.

Now soon Arch goes a little bit Hollywood. He becomes acquainted with Don Ameche, the actor. Ameche wanted a pro football franchise in the NFL, and so Arch appears before the NFL owners on behalf of Don Ameche for a Los Angeles franchise. He was turned down. And one of the guys who voted against him was his old buddy, George Halas of the Bears.

A little bit later—I can still remember the moment—Arch came up to me in our sports department and he says, "Ed, I wish I had enough time to go out and organize a new football league. I would do it."

Well, he did. Believe it or not, he organized the All-America Conference, what some of the Chicago writers later were to call the Arch-America Conference. Arch got all kinds of people, moneyed people, together and passed out franchises. And when the All-America Conference got started, the *Tribune* was its house organ.

The All-America Conference, of course, finished Arch's friendship with George Halas. Halas owned the Bears in the NFL, which is now the rival league, and Halas then began courting Don Maxwell, the editor of the *Tribune*. Later Maxwell got into oil deals with Halas, and all that stuff.

And this is where I got caught in the middle. Maxwell had been the *Tribune* sports editor before Ward, but never was too well known, certainly not like Arch. Arch became a national figure, with all of his promotions. Arch also had the confidence of Colonel

McCormick, the publisher of the *Tribune*. Arch would often be McCormick's spokesman at those national Associated Press publishers' conventions. He would make the main speech for the *Tribune*. And here's Don Maxwell, who outranks Arch on the *Tribune*, and he's burning.

The first year of the All-America Conference, the Chicago Rockets opened the season with Dick Hanley as their coach. But after the first few games, the owner of the Rockets, John Keeshin, fired Hanley. Ward and Keeshin were very close, and the next day Keeshin called me and said, "Ed, I'm offering Sid Luckman a contract to be player-coach of the Rockets."

I talked to Arch about this, and he said, "Yes, Keeshin's doing that." So I wrote the story, that the Rockets were now after Sid Luckman, Halas's great quarterback for the Bears.

Immediately Halas came back with a story that got into the *Tribune*—I guess through Maxwell—that Keeshin was guilty of tampering and raiding his ball club. Then comes another announcement that Luckman had turned Keeshin down and was staying with the Bears. I wrote that story myself.

But after the first edition came up, Arch called me into his office and said, "Ed, I just talked to Keeshin's secretary and she told me that Luckman had called Keeshin. He said he was sorry Halas had lost his head in saying that Keeshin was guilty of tampering."

Arch asked me to insert this in my story for the later editions and, like a fool, I did. The next day I get a call from Luckman and he says, "Who told you that I called Keeshin and said I was sorry that Halas had lost his head?"

"Sid," I said, "you're a smart quarterback. You figure it out."

He kept trying. He wanted me to admit that Arch had told me to insert it in my story, but I didn't say anything more because I knew he was calling from Halas's office. It turned out that Luckman's telephone call to me was being taped by Halas, and the next day the tape was delivered to Maxwell. They were trying to trap Arch through me.

The fact that I was caught in the middle made me work harder. I knew that Arch was in my corner and that Maxwell resented me because I had stayed loyal to Arch. But I was also smart enough to know that Arch could never beat Maxwell. So not wanting to give

Maxwell any chance to criticize my work, I worked about twice as hard as I would have in a normal situation.

Many years later, when Arch died in July of 1955, I had this moment with Maxwell. We were in the funeral car going to the cemetery with Wilfrid Smith, George Strickler, and Dave Condon. On the way, Maxwell speaks up and says to me, "Ed, Wilfrid Smith is the new sports editor, Dave Condon will do 'The Wake,' and George Strickler is the assistant sports editor."

I just said, "Well, that's fine, Don."

But I have to say this now—and I hope Don reads it. I thought it was a very rude thing for him to say. Very bush league. We're riding right behind the hearse. Arch isn't even buried yet, and Maxwell's in such a hurry he's rearranging the department. I guess he figured he was going to tell me something I didn't know. What did he think I was going to do, jump out of the car?

I was always afraid of managing editors. The only thing I ever wanted to do was write sports. In 1942, with a lot of the younger writers in the service, the *Tribune* wanted to send me to Washington. But I had no interest in it. The *Tribune* had it in for Franklin D. Roosevelt, and I told Loy Maloney—he was then the managing editor—that I wasn't mad at Roosevelt. Still, he wanted me to go down and join the Washington bureau. We kept sparring around. Finally I talked him out of it.

The *Tribune* called itself "the world's greatest newspaper," but taking my whole newspaper career into focus, I would have to say that I wasn't all that taxed in my thirty-one years working on the *Tribune*. It was tougher for me working for two or three other papers that folded. The *Tribune* is a very good newspaper, though I wish it had kept its traditional makeup. The *Tribune* got suckered into this typography explosion. I don't know why it had to go in for the modern jazz, the flashy heads. *The New York Times* was smarter. The *Times* kept its traditional makeup. It still has character.

The thing I'm proudest of is that I did almost every kind of work for a big newspaper. Hell, I was a working man. I did hundreds of columns for Arch, traveled with ball clubs working every day, seven days a week, and I did a lot of magazine stories on the side. But I never figured I was a writer. I figured I was just a reporter.

A lot of people seem to think that because they're in the newspaper business they're something special. I don't think it's special, no more special than working in a bank or in a grocery store. We go overboard in thinking we're so important—the fact is that the people we write about can't fight back. I was always conscious that the newspaper has a little edge over the ball club. But it's a tough business, tougher today with sports having developed so much. I feel like the guy who has run in the marathon. There's a lot of satisfaction knowing not only that you made it but that you got there before you had a heart attack. It's a rigorous job.

I think the sportswriters today depend too much on quotes from the dressing rooms. They've become nothing more than messenger boys. They rush to the athletes after every game for quotes, and often the answers are silly and repetitive. I tried to write the game the way it happened and went on the premise that what goes on on the playing field is more important than the stuff in the clubhouse.

I just love being a reporter. I retired from the *Tribune* three years ago, but I'm still working. I live out here in Arizona, where the Cubs train, and during spring training I cover a couple of the Cub farm teams—for Midland, Texas, and Quincy, Illinois. The papers there don't have regular baseball writers. Then, I do an occasional piece for *The Sporting News*, and lately I've taken the job as the publicity man for the Pacific Coast League.

I get just as much of a kick writing for the Midland *Reporter Telegram* as I did for the *Tribune*. It's doing the thing. Like last week, I found out that Dave LaRoche, a pitcher with the Cubs, was going to marry a gal named Patricia Regan in, of all places, my home town of Pittsburg, Kansas. I got all the details and wrote a letter to the publisher of the Pittsburg *Headlight Sun*, and they had a big three-column advance story on the wedding. It was probably the biggest wedding story in the history of the paper.

George Strickler

George Strickler, who once batted against the legendary Walter Johnson (and doubled to center field) had a varied career divided between newspaper and publicity work. He earned his college tuition, and more, as Knute Rockne's student publicity man at Notre Dame and later, while serving as assistant to the commissioner of the National Football League, the late Bert Bell, became the NFL's first public relations director. Mr. Strickler subsequently left the League office to become the assistant general manager and public relations director for the Green Bay Packers.

Mr. Strickler was born on August 12, 1904, and began his newspaper career in his home town of South Bend, Indiana. He had two stretches with the Chicago Tribune where he gained national prominence as a professional football writer. A reporter with a reputation for accurate and thorough accounts, he won the Tribune's Beck Award for best foreign news reporting with his coverage of the

1968 Olympic Games in Mexico City, and was the winner of the first Dick McCann Memorial Award, in 1969, which simultaneously elevated him to the Pro Football Hall of Fame in Canton, Ohio. Mr. Strickler retired as the sports editor of the Tribune *in 1969. He died at his home in Evanston, Illinois, on December 7, 1976, at the age of seventy-two.*

You can't build the heroes today the way you used to. In 1924 you could write about Red Grange or the Four Horsemen, and they were very romantic figures, big heroes. Very few people saw them, but everybody could read about them. You'd get a guy like Grantland Rice taking off on them, or Davis Walsh, or W. O. McGeehan, or Gallico—any of these fellows who could really write—and you're home reading the paper and you say, "Gee, I'd like to see those fellows play. They must really be something."

But I don't think we'll ever again see a Grantland Rice or a Damon Runyon or a Paul Gallico. They couldn't write sports today. Your stories today are shorter because of the economics of getting out a newspaper. Your columns are narrower. Your type is larger. And when you start to trim a Grantland Rice or a Davis Walsh, you get down to the straight Associated Press story. You trim out the little touches, the man's nuances. You trim out the man himself. So how are they going to build up another Red Grange?

How many people did Grange play to? Supposing he played to an average of sixty thousand people in those stadiums back in '24. He played nine games a year. That's a half-million a year. He played three years. That's a million and a half, and there were a lot of repeaters in those crowds. So you didn't have that many people. Today, with television, a guy comes along and in one afternoon, in one game, 64 million people see him.

When you see a player, in the flesh or on television, it takes a lot of the romance out of it. Like the Four Horsemen of Notre Dame. They were good for their time, but they were small. You'd have difficulty playing them today. Sure, they whacked things around pretty good and they were excellent football players. They were national champions under Rockne and won the Rose Bowl. But the sportswriters built them up, and there was that famous picture of them. You couldn't see them on television. The distance lent enchantment.

I dropped the idea for Granny Rice's lead on the Four Horsemen. It's probably the most famous lead in sportswriting history. Granny picked it up from something I said. I was then in my second year in college and was Rockne's student publicity director at Notre Dame. I came to New York with the team for the Army game.

It was between halves when it happened. I think the score was tied at 7-7 at the half. Notre Dame only won the game by one touchdown, 14-7. I was standing in the aisle of the press box between halves and was talking to Grantland Rice and Davis Walsh and Damon Runyon and a fourth fellow who I believe was Jack Kofoed. I'm not sure. Anyway, the four of them were discussing the Notre Dame backfield and how it was handling Army.

Now the night before we left South Bend, a Wednesday, they had this picture, *The Four Horsemen of the Apocalypse,* showing at Washington Hall, the recreational hall on the campus. I went to see it for about the seventh time. It was a tremendous hit, one of the milestones in motion picture history. I don't remember too much about the story. But I can still see those ethereal figures charging through the clouds—Death, Pestilence, Famine, and War.

They just rode over the world, through the clouds. One of them was Bull Montana, a character actor who later became a wrestler. He may still be living. Another was Boris Karloff. That was the movie where Valentino made his first big hit. The only thing I remember about the story was that Valentino did the tango in it. But I'll never forget those Four Horsemen riding across the sky, always to the musical accompaniment of the "Ride of the Valkyries."

So we were talking about what a tremendous job the Notre Dame backfield was doing, how they were cutting the Army down, and I said, "Yeah, just like the Four Horsemen." That's all I said.

We stayed in New York that night and went to the Follies. We saw Will Rogers and Marilyn Miller. I'll never forget Rogers walking out with a big Notre Dame sweater on. We were all sitting down in the front rows, and a big cheer went up.

Marilyn Miller stuck her head out from the other side of the stage and asked, "What's going on out there?"

And Will said, "I don't know. Unless they're cheering my North Dakota sweater."

When we got back downtown to the Belmont Hotel, stacks of

the New York *Sun* were on the newsstands. And there was Grant-land's lead:

> Outlined against a blue-gray October sky, the Four Horsemen rode again. In dramatic lore they are known as Famine, Pestilence, Destruction and Death. These are only aliases. Their real names are Stuhldreher, Miller, Crowley and Layden.

I don't remember that Granny ever thanked me. The last time we sat down together was at Notre Dame for one of the Oklahoma games. We were at the bar in the Oliver Hotel. Granny acknowledged he had heard it from me, but in his book he was confused on where he got the idea. He tied it up to something he had written the year before. But, heck, he only saw Notre Dame once in '23, when they played in Brooklyn, and they didn't do much. The Four Horsemen weren't even the regular backfield that year.

I asked him what would have happened if all four writers had used the same idea for their lead, and he said, "Well, I don't know. Maybe it wouldn't have been so good if everybody had used it."

One night, also years later, I asked Davis J. Walsh the same question. I still remember Walsh's answer. He said, "We'd have probably all been famous like Rice."

The ball club went back to South Bend on Sunday morning and was to work out Monday afternoon because the following Thursday we had to leave again. We were going to play Princeton. Just as the team was leaving New York I got the idea for the picture, of putting the Four Horsemen on horseback.

I wired my father. My dad was working at Notre Dame, worked for 'em for years. I asked him to see if he could round up four horses. The next afternoon, as soon as my train got into the depot, I called my father. He had the horses lined up at a coal and ice house which was about four doors away from my father's favorite saloon. They were supposed to be riding horses, but it was fall and nobody was riding. The horses weren't very well taken care of. But they were saddled, ready to go.

I got on one of the horses and started pulling the other three. I got pulled off that horse three or four times, and I had a hell of a time getting back on. Then, when I got to the football field I had to talk the guard into letting me get into practice. I broke up Rock's practice to get this picture. My photographer was already there. I led the horses onto the field, put the Horsemen on them, and took the picture.

I didn't have any trouble getting the horses back. Then I went to the gymnasium, to my office. I had a bare room, nothing but a desk and a chair. Practice was over and Rock gave me a little hell. He didn't like the idea of my breaking up his practice. He said he only had a couple of practices before the Princeton game and that I should have made other arrangements.

I said, "I didn't have a chance."

He kept giving me hell, but he wound up saying it was a good idea.

Harry Elmore often gets credit for taking that picture. He was the fellow on the South Bend *News-Times*. He did all the photography for Arch Ward and Frank Wallace. They were the Notre Dame student publicity men before me. But Elmore didn't take the picture, because I didn't like his prints. I had a commercial man whose office was across the street from the city fire department. His name was Christman. I don't remember his first name. Christman took all my pictures.

Harry Elmore got into the act because a number of years later Christman died and Harry bought his entire plant. Among the things he found in there was the original negative of the Four Horsemen. Harry blocked out the background, blew it up, and cropped it. He sold a lot of those pictures.

The picture was reprinted all over the country. Pacific and Atlantic bought it immediately. I sold it to them for a couple of bucks, but I kept getting royalties. Every time the picture was used I got some dough. I made about ten thousand dollars that year as publicity man for Rockne. Most of it was on that picture.

I had to put myself through school. We never had any extra money at home. My father was the butcher for Notre Dame for twenty-five to thirty years. In those days Notre Dame had its own farm, its own slaughterhouse. My father did all the butchering during the school year for the sisters to cook the meat. In the summer he ran their threshing outfit.

Brother Leo used to carry on all of the farm operations. He would go down to Texas, bring cattle back by the carload, and my dad would feed them. Then, in the fall, when they were taken to the stock show, they were so big and fat that the classes of animal husbandry from Purdue would come and watch. I was just a small shaver working with my dad. Although he was a butcher and killed all the time, he had such an attachment for some of that prize cattle that after they were sold for slaughter we wouldn't find him for a week, couldn't locate him. He'd go on a good drunk.

I was born in South Bend and was never really too anxious to go any place else. I figured no matter where I went, or what I did, I'd wind up where I started. I was born right across the alley from the city cemetery, so I didn't have very far to go. I had a normal Hoosier upbringing. Very strict mother. Very fine, generous father who worked hard.

My dad used to take what little money he got from Notre Dame, and on Saturday he'd go downtown with a big shopping list and buy all the groceries and everything we needed for a week. And if anything was left over he went to the saloon and got himself a nose full. They'd put him on a streetcar toward Notre Dame. When the car stopped, Mother and I would go out and take off all the packages, including Dad. He died of septicemia poisoning, from plucking chickens. They'd kill it off in twenty-four hours today. He was fifty-six years old.

I went to a little country school three miles north of Notre Dame. District number three. Carved my initials in the same seat my dad used. I was there about eight years, then went to South Bend Central High School. That was in 1918, when I was fourteen. I reported for football my first day there and played for four years.

In those days you had to bring your own equipment, and I got mine from the boys at Notre Dame. I had been batboy for Jesse Harper's baseball team in 1915 and 1916. I had Leo DuBois's old shoulder pads. He was a halfback. They came all the way down to my elbows when I put them on. I had Bodie Andrews's pants. He was the captain one of those years. I pulled them up under my armpits. They got me a pair of shoes that fit and the helmet that Rockne had worn. It was flat-level and had a lot of names on it, people who had worn it, including Rockne's. It's in the football Hall of Fame at Canton, Ohio.

I played a lot of football and baseball. There wasn't anything else for us to do, except work. We had a football camp in the summertime, and Rockne used to come down and coach us. The first time Nebraska played Notre Dame, our high school, South Bend Central, played the preliminary. We won about 87-0. I was a senior that year and did all the kicking. I got hurt in that game, after we had about a seventy-point lead. I ran downfield, on a kick, tried for one of those spectacular and foolish tackles. I did a handstand and while I was still in the air, a guy fell on the right arm, at the elbow. Didn't break it, just tore it all up.

They strapped my arm and I played the next week, but I couldn't move it. They just put my right arm across my body, with the hand under the left armpit. After the bandages came off, I went to the YMCA every day for six months and ran hot water on it, as hot as I could stand. And big George Cooper, the athletic director at the Y, used to massage it. I got it moving but from then on I couldn't throw, so I knew I probably wouldn't be able to play college baseball.

But football still looked pretty good. I thought there was no question about my going to Notre Dame, with my father there and my having worked there and knowing Rockne. But I had to have some scholarship help. When there wasn't any forthcoming, I applied at Indiana University and got a scholarship through Jim Stiehm, who was the coach there. Only I didn't play for Stiehm. He died before the season started.

They brought Navy Bill Ingram to take over as the head coach, and then I got hurt in a spring scrimmage. I took off downfield with the ball and was slowing up to give a little hip switch when a crazy quarterback named Ted Smith hit me from behind and knocked me about ten yards. I wound up scoring, but I ended up with a bad knee.

I stayed out of school the next year. I had done some correspondent work while I was in high school for Gene Kessler—a wonderful man. He was the sports editor of the South Bend *News-Times,* and I went back and joined their advertising department. The knee got stronger, and the next fall I applied again at Notre Dame. This time I got some scholarship assistance. When I got there, Rockne said, "Just stay with the varsity. Never mind reporting with the freshmen."

About the second day of practice he caught me going down on passes. Well, my knee would lock, but I would just hit it and it would be okay. Rock caught me doing it and sent me into Doc Glimstead. He examined it, and after practice that day Rock told me, "Turn in your uniform. You're through."

I knew I was in trouble because without football I wouldn't get any financial help. So I said, "Well, I'll go down to Indianapolis to the Indiana University Hospital and let them operate on it."

Rock hit the roof. He said, "No operation! Positively not! You might get an infection and have a stiff leg for the rest of your life, and football isn't worth it."

This was in 1924, and in those days Rock wasn't operating on knees. About three or four years later he would bring in as many as a half-dozen at a time into Chicago to Dr. Danny Leventhal, and let him operate on them. But in '24 he wouldn't let anybody operate on knees. I figured that was the end of it, but about four or five days later Rock drove out to my house. He came out at night, after dinner. He said, "I hear you quit school."

"Yes, I've got to have help, and I don't know how I'm going to get it if I don't play football."

Rock hemmed and hawed a little bit. Then he said, "You're a newspaperman, aren't you?"

Well, he knew that all through high school I'd been writing for Gene Kessler and that I was filing stuff the year I was down at Indiana. So he said, "Come over to see me tomorrow. We'll see what we can work out." The next day he said, "You're my publicity man."

Notre Dame didn't have a full-time publicity man in those days. They used students. Arch Ward was the first one, and after he left Francis Wallace had it for two years. Frank graduated in '22. The job wasn't filled in '23, which was the year before Rock hired me. I was responsible to Rock only. I worked for him. The only pay I got was space rates from whatever papers used my stuff. Rock controlled everything so well that nobody else could send anything out of South Bend about the Notre Dame football team. If anybody sent anything out and Rock found out about it from Western Union or Postal, where he had connections, he would right away get the kid in, if he was in school, and say, "Look, if you want to stay in school, stop writing about the football team. Nobody writes about the football team except Strickler."

That's how Rock protected me. I didn't get any money from the school. He had the same arrangement with Ward and Wallace, and after I left, the next year, he gave the job to Paul Butler. Paul lived next door to me in the country out there. I had given him my high school job with Kessler, and then Rock gave him my job at Notre Dame. Butler later became the national chairman of the Democratic Party during the Roosevelt regimes.

Rockne was one of the most remarkable men I have known. All the things you hear about him were absolutely true. He was a tremendous psychologist. He had a brilliant mind and he was a great leader, a genuine inspiration. He could walk into any meeting, and the instant he stepped into the room you knew he was there. It was electric. Rock wasn't quite as ruthless as Vince Lombardi, but he exerted more influence.

My brother worked in a bookstore in South Bend, and he would take anywhere from two to five books a week out to Rockne. Either Rockne would order them or my brother would pick out the books that he thought Rock would like. Rock read all the time, heavy stuff, not much fiction. He was an intellectual and read books on science, law, history. He could have been the head of the chemistry department at Yale, but he stayed at Notre Dame to do his athletic work and also to work with Father Neiwland, the famous priest who discovered synthetic rubber. Chemistry was Rock's major, and I remember him teaching chemistry at Notre Dame. Everybody always fought to get into his classes.

He was as fair as they come but very stern. I once saw him order the president of the university and one of its biggest donors right off the practice field. He was working with some kid, trying to embarrass the kid a little and get to him, which was Rock's way of breaking the tension. The president of the university and this big hotshot from New York laughed. Rock stopped and went right over and asked them to leave the field. There was a priest with them, and Rock said to the father, "I don't come into your classroom and laugh when some of your students do silly things. This is my classroom."

George Gipp was gone when I got to Notre Dame, but this

buddy of mine and I were the last people to see him before he went into the hospital. Each year Kiwanis and Rotary would have a luncheon for the Notre Dame ball club, and the high school ball club. The luncheon was held in the Oliver Hotel. My buddy and I were late getting there, and we met Gipp on the mezzanine. Gipp knew us and knew we were friendly with Rock, and he said, "Tell the old man I'm not feeling well. I won't be at the luncheon." He was living in the hotel and went up to his room. Rock went up after the luncheon and found out Gipp was sick and took him to the hospital. Gipp never got out.

After the '24 season, that next summer, I got married and worked on the *News-Times*. I also played baseball for the South Bend Independents, a team owned by Louie Batchelor, a promoter around there. The manager was Ben Koehler, who had played for a couple of years with the St. Louis Browns, in their early days. I played second base and the outfield. I couldn't throw worth a damn because of that high school elbow injury, but I could hit. The Designated Hitter, this new rule they have in the American League, would have been perfect for me. But it came fifty years too late. I could hit anybody. I could hit like hell. No question about that.

I once batted against the great Walter Johnson. I hit a line shot right over Sam Rice's head, in centerfield. It was in '25. The Washington club was on its way to Chicago, to play the White Sox, and stopped off in South Bend for an exhibition. I only had that one time at bat against Johnson. He pitched one inning, faced four men. I remember his first pitch to me was a little swift and was high and inside. I stepped back and raised my arms. Muddy Ruel was catching and he said, "Don't throw your arms up, sonny. Keep your hands down." He was afraid if I put my arms up in front of the ball, I wouldn't have time to get away from the pitch.

We played the Pittsburgh Pirates that same year, in another exhibition. I hit against all three of those big pitchers Pittsburgh had—Kremer, Yde and Meadows. I remember Ben Koehler introduced me to Kiki Cuyler. That was quite a thrill. Cuyler had a way of lining his pants around his knees, but it didn't have the bloomer effect. And Cuyler lifted his knees high when he ran. He looked like the nicest thing that ever stepped on a ball field.

In about July of that season Dick Kerr, the Black Sox World Series hero, joined our club. He had won two games for the Black Sox in the 1919 Series, then jumped his contract. He couldn't agree with Comiskey on salary. Kerr played a little independent ball for the next few years, and in '25 he applied for reinstatement. Judge Landis put him on a year's probation and gave him a choice. He could play with the Kelloggs out of Kalamazoo or the South Bend Independents. He picked our club.

Dick and I got to be good friends. We only played two games a week, at the most, but he and I would work out every day. I'd go down to the *News-Times* in the morning. That would take me about an hour, covering my beat and picking up the ads from a couple of stores. Then I would meet Dick and we would go out to Springbrook Park, a big amusement park between South Bend and Mishawaka.

Across from the park there was this roadhouse, and we would knock on the door and wake up the bartenders, the pimps, the croupiers. This was bootleg time. We would rout them out, and they would come over and get their exercise shagging flies. I'd back up against the stands, and Dick would pitch to me for an hour. I'd hit and those guys would chase the ball.

When we got through we'd get in the car and go to the west side of South Bend, to the Polish district. We would go in the back door of this place, sit down at the kitchen table, and Dick would have two bottles of beer, home brew beer with about two inches of yeast in the bottle. Mrs. Kerr used to give him a half a dollar a day. That's all he had. And he'd open this little purse and put the two quarters on the table.

I never asked him about the Black Sox, and he didn't talk much about them. The only thing I remember him saying was that they knew when the Series started that there was something on. They knew who the guilty ones were because in the dressing room, Kid Gleason, the manager, said, "Now some of you fellows on this club have arranged to throw the Series."

Dick said that the minute Gleason broached this, the innocent guys looked up and said, "What the hell is this?" And you could pick out all the guys who were involved because they kept their heads down. This was just before the first Series game. Gleason had called them in after their warm-ups. Cicotte was supposed to pitch the first game, but after that meeting in the dressing room Gleason changed pitchers and picked Dick instead.

I finished that season as a full-time professional ball player. I went to Janesville and played in the Wisconsin State League. Hit a home run off a hotshot pitcher who was supposed to be called up the next year by the Philadelphia Athletics. But about the time Pittsburgh was playing Washington in the World Series I was in Chicago and got a job as a sportswriter with the International News Service. I never went back to college. I knew with my bum arm I couldn't make it in professional baseball.

Two or three years later I caught on with the *Herald-Examiner,* one of the Hearst papers in Chicago, and then they sent me to Atlanta as sports editor of the Hearst paper there, the *Georgian.* I replaced Ed Danforth, who had gone over to the *Constitution.* I stayed in Atlanta about seven months. My father died and I didn't want to be that far away from mother. So I came back to Chicago and got lucky and fell into a job as the publicity man for the Chicago Stadium for $250 a week, a hell of a lot of money in those days.

Then one afternoon, in the summer of '31, I was on the beach at Argyle with a girl friend. The Outer Drive was then under construction and a canoe tipped over in the big lagoon they had just built. A guy drowned. I saw the canoe turn over and the lifeguard run out. This guy, even though he was a good swimmer, drowned in about eight feet of water. He had a heart attack.

Three days later I was at the Midnight Frolics, a nightclub down on Twenty-second Street, when I was told that Harry McNamara had been trying to reach me. McNamara was a sportswriter, a good friend. I got in touch with him at Mills Stadium, where he was covering a fight, and he said, "Christ, get over to the *Tribune.* They've been looking for you. They want to put you to work."

I knew that the stadium publicity was a shaky deal and wouldn't last. So I went down to see Arch Ward and he said, "We've been looking for you for three days. Our man Twohill drowned out at the lagoon the other day." Twohill had been working on the copy desk and I had seen him drown, not knowing who he was. I took his place at the *Tribune.* But I didn't stay on the desk very long. Pretty soon I was out covering professional football. This was in the days when pro football didn't have much coverage.

I worked for Arch Ward from then on until 1941, when I went with the National Football League as an assistant to Elmer Layden, one of the Four Horsemen who had been elected the commissioner of the NFL. Ward was a good guy to work for. He was into so many things. He was so intense and worked so hard he kept everybody else hard at it, too. But he wasn't overly generous from the standpoint of a pay envelope.

After I left the *Tribune,* Arch and I would still have lunch together occasionally. We had a few bad moments. Once we were having lunch at the Medinah Club and were talking about a magazine piece that Red Smith had done called "Don't Send My Boy to Halas," in which Bill Hewitt, a Bear player, told of only getting $125 a game.

Ward got all excited. He said, "This is terrible! This is awful! A great star like Bill Hewitt only getting $125 a game!"

Ward had just started the All-America Conference and insisted this was one of the things he would straighten out. The All-America Conference was then a rival for the National Football League, and was, supposedly, going to pay bigger salaries. And here I am working for the NFL at the time.

So I said, "Well, Arch, we're going to pay the players just as much as we have to and no more. When I worked on your copy desk you didn't come around and say to me, 'Hey, you can't work here for fifty dollars a week. You've got to make two hundred.'" After that Arch didn't talk to me for about six months.

Arch was a great promoter. No question about it. And having the *Tribune* behind him—a big, powerful paper at that time— meant a lot. What Arch did was create a new conception of newspaper sports promotion. In those days you had all these promotions open to participants. Soapbox Derbies. Silver Skates. Golden Gloves. And Arch said, "Anybody can put on a Silver Skates or a marble or a fishing tournament. But can you put something on that people have to pay to see, and make a success out of it?"

He sold this idea to the *Tribune.* It went with their slogan, "The Tribune Can Do It Alone," which was the basis on how they sold their advertising. Ward's whole promotional program was done to convince the advertisers of the power of the *Tribune.*

Most of the ideas had been around for a long time. The All-Star baseball game, for instance, had been talked about for years. It was thought to be impossible. But Arch had sufficient persuasion and was enough of a politician to put it over. It almost didn't go. The American League, which was headquartered in Chicago, was all set, but the National League almost killed it. Arch had to put the pressure on the Boston Braves and Judge Fuchs. Arch called Fuchs and said, "Look, we're going to announce this the day after tomorrow, and either we're going to announce there is a game, or that we almost had one and didn't because of you. Now can you and the National League stand that kind of publicity?" That's the way he forced them into it.

Later, when they were starting to handle tickets, I went out to Comiskey Park for Arch, to represent him. Harry Grabiner, the general manager of the White Sox, didn't know what was going on. Grabiner was frightened and thought it was going to be a flop, that there would be nothing but empty seats. I was out there for about five hours. When I came back Arch said, "How's everything?" and I said, "Well, they're busy returning ticket applications." The players selected for the All-Star teams were chosen by popular vote, which was conducted essentially by the *Tribune*.

Ward started the All-Star football game the next year. This pitted the best college players against the pro champion and made him a powerful figure in football. I was still working for Arch when the NFL offered him the job as commissioner. This was in 1940, the first time. They offered him $25,000 a year and he turned it down. The next year they offered it to him again and he accepted. I found out about it through Curley Lambeau, who was a good friend of mine. Curley ran the Green Bay Packers. We were together for two weeks on the West Coast, first for the Rose Bowl game and then the Pro Bowl game. Curley told me, "This will be your last assignment for the *Tribune*. When you get back Ward will be the commissioner of the league and you're going to be his assistant." But then Ward changed his mind and turned them down again.

The committee of owners that dealt with Ward had to look for another commissioner. This went on, I guess, until February or March, maybe even later. Finally, they had a meeting here in Chicago at the Blackstone Hotel. The night before the meeting I had dinner with George Marshall of the Redskins and he was telling me how they didn't know what they were going to do.

So I said, "Why don't you get hold of Ward and ask him? Maybe he's got some ideas. Anyway, Ward ought to be over here thanking you people for the opportunity you've given him and explaining why he turned it down."

Ward came over the next night and recommended two people—Frank McCormick, the athletic director at the University of Minnesota, and Fritz Crisler, the Michigan coach and athletic director. The owners didn't care for either one. Then, at a subsequent meeting, Ward suggested Elmer Layden. Layden had a coaching contract at Notre Dame, but it wasn't much of a contract and was only for one year. Ward sold the league on him. When Layden agreed, he took me along with him.

My title was assistant to the commissioner, but I was also handling the league publicity, the first full-time publicity man they'd had. I was with Layden for five years, until he was replaced by Bert Bell. The owners rewrote the book for Layden, gave him more power than Judge Landis. But Layden wouldn't use it. He was still back in college. He wouldn't make a decision. He always felt, "Well, if that's the way they want to do it, it's their league. Why should I step in?" I was just beginning to get him out of college, to get him to operate, but then his five-year contract was up and they wouldn't stand for any more.

For instance, I wanted him to fine Marshall five thousand dollars for a hassle during a playoff game at Wrigley Field between the Redskins and the Bears. In the last five minutes of the second quarter, Marshall came out of the stands and sat on the Bears' bench. George Halas was away in the service, and Ralph Brizzolara was managing the Bears. Brizzolara looks up, and there's the owner of the opposition sitting with his team. He ran him out of there, not only off the bench, but out of the park. I wanted Layden immediately to fine Marshall five thousand dollars for causing this scene—for Christ sake, during a championship playoff! Layden hesitated and hesitated. Finally, he fined him five hundred dollars.

One of our problems with Layden was over the organization of the All-America Conference. Layden refused to believe that his friend

Arch Ward would do this. Layden was so damn naïve. But Ward started the All-America Conference, and in retrospect, it helped in the growth of professional football. It focused an awful lot of national attention on pro football because of the fight between the two leagues, and of course, now more major cities were involved. In that way Arch helped pro football. Helped a great deal.

Arch promised the All-America Conference he would get them into the All-Star game. But this was one time when the *Tribune* didn't stand behind Ward. The *Tribune*'s contracts with the NFL weren't of such long duration, and Arch advised the NFL owners the *Tribune* wasn't going to renew. I was at the league meeting of the owners when this thing came up, and they said they were going to Chicago to see Colonel Robert McCormick, the publisher of the *Tribune*. They figured the colonel would be in their corner.

I said, "Don't do that. Don't see the colonel. He'll do what he always does. He'll say, 'Well, that's Ward's department. Go down and see Ward.' "

I told them to see J. Loy Maloney, who was then the managing editor. And that's what they did. Maloney got it before the board of directors of the *Tribune* and the directors voted to continue honoring the original contract with the NFL. That may have been the only time Ward lost.

After the owners fired Layden, Bert Bell took over. I worked with Bell for two years. Then I resigned. Bell was afraid of me for some reason, afraid I was trying to get his job. I had no designs on his job, but he felt that way and I never could convince him otherwise. He stayed in Philadelphia but moved the NFL office to New York, in the same building with the Giants, up at Fifth Avenue and Forty-second Street. Bell thought it was advantageous to have an office in New York from a publicity standpoint.

About all I did in New York was go to lunch with Tim Mara, the owner of the Giants. He would take me to the Harvard Club. Mara wasn't a college man, and he used to get a great chuckle out of sneaking a Notre Dame into the Harvard Club.

The day I resigned I got a call from Curley Lambeau. He wanted to know what was the matter. I told him and he said, "Hell, I've got a job for you." So I went to Green Bay and was with the Packers for three years, as the publicity man and assistant general manager. When Curley died, Ward called me and wanted to know if I'd like to rejoin the *Tribune*. Ward needed a man to write his column, "In the Wake of the News." Dave Condon had been doing it, but Condon wanted a year's leave of absence to go home and straighten his affairs. Ward asked me to fill in for Condon. But when the year was up I stayed at the paper. This was in April 1950.

Ward died in '55, and Wilfrid Smith took the job and I was named Smitty's assistant. And when Smitty left in '67 I became the sports editor. Smitty was one the greatest friends I ever had. He didn't have to retire but literally walked out to give me a chance to become sports editor, so I could get into the executive echelon and improve my pension. So I had that for three or four years, and when I became sixty-five I was tossed out, but they let me stay until the end of the year. My last assignment was Notre Dame and Texas in the Cotton Bowl.

It got to be kind of funny in the latter part of my career. I'd walk into a press box and look around and see nothing but a lot of young people and not know any of them. I would wonder, "Who the hell are these young punks?" And then suddenly I would realize that they were saying, "Who is that old fossil?" So I'd sit down and go to work and keep quiet.

I was amused when I went around to these different stadiums—many of them are new—and hear these fellows griping about the hospitality room back of the press box, with rugs and settees and lockers for the writers. It gave me a chuckle. I remember the days when the press boxes weren't quite so elaborate. For years when I went to Green Bay, for the *Examiner* and the *Tribune*, our press box was a row of chairs on the track right behind the bench. And when the fans left the stands, after the game, they'd come down to the track on their way out, and would look over our shoulders to see what we were writing.

One time, after a very exciting Bear game, I thought I had a real good lead. I figured this would get at least an honorable mention from the Pulitzer Committee. Some big Belgian behind me was chewing tobacco, and I guess he didn't like my lead because he let one go right over my shoulder that just blotted the entire page of copy.

Abe Kemp

Abe Kemp began his newspaper career in 1907, at the age of fourteen, and continued as a sportswriter for sixty-two years, dividing his time almost equally between baseball and horse racing. Unlike most turf writers, who also double as handicappers, Mr. Kemp often played his own selections. He had a large following, several times picked the card, and over the ten-year period up to his retirement showed an aggregate profit on a two-dollar win bet, a rare achievement for a newspaper handicapper, who must make selections on every race.

The son of a tailor whose shop was destroyed in the 1906 earthquake, Mr. Kemp started as an office boy on the San Francisco Bulletin. *He left San Francisco briefly for stints in Los Angeles and Spokane, but rejoined the* Bulletin *as sports editor and then moved to the* Examiner *where he remained for forty-three years. A witty storyteller, Mr. Kemp was among San Francisco's best-known toast-*

masters. He was presented at his retirement banquet with two round-trip tickets for a South American vacation, but said that since neither he nor his wife spoke Spanish he didn't see any sense in going to South America. Instead he used most of the money to purchase daily double tickets. He died in 1975 at the age of eighty-one.

I was a lousy baseball writer and a lousy sportswriter and a lousy newspaperman because I never believed in the concept. I went my own way, figured out my own concept of what I wanted to write about. I wasn't interested in scoops, I wasn't interested in routine stories. I was interested in the unusual, the bizarre, the esoteric. I devoted sixty-three years to pursuing that line and as a consequence came up with more God damned stories than any sportswriter who ever lived. And that's the theme of my book—the unusual. Nobody will believe what I write, and I don't give a good God damn if they do or they don't. I've entitled my book *Almost the Truth—So Help Me, Ananias.* Ninety percent of it is the truth and five percent is hyperbole. The rest is imagination.

What the hell, you can't be perfect. Every sportswriter has his own ideas. You take today. You know what I term these modern-day sportswriters—inspired idiots. I'll be a sonofabitch if I know what they're thinking about. They're not writing sports. They're telling the manager who to hire, who to fire, how to coach, who to play. I don't think that's the prerogative of the sportswriter. All of 'em are trying to emulate Brann The Iconoclast. Brann was the most famous iconoclast of all time, and a terrific writer. He knocked and damned everything. But the guy could write.

Let me try to illustrate by a story—and a true story. Did you ever know Bill Byron, the umpire? Well, he was quite a famous guy. He umpired in the National League, umpired in the Pacific Coast League, and I don't know how many other leagues. He was typical of an umpire. Don't touch the blue uniform. It's sacred, you know. He was a good friend of mine. John McGraw called him the "Hummingbird" because when ball players were arguing with him, he'd hum "Down by the Old Mill Stream," or whatever the hell it was.

In the old days, here in San Francisco, they played baseball at Recreation Park, down on Fourteenth and Valencia Street, a ramshackle two-by-four ball park. You could kick a ball over the right field fence. One day Byron and I walked from the umpire's dressing room to home plate. Now in those days they had a place called the Booze Cage underneath the grandstand. The admission price to the bleachers was twenty-five cents, but to get in the Booze Cage you paid forty cents. For the extra fifteen cents you either got a shot of whiskey or a stein of beer. Or a ham and cheese sandwich. Christ, the guys in there were tough, particularly on umpires. They were all drunks. They got on everybody, and as we're walking past the Booze Cage they started on Byron. They called him everything. Byron held up his hand. Strangely, he got silence. He said, "Gentlemen, years ago a namesake of mine wrote some famous lines."

One drunk yelled out, "What the hell were those lines, you blind sonofabitch?"

Byron said, "He wrote, 'It takes years for a man to learn his trade but critics come ready-made.' "

Now you think about that and sportswriters. What the hell, they can take you off the sandlots, give you a typewriter, and now you're telling Ty Cobb how he should play, Walter Johnson how he should pitch. Think about it.

I started writing baseball in 1908 when I was fifteen years old, for the San Francisco *Bulletin*. I was the youngest baseball writer in the United States with a daily by-line—"Abe the Irrepressible Rooter." I was a Seals fan, and sometimes when I was rooting for the club I used to climb up the screen. Three times I was thrown out of the ball park for disturbing the spectators.

In those days most writers resorted to slang, and I was trying to outdo 'em as best as I could in my feeble way. I wrote the old clichés—he "rammycackled the old tomato." He "ripped the stitches off the ball." That's the best I could do. Christ, all I graduated from was grammar school.

I was helped by a lot of old-timers, no newspapermen particularly, but the linotype operators. They liked me. They'd edit my copy so I didn't make too many God damned mistakes.

Actually, my first job at the paper was as an office boy. The *Bulletin* had a woman writer, Bessie Beatty, a terrific sob sister. But she was a sonofabitch. Mean. She later became the editor of *McCall's* magazine. She was the original woman suffragette. She didn't have any use for men. She used to stand on a chair and look at the editorial department and say, "Mere men."

One day she said, "Boy," and I came over and she said "Get me some copy paper."

I said, "Bessie, the copy paper is in your drawer."

She said, "Open the drawer."

I said, "Go to hell!"

She reported me to the city editor, whose name was Jack Dunnigan. He was the prototype of all you've read about tough city editors. He sent for me. He said, "Did you tell Bessie Beatty to go to hell?"

"You're God damned right I did."

He leaned over and said, "Go tell her again and I'll give you a quarter."

So I went over and I said, "Bessie, how would you like to go to hell again?"

I was working at the time for Fremont Older, who was a famed crusading managing editor in those days. My main job was to go out and pick up his cigars every morning. This was right after the earthquake, and everything downtown was burned out and the closest cigar store was at Geary and Van Ness Avenue. Older had a charge account there. He would give me ten cents, a nickel carfare each way.

He smoked Van Dyke cigars, two for a quarter. I was fifteen years old but I was smoking cigars then, only I was smoking White Owls. That's all I could afford. One day I picked up his twelve Van Dyke cigars, and coming back on the streetcar I said, "I think I'll substitute one of my White Owls for one of his Van Dykes." It was a dangerous swap because White Owls had the word "Owl" superimposed on the leaf of the tobacco. O-W-L. Well, I took a chance. He didn't say a word.

The next day he sent me out again, and before I picked up the cigars I got into a crap game and won three and a half dollars. So I used the money to buy more White Owls. I said, "What the hell, I'll try two." Eventually, I wound up substituting six Owls for six Van Dykes. One day Older sends for me and says, "I went to see my doctor yesterday, and he told me I can't smoke these heavy Van Dykes anymore. So, when you go out today pick me up twelve White Owls."

I looked at him. Jesus, there was no expression on his face. Well, he never said anything to me, but Hyland L. Baggerly was the sports editor of the *Bulletin* and he was Fremont Older's brother-in-law. Later, when I started to write baseball under Baggerly, I told him the story. He told it to Older, naturally. But Older never said anything to me.

I'll tell you about Baggerly. I really think he's the man who promoted the sports page in America, made it something special. Oh, there were sports pages all over the country, but nobody ever devoted his whole time to it like he did. He developed some of the greatest sportswriters and beyond any question the greatest sports cartoonists in history. He developed Ripley. He developed Tad. He developed Goldberg. He developed Pete Llunaza. He developed Billy Hon. He developed, in my mind, the greatest sportswriter of all time—Charley Van Loan. Van Loan was working for the Pacific Gas and Electric Company in San Francisco. He turned in a story to the *Bulletin* on an amateur baseball game, and Baggerly was impressed by his style and hired him. Later Van Loan became the sports editor of the Los Angeles *Examiner*. He left Los Angeles to become the sports editor of the New York *American,* and then he wrote all those famous magazine articles—"The Greatest Double Play of All Time: Sanguinette to Schultz to Sweeney." Van Loan had Runyon cheated in a hundred ways, but in a different vein. Runyon was what I aspired to be—a character writing about characters. That's what I devoted my whole life to.

I was brought up under a strange philosophy that I wouldn't advise anybody to pursue today. But I pursued it and I don't regret it. I was a Pollyanna. When I broke in under Baggerly, the only advice he gave me was "Abe, I'm not telling you to do this, but if you can't write something nice about a ball player, don't mention his name."

I pursued that policy the rest of my life, and nobody could sway me. Managing editors tried, but I didn't give a shit. I hewed to the line. Now, I don't recommend it. I don't say it was good. You couldn't get away with it today, not in this critical day and age. No earthly chance. Hell, I could have written some of the most scandalous stories of all time. But I didn't. I'm not patting myself on the back because I didn't. I didn't believe in it, that's all.

What the hell, when a guy dies they praise the hell out of him. But he doesn't know what the hell it's all about. I believe in Felicia Hyams's poem: "Roses to the living are better than sumptuous wreaths to the dead."

There was a groom at the racetrack, Tom Farrell, a hell of a guy. He was at a funeral and another racetracker comes rushing into the funeral parlor too late. And he said to Tom, "Jesus, has the body left?"

Tom said, "Yes."

"God damn it," he says, "I wanted to get one last look at him."

Tom said, "Hell, it wouldn't have done you any good. He wouldn't have recognized you, anyway."

If you can't pat a guy on the back when he's doing something good, why the hell destroy him because he does something bad? Christ, they overemphasize the errors. Let me ask you a question. You say you've been writing sports for thirty years. How would you go about it if every game you ever covered—baseball, basketball, football, ice hockey—was perfection? What would you have? You'd have no score, wouldn't you? It'd be nothing-to-nothing. Would you like that?

Right after I started to write baseball, a shortstop named Roy McArdle made an error on a ground ball and it cost the ball game. I was a rabid nut, and I went back to the office and I was going to roust the hell out of McArdle, knock the hell out of him. Then I remembered what Baggerly told me.

I went over to the hotel where the ball players were staying, and I got on the house phone and asked for McArdle's room. A voice came back and said, "You can't talk to him right now."

I said, "Who's this?"

He said "Doctor so-and-so"—whatever the hell his name was.

I hung up and I went to McArdle's room and knocked on the door. The doctor let me in, and I found out a pebble had lodged in McArdle's eye. The doctor had to take five or six stitches. So I thought to myself, I could have done a rank injustice to that ball player. That stuck in my craw for years.

Your mind plays strange pranks when you get as old as I am. Some things I can remember vividly, and some things I can't remember at all. I can give you the batting lineups of fifty, sixty years ago, but I can't tell you what day yesterday was. Or what the hell I ate for dinner. It's events that I remember. Dates don't mean anything to me. Statistics, I detest. They're the scourge of the American sports page. The fifteenth time he wiped his ass; the sixteenth time he rubbed his nose. You're writing a story and you say he's six foot seven, he's four foot two, or his earned run average is —— that's a lot of crap. You disturb the continuity of the story. But that's all you get today.

There were some great baseball writers out in this part of the country years ago. Names that wouldn't mean anything nationwide. But clever writers who knew their business.

We had a sportswriter here named Al Joy. He worked for the *Examiner*, a brilliant sonofabitch. One of the best of all time, but his activities were confined to San Francisco, and back east they never heard of him. As a cub reporter he was assigned to interview a coed at the University of California who had won some kind of prize for scholastic brilliance. He went to interview her, and in the course of the interview she attributed her brain acceleration to a fondness for beans—string beans, pinto beans, black beans, pink beans. All kinds of beans.

This story was right down Joy's alley and he wrote it. But it wasn't the story that had everybody in San Francisco talking for weeks. It was the headline:

COED EATS BEANS TO MAKE HER ASTUTE

The philologists, or whatever the hell you call them, argued for a month. Torrents of letters poured into the *Examiner*. Hell, it was a blizzard. But the guy who wrote the headline didn't do anything wrong. He used the right word.

I knew Charlie Dryden, a hell of a writer. Some people insist he was the best baseball writer of all time, and I'm not going to argue. He worked out here on the San Francisco *Examiner* in 1908, and in those days Hearst gave a weekly five-dollar prize to the reporter who turned in the most original story.

Dryden's in a beer joint run by a Dutchman, trying to think

how the hell he can win that five-dollar prize. I don't remember the Dutchman's name, but he had a luxuriant beard. Trailed way down.

The Dutchman was talking to him and Dryden got an inspiration. He had a box of pressed matches, big matches, and he lit one and applied it to the Dutchman's whiskers. Down at the end of the bar was an alarm that went to the fire department. Dryden pulled the alarm. When the firemen get there, the Dutchman's beard is smoldering. And Dryden's squirting a bottle of seltzer water at the Dutchman's chin. Then Dryden went back and wrote the story how he put out this fire. He won the five-dollar prize.

Jesus, we had characters out here. Back in 1910, when I was still a punk baseball writer, this big, hulking guy comes out to see Dan Long, who was then the manager of the Seals. He told Long he wanted a job as a pitcher. Long questioned him, asked if he'd had any previous experience. He insisted he'd pitched some as a professional but he wouldn't amplify on it. To all the questions Long asked, he was evasive as hell. He wouldn't say where he had pitched or what clubs he pitched for. All he said was that his name was Mitchell.

Long asks him, "Are you on the blacklist?"

He says he isn't and he tells Long that if he doesn't win two-thirds of his games the Seals won't have to pay him a nickle. They signed him, but that wasn't incorporated in the contract. That was verbal.

Well, he was a helluva pitcher—a spitball pitcher. But he was eccentric as all outdoors. And he wouldn't talk to the baseball writers, nothing more than hello and good-bye. He wouldn't permit any photographers on the field. In those days they didn't have these long-lensed cameras. You had to snap a picture close up or you didn't get it. And if he saw a guy in the box seats leveling a camera at him, he put his glove over his face and made the umpire shoo the photographer away. One of the writers dubbed him Mysterious Mitchell.

To help keep his secrecy, he lived in a place called the Manx Hotel, on Powell Street, and he warmed up on the roof of the hotel on the days he was supposed to pitch. He got one of the bellhops who had been a semipro catcher to warm him up. Then he got into a taxicab with his guitar and he strummed his guitar all the way to the ball park. Flocks of people tried to get within photographic distance but none ever succeeded. Finally, the ball club got tired of paying his taxicab fare. They put a stop to it. So he rode downtown on a streetcar but he put a newspaper over his face. They had photographers galore on the streetcar, and cartoonists, but he never removed the newspaper from his face.

Well, he was a sensation. Every newspaper in San Francisco offered bonuses to anybody who could find out who he was. People called up, giving us leads. But they didn't know a damn thing. I followed dopeheads, heroin addicts, whores, pimps, everybody. But I never got close.

This went on for weeks, and one day I'm in the clubhouse with Denny Carroll, the trainer. All the players were out on the field and Denny says to me, "How would you like to find out who Mysterious Mitchell is?"

I said, "Denny, quit hamming me."

He said, "I'm not hamming you. Put the padlock on the door."

I put the padlock on the door.

They had a trunk for the players' valuables. Denny opened the trunk, and there was a little shammy bag with a watch in it. He pulled out the watch and gave it to me and said, "Open the back cover."

I opened the cover and there was an inscription: "Presented to Clarence Walker, captain of the U. of Chicago Football Team, 1906."

Denny heard footsteps. He put the watch back in the shammy case, put the case back in the trunk, and made me open the door. A couple of players came in. They suspected what was going on. One of them said to me, "Now you got your story."

I rushed down to a sporting goods store and asked if they had a 1906 college football guide. They had one and, sure enough, on one of the pages was a picture of the University of Chicago football team, coached by Alonzo Stagg, and in the center was a lifelike picture of Mitchell. And that's how I got the exclusive on who in the hell Mitchell was.

Years later I ran into him, when he was pitching for Newark in the International League. We talked old times and I asked him why he didn't want anybody to know who he was. He then told me the full story for the first time.

He was pitching for the New York Giants and got hold of some chambermaid at some hotel in New York. He wrestled with her. She fell down a flight of stairs, and that was the end of her. They got out a warrant for his arrest. McGraw gave him his unconditional release and told him to get the hell out of town. So that's how he came out to San Francisco.

I don't suppose many people know it, but a guy from San Francisco, Ping Bodie, was the inspiration for Ring Lardner's "You Know Me, Al" series. Lardner wrote about Bodie when he was with the White Sox, but Bodie played out here. He had a boy five years old when he was playing with the Seals. His boy would go through the stands and he'd buttonhole any spectator, it didn't make any difference who it was, and he'd say, "Who's the best hitter in the Pacific Coast League?"

The guy would usually say, "I don't know, who?"

Then the Bodie kid would say, "My father."

"Well, who's your father?"

"Ping Bodie."

"What makes you think he's the best hitter in the Pacific Coast League?"

And the kid says, "Every night at supper my father tells me he's the best hitter in the Pacific Coast League."

Damon Runyon came to me in 1922 and offered me a job writing baseball for the New York *American*. This was when Runyon had switched from becoming a drunkard to becoming a teetotaler. But he asked me so God damn many questions I got terrified. How much do you drink? How much do you smoke? I got scared. I thought to myself, "Holy Jesus, I don't want to work for any sonofabitch like that."

You know Vernon Gomez, don't you? Lefty Gomez. They just put him into the Hall of Fame. Well, he broke in with the Seals here. He had plenty of guts right from the start. Nick Williams managed the Seals, and Nick would look down the bench before the game and he'd say, "Anybody got guts enough to challenge the enemy?" and Gomez would speak up and say, "I'll challenge 'em."

Cy Slapnicka, a scout for Cleveland—he's the guy who later signed Bob Feller—was looking at Gomez. Cleveland secured a ten-day option from the San Francisco club to buy Gomez for fifty thousand dollars and three ball players. The Seals were home, and I'm sitting up in the tower talking to Charlie Graham, the vice-president of the Seals.

Slapnicka comes in and he says, "Charlie, is it all right if I go down to the clubhouse where the players are dressing?"

Charlie said, "Sure."

"Well, are you sure they'll let me in?"

So Graham phoned Denny Carroll, the trainer, and he said, "Slapnicka is coming down. Let him in."

After Slapnicka left, Graham says to me, "What the hell do you suppose he wants to go in the clubhouse for?"

I said, "Charlie, I haven't any idea."

About a half-hour later Slapnicka came back and said, "Charlie, I'm going to forfeit my option on Gomez."

Graham says, "Tell me something, Cy. Why did you change your mind from the time you left here until the time you returned?"

"Well," he says, "I'll tell you, Charlie. I saw Gomez undressed in the clubhouse, and anybody who's got as big a prick as he's got can't pitch winning ball in the major leagues."

I started to laugh like hell. Meanwhile, Slapnicka ducked out and Graham says, "What the hell do you find so amusing?"

I said, "I'll tell you what I find so amusing. This is the best God damned story in my life and I can't write a word about it."

I was at Seals Stadium the day Joe DiMaggio first worked out with the team. There were about eighteen kids on the infield, just an impromptu practice. I was sitting in the grandstand with Charlie Graham, and some kid picks up a ground ball and he heaves it right past Graham's head. And Graham says, "I'll say one thing about that kid, he's got a hell of an arm." It was Joe DiMaggio.

The Seals had a trainer, fellow named Bobby Johnson. Bobby had a penchant for big words, and he thought he'd improve DiMaggio by teaching him how to use big words. Now whether or not I was set up for this I don't know. But it so happened that DiMaggio had been reported as having a bad cold, and I walked into the clubhouse and I said, "You're late, Joe."

He looked at me kind of funny and said, "Yeah, I've just been perignating around the block."

"You've been what?"

He said, "I've been perignating around the block."

Joe coughed a little bit, and I said, "You got a cough, Joe?"

"No," he says. "Just a slight regurgitation."

I looked at Johnson, and there's a big smile on his face. I know damn well that sonofabitch has been tutoring Joe on these words. Then I forget what the hell I said to him, but DiMaggio used the word idiosyncrasy. In what context, I can't recall.

Now in those days I scouted for the White Sox. Did it for eleven years. Maybe you shouldn't call me a scout. I was their Pacific coast representative. They paid me a hundred a month. Well, anybody with two eyes in his head could see there was no way DiMaggio could miss. But one day, in getting out of a taxicab, Joe injured his right knee and every scout was leery. Harry Grabiner, the White Sox general manager, called me and asked me about Joe's knee. I said, "I don't know anything about his knee, Harry. Outside of that you can go the limit."

"How are we going to find out about his knee?"

I said, "I don't know."

Well, foxy Bill Essick was scouting for the Yankees. Essick was no dummy. Unbeknown to any of the rest of us, Essick took DiMaggio to see an orthopedic surgeon, a Dr. Bull. After two days of examination, Dr. Bull told Essick the knee would be as good as ever and that if he wanted he'd even give him a guarantee. And that's how Essick sneaked in and bought DiMaggio for $25,000 and five players. He just outsmarted all of us.

There was never any doubt Joe would be a major league star. But we had a hell of a time trying to find out if he got his contract from the Yankees. Joe's mother was impossible. You'd phone and ask for Joe and she'd say, "No, Joe da' home." That's all we ever got. "No, Joe da' home." So my boss, Curley Grieve, a damn good sports editor, says to me, "Can't you find out if he's got a contract?"

I said, "How the hell am I going to find out? I can't find DiMaggio. I can't get anything out of his mother. I can't get his father. His brothers, they profess ignorance." But I said, "Wait a minute, Curley, I've got an idea."

He says, "What is it?"

I says, "I'm not going to tell you. I'll try to work it out."

Bill McCarthy was the postmaster of San Francisco and a good friend of mine. Bill had been the president of the Pacific Coast League. I went to see him and I said, "Bill, I think you can help me."

"Anything. What is it?"

I told him my boss was bugging me on whether Joe DiMaggio got his contract from the Yankees, and that if it came it would come by registered mail and there'd be a receipt. He checked it out and came back and said, "Yep, he signed a receipt." So at least we knew he got his contract. How much it was for I never did find out.

My great stories were on the racetrack. That's where I spent the last forty years. I've got so God damned many racetrack stories you can't separate 'em.

I used to handicap the horses, and I picked the card a few times. It's a rare feat. I did it once at a little town called Dixon, just outside of Sacramento. Had eleven races and I picked all winners, but I never cashed a ticket. I bet on all the losers. After the ninth race I was tapioca. I went into the jockeys' room. I knew Allan Gray, the jock, very well.

I said, "Loan me fifty bucks."

He says, "Have you had any luck?"

I said, "Jesus Christ, Allan, I can't pick a winner."

He says, "I'll loan you fifty bucks on one condition."

"What's that?"

"Bet my two horses on the last two races. I'll win both of them."

Well, I didn't—and he won them both.

When I left the track I didn't realize I had picked the card. So when I got back to Sacramento—I was staying in Sacramento at the time—one of the guys who'd been at the track said, "Jesus Christ, you must be fat."

I said, "Fat? I had to borrow fifty bucks and I blew that."

"You picked the whole card."

I said, "Don't crap me."

So he showed me my selections, and damn if I didn't. But that's not uncommon for handicappers. You seldom bet your own picks.

The sports editor of the Sacramento *Bee* was Rudy Hickey. A real good guy if you could understand him. But few people could. I could. We were buddies. Oh, what a grumpy, grouchy sonofabitch he could be.

He'd drool at the mouth at a 2-5 shot. One day we're at the harness track at Stockton and he bet two hundred dollars on an odds-on choice to show. I think the horse went off at 3-5, or something like that. And the horse broke at the start and lost all chance. I'm sitting next to Rudy—we're not in the press box, but just below it. Rudy picked up a straw hat and heaved it, and it described a half-circle and landed in some woman's lap down in the grandstand. She turned around and glared daggers.

But the guy sitting next to Rudy, he tapped him on the shoulder. He said, "Mister, I know how it feels when you bet your good money on an odds-on horse to show and he breaks. I sympathize with you. But would you do me a big favor the next time this happens?"

Rudy, the grumpy, grouchy sonofabitch, gives this guy an angry look and says, "Do you what kind of a favor?"

And the guy says, "Would you mind throwing your own hat?"

Rudy bets the daily double, another day at Stockton. His first horse wins and they announce the possible payoffs on the second part of the double, and if his horse wins it's going to pay fifteen hundred bucks.

Rudy says to me, "I'm going to tear up the ticket. The sonofabitch has got no chance at all."

I say, "Now wait a minute, Rudy, the race hasn't been run. Don't tear up the ticket. Give it to me. I'll hold it for you."

"No, I'm going to tear it up."

Well, he didn't tear it up. Now, I've got my binoculars screwed on the race, and as they're turning for home, I said, "Rudy, start to root! You've got a chance."

He says, "Where's my horse?"

"He's fifth but he's moving up. Now go to root."

"He ain't got no God damn chance. I'll tear the ticket up."

I'd had it. I said, "Go ahead and tear it up."

His horse wins and he wins the fifteen hundred bucks. Now he goes back upstairs where the teletype machines are. He's got another bet, two dollars on some horse at Delmar—an even money shot. He comes back and says, "The blind, sonofabitchin' judges."

I say, "What the hell happened?"

"Why," he says, "that horse figured to win and he blew. God damn those blind bastards."

I said, "Wait a minute, Rudy. You've just won fifteen hundred bucks, and now you've lost a lousy two bucks on some horse at Delmar, six or seven hundred miles away. What the hell's the matter with you?"

And he says, "I'm going to roust those God damned judges at Delmar." The next day he wrote a whole column about the blind judges—after he'd just won fifteen hundred bucks.

Nobody who wrote sports met the characters I met—because I concentrated on 'em, like Runyon. My managing editor at the *Examiner* never believed anything I wrote. Nothing. I would keep digging up stories, but he wouldn't publish 'em. He said I faked 'em. There was no way you could convince him.

There was a fellow named Lawrence (Tulley) Sullivan, and he was quite a character. He traveled all over the country, from one racetrack to another, and in all his life he never paid a nickle's worth of fare. He's riding on the Pennsylvania Railroad in an open lumber car, heading for New York. There's a big rope tied around the lumber to prevent it from shifting, and when it comes loose all the hoboes had to dive over the side, or get cracked up. Tulley makes it, and then he goes into the station and steals a roll of toilet paper and writes a note to the president of the Pennsylvania Railroad upbraiding him for the loose conditions of the lumber car, jeopardizing the lives of the patrons. And he gave an address, which was his sister in San Francisco. He got a letter back from the president which, in effect, said, "Well, I'm sorry. I assure you that if you ever avail yourself of our convenience, it will never happen again."

Tulley comes into the *Examiner* office and shows me the president's letter. I thought it was a funny story—and I wrote it. Wrenn, he was the managing editor, comes storming in, abusing the hell out of me. "You and your God damned stories about Sullivan writing on soft tissue. I don't believe it."

I said, "Wait a minute, Bill. Look in the right hand drawer of my desk. There's five letters from Tulley in there that I haven't even opened"—because anytime I opened one it took me two weeks to decipher his scrawl. I said, "Open 'em up. See what they're written on." All five were written on toilet paper. Wrenn walked out. He never said another word.

Tulley was the only guy who ever touted Pancho Villa and lived to tell about it. He touted him on a loser. He told me the story and I said, "What happened?"

He said, "I swam the Rio Grande in a hail of bullets."

There was a fight manager, a friend of mine named Red Sammy McClintoc. He managed five or six fighters. He got a match for one of his fighters in Butte, Montana, but the promoter only sent him transportation for the fighter. He didn't send Red a ticket.

So Red hoboed his way, and when he landed in Butte, on a miserable, snowy day, he had fifteen cents in his pocket. He was cold and hungry. He went into the round station—what they call the railroad depot today. The wall was plastered with signs: "Coffee and —— 5 cents. Please Pay in Advance." And way in the corner, on a fly-specked sign, it read "Pork and Beans—15 cents. Please Pay in Advance."

They had a potbellied stove in the center of the restaurant, and Sammy's warming himself and he's debating whether to spend a nickle for coffee and doughnuts, or to spend the whole fifteen cents for pork and beans. It's a hell of a decision. He finally makes up his mind. He's going to have pork and beans. He goes up to the counter that's presided over by some harridan. And she says, "What the hell do you want?"

Sammy says, "I want pork and beans."

She says, "What'd you say?"

"I want pork and beans."

"Well, where's your money?"

So he forks out the fifteen cents. In those days the register was up on the ceiling. There was a rope attached, and every time you pulled it it registered a nickle. So she pulled it three times and then sang out to the kitchen: "Pork and beans! The Prince of Wales is in the house!"

Altogether I worked in sports sixty-three years, the last forty-one years for the *Examiner* until I quit. I didn't want to quit. They forced me out on account of my age. They couldn't fire me, so they stuck me on the copy desk and they knew I wouldn't take it. They had it all figured. I was God damn bitter at that time. But time does heal all wounds. What the hell. I was too old. They didn't want an old fart like me.

Yet the last ten years I worked, I was one of the few handicappers in the United States who showed a profit on a two-dollar bet. That's going some. Lots of guys picked more winners, but if you had followed them you could have lost your ass. You would have made money following me because I picked against the favorites.

I can't even win a mind bet anymore. Three days last week I went to this little place, in the neighborhood, to find out if anybody's going to the racetrack. I wanted to make some bets, but nobody's going. I lost out on a seven-hundred-dollar exacta, a three-hundred-dollar exacta, and a five-hundred-dollar exacta, 'cause nobody was going.

But a couple of weeks ago I got fairly lucky. I saw a guy walking up the street and he's singing a ditty about the spirit of '76. I had no intention of making a bet, so I wandered by this little store and a guy comes out and he says, "I've got a friend going to the racetrack today. Do you want to make a bet?"

I said, "Yeah, give me an exacta on seven and six."

He said, "You know anything?"

"I don't know a God damned thing."

"Why you playing seven and six?"

"I just heard a guy singing 'The Spirit of '76.'"

So I got lucky. The sonofabitch won and paid five hundred dollars.

You need luck. I'm at Golden Gate Fields this one day, when I was still working. I'd just invested forty-four dollars in daily doubles, and I went to the jocks' rooms. That was part of my ritual. Every day I went to the barn area. I talked to everybody who talked to me. The daily double machine is right next to the jocks' room. So I come out and I reach into my pocket and I've got six bucks. What the hell. Six bucks is no good to me. So I bought three more daily double tickets and one of 'em paid $4,199.00.

I had to pay Uncle Sam. That took quite a big bite out of it. And I must have loaned out eighteen hundred bucks. Never got a nickle back. And I gave away some money to guys that needed it. I didn't wind up with much—maybe twelve hundred bucks out of the whole thing. What the hell. Easy come, easy go.

I'm working on my book, every night. I can't stay at the type-writer very long. I can do about two pages and my fingers cramp up on me. I tear up the God damned sheets. I just don't like what I've written. I've torn up five thousand pages. I guess I shouldn't, but I do. I doubt if I'll ever finish the sonofabitch.

Al Horwits

The Philadelphia baseball writers, to fight the boredom, often amused themselves by tossing peanuts at each other. One day, during a Philly–Chicago Cub game at the old Baker Bowl, the scribes ran out of peanuts and began throwing paper cups of water. The water trickled through the rotted floor to the lower stand. Gerry Nugent, president of the Phillies, came huffing into the press coop. "Don't do that," screamed Nugent. "Don't you realize we have patrons downstairs?" There was a silence. Suddenly, Al Horwits of the Phila-delphia Ledger *leaped to his feet and said, "My God, what a story!"*

    Al Horwits always knew a story when he saw one. He covered the Philadelphia baseball teams over the fifteen-year period from 1927 through 1941, when the Ledger *folded. He spent the 1942 season as publicitor for Connie Mack's Athletics and subsequently went to Los Angeles to begin a new career as a Hollywood press agent. He became a fixture in the movie business and handled dozens of successful films, managing both publicity and promotion. A native Philadelphian and the son of a manufacturer of ladies' clothing, Mr. Horwits was a former national president of the Baseball Writers Association of America. He died in 1984 at the age of seventy-eight.*

I would say from what I've seen around the country that you could count a handful of writers who are real baseball writers. The others are just going through the motions. They depend on the publicity men to furnish a story for them. They don't get to the human side, nor do they explore the inside of baseball. Here in Los Angeles, you look at what we have. They can write, some of them, but here it's not a career. It's a matter of expediency. They keep changing all the time.

I've had two careers, but I don't think I would have been in the movie business if I hadn't been a baseball writer. It opened all the avenues. Even today I go into the cities and I'll talk to newspaper people and they know about my background. I've had great fun out here because I haven't taken myself seriously as making a great contribution to the arts of America, like some of the so-called producer-directors. I was fortunate to have had some talent that fitted in, but as far as the two businesses go I don't think this would have been possible without my baseball and reporting background.

My whole newspaper career, from 1922 to 1942, was with one paper—the Philadelphia *Evening Ledger.* I was born in Philadelphia and went to high school there. One of my classmates was the son of the guy who built the Arena at Forty-sixth and Market in West Philadelphia, the first arena the city ever had. I worked as an usher and they put me in charge of the press section. I was sixteen, still in high school, and through this job I got to meet the sportswriters. One of them, Lou Jaffe, was the boxing writer on the *Ledger,* and one day he said to me, "Why don't you come down and do some work? You could be our high school correspondent."

So I went to the *Ledger* office, and a fellow named Joe

McGlynn, the sports editor, said he wanted me to cover a soccer game the next day. Now this was in January. The next day was cold, with snow on the ground. I just figured they won't play today. So I never bothered going. Actually, I did call them at the field and they told me that one of the teams hadn't shown up. But when I called the paper a couple of weeks later I was told by McGlynn, "Well, we gave you an assignment and you didn't cover it." They thought that the team not showing up was a better story than the game would have been. That was my first lesson in journalism.

They gave me other assignments. I started to cover school basketball games and soccer matches, and during the summer they gave me a full job. When I got out of high school, I didn't go to college, though I had been accepted at Penn State. Instead I went over to the *Evening Ledger* and became a member of the staff. I helped cover the first National Open Golf Championship, in 1923 I believe it was, the year Bobby Jones won. I was working on space rates. Soon I was making so much money that the managing editor came in and said I would have to go on salary.

I started covering baseball in 1927, first with the Phillies. In 1932 I started switching, starting with the Athletics at their training camp and moving over to the Phillies after the first four weeks. During the season, I would cover both the A's and Phillies at home.

I got along well with the players, particularly the Athletics. I had a feeling for the players' plight. I knew they were underpaid, particularly in Philadelphia, and that most of them were being pushed around. Not just that they would be traded without notice, but in those days they had to pay their own expenses to move to another city. You just didn't have a good deal, unless you happened to be a superstar. Then you did fairly well, but even in those days— well, take Al Simmons, who was a superstar with the Athletics. He signed a three-year contract for $100,000. There's no telling what he would have made today with his kind of talent. I knew Simmons fairly well.

But more typical was Chuck Klein of the Phillies. He called me the day he got his contract to say how ridiculous it was and ask if I would help him. So I started a series about Klein being the top attraction for the Phillies and being underpaid, and eventually they paid him closer to what he was worth. So he always knew I was a good friend. So did the other players, and knowing this, they would tip me off to many a story.

The teams in those days were playing in the old Baker Bowl. It was a horrible, claptrap ball park with a seating capacity of nineteen thousand, which was never proved. It finally collapsed one day. The fans were stamping their feet after Cy Williams hit a home run and all the stands collapsed. That's when they moved to Shibe Park. But we had a lot of fun in that old ball park. You were right on top of everybody.

Baker Bowl was where the boo birds started. There were these two brothers, the Kesslers, who were really rough. They sold fruit around the neighborhoods, and would start early and be finished by the time the game began—which in those days wasn't until 3:15. One brother would sit on the right side of the field, near first base, and the other would be at third base. In Baker Bowl you could sit anywhere and just about shake hands with the players in the infield.

The Kesslers would hold conversations across the field and would get terribly abusive. These guys were needlers. They never let up. They were forerunners to the CIA. They knew all the ball players' habits, where they were drinking, and the girls they were with. And they would go out and yell the names. A ball player would really be upset when he found out that they knew the truth about him.

Connie Mack had this left fielder named Bill Lamar, who was a pretty good hitter. But Bill liked to spend his nights around the bars, and the Kesslers got on him. The guy was dropping fly balls in the outfield. They really had him intimidated. Connie took the Kesslers to court to try to get them to stop, claiming they were disrupting his club, and though Connie had friends in court there was nothing he could do about it. So he offered each of the Kesslers a season's pass if they would lay off his players. But they said they'd prefer paying and having the chance to yell.

The needling and booing caught on with the other fans and became a big thing. There was this time when President Hoover came up, though I don't think this was the regular boo birds. But I think they were the ones who started it. This was for the second game of the World Series, and Hoover was being driven into the stadium along third base, where they used to bring the equipment in. The presidential limousine stops in front of the dugout. Hoover gets out and from everywhere in the park the boos came. I never heard such booing in my life. Then they started yelling, "We want beer." It reverberated over the whole park. Of course this was 1930, when things were tough.

About the only ball player I had trouble with was Rube Walberg, a big left-handed pitcher. Jimmy Dykes used to call him Silly Charlie. Dykes always said that whenever Walberg was pitching and he started to smile, that was the signal for the infielders to play deep. Anyway, I had written something about Walberg that he didn't like, and one day on the train from St. Louis to Boston he grabbed me by the throat. He had a hand as big as a ham. He said, "I ought to strangle you for what you wrote about me."

I said, "Well, it was the truth. How about the things you've been saying about me?"

"Yeah," he said, "but when I say 'em, only three guys hear it. But when you write it, thousands of people read it."

I told him, "Well, let that be a lesson to you." And with that he let go.

One of my dearest friends in baseball was Jimmy Foxx. Of course everybody knows he died broke. He couldn't hold onto his money. He and his first wife came from a small town, Sudlersville, Maryland. Jimmy started as a catcher, but it wasn't until he switched over to first base in '29 that he became a big hero. He didn't make much money, but what he made he and his wife lived up to and then some. I remember, in '32 or '33, he lived out in Jenkintown, a suburb of Philadelphia, and he had a butler. That didn't last long. The players would kid him because whenever they'd call him up on the phone, the butler would answer, "This is the Foxx residence."

It was his wife who wanted this way of living. She had been a telephone operator in Sudlersville and had seen all this in the movies. She liked to travel, to move around in the right social circles, and I guess the more adulation Jimmy had the more he started believing, as she did, that that was the way to live.

Years later, when I was at Universal, I got a call from him one day. He was now remarried, living in Boston, and said he was coming out to Phoenix and could I find a job for him on the coast. I said, "Well, I think we could get you a job broadcasting the Hollywood Stars' games. I think it would be perfect for you. You come out and we'll arrange it."

Then I talked to some people and they thought it was a good idea. Jimmy got to Phoenix and he called me. I told him what we had lined up, and he said, "I'll call you when I'm coming." But he never did.

He was a coach for a while with the Phillies, but they had to let him go. The complaint I heard was that it wasn't so much his drinking but that he was taking the younger players with him. I always thought that Tom Yawkey would take care of him. Yawkey liked him very much. But Jimmy loused himself up in Boston. He would drink beer, whiskey, anything. And he liked the nightlife, too.

He could have been even greater than he was if he had taken care of himself. He was a terrific ball player, and easy to handle. He was a great fielding first baseman, and when Connie sold Mickey Cochrane, Foxx went back behind the plate. He could run, he could field, he could throw—a powerful arm. He cut his sleeves all the way up to the shoulders, to show his bare arms, the way Ted Kluszewski did. And you could see those muscles. It would have meant a lot to Jimmy if he had broken Ruth's record. But there wasn't much stress put on statistics in those days. And then the drinking affected his batting. He started getting a little heavy in the chest. This is where it affects sluggers. They can't get the bat around fast enough on the fastball. That's what happened to him.

Mickey Cochrane was another great athlete. He was quite a football player—once kicked a fifty-two-yard drop kick for Boston University. He was the only player in the history of baseball who, to buy him, they bought up a whole team. Connie bought the Portland club from the Pacific Coast League in order to get Cochrane. Connie was friendly with the Portland owner, Tom Turner, and he bought the Portland club in 1924-1925. But Mickey was badly hit by the Depression. He had invested heavily in the market, and when the crash came in '29 and things got worse in the next few years, it affected his play. In the '31 series, they stole a lot of bases on Cochrane. His mind wasn't on baseball.

Connie was also hit hard by the crash. He had a lot of money in the market from baseball, and I think he lost over a quarter of a million by '31. I remember one time I was coming back after a game and I ran into Connie in the lobby of the hotel. He was looking at the stock quotations, and he says to me, "You know, I used to buy shares by the thousands. Now I buy them by the hundreds."

A lot of guys on the club lost money. It was Ty Cobb coming to the A's who got them all interested in the market. He had them buying stock, although Connie was in it before. Cobb knew the market. He had original Coca-Cola stock. He knew people everywhere he went, people in financial circles and also in business. It helped him. Somehow he wasn't hurt by the crash. To begin with, he owned his stock outright. He didn't buy on margin. Cobb died a rich man.

I had a good relationship with Cobb. He used to call me and he'd say, "Let's go to a movie." This is when it was a rainy day, an off-day, and we'd go from one movie to another. He would see four or five in a day. I'd give up after the second. I had to go back to work. But he was smart. All the time he'd manage to give you enough information that you'd wind up with a story, and he still kept his name before the public. He had friends everywhere. He drank, but only wine. He loved champagne. His bathtub in the hotel was always filled with ice and champagne. I don't know what would happen if he had to take a shower or a bath. I guess he always depended on the ball park.

Eventually he moved to San Francisco, and I remember this time when we visited him in the forties, some of us newspaper fellows who were traveling with the Athletics. He gave each of us a bottle of wine with a label that said "Bottled especially for Ty Cobb."

He taught the A's a lot, too. He made real gentlemen of them, with the places he took them, the things he'd tell them. He had mellowed by the time he had got to the A's, though he still had his ego. He hit like hell in '27, but in his later years, when he had to be taken out of the lineup, he realized he was slowing up the ball club.

Another great ball player I got to know well was Lefty Grove. He was a crabby sort of a guy, not an educated fellow like Cobb. I wasn't in camp the time he reported, but they told me he had a hard time reading the menu and used to say, "I'll have the same thing." But I'll never forget one thing he said to me. He lived in Lanaconing, Maryland, in the off-season, in the hills, and I asked him if he was going to hang around Philadelphia after the season. He said, "No, I'm going back to Lanaconing. It only costs me eight dollars a week to live there." But he could pitch. He could really burn them in. Jesus, he was fast. He'd knock you down, throw at you, do anything.

On the management side, I got along fine with Connie Mack, but the Phillies were run by a guy named Gerry Nugent. He hated me and I hated him. He was a devious guy. Bill Terry told me that every time he made a deal with the Phillies there was always some extra compensation that they had to pay to Nugent under the table —cash, not a check.

One time I had a story that the Phillies had sold their radio rights for five years in order to get money to operate their spring training camp, and that they had borrowed the money from various individuals. I knew about this because someone at the bank was a friend of mine. He had seen the check go through and tipped me on the story. I wrote it and Nugent raised hell. He came down to the paper with his lawyer demanding to see Stanley Walker, the city editor. Walker had just come down from the New York *Herald Tribune.* He lasted a couple of months. He just couldn't take Philadelphia. This was his second day on the job when Nugent walks in saying, "I want this man fired. He writes things about me, he's always hurting me."

Walker said, "Well, Mr. Nugent, first let me ask you: Is this story true?"

Nugent said, "It's a damaging story."

"Is it true?"

And Nugent said, "Yes."

So Walker says, "Well, you're wasting my time. I would suggest you leave." He left, and Walker gave me a raise.

Nugent tried to get me fired several times. I had a story one day that the Phillies were going to sell Bucky Walters to the Cincinnati Reds. I got it from a telegraph operator who I used to dictate to, to send the play-by-play. In the mornings he worked downtown in the Western Union office, and this one Saturday he told me he had sent a telegram from the Phillies confirming that Bucky Walters was going to Cincinnati for $45,000.

I went to the phone and dictated it straight to my office. And when the story ran, all hell broke loose. Nugent started to track it down and accused Western Union of giving me the story. He didn't know where else I could have gotten it. So they brought this telegraph operator in. His name was Visicki and he had one eye. He had lost the other eye in the war. And they asked him what he knew about it. He insisted he didn't know anything. Three days later the Phillies sent another wire to another club about a trade. It was a phony. Visicki came to me and told me about it, and I said, "I don't think that's so. Let's not do anything about it. They're trying to hook us." So nothing appeared on this thing and Visicki was absolved.

Connie was a different kind of guy. In the same kind of situation, at the end of the '33 season, I got the story that he had sold Cochrane to Detroit and Grove and Walberg to Boston. Connie just unloaded the team. I wrote the story and it was the lead on page one. The other writers started calling Connie and he had to deny it, and up in Boston they were denying it, too.

But I stuck to my guns because I got the whole story from Jimmy Foxx. After the story broke, I went down to Easton, Maryland, where they were giving a dinner for Foxx. Connie was there, and he called me aside and said, "What are you doing? Breaking up my club?"

I said, "No, Connie, it's too late. You've already done that."

He smiled and said, "We'll talk later."

He was smiling because I think he remembered an earlier time when I had checked with him on a story and he had denied it. I didn't write it, but the story turned out to be true. The next day, at the ball park, he called me over and said, "Listen, the next time you get a story like that—you print it—and then call me and I'll deny it. And then you'll have two stories. This way you don't have any." He was a pretty smart and cute old guy.

Actually, he was great with the writers. He helped you with your stories. He knew what it meant to get a good story. On rainy days he would always make himself available in the hotel. He'd call and say, "Do you need any help? Come on up and we'll talk."

He was fond of most of the Philadelphia writers, except maybe for Cy Peterman. There was this annual award, the Bok Award, that was presented every year to the outstanding Philadelphian. I think it was in 1935 they awarded it to Connie Mack. This was after he had sold all his best players. The team just couldn't take in enough money to meet its payroll. Cy Peterman wrote a story about Connie selling all the players in which he said, "If he could have sold the Bok Award he would have done that, too."

Well, that was a nasty crack. So a couple of days later I was walking down Lehigh Avenue with Connie, and Cy Peterman is coming up the street. Connie stops him and says, "Cy, how are you?" He made a big fuss over him, friendly as can be, and then we continued on.

So I said to Connie, "After what he wrote about you, how could you make that kind of fuss over him?"

"You know what Cy's thinking right now?"

I said, "No."

Connie says, "He's saying, 'Jesus, I guess he doesn't read my column.' "

Connie was a great manager, no question about it, but he was a hunch player. He knew how to handle pitchers and he knew how to place his outfield. Everybody knows the famous business of the scorecard. He would sit in the dugout and wave the outfielders around with a scorecard, even when he was managing in his sixties and seventies. The players never laughed at him. They all called him Mr. Mack. The only one around who called him Connie that I remember was Eddie Collins.

But in the late thirties and in the forties, when the team was going nowhere and he was a bit senile, they weren't paying too much attention to him. Yet he never thought of himself as being an old man. I remember in '42, we were in Boston and Connie's in the hotel lobby when some guy stops him and Connie makes a big fuss over him. He called me over and said, "I want you to meet my old friend Sweeney. He pitched to me in Holyoke. How old are you now, Sweeney?"

"I'm seventy-four," Sweeney says.

"Isn't that wonderful? Seventy-four years old and look at him." Connie was then seventy-eight.

But Connie was great in the early years. He got Ty Cobb in '27. In 1928 he had Cobb and Tris Speaker on the same team, Speaker playing center and Cobb in right. Of course business picked up terrifically, but the team kept losing. Toward the end of the season Connie took Speaker out and put Mule Haas in center. Then he took Cobb out and put Bing Miller in right. And this took guts. He moved Foxx from third base to first base, and he put Jimmie Dykes on third. The team finished great, almost won the pennant. They were 13½ games behind and came back to tie the Yankees but then lost the big final series with the Yankees, and that finished them.

Connie knew how to use psychology. I remember Jimmy Foxx telling me how one day he had popped up. When he came back to the bench and sat down, Connie said, "What have you been drinking lately, Foxie?"

After the game Jimmy went to him and said, "Mr. Mack, I haven't had a drink in months."

He said, "I know, Jimmy, but the fellow sitting next to you had." He made his point through Jimmy because the guy sitting next to him on the bench had been on the stuff.

I did an article with Connie for the old *Saturday Evening Post*. It was a story about managerial strategy and psychology, titled "Winning Them in the Clubhouse." Connie, for the first time, told how and why he picked Howard Ehmke to pitch the opening game against the Cubs in the 1929 World Series. Ehmke's selection as the starting pitcher in that game was one of the greatest surprise stories in sports. Nobody figured on it.

Late in the season, in August, Connie called Ehmke into his office and said, "Howard, this is bad news I have to give you. But I can't help it. I have to let you go."

Tears came into Ehmke's eyes. He was having a terrible season and he knew it. He says, "Gee, Mr. Mack, I've never been on a pennant winner before, and here this club is winning the pennant. I'd always dreamed that I could pitch in a World Series, and now you're giving me my release."

"Do you think you could pitch in a World Series?"

"There's one good game left in this arm," Ehmke says.

Connie told him, "If you feel that way, all right. But I don't want you to make the next trip with the club. The boys don't want you around. They think you can't pitch anymore. I want you to stay home, and when the Cubs are playing in Brooklyn and in New York, go over there and scout them. And when they're here against the Phillies I want you to watch them."

Then Connie says, "Howard, tell me which game you want to pitch against the Cubs and you'll pitch it."

Ehmke says, "Mr. Mack, I want to pitch the first one."

Connie just used that psychology on Ehmke, and of course, Ehmke not only beat the Cubs but he set a World Series record of thirteen strikeouts.

When I got the check for this story I told Connie, "We sold this article on the strength of your name. You're entitled to the major portion of it. You tell me what."

He said, "Who's it made out to?"

I said, "Connie Mack."

He took it and endorsed it and said, "It's all yours. All I did was spend a few mornings with you and tell you what you wanted to know. It's good for baseball. The check is yours."

It was Connie's use of psychology that got him Cobb in '27. Cobb was thinking of retiring. He had had one or two other offers, but actually he didn't need the money. He was a rich man by then. But Connie went down to Augusta, Georgia, to see him in the off-season. Cobb was so flattered that Connie would come down to his home and talk to him that when he made him his offer Cobb accepted it.

Cobb hated to be told what to do. At first, when he was playing right field and Connie waved his scorecard at him, Cobb acted as though he didn't see it. But finally Connie got him over there, and the very next batter hit the ball right at Cobb. He didn't have to move to catch it. He said afterwards he would never challenge the old man again.

Bringing Cobb and Speaker together in 1928 for their last year was a great piece of showmanship. They didn't win the pennant for Connie. In fact, they didn't even finish the season as regulars. But they did a lot of business and were a great draw on the road, too. Connie had come to their rescue. They were in trouble at that time, because both had been under the scrutiny of Judge Landis. There was talk they were involved in betting on games. There was still the specter of the 1919 World Series. But then Landis held a hearing and both were absolved. That's when Connie hired them.

The game today lacks showmanship, and that was one thing

that Connie had. He just had a natural instinct for it. People thought that because of that high stiff collar he was a prude, that he just sat there and had no idea of what was going on around him. But he was a good showman. He knew how to build up the crowds.

Landis was another great showman. He always had the press on his side because he played up to the press. He was smart. I remember this one time we went back to Chicago, for the baseball meetings, when Nugent was up before the judge for a drafting violation. The Phillies had drafted a player for the Brooklyn Dodgers. They didn't want this player for their club, but MacPhail of Brooklyn told Nugent to "draft him for us" because the Phillies were always last and they had the first crack in the draft. The understanding, of course, was that the Phillies would then sell him to the Dodgers, which was against the rules.

Landis called a hearing with MacPhail and Nugent, and there were about ten or twelve writers outside the office. Before the meeting started, Landis opened the transom door to the office, so we'd be able to hear everything that was going on. Landis knew that baseball could always use publicity. He wanted us to know he was disciplining Nugent and MacPhail without his making a statement. He let us hear the whole thing.

The Phillies were always losers while I was in Philadelphia. After 1933, when the Athletics started to sell all their ball players, they also went downhill. It was brutal because there was no interest. Our work suffered. We'd get to the ball park just as the game was starting. Maybe twice a week we'd bother going down to the field. But covering all those losers had its lighter side, too, especially in spring training. We never had to worry about anything.

I always got into uniform and worked out with the players. I'd pitch batting practice, and they'd try to hit me on the shins. I remember when Cy Peterman started on the *Bulletin*. He liked to play golf and he hardly ever came to practice. Cy was a gullible guy. After the first ten days of camp he asked me, "What's going on?"

I said, "Well, Rodriguez looks awfully good."

He said, "Who? He's not on the roster."

I said, "He just dropped into camp and asked Connie for a tryout. Connie put him at second base, and it looks like he's going to start the season there."

Cy wrote about Rodriguez for the next three or four days. Every night he'd see me and I'd say, "Jesus, Rodriguez had two hits in the camp game."

Finally, it's getting close to the first exhibition game and Cy came out for practice. He walked up to Connie and said, "Connie, I understand Rodriguez looks pretty good."

Connie said, "Rodriguez?"

Then he called his son Earle. "Earle, do we have someone named Rodriguez?"

And Earle said, "No."

So Cy found out I pulled this rib on him, and now he's embarrassed at the office. So he sends in a short piece saying that the A's have decided to give Rodriguez his unconditional release. But then the strange thing. I got a wire from my paper, wanting to know why I didn't have a story on Rodriguez.

A lot of gags. This was a last-place team. What else could you do? I remember Tom Meany, a very funny guy. Tom and I were sitting in the Shibe Park press box, and in those days you had the C & D wire which gave you the running line scores of every inning of every game in the major and minor leagues, also the home runs. It would say "Hank Greenberg, HR, 3d inning, one on."

I'm looking at the scorecard and I notice this ad for a bar named McCaffery. I showed it to Meany and we get it on to the wire, "McCaffery, HR, two on."

That started a gag. We'd go into different ball parks and report McCaffery hitting another home run. Jerry Mitchell gave him a first name—Bingo.

McCaffery hit ninety home runs that season—sixty in the day games and thirty in the night games. McCaffery became a big subject. There was a laugh everywhere we went, in every press box. He went on for quite a few years. At the World Series one year, I think it was in Washington in '33, we posted a note on the press room bulletin board that McCaffery had been sold to the Senators. The Washington writers started to look around. They were in the American League and weren't in on the gag. Christ, this thing was blown out of all proportion.

After the war came in '41, Tom Meany and I decided we had to get rid of McCaffery. Here's how we did it. We announced he was drafted into the army and refused to report, and that Judge Landis ruled him a slacker and ordered him off the turf for life. McCaffery wound up in Alaska playing for the Nome Yessims. That was the end of McCaffery.

We had all kinds of guys with great ideas. Did you ever hear of Caswell Adams? He wrote boxing and baseball for the *Herald Tribune*, and one night, in '39, we were in New York at Jack Bleeck's bar, the Artist and Writers Restaurant on Thirty-ninth Street, next to the *Tribune*, a big hangout for writers and movie people.

The Pope had just died and there was talk about who would be the next Pope. So Cass says, "We'll take bets." The Pope doesn't necessarily have to be Catholic. We could pick anybody. Back in 1216 there was a Pope selected who wasn't Catholic.

Cass makes up the odds and lists the entries on this big board. He had Groucho Marx down at 30-1. The favorite was Leo Pacelli, at 6-1. Humphrey Bogart puts five dollars on Leo Pacelli. Cass collected all the bets. It came to about four hundred dollars. I think we spent it all that night on a big party.

Now, it's about fifteen years later, I'm at Columbia, and we've made a picture called *The Harder They Fall*, starring Bogart. He plays a sportswriter who becomes a press agent. That was the year Marciano fought Moore in New York, so I called the sports editor at INS and said, "Listen, would you be interested in Bogart covering the fight for you? Won't cost you anything."

He says, "Sure," and so we're in New York for the fight, on September 19, 1955. But it rained that day and they postponed the fight to the next night. So we had a free night. Bogart had just made a picture for Paramount and the people from Paramount had sent him a case of scotch and they sent Baby, his wife, Betty Bacall, a case of Jack Daniels. She was a bourbon drinker. So I said to Bogie, "We've got all this booze. I'll invite a lot of sportswriters and we'll have a cocktail party."

He says, "Great."

I go over to the Garden and I get all these guys. Red Smith shows up and Shirley Povich and Vince Flaherty, all the top columnists. We're up in Bogie's suite, drinking away, and in walks Cass Adams. Bogart looks at him, and says, "Hey, buster, you owe me thirty bucks. I had a fin down on Leo Pacelli."

I got into publicity in 1942 when the *Evening Ledger* went out of business. I heard the paper was going to fold. I went to Connie and he said, "If that happens you have a job with me." I was to be the A's publicity director.

When the closing of the paper was announced, Connie said, "Al, I must tell you. I've been running this club all these years. I've never had any trouble or anyone question anything I've done. But my sons, Roy and Earle, are opposed to you joining the organization. They don't want you."

I said, "Hell, Connie, if they don't want me there's nothing you can do about it."

But he says, "I do want you and I'm going to pay you out of my own pocket. I'm not going to let the club spend this money. My sons want to run it this way—fine. As a matter of fact, I've resigned over this, but they won't accept my resignation. I've told them I'll manage the club but that's all I'll do. I've resigned everything else. I'm going to hire you for this year and give you a chance to find something because it wouldn't be good for you to be involved in this atmosphere."

I said, "Connie, I wouldn't want to."

And he said, "I gave you my word that you had this job, and you do. And when you file your income tax, I'm your employer, not the Philadelphia Athletics."

The trouble was, Earle and Roy resented me because I was Jewish. They were anti-Semitic. That was the reason they didn't want me around. There weren't too many Jews in baseball then, outside of Moe Berg and Andy Cohen of the Giants. Morrie Arnovich came later. The Macks were devout Catholics. Management was partial to players who were Catholic, and those on the club who were Catholic, and this included all the hired help, would have to go to mass to stay in the good graces of the management. Now, not only was I a Jew, I was the first Jew elected president of the Baseball Writers Association. I was the national president of the Baseball Writers that year. That's why I wanted to stay in baseball for one more season. I had no paper, but I was the president.

I traveled with the A's and made a few trips. Toward the end of the season Judge Landis asked me to be the official scorer for the World Series. I finished the season with Connie and scored the Series. After that I wanted to get out of Philadelphia, and somebody suggested I go into the movie business. I went to New York and had an interview at Universal with Maurice Bergman. I told him my background and he said, "Say no more. I'm going to recommend we hire you because I'll have someone to go to the ball games with."

But the thing stalled on and on, and so I called George Stevens, one of the top directors. I had been friendly with him. He says, "Oh, I know some people at Universal. I'll call." That's how I got the job. I started with Universal in New York in December 1942 and stayed there until 1949 when they brought me out to California to head the studio department. I've been in Los Angeles ever since.

I opened my own publicity office in '52 and kept it until '55, when Harry Cohn of Columbia asked me to head up the department there. I stayed at Columbia four years, until Cohn died. I got out before my contract expired because I had a deal on. I had started negotiations to buy the Hollywood *Reporter,* the trade paper here, with two friends of mine, this George Stevens and Bill Goetz. They agreed to put up the money for me. We were to be equal partners, but they would have nothing to do with the operation of the paper. I would be the sole operator, editor, and publisher.

We put accountants on the book and found that the paper was making more than $200,000 profit, although actually it was much higher because the guy who owned it, a fellow named Billy Wilkerson, was using it to pay for his travel and home and cars and everything else. Stevens and Goetz put up a million dollars. We had a handshake on the deal and were supposed to close on the morning of July 16, in the lawyers' office. But Wilkerson took off for Europe and called the deal off. Oh, what the hell! If that deal had been consummated I'd have been a millionaire today.

I hooked up with Stanley Kramer. I worked for Stanley for eight years, on some great movies. *Judgment at Nuremberg, Inherit the Wind, Ship of Fools.* Then Stanley didn't have anything going, and Columbia asked me if I would work with Richard Brooks. He was coming out with *The Professionals* and was about to go into production on *In Cold Blood.* I went with Brooks. He's one of the most talented men in the business. Creative. He writes and directs. I'm still with him.

I had it pretty good as a baseball writer. The ball clubs paid our expenses in those days. Even when the A's had lousy clubs and you were rapping the club, they never bothered you. You wrote as you pleased. There were no strings attached. They paid your way during the season, and you got a meal allowance of $3.50 a day. They also paid your laundry and pressing.

But when I got into the movie business, my God, what a difference. Money was plentiful. The salary I started at was twice what I made as a baseball writer. I no longer had a lower berth. I was now traveling in compartments and drawing rooms. When I'd go into any town, I'd have a suite. All I did was sign. My bill at "21," when I was in New York, used to run from six to eight hundred dollars a month. Just in that one place, for entertaining. Stork Club, the same thing. When Connie came up to New York I took him to lunch one day, and he offered to pay. But I said, "Not now, Connie. You're my guest."

I remember the last time I saw Connie. He came out here after he had retired. He didn't have all his faculties then. He had a hard time remembering and talking. I got a call at the studio from his cousin, Ralph Gutzhell, an attorney, and he says, "Connie would like to have you come down and have lunch."

So I went down to the Town House and we had lunch together. Connie was trying to tell me something. But he couldn't get it out. The gist of it, I thought, was that he was trying to tell me what a good friend I had been and how much he appreciated it. But he had a hard time trying to express himself. I think he was ninety-three.

○ ○ ○ ○
○ ○ ○ ○
○ ○ ○ ○

Ford Frick

"I'm a newspaperman at heart. I still think of myself basically as a baseball writer." So said Ford Frick at the age of seventy-eight, having been the only sportswriter to make the leap from the press box to the highest administrative office in sports—that of Commissioner of Baseball. He presided as baseball's so-called czar from 1951 through 1965, a difficult period in which he made seventeen appearances before a seemingly endless succession of congressional committees unsuccessfully challenging baseball's antitrust exemption.

During this time Mr. Frick was often criticized by some of his former sportswriting colleagues and, in retrospect, may have been the victim of both jealousy and objective reporting. Mr. Frick was depicted as a compromiser who lived in fear of the club owners who had knighted him. Nonetheless, baseball maintained its integrity and increased its attendance under his stewardship and, more important, led the nation in showing that racial integration was not only possible, but desirable. Mr. Frick, in one of his finest moments, squelched a budding players' boycott against Jackie Robinson, threatening the dissidents with expulsion.

Mr. Frick was born on December 19, 1895, on a farm in Noble County, Indiana, an only son in a family of five children. He worked his way through college, setting a pattern for many years to come of holding two jobs concurrently. He began his newspaper career in 1915 on the Colorado Springs Gazette and moved to New York in 1921, at the behest of Arthur Brisbane, then the chief editor in the Hearst empire. Mr. Frick was a baseball writer for ten years, doubling as a radio announcer, and in 1933 was appointed publicitor for the National League. He was named National League president a year later and served in that capacity for seventeen years prior to being selected as commissioner. A stamp collector and an expert on American Indian lore, Mr. Frick lived with his wife, Eleanor, in Bronxville, New York. His memoir, titled Asterisks and People, *was published in 1973. He died ten years later at the age of eighty-three.*

I was a hell of a typist. Maybe I wasn't a good writer, but I could type. I had a reputation for it. I could turn out a hell of a lot of words. When I graduated from high school I decided I was going to be a newspaperman. I was a young kid, fifteen or sixteen, and somebody told me you had to know how to type. So I went down to Fort Wayne one summer and took courses in typing and stenography. It was the International Business College.

There were no journalism schools in those days, and I figured that sort of stuff could be the beginning thing. The next year—in the fall of 1912—I enrolled at DePauw University in Greencastle. I worked my way all through school. One of the things I did was correspond on sports stuff for the Indianapolis and Terre Haute papers. Occasionally I did special assignments for the Chicago *Tribune,* like when we had our traditional football game with Wabash College, or when the Notre Dame baseball team came to town.

I played a lot of baseball. I wasn't very good, but I got my letter at DePauw. Later, when I went to Colorado, I played some semipro, in the coal mining leagues out there. I was a first baseman but couldn't throw. I had to wind up to throw to third. Ball players are born with a good arm, I think. You either have it or you don't. I don't think it's one of those things you can develop. It could be that I hurt my arm as a boy. I can't recall any specific injury but I've always had trouble with my arm.

I had the usual kind of boyhood. We were farm people. I was the only son but I had four sisters. We lived in a little village with about 250 or 300 people. This was in Bloomfield, Indiana. We did all the things country kids did. I suppose, by modern standards, we were underprivileged because we had no organized program, but we had the whole world to ourselves. We had the woods to play in and the rivers and the lakes to swim in. We skated in the winter and played baseball in the summer. We made our own recreation, and I think that's really good. We never thought of ourselves as underprivileged.

It would have taken all the kids in the three neighboring villages —and a lot of equipment—to have a football team. But baseball was easy. You could go out in the cow pasture, after the hay was cut, and take four or five bricks for bases and take a slab of stone for home plate, measure it out, and you had a ball field. If you had nine men on a side, swell. If you had only seven, that was all right, too. You just moved them around.

We made our own baseballs, and the guy who had the best baseball was captain of the team—until that baseball was lost. If you had a bat you made the team. Everybody used the same bat. We had gloves that were interchangeable. Someone else used my glove when my side was at bat. Baseball was standard in rural communities in those days. It was a rural game.

My mother was a very saintly person. My father was stern but very generous and honest. He was a reader, and so was I, though we didn't do much reading together because he was always busy. My parents were always working. When you work a farm, you start at dawn and don't quit until sunset. It was a general farm—corn, wheat, and potatoes, and hay and alfalfa. We were 136 miles from Chicago, and in those days that was a long trip. Lord, when you went that far you packed a trunk. None of that running back and forth.

The people who were my greatest heroes were the big fellows who played on the men's baseball team. They stood for something in the community. My first major league hero was a fellow named Big

Bert Inks, who pitched for about five or six different teams from 1890 to 1900. He was the first major leaguer I ever had an opportunity to look at, to shake hands with, and he came from our community. Lord, he was more important to me than John McGraw or Connie Mack or Christy Mathewson, or any of the great performers of that day. I used to send him passes to the ball games when I was president of the National League.

Good Lord, I didn't want to become commissioner. When my name was being bandied about as the next commissioner, I didn't want it. Happy Chandler was out and the job was open, but I wasn't interested. I saw my old friend, Frankie Graham—we had been baseball writers together, had even roomed together one year when we were both with the Giants—and I got him into a corner and said, "Do me a favor, will you?"

He said, "Sure."

I told him I wanted to say in his column that I wasn't a candidate, that I was happy in the National League.

Well, he wrote that. But the old sonofagun. He wound it up with one line across the bottom: "I told Ford Frick I would write this story. I've written it. But my candidate for commissioner is Ford Frick."

Any man who is doing something he likes to do in a profession he respects and enjoys can be happy. Writing was a wonderful job and I enjoyed it. I had contacts and a breadth of acquaintances that you probably couldn't get in any other profession. Then, I was very happy as league president, because I still had a lot of close personal contact with the ball players, the people I had known. The greatest change happened when I entered the commissioner's office because then you're through with your close contacts. You are sitting up there in a position where you can't afford, and they don't want, the personal contact. You miss a lot of the fun.

The thing I'm proudest of in baseball is the Hall of Fame in Cooperstown. That's my baby. I started it. This was about in 1936 when I was still president of the National League and Judge Landis was the commissioner. There's a big portrait of me up there, that the league had printed, a picture of me which I don't like. It says I was the father of the whole thing.

Judge Landis never liked the idea, never warmed up to it, probably because he didn't think of it first. Maybe I shouldn't say that because I loved the judge. He was a great guy but a stubborn sonofagun.

Once the Hall of Fame was established each of the two major leagues would set aside five thousand dollars, a subsidy to help run the place. The owners would get together at the annual joint meeting, and every year I'd make the motion to renew our pledge for the five thousand dollars. And every time it came up the judge would say, "What is this God damned Hall of Fame business?"

Finally, I got mad and said, "Now, listen, Judge, you've been asking that for the last four, five years, and I've always answered. If you don't know by now, to hell with it!"

The judge was a funny fellow. Oh, he was an ornery sonofabitch. But he was an honest old guy and he was good for baseball. The public had great confidence in him.

He was one of the most profane men I ever heard in my life. His profanity was on the sublime. I can't remember all the terms. Once he was talking about his golf game—he wasn't too good a golfer—and somebody asked how he had done. He said, "I bitched my drive, boogered my mashie, I fucked up my approach shot." I don't remember the whole sequence. But he just kept using words, every one of them worse that the one before.

I had always been an American history buff, colonial history particularly. The judge knew that. I was in Chicago, at his office, in September of '36—the year Landon was the Republican presidential candidate. We transacted our baseball business in a few minutes, and then he started talking and asking questions. He always called me "Mr. Fo'd. Mr. F'od."

He said, "Mr. Fo'd, who's the lousiest President the United States ever had?"

"Oh, Judge," I said, "a lot of people. Lots of difference of opinion. Harding was no bargain. And Andrew Johnson."

"Andrew Johnson, hell!" he roared. "The lousiest President the United States ever had was Calvin Coolidge. Did you ever hear the man talk? Ever read anything he wrote? 'Course, he was the lousiest President we ever had. And now they're calling this man Landon 'The Kansas Coolidge.' You know what I think of Landon? I think he's a beer-bellied, pinch-pennied Presbyterian sonofabitch."

And he was pointing that finger at me all the time, thumping his finger into my chest.

"But I'm going to vote for him, anyway, 'cause he's the kind of man this country needs."

When the judge went into law the world lost a great Shakespearean actor. Oh, he was a dramatic cuss. Everything he did was dramatic. He had a flair. That old hat he wore. That funny cane he carried. He used 'em as props. I don't think he needed a cane. And he certainly could afford to buy a new hat.

The judge, being a lawyer, knew that certain things we were doing in baseball were pretty doubtful, legally. He was always worried about the reserve clause and all that antitrust stuff. But you could get away with a lot of things in those days that today you'd get called on.

Some lawyer once told me, several of them did, actually, that the judge had more cases reversed by the Supreme Court than any federal judge in the country. That $29 million he fined Standard Oil— that was the case that made him famous—well, that $29 million finally got down to $3 million, and I don't think it was ever paid. But I'm not putting any of that stuff in my book, because that had nothing to do with baseball. That was before he became the commissioner.

The judge never did warm up to the Hall of Fame idea and I never tried to probe him. He did go up there in '39, made a beautiful dedication speech. But he never went back.

I've heard people say the Hall of Fame is a publicity man's dream. Maybe it is. But I think of it as more than that, something more substantial. I like to think of it as tying together yesterday and today. It keeps the continuity and it gives the oldsters a chance to discuss and relive their times. You can compare the moderns with the ancients. I always believed history is important, that we should mark what has gone before.

One of the greatest things is the Hall of Fame dinner, when all these old guys come back. Every player in the Hall of Fame is invited back to Cooperstown every year, all expenses paid. They participate in the ceremonies and welcome the new players being inducted. Between twenty and twenty-five Hall of Famers come back every year. They get there about two days early and they sit, late at night, drinking beer on that big porch at the Otsega Hotel and swapping lies and reliving the old days.

Waite Hoyt. Charlie Gehringer. Bill Terry. Zack Wheat. Eddie Roush. Red Ruffing, and many others. Cy Young came back year after year until he was unable. Ed Walsh never missed. Even Ty Cobb. He softened in his later years. He was always there. I suppose you can say that in the beginning the Hall of Fame was a vision— and it came to pass.

It will always be a happy time for the people who are there, and as people pass on someone takes their place. Other fellows come along. I thought when Cy Young was gone, and Connie Mack, that that would change the atmosphere. But it didn't. Ed Walsh died. Eddie Collins died, and the Babe died, and Alexander died. It didn't change. Last year it was George Weiss and Heinie Manush. This year three of them won't be there—Zack Wheat, George Sisler, and Frankie Frisch. Two or three die every year. But everybody talks about these guys as if they were still alive. They're just not there, that's all.

The whole thing started with the discovery of the so-called Doubleday Baseball. That was the excuse. This old ball was found on the Graves farm, around Cooperstown, in an old trunk. Abner Graves supposedly had played baseball with General Abner Doubleday. Stephen Clark, a resident of Cooperstown, heard about the ball and bought it for five dollars. Mr. Clark is a historian, a philanthropist, very museum-minded. He is a collector of early Americana. He had a baseball collection of his own, old paintings and prints. He took this Doubleday Ball—it's all falling apart—had it mounted and put on display with his other stuff in the Otsega Historical Society. And he assigned a member of his staff, Alexander Cleland, to look around and find other authentic baseball relics.

Mr. Cleland then came down to New York, to the National League office, to see me. I had known him from several years before. I'd been up to Cooperstown when I was a sportswriter. I had done a few stories. And he said the people in Cooperstown wanted to have some sort of baseball celebration. They wanted to get some publicity and get the newspapermen up there. He suggested we pick an all-star team and play a game up there—sort of a one-day holiday.

I said, "Hell, why do that? If you're going to do that, why not start a baseball museum—a Hall of Fame, and have something that will last?"

That's the way the Hall of Fame started. Mr. Clark was the financial angel. He was a businessman, in Singer sewing machines. That's where the family got their fortune.

I called a meeting with the wire service writers. I can tell you who was there—Davis Walsh of the International News Service, Alan Gould of the Associated Press, and Henry Farrell of the United Press. They picked it up and said they would recommend it to the Baseball Writers Association. It was Alan Gould who said that seventy-five percent of the votes be required for induction. That rule still stands today. Five players made it in the first election—the Babe, Honus Wagner, Cobb, Mathewson, and Walter Johnson.

It's a funny thing about us writers. We build everybody up but we forget ourselves—our own kind, our comrades who through the years made America a great sports nation. One of the reasons I wanted a library at Cooperstown was to take care of all the records, and to gather some of the written material of the past. Now someone who wants to do research, whether for a magazine or a documented book, can go to Cooperstown and find all the material.

And we have one corner in the museum dedicated to the baseball writers. Lord, that's the way it should be. The names of all the presidents of the Baseball Writers are listed. We have some old typewriters and a big, broken-down camera, and Graham McNamee's mircrophone, the one he used. And across the way we have a room dedicated to cartoonists, with original cartoons by Tad, Bob Edgren, and Davenport, and all those fellows who started the cartooning business. Willard Mullin gave us his drawing board. We've got that up there. At first, a writer, before he was elected to the Hall of Fame, had to be dead. But this year, for the first time, two writers will be inducted who are alive—Dan Daniel and Fred Lieb. That's the way it should be. After all, it's nice to smell the roses.

Many people think I started as a sportswriter. But that isn't true. I was a schoolteacher. Taught school for two years in Colorado Springs. I guess you can say I took Horace Greeley's advice. I went west, after I got out of college. I taught English in high school, and at Colorado College—what they called business English, commercial English.

The money was pretty skimpy. I was married and had a child, so I found I had to do something else, and the natural thing was to start work on a newspaper. I started my serious newspaper career out there, on the *Gazette* in Colorado Springs. It was later combined with the morning paper and became the *Gazette-Telegraph.*

I did everything on the paper. Good Lord, I wrote editorials at space rates. That's where you made your money. I probably wrote the longest editorials in the world. I did police, some sports, hotel interviews—everything. Colorado Springs was a great resort city. First time I met Al Smith was in a hotel out there. Al Jolson, too, and Ethel Barrymore and Madame Schumann-Heink. She was a diva, one of the big opera stars of the day.

Some printer out there knew Arthur Brisbane, the big editor of the New York *American,* and he clipped a lot of the stuff I had written and sent it on to him, in New York. And Brisbane sent for me. This was in late 1921, after I'd been in Colorado Springs for about five years. Once I came to New York I was definitely a sportswriter.

I went to work for the *American*—the Hearst morning paper— and when Brisbane took over the *Journal* he took me with him.

I'll never forget the day I moved from the *American* to the *Journal.* I was covering the Giants. The game was rained out and I was in the office writing a rainy day story, and the office boy came in and said, "Mr. Brisbane wants to see you."

I went to Mr. Brisbane's office, and he told me he had taken over the *Journal* and was switching me over. He already had an assignment for me, to go down to Atlantic City and cover the Firpo camp. I started to walk away and he said, "Where are you going?"

"I'm going back to the *American* to finish my story."

And he said, "To hell with the *American.* You're working on the *Journal.*"

I never did go back. As far as I'm concerned that rainy day story, on the Giants, is still in the typewriter.

New York was full of newspapers then. Good Lord, the Giants always had fifteen writers traveling with them. The day I went to work on the *American*, I reported to Mr. Brisbane, chatted with him for a few minutes, and signed a contract. Mr. Brisbane then introduced me to Bill Farnsworth because I was going to work under Bill. He was the sports editor.

And because I came from Colorado, Bill thought it would be a good idea to have Damon Runyon take me around. Damon was a Colorado boy. This was in the winter, and in those days there were only about three sports that you could count on to be the basis of your sports page—boxing, horse racing, and baseball. Football was becoming strong as a collegiate game, but it was pretty much sectional. There were three baseball stories in the paper every day, one on the Giants, one on the Yankees, one on the Dodgers. This was a major part of the sports section—all winter long. There was no radio or television in those days.

It was routine for the whole staff of writers, always a coterie of guys, to go to the Yankee office and to the Giant office. You'd punch the bag with Miller Huggins, or with Ed Barrow, or McGraw, or Eddie Brannick, or somebody. This was every day. That's the way you got your ideas for stories.

There used to be a little kosher delicatessen on Forty-second Street, next to the Yankee office, where we stopped for coffee. The first time I was there, a wide-eyed kid from Colorado, Ring Lardner, came in. Granny Rice was there. Heywood Broun and John Kieran. Bugs Baer. Sid Mercer. Frankie Graham. And of course, Damon Runyon. Damn, you could go on and on. Just topflight guys. Good Lord, I was goggle-eyed, scared to death, but it was a great experience.

Well, everybody talks about that particular period—the Golden Age of Sports—but maybe it was and maybe it was not, but it was certainly an exciting period. It was right after the war and we had a lot of stars in the sports world. Jack Dempsey was just coming along and he had color. Walter Hagen was breaking into golf, and Hagen was one of the most colorful guys you'll ever know. Ruth was starting his baseball career. And Cobb and Speaker and Pete Alexander —all those people were around. It was a great era.

Brisbane was a rough, tough guy, a smart guy. He was very opinionated, very cold. He wasn't the kind of guy you'd have any feeling of warmth about. He was about medium height, stocky, had a big head and a protruding brow. Brisbane was the biggest name in New York in those days, both as a writer and editor. He wrote a column called "Today," comments on the day's news. That's when he pulled the famous line that he kept repeating, that one gorilla could lick twelve Dempseys. He had been a sportswriter. He covered the John L. Sullivan–Jake Kilrain fight, the one that went seventy-five rounds.

I wasn't his protégé. I never saw him outside the office. He was a cold guy, unsympathetic. He was selfish and he loved the dollar. He accumulated a fortune. He got a big salary, thousands of dollars a year, and then Hearst took him in on projects. One of the projects was the Ritz Towers in New York, when that was built. Brisbane was a great friend of Joseph P. Day, a big real estate man in New York in the twenties. He was in on a lot of Day's real estate deals.

His family background was good. I don't think he was in the Four Hundred socially but he was well educated. He wasn't a social or society person. He was a businessman—a businessman-writer, a rare combination. He was very interested in circulation, and he concentrated completely on the job he was doing. I don't think he had any recreations. He didn't play golf. He didn't go fishing. He didn't do any of those things. He read a great deal. His avocation and vocation were wrapped up in editing the newspaper. He was a brilliant man, quite a brilliant mind.

You saw him only when he wanted to see you. He sent for you, and he was always a thought ahead of you. You never had the slightest idea why he was calling you in. It'd be bang! bang! bang!

He called me "young man." He never called me anything but "young man." One day I answered his summons, and he said, "Young man, how fast can an elephant run?"

I didn't have the slightest idea.

"How far do you mean? Do you want the speed on him for a mile? For a hundred yards?"

I called the circus. The headquarters were up in Connecticut in those days. I got hold of an animal trainer, various people, finally got someone to guess an elephant could run a mile at such and such speed. Put yourself in my place. You're finding out how fast an elephant can run, and you're going to tell Mr. Brisbane and you haven't the slightest idea why he wants to know.

The Sunday paper came out with an editorial clear across the top with a Hal Coffman cartoon, with a guy in an automobile, a guy on horseback, a man running, a man on a bicycle, all these things, and the story featured an elephant. Brisbane was one of those guys who always contended that nature endowed men with two legs and a brain but shortchanged him on a hell of a lot of things. That's why he used the line about one gorilla licking twelve Dempseys. The automobile, of course, was first; that was part of the editorial, that man was puny and so he invented things. I think the horse was second and the elephant was third. The guy running was way behind. I clipped that out, saved it for years.

Oh, he'd give me the damnedest assignments. We had a circulation manager named Joe Bannon. He was very close to Brisbane. They'd go out together. I think they gypped each other on their deals, took advantage of each other. Joe liked to put one over on Brisbane and vice versa.

Anyhow, Brisbane called me in—this was after the first Dempsey-Tunney fight. He said, "I just had lunch with Joe Bannon. He was explaining to me how Dempsey was going to take Tunney the next time they fought, and I want you to go in and talk to him—and write it just as he tells it to you."

Bannon was a dese, dose and dem guy. I talked to Joe and wrote the story, wrote it dese, dose, and dems, as Brisbane told me. I took it back to Mr. Brisbane and he said, "That's swell. Now show it to Bannon."

I knew I was in trouble. Bannon said, "I don't talk that way."

So I'm in the middle. I rewrote that story three or four times and finally sent it to the composing room—the hell with it! I never did know what Brisbane was trying to prove. Listen, he never explained anything to me.

Brisbane went to sports events, occasionally. When Red Grange turned pro he was at the Polo Grounds and saw that huge crowd on Sunday. Monday morning, first thing, he sent for me and he said, "I want you to follow this guy Grange around the country." Grange was barnstorming, playing three, four times a week. He said, "I want you on their train, and stay with them until I call you back."

"Jesus, Mr. Brisbane, I haven't any clothes, haven't any bag."

And he said, "To hell with it. Get whatever you need."

I had to call my wife and say I wouldn't be home for dinner. I was gone for three weeks. It was a good circulation builder and a good sports story because the Grange thing got a hell of a play.

Everybody was afraid of Brisbane except Tad, the cartoonist—

Theodore Aloysius Dorgan. Tad was a genius. Tad called him George. I never did know why. In the old days the *Journal* and the *American* were published at 230 Williams Street, in an old loft building. The editorial rooms were on the seventh floor. It was kind of a V-shaped building, and Brisbane's office was at the head of the V; on one side was the *Journal* and the other side the *American.*

Down at one end was what we called the Chamber of Horrors—where the cartoonists hung out. George McManus—he started Jiggs and Maggie—and Tad and Coffman and Joe McGurk. Brisbane was tough on gambling of any sort. Staff gambling, too. And they had a crap game going down there one day, and Tad is down on the floor with the dice in his hands. Brisbane comes in the door. Everybody's frightened. Tad looks up and says, "Hey, George, couple dollars open. Do you want to cover it?" And Brisbane turned around and walked out.

All this time I was writing baseball. I wrote baseball from 1922 to 1931 or '32. Sure, my favorite player has got to be the Babe. There's no question. He was the greatest, with all due respect to those who went before and to those who have come along since. The Babe had everything it takes, including a lovable personality. Hell, he was the best left-handed pitcher in baseball, when he was pitching—and he was the best hitter.

He told me himself, and I believed him, that he wasn't paid to go up and hit singles or doubles. He could have hit .400 every year. I saw him when they pulled that Williams shift on him. I think it was Bucky Harris who did it. And Babe got up there—he was pretty fat then, wasn't the trim athlete he had been earlier—and he looked around and hit it out past third base. And he walked to first base. They pulled it on him twice. Second time he got a two-base hit. I can still see him dusting himself off at second base, that old belly just bouncing up and down. They never tried it on him again.

I was Babe's ghost-writer from 1924 until I stopped working. I think we wrote a schedule of three stories a week. I know we did more than one. Lots of times I would talk to him, but there were times when I'd pick up a story and didn't talk to him. But I lived with the old guy, really. Babe was always around and I was traveling with the ball club, and so there was no excuse not to contact him. I always believed he felt that these stories were important. But he never showed much.

I didn't use the word "asterisk"—when Babe's record was being threatened. I think it was Dick Young who first used it. There was this press conference and I was asked what I was going to do if Roger Maris broke Babe's home run record—his record of sixty in one season. Babe did it in a 154-game schedule. Then we had expansion and the schedule was lengthened to 162 games.

I said if Maris does it in 154 games, then he will have broken the record. But if he does it in 162 games, there will be two records —the Babe's in x number of games, and the other. What the dickens, I tried to protect the Babe because his record should stand until it's honestly beaten. Anyway, the word "asterisk" has stuck all these years. I'm even going to use it in the title of my book—it's going to be called *Games, Asterisks and People*.

Now Hank Aaron's going for Babe's lifetime record of 714 home runs. Well, if he breaks it, he breaks it. But I'll never change my mind about Babe Ruth. Hell, Hank Aaron's already had two thousand more times at bat than Ruth had in his whole career. And the seasons are longer, you know, more games. He gets more opportunities. But if Aaron breaks it, it's a hell of an accomplishment and certainly it's a lifetime record. No question about it. It'll go into the books as a lifetime record.

I stopped writing, professionally, in '34 when I went with the National League. I had started on radio a few years before. I did a twelve o'clock news broadcast. Then I wrote a six o'clock sports broadcast and had my own sports show at seven o'clock. This was while I was working at the paper. I was writing a column called "Ford Frick's Comments," but it was a lousy column because I didn't get around too much. It was a very demanding schedule. I saw very little of my family. The last year I was on radio I never had a single dinner at home except on Sunday night.

And I was always picking up a few M.C. jobs on the side. Money-wise, I wasn't an Ed Sullivan, but hour-wise I was. I was the M.C. for the Chesterfield Show and the funny part was that I know nothing about music. I can't even keep time. It was a high-class musical show. Everyone was in dinner clothes and Andre Kostelanetz and I wore white tie and tails. It was three times a week for thirty minutes. I was the M.C. for about a year. I broke my contract when I became president of the National League.

When I went with the league I succeeded Cullen Cain. He was the league's first service bureau man, what you'd call publicity man today. I've always thought John McGraw was responsible. I never asked him, but that's the only way I could figure—that he suggested me for the job. I had gotten along with him all right, when I covered the Giants. But when Mac was drinking he was a bad guy. But what the hell. I'd stay away from him.

The Giants had been antibroadcasting in New York. The Yankees, the Dodgers, and Giants got together and decided radio was bad—that you shouldn't give away what you were trying to sell, the old theory. In '33 the Giants and Dodgers were in a pennant fight, so I recreated, by Western Union, the games on the radio. I took it off the ticker, pitch by pitch. This was the first recreation of games in New York though it had been done elsewhere.

And when I was on the air I told the people listening to write and send postcards to the Giants to show their appreciation. The Giants must have received thousands of letters and postcards. This impressed McGraw. So he invited me to be his guest at the World Series. I was going as a writer anyway. I was still covering. But he extended the invitation, and when the Giants won the Series, against Washington, he invited me to be his guest at the victory dinner.

In February I got a call from Mr. McGraw—the National League was meeting at the Waldorf—and he asked me if I would come up there. They offered me the job in the service bureau. The salary was about ten thousand dollars. They said I could keep my radio connections, which I did, and then in November of that year John Heydler retired. He had been the league president. I have a hunch that this was all part of a plan. But I had no idea it was going to happen that soon.

I was the National League president for seventeen years, the longest anybody held the office, and then I was commissioner for fourteen years—two seven-year terms. I always felt, in handling both offices, that you were doing a pretty good job if you kept out of the headlines, like an umpire.

Every now and then people recall unpleasant incidents that happened in baseball and they say, "Oh, you must hate so-and-so."

My answer always has been "I don't hate anybody. I don't have time to hate anybody."

It takes time to learn to hate. You've got to work at it. I've always had too many other things to do.

There are people who I like better than others, people I would rather associate with, spend idle time with, than others. There are many people I disagree with, but I honestly believe that I have never hated anybody in my life. You get the reputation, publicly, of being soft, of being a compromiser, and all that sort of thing. Those criticisms are untrue and unfair. I've always believed that a soft word, listening to the other guy and laying it on the table, factually, and without vehemence and without prejudice, you solve many problems.

I got panned frequently. Oh, I don't think I was criticized anymore than anybody else. The writers, many of them, always were insisting I didn't make enough decisions, enough rulings. They would get on me, insisting I was always saying this or that dispute "is a league matter." I was panned a lot for that. But I followed pretty good precedent. Judge Landis would never step into a league controversy—unless it had to do with the honesty and integrity of baseball. Then he'd step in. He had authority to do that.

I think the commissioner today is the victim of the changes that have come in baseball. The sole purpose of the commissioner's office is to maintain the integrity of the game. Nowadays these guys, the owners, are throwing a lot of things in the commissioner's lap that were never meant for the commissioner to decide. You can't remain at a judicial level, protecting and guarding honesty and integrity and holding the confidence of the fans, if you're going to be required to roll in the dirt down at a lower level.

I didn't resent the criticism. I used to resent, very much, the guys who would write a story without checking. As long as the people who were writing the story would call me on the telephone, or come by the office to find out my side of the story, I had no complaint.

But I did resent the guys who never checked. The years I was commissioner there were three or four writers, some of them old friends, who were never in my office and never called me up. It seemed that they did go out of their way to be critical. I don't know. Maybe it was their style of writing. Commissioner Chandler was heavily criticized, too. So was Mr. Eckert. That's part of the job. But any man who says he doesn't pay attention to criticism is crazy. In your heart there is a scar.

oooo
oooo
oooo

John Drebinger

Of all these sportswriters, John Drebinger, a gentleman of the New
York Times, *may have come closest to fitting the traditional image of
the ideal baseball Boswell—a kindly and benevolent veteran with an
endless fund of tales to fascinate the younger players, yet a man who
often offered significant counsel to veteran players and their coaches
and managers. He retired from the* Times *in 1964. Ten years later,
when I was interviewing him, he spoke with a wonderful spirit and
good fellowship. Typically, in recalling his career, he several times
said, "My God, look at all the fun I had."*

*Mr. Drebinger was born on March 23, 1891, in New York City.
He was an only child, the son of a violinist with the New York
Metropolitan Opera Company, and was an accomplished pianist at
the age of eighteen, when he suffered a severe thumb injury. He*

turned to newspaper work, joined the staff of the then weekly Staten Island Advance *and, in a memorable promotion stunt that sent circulation booming, led a heroic attempt to cross the country from New York to San Francisco in a covered wagon. He joined the* Times *in 1923, wrote baseball for thirty-seven years and did the lead story for the* Times *on 203 consecutive World Series games. A connoisseur of drink and song, Mr. Drebinger was inducted into the Baseball Hall of Fame in 1974. He died in 1979 at the age of eighty-eight in a nursing home in Greensboro, North Carolina.*

I set an Iron Man record at *The New York Times*. They called it the Lou Gehrig record and I don't think anybody's going to bust it, not for a long time. Starting with 1929 and running through 1963, I wrote the page-one lead story of every World Series game. I think it was about three hundred. The *Times* could tell you how many it was. Then, in 1964, I reached seventy-three. That's when I had to go. I'd been there forty-one years.

At the finish, Mr. Clifton Daniel, the managing editor, was one of my best friends. This was in my final years there. He came to me with some nice condolences when I was leaving. I told him, "Hell, you've got to remember, this wasn't just a job. This has been my life. There was no other job on the paper I would have taken."

He said, "No other job?"

"Hell no! And I sure wouldn't have taken yours."

That floored him. "Do you mean that?" he asked.

I said, "Absolutely."

I couldn't have worked indoors. Look at the fun I had, meeting all those people. Carl Hubbell. Mel Ott. McGraw. Ruth. Gehrig. The Waner brothers, all the way back to Christy Mathewson. By God, it was a tremendous thing to have known all those players. I knew everybody in the Hall of Fame—except Cap Anson. Only Dan Daniel met Cap Anson.

I started with the *Times* in 1923, a few weeks after the opening of Yankee Stadium. I didn't start as a baseball writer. They had a system then that called for you to work on the desk for your first two years. Jim Harrison was the number-one baseball writer. He covered all the home games of the Giants and the Yankees. Dick Vidmer was there, too, and Harry Cross and Bill Corum. By 1927 Cross had quit and Corum had gone to the *Journal*. So I became the number-three baseball writer—after Harrison and Vidmer. I covered the Dodgers.

Then I got my big break. Toward the end of the '28 season, Gene Fowler got involved in the purchase of the *Morning Telegraph* and became their top editor. He was going to develop and promote "the greatest sports page in all history." That's the way they billed it. He was offering fabulous sums—to Harrison and Vidmer and Dawson, to writers from all the papers. I was getting $150 from the *Times*, and Fowler offered me $300.

That was one time Jim Dawson did me a favor. I told him about the offer and he said, "Don't be a damn fool. How long do you think it's going to last? You stick with the *Times*. They'll take care of you the rest of your life."

Prophetic, wasn't it? Harrison and Vidmer jumped and went with Fowler. I stayed with the *Times* and became their number-one baseball man. And as Jim Dawson predicted, the *Telegraph* folded in about a year. Vidmer bounced around, went to the *Tribune* for a while, and became a column writer. He was quite a capable guy. Harrison was a brilliant writer. But he got sick shortly after going over to the *Telegraph* and died.

The sports editor of the *Times* was Colonel Bernard Thomson. He made you feel that being on the *Times* was something. He was extremely fussy, a sort of dedicated bloke on the traditions of the paper. He was very English and spoke with an accent. I believe his father was a great lexicographer in Canada.

The basic thing he used to bang into our heads was, never show any prejudice or bias. Do your utmost! Always report objectively! Report it as it happens! If it's funny and has a humorous twist, by all means let's have it. But don't strain to be funny! And above all, don't slant your stuff!

There was this time when Harrison covered a Harvard-Yale football game. His story of the game belittled the kind of football that Harvard and Yale were putting on, implying that it wasn't up to the standards you might expect when Michigan played Chicago, or teams like that.

Early the next week I came bumping into the office and Thomson called me over. He said, "Hrrruummmph! Did you read Harrison's story?"

I said, "Yes, sir! I thought it was very good."

That put my foot in it. Colonel Thomson proceeded to give a little lecture: "We must assume, whatever we believe privately, that the colleges are putting on the best they have, the best they are able to recruit from their classrooms. Now whatever you may think these other colleges do, if it were known for a fact that professional players were on these clubs, that would be a separate story. You write that if you got it.

"Now when you are covering a game don't take the attitude of criticizing the teams because they haven't got better players. They are recruiting amateurs. Your field is baseball, professional baseball. You are at liberty to criticize the players. Go right ahead. But you should never belittle an amateur."

Even covering professional baseball, I gave the teams the benefit of the doubt. Sure, if a guy played lousy, I wrote it that way. But if a manager's strategic moves weren't as sound as they might have been, I wouldn't try to make myself the expert. I would just write that others had a different opinion. Anyway, there's no end to what you could argue about. Rogers Hornsby once said there wasn't a game played that you couldn't second-guess, unless it was a no-hitter.

I was once put into a very crummy position on knocking a ball player. Jimmy Jemail called me on the long distance phone in spring training one year. He used to be the inquiring photographer for the *Daily News* and wanted me to come in with him and about seven or eight other guys around the country for a story in *Sports Illustrated*. We were to write on the topic: "If you were a manager, who would you rather have on your team, Stan Musial or Ted Williams?"

I wrote this stupid thing. I gave my honest opinion, that I would take Musial because he was far more of a team player. I told how one day at Fenway Park, in Boston, Williams hit a smash off the screen. The ball bounced back onto the field and Joe DiMaggio booted it. And here is Mr. Ted trotting into second base. Hell, he should have had an easy triple. He was the tying run, with no outs, and the next two men went out on long fly balls. If Ted had been on third he could have tagged up and scored. So that's what I wrote.

The next time the Red Sox came into Yankee Stadium this Boston writer comes up to me and says, "Hey, Ted was reading this thing in the magazine and he asked me, 'Did Dreb really write that?' "

I said, "Tell Ted I can't afford a ghost-writer. I had to write it myself."

The next day, before the game, I went down on the field. I went right up to Ted as he was taking batting practice, and I put my face up to him and I said, "Well, how about it, Ted? Do you want to knock these teeth out?"

He said, "Hell no, that was thoroughly all right. I can understand how you feel about some of the things I do. I feel sorry myself when I do them."

I was John McGraw's ghost-writer for a while. I didn't like being a ghost, but I did it once or twice for him because he was such a fascinating buzzard. God, he was an amazing man. He did everything. Signed the players. Fired them. Paid them. Ran the show. He lasted thirty years, won ten pennants, and finished second eleven times. Imagine that: twenty-one years no worse than second. And he had the most amazing memory.

When we were on the road, usually once or twice during a trip, Eddie Brannick, the traveling secretary, would get us together and say, "The old man wants to take you out to dinner tonight."

McGraw's pet act at these dinners, before he drank one or two too many, was having us ask him questions. When did so-and-so happen? When was this? Who won the Brooklyn Handicap in 1905? All kinds of sports questions, like the $64,000 Question.

Tom Meany was with us, and at that particular time he was doing "Twenty-Five Years Ago" for the *Telegram,* so he'd have all the questions scribbled down. We'd fire them at McGraw, and my God, he knew all the answers. He not only knew who won the Brooklyn Handicap every year, but he'd tell you who placed and showed, the odds, the jockeys, everything.

Once he asked me what was the first ball game I saw as a kid, the first game I could remember. I told him, "It was the Giants against the Pittsburgh Pirates at the Polo Grounds. Sandow Mertes cleared the bases with a triple."

McGraw nodded. He said, "Yes, I remember that, and three days later George Van Haltren broke his leg. Now, when you get back to New York look it up in the files."

For the hell of it I looked it up. It wasn't three days later. It was four days later. The reason McGraw was confused was because there was an open date in between. Jesus, what a mind he had.

Babe Ruth's memory was a funny thing. He had an awful tough time with names. One night we were in a speakeasy in St. Louis, sitting on a couch, quietly by ourselves, and all of a sudden he said, "You know, it's damn embarrassing. I can't remember names. I can remember every ball pitched to me, what I hit, and what I didn't hit. But names go like that. Like the other day this guy comes in to pitch against us. I've known him for ten years but I couldn't remember his name. So I called over to whatchamacallit in centerfield."

Of course that was Earle Combs. Babe couldn't remember Combs's name, either.

The Babe goes on. "But the wife is on top of me about this. She's raising hell." The Babe orders another drink and then he says, "But I think I'm getting better, Joe."

I almost slid off the couch. To his dying day, he never called me anything but Joe. And now—the damnedest thing—I'm having the same blasted trouble with names myself.

You've heard that the Babe and Lou Gehrig didn't hit it off. You've seen that written. Well, that's baloney. Gehrig idolized the Babe, and the Babe was very fond of Lou. But Gehrig never could forget he had been a poor boy. He was always worried he was going to lose his money.

Gehrig envied the careless way the Babe tossed his money around. We used to play poker on the trains with the Babe. Five-card stud. The Babe would bet like the devil, just taking wild gambles. He wouldn't drive you out, but he never folded. Always played down to the last card. Most of the time we'd clean up on him. Gehrig would be sitting across the aisle, watching the game. The Babe would be throwing his dough around in this fine style, and Lou would look at him and say, "My God, isn't that wonderful."

Gehrig was a very straightforward, honest guy. Once he did an advertising spiel for Corn Flakes, and at the end of this spiel they asked him, "And, Lou, what is your favorite breakfast food?"

He answers, "Wheaties!"

Of course that blew it. This was a live commercial, in the studio. But they still wanted to pay him. But to show you the kind of guy Gehrig was, he wouldn't take the money. But they kept insisting. So he just turned it over to some charity. He wouldn't touch the dough.

Another guy I just loved back then was Rogers Hornsby. I always felt sorry about his reputation. But in my book he was a tremendous guy. He was blunt and outspoken and as honest as the day is long. If he thought a certain player was a punk, he told you so. He told you his opinion on everything. And of course, that got him into trouble.

Once when he was with the Giants, McGraw was sick and Hornsby was managing the club and the writers got on him for not playing this one guy, a catcher. Hornsby never read the papers. He was always worried about his eyesight. And so he got me in the lobby and he said, "Have the writers been knocking me?"

I said, "Hell no, everybody's in your corner. You ought to know that."

And he said, "Anytime you fellows want to know anything, I'll tell you. Like I'll tell you why I didn't put him in yesterday. It's because he's a big, fat lardass and I was afraid of the double play. I had to get the runner down to second base, or at least give up no more than one out."

I felt sorry in the later years when the younger writers got Hornsby wrong. One or two times I straightened them out. Once up in Boston, after he had supplanted Jack Slattery as manager. Of course Jack was Irish, and the Catholics were very strong in Boston. And when Hornsby replaced him the Boston writers were saying he had railroaded Slattery. They even hinted Hornsby was a Ku Kluxer.

So one day I said, "Hey, Rog, I'd like to pop off on this."

He said, "What do you mean, pop off?"

I knew Hornsby's wife was a Roman Catholic and I said, "Let me give it to these Boston guys. I'll let them know you're about as much of a Ku Kluxer as I am."

But Hornsby was tough. He said, "Let the bastards find out for themselves. And if you tell them, I'll never talk to you again." That was Hornsby. He never soft-soaped anybody in his whole life.

I knew him to the very end, and it was a peculiar thing because after we'd known each other all these years we found out we had the same philosophy about life. He was working for the Mets then—George Weiss had given him a job as a scout. We were on a flight to Houston, and all of a sudden it got very stormy and rocky. We were really getting bounced around and I said, "Jesus, Rog, this bothering you?" I was thinking maybe he had an upset stomach, something like that.

And he said, "We shouldn't be worried. What better way is there to end our lives than right here? This has been our racket. This has been our business. It'd be a hell of a lot better than dragging out your life for three or four years in a wheelchair."

But the poor guy. He wasn't that lucky. He had cancer. He wouldn't let anybody see him in the last few months. And you know, it was an ironic thing. He had always had that fear about his eyes. He had marvelous eyesight. But he was going blind when he died. He had glaucoma and it affected both his eyes.

It's a terrible thing when you think about these guys who were such physical marvels and had to wind up like that. There was Gehrig, the Iron Man, and Jesus, he couldn't lift a piece of paper his last years. Babe Ruth collapsed completely. Gil Hodges. Another strong man, and he dropped dead before his time. And then, of course, there was Jackie Robinson. It's about as brutal as anything that can happen to a guy.

The guys back in the old days used to drink a lot more than they do now, but they seemed better able to handle it. I saw Babe Ruth take down a Coca-Cola bottle full of whiskey one time. Gurgled it right down. Drinking didn't in any way handicap him. In fact, I think it helped him relax. I still contend that Mickey Mantle, if he had been able to drink the way the Babe could, he would have smashed all the home run records. When you get up to fifty home runs there's a lot of pressure. Drinking would help anybody relax. But Mantle couldn't drink. He'd take a few and he'd get silly.

I'll tell you who could relax on the stuff. Paul Waner. He was really something. One time he tied the lifetime record of that period for hitting doubles and didn't know what the hell he was doing. It was a hot day and he'd been drinking beer all through the game. He had this fellow who brought him another cold bottle every time he'd give him the signal. And Paul won the ball game with a double that drove in the winning run. He didn't know it was a double. He told me later, "Dreb, all I remember was that I hit the ball into left center and that I hit it good. I rounded first base, just kept going, and slid into second, and that's how I tied the record."

Another guy who drank heavily and could handle it was Pete Alexander. There was the time he struck out Lazzeri. It was in the 1926 World Series, against the Yankees. Alexander had pitched and won the day before and thought that was his last appearance. So he had been out drinking the whole night. Hornsby was managing the Cardinals and found himself in a tough spot, leading by one run in the seventh. He called in Alexander, who was in the bullpen sleeping off his binge. And by God, Alexander struck out Lazzeri with the bases loaded, and then pitched the next two innings and saved the game.

Years later Hornsby and I were fanning around and he says to me, "Hey, remember when I brought in Alex? Do you remember whether he took any warm-up pitches when he got to the mound?"

I said I couldn't remember because I was too busy banging on the typewriter.

"Well," he said, "he never did. I was out there when he came in and I said, 'How are you, kid?' and he said, 'Okay, but no warm-up pitches. That would be the giveaway.' "

The study of drinking has been something of a hobby with me. I used to watch the various drinkers from the days of Bozeman Bulger. He was one of the senior writers when I was breaking in. He and McGraw were great pals. Bulger, now there was really a congenial drinker. The more he drank the happier he became. He'd make friends. He'd go into a bar and in ten minutes he knew everybody.

It was my father who taught me how to drink. I used to say that my father left me two legacies, one was the fiddle, which I couldn't play, and the other was a drinking education. When I would slop over in my younger days, he used to lay it on the line. He would say, "That's a weakness of character. Standing up at a bar and just swilling drink is nothing."

The key line of his lectures would be "Drink only what and when it is palatable. Drink just for the taste of it." In other words, don't swill it. Well, that got me into the habit of shifting drinks.

They say you can't shift drinks, that you get drunk. But that isn't true. I can start with a martini, and then have a bloody mary, and then maybe a manhattan. I drink everything but scotch.

Casey Stengel got into the habit with me. We'd have a cocktail or two, then take a bit of something else, and yak away. Then we'd switch to another drink. I remember one time when Casey overdid it. The Yankees were in Tampa and somebody was throwing a big dinner for the baseball people at one of the more distinguished restaurants there. As we're going in, Casey says, "Hey, Dreb, what's good to drink here?"

I said, "Casey, they make the finest daiquiris this side of Havana."

I didn't see much of Casey the rest of the evening, but I heard he got himself pretty well plastered.

The next day, after an exhibition game in St. Pete, I'm coming down the hall of the Serena Hotel and I hear that raspy voice of Stengel's: "Sure, I had too much, but where is that God damned Drebinger? He said you could drink those daiquiris like lemonade."

So I said, "Now just a minute, Casey. Maybe I did. But I didn't recommend a bottle of bourbon on top of them."

My father—now there was a drinker. He was a connoisseur. He was a musician, a violinist in the Metropolitan Orchestra. He played under all of the great conductors—Toscanini, Damrosch. Everybody. He loved boxing, and Bob Fitzsimmons was one of his closest pals. One time he was on tour with the Metropolitan and was playing in Cincinnati, at the old opera house there. And here's Fitzsimmons sitting in the front row.

After the show my father took Fitzsimmons backstage and introduced him to the director, a man named Antoine Seidl. Fitzsimmons was mad on music. He had those big, broad shoulders, tremendous paws. He shook hands with Seidl, nearly broke his knuckles, and said, "Mr. Seidl, I want you to know you've got a damn fine band." And Fitzsimmons slapped him on the back and dislocated his shoulder. Seidl couldn't wave his stick for a week.

And Seidl said to my father, "Don't ever bring those God damned prize fighters around here again."

I might have been a musician myself. First, I took up the fiddle but that didn't work, and then the piano. I studied the piano for ten years, until I was eighteen. Then I had an accident. The scar is still there. I was ice skating and trying to dig a hole into the strap of a skate. The knife slipped, cut me right through, and severed the nerve of the thumb. I didn't play at all for a couple of years, and when I did it bothered me. So I gave it up. To this day, when I turn my thumb, like when you're running a scale, it hurts.

I was born on the sidewalks of New York. I went to grammar school up at Eighty-fifth Street and Madison Avenue. In 1906 the family moved to Staten Island and I went to Curtis High School, which had just started. I took up track and was one of the first schoolboys to run a hundred yards in ten seconds. Ten seconds flat was very fast in those days, and a couple of years later, when I went to work for the Staten Island *Advance,* I took the nom de plume of "Ten Flat." Some guys used to call me that. I ran for the Irish Athletic Club for a couple of years after high school, but my running career ended when I busted a muscle in my leg, a hamstring. Tore it bad.

With my running record and everything I had several scholarships offered, from Columbia, NYU, and a few others. But working for the *Advance* sounded more appealing. A friend of mine, Eddie Johnson, was the editor at the *Advance.* Johnson had been a reporter on the old New York *Sun.* In those days the *Sun* was like the *Times* and the *Tribune* became later, a beautiful paper.

Johnson lived on Staten Island and moved around in society circles. He knew William G. Wilcox, the head of a marine insurance firm, a wealthy and successful man. Wilcox had a brother who died and left him quite a lump of money, but one of the stipulations was that he should use this money for some sort of public utility. So Eddie Johnson told Wilcox, "The finest public utility you can have is a newspaper with no political ties of any sort."

They had two papers on the island then. One was a weekly which was the official arm of the Democratic party. The Democrats ran the island three to one. The other was a little Republican sheet called the *Advance.* It made no pretext of being any kind of paper. Wilcox bought the paper and it became a tremendous success. In fact, the Columbia School of Journalism used it as their model for a weekly paper.

My main title was sports editor, but I covered politics and police stories, too. One day—this was in 1915 when I was twenty-four —a fellow named Billy Stephens, a promoter, a circus sort of guy, comes into our office. He says if the paper will finance him to drive a horse-drawn prairie schooner across the United States he would take a writer with him, would pay all his expenses, and then the outfit would be his when the trip was done. The idea was to go from Staten Island to San Francisco, which was having a World's Fair.

Eddie Johnson listened to Stephens and was brighter than that. He told Stephens, "I'll do better. I'll get the Staten Island Chamber of Commerce to finance this, we'll put a man on it, and he'll write stories for the paper, and if you ever get to San Francisco you can keep the wagon and sell it." So that was it. I went off with Stephens and a third guy, a roughneck. I wrote stories for the paper every week. It sent circulation booming.

We left New York on Washington's Birthday and had quite a send-off. The mayor was there, and everything. In all the cities we went through, the mayors came out and gave us a big to-do. In Washington we met President Wilson. He was very busy and pushed us into the arms of William Jennings Bryan, his secretary of state. Bryan was very pleasant. He asked me, "Are you doing this for your health?"

I said, "Partly."

We went south around through the Cumberland Gap. And then came some difficulties. Billy Stephens got sick, and by God, he died in a hospital in Kentucky, around Murphysboro. We had to send him back. So it was just the roughneck and I. We went into Missouri and ran out of funds in St. Louis. The Chamber of Commerce wasn't coming through quite as big as we had hoped. I canceled my salary. What the hell, I was single then. They didn't pay me much, anyway.

We waited in St. Louis for three or four weeks until a fellow from Staten Island, Christian Storberg, came out to finance the rest of the trip. He was a Dane and owned a chain of grocery stores all through New Jersey. He was probably the only man who made a trip of that kind in a boiled shirt. Storberg took over and was on the wagon when we went through Missouri. Route 40 was a mud road then. This was in July, and good God, it rained like the devil. Every morning it was muddy, and by noon it would be so boiling hot we'd have to stop.

When we got to Kansas City I had a brawl with the roughneck and he just took off, left us flat. Storberg had been sick all the way from St. Louis, and he quit, too. I went on alone, all the way up to Denver, and by then it was almost October. I was out of money again and telephoned Eddie Johnson. We called the whole thing off. The snow was on the Rockies and I couldn't have gotten over them.

I sold the whole outfit. I had three horses, but they were pretty well worn out. I got about five hundred dollars and kept that. Then I went on to San Francisco. There were quite a few Staten Islanders out there waiting for me at the fair, ready to give some big parties. It wasn't quite what they had planned, but they gave the parties anyway, and that ended that. The whole thing took ten months. I wrote a story a week, each of them about three or four thousand words long. The circulation of the paper really rose, and within a year we became a daily.

In the spring of 1923 the paper changed hands. Johnson and I thought we had an agreement that we could buy the paper when it got out of the red. But there was a mix-up. Mr. Wilcox never consulted us, just sold to a fellow named Newhouse. The new ownership wanted me to stay but I said, "Absolutely not. If I want to continue on salary, I'll go across the bay and work in New York."

I stayed at the *Times* forty-one years, and of course, almost all those years I was out on baseball. I couldn't have worked inside. Meeting people to me was everything. It was the main thing. I traveled everywhere, but I never cared much about scenery. I've seen it all. Pikes Peak, Short Peak, Long Peak, all the other peaks you've got. When I bumped into the scenic effects I looked at 'em and that was it. It was the people I met. That's what made it such a great job.

There was some confusion about my retirement from the *Times*. When Gay Talese wrote that book on *The New York Times*, he made it look like there was this new regime coming and throwing out all the old guys, that there was this big uproar because they were forcing out old-timers like Brooks Atkinson, the drama critic, and John Drebinger, the baseball writer.

I told Talese, "You knew damned well we weren't forced out.

You were right there when it happened." As a matter of fact, the *Times* was probably the first paper that had pensions for its writers. Adolph Ochs set that up back in the twenties. Talese wrote a very slanted book. He made no mention of this fine pension setup that we had.

It's when you retire that you find out who your real friends are. The Yankees owed me nothing. The stigma was on me from my early years because of my close relations with McGraw. When I'd switched over to the Yankees, they'd see me and they'd say, "Here comes the guy from the Giants," that sort of stuff.

And yet who offered me a job? When the Yankees heard I was retiring from the *Times*—I had just turned seventy-three—they asked me to come with them. Ralph Houk was then the general manager and Houk said, "Hey, Dreb, what are you going to be doing?"

I really hadn't given it much thought and told them I didn't have to worry. I had enough money. But Houk says to Bob Fishel—he's the Yankee public relations man—"Can't we fix Dreb up with something?"

"Now wait a minute," I said. "I don't want a regular job. I couldn't do it."

"Oh, no," Houk says, "we'll get you something better. Supposing you come in as a public relations assistant to Bob. All you have to do is come up to the press box on the days of home games. No travel, no nothing."

I was astounded. I went over with the Yankees for seven more years, until I was eighty, and they paid me some damn nice money. That was a wonderful thing they did for me because I had never leaned over backwards for them. Not that I had anything against them. But it was this constant winning. You get tired of writing about the Great Yankees. We took them for granted. I'm for the underdog, the guy that's not supposed to win. He's the one that makes a good story.

Laraine Day—when she was married to Leo Durocher—had a radio program in New York. Leo was managing the Giants then, and Laraine had me on her show. She was a good student of baseball. When we're on the air, she says, "But on the pennant race this year, you really do kind of lean toward the Giants, don't you? You'd like to see them win."

I said, "Just a minute, Laraine. Us writers are a little selfish about these things. Whoever wins, it's not going to slay me because I don't work for either team. What I'm always hoping for is a close race because it gives me good copy. If the Yankees or the Giants win by ten or fifteen games, I haven't got anything."

The only other interest I had, that is in newspaper work, was in politics. But that was strictly as a spectator. I was nonpartisan, strictly neutral. I just kept watching the show. I always knew a few politicians. I've known every mayor of New York starting with Gaynor. Jim Farley is a friend of mine from way back. He always used to send me cards on my birthday. When I passed my eightieth he sent me a telegram, saying "Welcome to the Octogenarian Club."

I always plagued Farley with questions about politics. One day he said to me, "John, why don't you write politics if you're so interested in it?"

I said, "Jim, there's only one reason. In politics you only have a World Series once every four years, and that's too long to wait."

Harold Parrott

Harold Parrott, a graduate of St. John's University of Brooklyn at the age of eighteen, was fifth in the holy succession of baseball writers for the old Brooklyn Eagle *that began with Henry Chadwick, the "father of baseball" and inventor of the box score. In addition to his vigorous coverage of the Dodgers, Mr. Parrott did a daily column, "Both Sides," and was a frequent contributor to such premier magazines as the old* Saturday Evening Post, Collier's, *and* This Week.

He was also a prolific literary ghost. Often he did the "Looping the Loop" column for J. G. Taylor Spink, the late publisher of The Sporting News; *he was responsible for* The Dodgers and Me, *the Brooklyn life and travails of Leo Durocher; and had the distinction, perhaps without precedent, of having been the daily postgame ghost for Lou Gehrig of the Yankees and Carl Hubbell of the Giants when the two played on opposite sides of the same World Series.*

After nineteen years as a sportswriter, Mr. Parrott was sepa-

rated from his typewriter in 1944 when the Dodgers hired him as their traveling secretary. Thereafter he was employed in the front office of major league baseball clubs and participated in the opening of three new California stadia—at Los Angeles, Anaheim, and San Diego. He died in Nyack, New York, in 1987 at the age of seventy-eight.

Leo Durocher and I were in a lot of hot water with the commissioner, the so-called commissioner of baseball, Happy Chandler. Leo was always doing something controversial. I remember one time, in Cincinnati, he was thrown out of a game. He came and sat next to me in the club box and told me to give the signs. It was illegal for him to run the club, but there he was whispering to me.

"All right," he said, "pull your nose with your left hand. Put your right hand up to your ear."

And I was putting on the take sign, the bunt, and the hit-and-run. We won the game, 3-2, on a squeeze play in the ninth inning. Leo was so delighted. He felt he had put one over on the umpires.

But characteristically of Leo, he couldn't keep it to himself. In the drawing room that night, on the train, he told all the writers how he worked this thing, and a day or two later he was fined five hundred dollars by Ford Frick, the National League president. Frick censured me, too, for being Leo's accomplice.

In those days those were big adventures. I remember Leo took me across the river in Cincinnati and introduced me to three people in racing, and these were their real names, not Runyon inventions: "Sleepout Looie," "Cigar Charlie," and "The Dancer." My eyes were the size of saucers. I just loved being with Leo, and of course, I'm very fond of Laraine Day, who is just as unlike Leo as she could be.

We wrote *The Dodgers and Me* and before publication one chapter was picked up by *Cosmopolitan* or *Redbook*, I forget which. We got a lot of money for the forties, two thousand dollars, and the name of the chapter, oddly enough, was "Nice Guys Finish Last." I heard Leo make the remark to Frank Graham of the *Journal*, and he used it in his column.

Frankie Graham, now there was a great writer. Possibly if I

have to name my idea of the number-one writer, it would be hard for me to place anybody over Frank Graham. He was so genteel. He had a code which he held to very rigidly. He never hurt anybody. And he had the faculty for quoting people so correctly. He never shook them up by making a lot of notes in front of them. I think this ruins more stories than anything. If they see you writing something down, they stop talking. But Frank had a reproductive type of mind. Another thing that impressed me when I was so young among these greats—the Ruths, Gehrigs, the Hubbells—if I entered a group of writers, Frank would always stop the questioning and make sure that myself or any other young writer met every one of the principals involved. Frank had the kind of muscle to do that.

To get back to Leo. He was managing the Dodgers, and we were up at the Polo Grounds to play the Giants. Some of the bad boys on the Giants were taking advantage of their manager, a very fine gentleman, Mel Ott. Leo was making the point that you have to have discipline and rules, and I think if his remarks were kept in context he wouldn't have been subjected to the criticism over the years, because from then on every time a nice guy won something they would say, "Ah, there you are, Leo Durocher. You were wrong."

But what Leo meant is that you can't be a nice guy, a so-called nice guy, and win. You have to have discipline and rules. And oddly enough it was Ott who Durocher succeeded. It was the most bizarre shift of managers the game has ever known, because the Giant rooters hated Leo with his swaggering style, and this happened when our book was booming. Naturally, the sale of *The Dodgers and Me* just about terminated when Leo became manager of the Giants.

We were sued on that book because Leo insisted on putting a chapter in there. He insisted a writer named Tim Cohane had listened at the door, eavesdropped, and found out something that he wrote the next day.

I said, "Oh, I think we ought to leave that out of the book."

"Why? It's my book," Leo said. "Why can't I say it? Let's put it in there."

Before publication we were sued for $75,000. It was a futile suit, but it helped the sale of the book. Cohane was just doing it to hurt Leo, but it had the opposite effect. The suit was never carried through. Cohane didn't have a leg to stand on.

Here's what had happened. A couple of players in the Dodger clubhouse had engineered a player strike. Bobo Newsom was the ringleader. They thought some of Leo's rules and regulations were unfair. There were some players who definitely balked at putting on a uniform for a while, but it was straightened out. Cohane wrote one facet of it that Leo thought was private and he had gotten by eavesdropping. It was just one of those little episodes that made life so interesting.

I roomed with Leo, off and on, for three years, and there are so many fine things about Leo that are unwritten. His affection for children is genuine. When my two oldest boys made a road trip with us, he'd say, "Get lost, Dad. The fellows are in with me in the drawing room."

I like to tell this story because of Durocher's pride and his love of protocol. He would no more think of sleeping in an upper berth than he would of flying. But I knocked on the door one morning to see if I could take the youngsters to breakfast. There he was in the upper. He put them in the lower so they could look out the window in the morning.

He used to take them on spring training trips. He would talk their mother into letting them stay an extra week. We were going through Arkansas and Tennessee. We played games in the afternoon, and every night Leo would take them to see another Hopalong Cassidy movie. I said, "Leo, how can you look at those things?"

"I don't look at the movie," he said. "I just watch the kids' faces. They enjoy it so much."

I've always thought that if I do another piece on Durocher I'd open it with this anecdote. We were playing bridge one day. He and Branch Rickey against Hector Racine, who at that timed owned the Montreal club, and myself. Leo is very positive, and he's an excellent card player. He has an impeccable memory for cards that are played, and Rickey made the conventional bid of four no-trump—Blackwood—and Leo said, "I pass."

"You can't pass," Rickey told him.

"I did," Durocher replied.

Rickey was upset. "My boy," he said, "when you sit down to play with a set of conventions and you agree with them, you must follow through and this is a demand bid."

"You don't know what you're talking about, Branch," Leo said. "The greatest card player in the world is in the next room, and I'll get him and you'll see you're wrong."

So he went into the dining room at the Bear Mountain Inn, and he brought in P. Hal Sims, who was a great card player and plunger of those days. Leo patiently explained the whole situation and Rickey was looking out from under his bushy eyebrows, and Sims, at the conclusion of this presentation, turned to Leo and said, "I'm sorry, Leo, but you're wrong. You must respond to Mr. Rickey's bid of four no-trump as long as you're going by the Blackwood convention."

Leo said, "Well, what the hell do you know about it, anyway?"

I've written under a lot of pseudonyms, ghostly by-lines. As a matter of fact, when I was working on the Brooklyn *Eagle* and the paper had a circulation of about 100,000, I ghosted the World Series for Hubbell on one side and for Gehrig on the other, and Christy Walsh estimated I was writing for about sixty million people, and of course, it was canned, low-grade stuff compared to what I was doing for my own little paper.

Salaries weren't so great in the newspaper business in those days, and I did a lot of writing for magazines—*Saturday Evening Post, Collier's, This Week* magazine, a Sunday supplement. One of those pieces was about Branch Rickey, who was a much-maligned man of the time because of his authorship of the so-called chain gang and pinch-penny tactics, which led him to be called El Cheapo by Jimmy Powers, unfairly, I thought. Anyway, Rickey had built up quite a wall between himself and newspaper people. He was afraid of them, really. And I did this magazine piece about him which he liked, and in 1943 there was a tremendous upheaval in Brooklyn and Branch Rickey moved in to take Larry MacPhail's place and rehabilitate the franchise, which was going bankrupt. One of the first things he did was ask me to join him. He had remembered the friendly piece I wrote. At least he thought it was fair.

I was a compulsive writer. I wrote a lot of articles for *The Sporting News*—under Taylor Spink's by-line. I was always proud to do that. I used to turn out a lot of copy. I covered the minor league convention in Buffalo one year and *The Sporting News* didn't want to put "By Harold Parrott" on another piece, so they put "By N.

Falls," the allusion being to nearby Niagara Falls. That was the phoniest by-line I ever had, but every time I look at Joe Falls's column in *The Sporting News* I think of that.

Mr. Spink was one of the most zealous news hounds who ever trod an editorial floor. There was this pitcher in St. Louis, Blix Donnelly. He disliked Eddie Dyer, his manager with the Cardinals. He disliked him very much. Dyer went to the mound one day to take him out of the box. Donnelly warned him, "Advance one step further, Dyer, and I'm going to let you have the ball right between your eyes."

This was at the time when I had ended my career as a baseball writer. Mr. Rickey had hired me as the traveling secretary of the Dodgers, and I thought it would be indiscreet as a baseball executive for me to write any controversial things like that. I begged off. The more I begged off, the more desirable the story seemed to Taylor Spink, and I was the only one who could do it. He used to call me "Bonfire." He'd send wires to press boxes just addressed to "Bonfire."

So he said, "Bonfire, you've got to do this!"

I said, "Taylor, it would be bad taste."

He never sent anything by ordinary mail. It was always airmail special delivery. And by airmail special delivery there came to my fourteen-year-old son a check made out to Todd Parrott for one hundred dollars. The boy was, of course, delighted with this gift from heaven.

In about three days Mr. Spink called and asked, "Have you got that story done yet?"

I said, "Taylor, I told you I couldn't handle that. It's a hot potato story."

He said, "You mean, you're going to take that money right out of your kid's pocket."

I never tired of writing. It was never a chore. Never once can I remember when doing a piece was a chore. When the *Eagle* went through bankruptcy I used to worry that I would be laid off, and as I look back on it now they would have had to hire three men to take my place. We had an interesting column. I was a voracious reader of out-of-town newspapers, as I still am. The by-line on the column was "Shortstop." I had too many by-lines in the paper already, and I did paragraphs of interest about other ball clubs. This was a takeoff on a famous column the New York *Sun* ran for years, called "By the Old Scout." It was a very popular thing. It was a gossip column, you know, about who could hit left handers and what kind of a curve so-and-so threw.

I haunted that newspaper office. It was a magnet for me. My mother started complaining that I wasn't getting my proper sleep, but I just loved every minute of it. It gave me a real pang the other day to go by the spot where it used to be, to see it's now a park. There's not a vestige of the old *Eagle* building left.

I began working while I was at college, at St. John's University in Brooklyn. There was a fellow who reported all the games our teams played for about four different Brooklyn newspapers, and when he got ill one week four of us agreed to each take one paper and take the game down and write about it. I had had some experience on the college paper writing a column, and just by chance the paper I chose was the Brooklyn *Eagle*.

There was a real old-line newspaperman there named Jimmy Murphy. He had been with the paper for forty years, and he liked the few paragraphs that I wrote and pretty soon he asked me if I'd like to do some part-time work in the summer. The first assignment he gave me was to do some human interest stories on the grey-hounds, on Staten Island. It was one of the first greyhound tracks. I came back with a story that particularly delighted Jimmy Murphy. It was about how they brushed the teeth of the greyhounds, how they were very careful about the diet, and things like that.

We had a couple of older writers on the paper. One of them was Thomas S. Rice. He was a criminologist and the third in a line of great baseball writers who covered the Dodgers for the *Eagle*. The first was Father Chadwick. The second was Abe Yaeger, and third was Thomas Rice. Tom lingered too long over the bar some evenings, and he used to ask me to do his piece for him. Rice used to give me his pay from *The Sporting News*. His weekly stipend then—this was in the twenties—was five dollars. I wrote "By Thomas S. Rice," and I was so proud to see the words that I had put together appear under Rice's name. And it went on from there.

The night editor was a fight referee, a well-known man named Eddie Forbes. He had refereed the Tunney-Heeney fights and other big fights. Whenever he had a fight he used to put me in charge of the desk, and that was a ten-dollar bill every night. And when he found out I could do a good job on it, he started taking a few nights off. To me, it was the greatest training in the world because I worked in the afternoons with Murphy on the makeover edition. We had an edition every hour. And then I was the night editor at night. Pretty soon I was up to my armpits in printer's ink.

I worked summers until I got out of college. I got a Master of Arts degree by the time I was twenty. This was in 1927. My first big assignment was going south with the Dodgers in 1934. We had a managing editor who was a golf nut, and I used to write color on all of the big tournaments, the Open and the Amateur. This was in the days of Tommy Armour and Leo Diegel and Sarazen. Then I got on the tennis beat because I played a lot of tennis myself. Sometimes I'd be out of the office for four, five weeks at a time, wiring in my stories from Seabright and Southampton and so on.

I remember my first day on the baseball beat. I had two full columns to fill, and you were not facetious about the Dodgers in those days. It was very serious in Brooklyn. I went to Stengel. I was looking for a feature story, and we had just acquired a new outfielder who reported with a violin and a mustache and his name was Frenchy Bordagaray. I was looking for something to hang the story on and I knew that Bordagaray could run well, and I said to Stengel, "Is he the fastest man on the club?" And Casey pinched his chin and pulled on his ear, the same mannerisms that he has today, and he said, "Well, I'll tell you, Parrott, you can say he's the fastest man on the club running to the wrong base." There I was—I didn't have any more of a story before I asked the question, but Stengel was always the clown, I mean an affable, fine clown.

Just the other day I asked Babe Herman, trying to check up on a rumor, "Was he ever really hit on the head by a fly ball?"

"Absolutely not, Harold," Babe said. "On the shoulder, yes, but not on the head."

I was a great admirer of the baseball writers of that era. They were a colorful lot. They didn't deal in the gossip that you see today. They delighted in colorful, flamboyant anecdotes about the ball players, and they hung outrageous names on them.

This was the age of the triple-barreled name. For instance, Grover Cleveland Alexander and there was George Herman Ruth. That, of course, was Babe Ruth, the Sultan of Swat and the Bambino. Lefty Grove? No. He was Robert Moses Grove. Joe McCarthy, the very successful manager of the Yankees, was Marse Joe McCarthy, probably because he managed so successfully in the bluegrass country in Louisville. Even the commissioner, baseball's first czar. Was he Judge Landis? No, he was Kenesaw Mountain Landis. There was King Carl Hubbell, there was Prince Hal Schumacher, and names which I found out later were just colorful, but not authentic. Cincinnati had a famous left-hander named Eppa Jeptha Rixey. I always supposed that was his given name, but the Jeptha part of it was just fanciful.

Some of the others, like Frank Frisch, automatically, when you referred to him he was the Fordham Flash. Herb Pennock, the great left-hander of the Yankees, was identified as the Squire of Kenneth Square. Possibly one of the most interesting names in this era of fanciful baseball writing was Waite Hoyt. He was originally the Flatbush Schoolboy. He was a handsome youngster, but the Flatbush Schoolboy handle stuck to him even after he was thirty-five and still pitching in the majors. I think he married a girl whose father owned a string of undertaking shops, so Hoyt was also the Flatbush Undertaker or the Brooklyn Undertaker. When Hoyt won a game, as he often did, the writers would say that "Waite Hoyt interred so-and-so" or "He laid them to rest yesterday without trouble of many base hits." In that connection, another fanciful euphonic name was pinned on Colonel Ruppert's partner, Tillinghast L'Hommodeau Houston. The writers delighted in this. It filled a few lines and was a sign of the flamboyant writing of the times.

Then we came to the rhyming era. This was probably started by Bugs Baer of the Hearst chain, but certainly one of the greatest exponents of it was George Phair, a little man with a great mind. He wrote for Hearst, too. I remember George Phair made a spring training trip with us to Orlando, Florida, and never got to the ball park. But his little doggerel, his little quatrains at the top of his column every day, were among the most fanciful things ever created. You remember Manny Vaughan and Irving Vaughan in Chicago. They were baseball writers. Manny worked in Milwaukee and Irving in Chicago. Manny passed away. Irving was rather a sourpuss writer.

Manny was very popular, and George Phair was asked to do a few lines on the decease of Manny. He wrote as follows:

> Manny Vaughan dead and gone.
> To his ideals he was unswerving.
> Too damn bad it wasn't Irving.

Then the writers exerted a lot more power, I think. They had campaigns to get rid of managers they didn't like. The most noteworthy was the campaign to get rid of Bill Terry, who was a successful manager with the Giants. Won pennants. But Terry had the same low opinion of some of the writers who criticized him as Ted Williams did in a later day. But they kept jabbing at him. I remember one baseball writers' dinner in New York. Terry had just won the pennant and was having a mock press conference that the writers constructed on the stage, and here's the way it started:

> The Tennessee Colonel,
> Flushed with success,
> Was tossing his pearls
> To the swine of the press.

It was difficult for Terry to strike back. He was, of course, a fine manager. I learned a lot of my baseball from him because I refused to go along with the criticisms, and he spent a lot of time with me. He told me the percentage plays, why he bunted, how he arranged the defense. I learned a great deal from Bill Terry and I like him very much.

The *Eagle* was a comparatively small paper, and I didn't have a name like the writers of the era, although at times I did stories for all of them when they were indisposed. I'm talking of the Runyons and the Peglers and the Heywood Brouns and Tom Meany. I think the writers loved the game more then and they had more violent antipathies and more violent prejudices.

Pegler and Runyon had a terrific way with words that we don't find. They would travel with a ball club from time to time, unless there was a big trial or a big story they would be taken off for. They left a mark on the game. It got their foot in the door. Bob Considine is another I could mention who is still operating. Pegler? He was a sour fellow, and I think in some ways it was a defense he had, a mask. Do you remember the old movie actor Ned Sparks? I often thought that Pegler affected a pose like that to be cynical, something to hide behind. Runyon was, of course, suffering a lot. He was ill in the days I knew him. He had throat problems. I couldn't name the best writer, but I think there were so many more men of talent around and on the sports page than there are now.

We weren't rushing for editions in those days. Tomorrow's paper didn't come out until tomorrow. The writers went down and spoke to the people they were writing about. Today the writer hammers away in the press box and the canned quotes are brought up from the clubhouse by a press attaché or by the traveling secretary, or whoever. I just think this is an oversimplification of the thing, a corruption. I don't think you can really quote a man unless you see him and hear him say the words. The inflections and the surroundings are so important. Possibly some of the things he says are said with tongue in cheek, but when you get them without being present, when they are brought to you, I think reporting loses a lot of its sting.

In those days there was a lot more contact between the writers and the players and the managers and coaches. We traveled in the forties and into the fifties almost exclusively by train. I was the traveling secretary in those days. We had two sleepers and a diner which, later in the evening after everyone had dined, was turned into a workshop for the writers. When we left Cincinnati, for instance, on the run to St. Louis, I knew when all the players were on the train and I gave the sign to the conductor and off we went. And I think there was a lot more sleep for the players and a lot better food than in this day and age where everybody is rushing by jet and where everybody has to go to sleep, if the schedule calls for it, at six in the morning. Some people can't sleep at six.

I remember those drawing room poker games with Durocher and Charley Dressen and the other coaches. There was a lot more baseball talk between hands and a lot of kidding and a lot of good spirit. There was always a buffoon in the press corps, a straight man. In our group it was Arch Murray. But I think the relationship was a lot different than it is today, where there seems to be a cellophane wall with a lot of the players and managers on one side and the writers and broadcasters on the other.

When I first got into it, baseball didn't have many knockers. There was nobody who called the powers to be "the Lords of Baseball" as Dick Young of the New York *Daily News* does now. I admire Dick Young personally and count him among my friends. I don't think he does anything which he feels will harm the game or tear it down. But I think Dick has appointed himself as a policeman. I went into that on his last visit here. He has mounted a campaign to keep Lance Rentzel from playing football. This stirred up John Hall of the Los Angeles *Times,* and he wrote an anti-Young column in which he said, "Dick, you police New York and leave Los Angeles to the writers here."

This kind of thing has been going on for years. It reminds me of the first exchange between Young and Bob Hunter of the Los Angeles *Examiner.* Young was very bitter about the departure of the Dodgers and Giants from New York and it clouded his judgment, possibly, at the start, and he was really chagrined at the crowds we drew. When the Dodgers were drawing big crowds at the Coliseum in Los Angeles, Young wrote that it was because people had to go to the game to find out what was happening because there wasn't a writer on the west coast who knows how to write baseball. People had to go to the games to be informed.

Young has made a few enemies going through life. I feel at this point he regrets having made an enemy of old Burt Shotton, the manager of the Dodgers. They never got along. Shotton lived in a different era where people didn't say critical things about the ball players or criticize the manager's tactics. He never quite stomached some of Young's criticism. I'll never forget one confrontation in the dugout. Shotton looked at Young and he said, "Dick Young, the first time I met you I knew you was no good." So you can understand it wasn't a one-sided argument. Young had some justification for striking back.

Young is an extraordinary writer, certainly the most influential baseball writer of our time. But in my own mind no one can compare with Frankie Graham. He had such personal integrity. He very seldom did a think column. We all know that columnists take days off and write controversial things by never moving out of their chair.

Graham always got other people's opinions and commented on them, but his own remained subdued, you might say. Now, Frankie Graham would start a column by saying, "This was a Thursday afternoon in the Polo Grounds and the reporter asked John McGraw why Dolph Luque was throwing so many curve balls." Well, the reporter was, of course, Frankie Graham, and by using that style which has become quite popular he kept the first personal pronoun out. I know so many egotistical-type writers who would say, "I was at the Polo Grounds yesterday and I said to John McGraw, so-and-so and so-and-so." But Graham had a more tasteful way of doing it. And the most outstanding thing about him is that he abstained from hurting anybody. If it had to be a damning column, he would find another subject. I think Bill Corum was a writer in that same tradition. Of course Graham had been a standby on the *Sun* for years, and when the *Sun* folded Frank Graham went to the *Journal* and he and Corum were on the same paper. Incidentally, they tell a funny story about Graham's predecessor on the *Sun,* a man named Joe Vila. He used to cut up press releases and write a few words of introduction, and if the column wasn't long enough he'd say, "And the Cincinnati Reds will be in town today, the roster of which follows."

Graham was controversial, certainly. But he dug it up and not out of his own mind and not with anonymous quotes. He would go to somebody and ask, but these were not Graham think pieces, not composed in any easy chair. I just think that many writers take the easy way out. They dream up a controversy or they light a fire right in their own typewriter.

◦◦◦◦
◦◦◦◦
◦◦◦◦

Red Smith

Born in Green Bay, Wisconsin, on September 5, 1905, the son of a wholesale grocer, Walter (Red) Smith was, most likely, the best sports columnist-reporter in the history of American journalism. He was chosen the nation's best sportswriter in a vote of his peers, five times won the Pulitzer Prize for distinguished commentary, the Headliners' Award, the George Polk Award, the Grantland Rice Memorial Award, and multiple honors from the American Newspaper Guild. The University of Notre Dame, his alma mater, conferred on him an honorary Doctorate of Laws in 1968. La Salle College of Philadelphia also awarded him an honorary degree.

Mr. Smith was a working newspaperman for fifty-four years. He started as a cityside reporter on the Milwaukee Sentinel, *did both sports and local reporting for the St. Louis* Star *(later the* Star-Times), *and began devoting total attention to sports in 1936 when he joined the now defunct Philadelphia* Record. *He gained national prominence after moving to the New York* Herald Tribune. *He joined the* New York Times *in 1971 at the age of sixty-seven.*

His columns, though written with a rare literary elegance, are, nonetheless, extremely informative. Having been in the trenches himself, traveling with teams for two decades, Mr. Smith had an expert's knowledge and interest in all major sports, except basketball. Hemingway, after searching for the ultimate sportswriter, settled on Red Smith. Later Mr. Smith, having grown more skeptical of the sports establishment, often attacked with the power of a heavyweight, though he retained his characteristically light and whimsical touch. Some of his columns have been collected in two books, Out of the Red *and* The Best of Red Smith. *He worked until his death in 1982, in Stamford, Connecticut, at the age of seventy-six.*

I never felt that I was a bug-eyed fan as such. I wasn't one of those who dreamed of being a sportswriter and going around the country traveling with ball players and getting into the games free and, oh, dear diary, what a break. I'm not pretending that I haven't enjoyed this hugely. I have. I've loved it. But I never had any soaring ambition to be a sportswriter, per se. I wanted to be a newspaperman, and came to realize I didn't really care which side of the paper I worked on.

I'm too lazy to change over now, to start something new at this stage. I just got so comfortable in so many years in sports. But otherwise I still feel that way. I never cared. When I went to Philadelphia I didn't know what side of the paper I'd be on. I had done three or four years of rewrite and general reporting in St. Louis when I accepted the offer in Philadelphia. I knew how many dollars a week I was going to get. That was the essential thing. I never asked what they wanted me to do.

The guy I admire most in the world is a good reporter. I respect a good reporter, and I'd like to be called that. I'd like to be considered good and honest and reasonably accurate. The reporter has one of the toughest jobs in the world—getting as near the truth as possible is a terribly tough job. I was a local side reporter in St.

Louis and Milwaukee. I wasn't as good as some. I wasn't one of those who could go out and find the kidnapper and the child. But I got my facts straight and did a thorough job.

I like to report on the scene around me, on the little piece of the world as I see it, as it is in my time. And I like to do it in a way that gives the reader a little pleasure, a little entertainment. I've always had the notion that people go to spectator sports to have fun and then they grab the paper to read about it and have fun again.

I've always tried to remember—and this is an old line—that sports isn't Armageddon. These are just little games that little boys can play, and it really isn't important to the future of civilization whether the Athletics or the Browns win. If you can accept it as entertainment, and write it as entertainment, then I think that's what spectator sports are meant to be.

I've been having fun doing this seminar at Yale, once a week. They call it Sports in American Society. I don't know what that name means, but obviously it's a big, broad topic and I have got guys up to help me. It's a round-table discussion, eighteen students, but usually there are a couple missing so it's about fifteen. We bat around everything from the reserve system to amateurism and professionalism, and yesterday they wanted to talk about sports journalism, a subject I have been avoiding because I wanted them to do the talking. As a rule, I fire out a subject and say, "What do you think about this?" and they kick it around. I like that better. I knew that if I was alone I'd do all the talking so I got Leonard Koppett of the *Times* up there to help. And Koppett said that generally speaking sportswriters aren't the most brilliant people in the world because really smart people do something else besides traveling with a ball club for twenty-five years. I don't know. Did you ever feel discontented, feel the need to do something that other people would say was more important?

During the war, World War II, I was of draft age. By that I mean I hadn't yet gotten to be thirty-eight. I was registered for the draft, but I had a family and didn't think I could afford to be a private in the army and I didn't want to go looking for one of those phony public relations commissions. So I just kept traveling with the last-place Philadelphia Athletics and, oh boy, more than once I thought, "What the hell am I doing here?" But that was during the war. Outside of that I never felt any prodding need to solve the problems of the world. You can help a little by writing about games, especially if you're writing a column.

Oh, I don't know if I've ever helped, but I have tried to stay aware of the world outside, beyond the fences, outside the playing field, and to let that awareness creep into the column sometimes. Occasionally, I've thrown a line about a Spiro Agnew or a Richard Nixon into a piece. I wouldn't imagine I had any effect, excepting to make an occasional reader write and say, "Stick to sports, you bum. What do you know about politics?"

Sure, I respect the Tom Wickers. He's certainly more effective. But somehow I have felt that my time wasn't altogether wasted. I haven't been ashamed of what I've done. I seem to be making apologies for it. I don't mean to, because I feel keeping the public informed in any area is a perfectly worthwhile way to spend your life. I think sports constitute a valid part of our culture, our civilization, and keeping the public informed and, if possible, a little entertained about sports is not an entirely useless thing.

I did get a kick out of covering an occasional political convention, but even then my approach to it was as a sportswriter viewing a very popular spectator sport, and I tried to have fun with it. I did the presidential conventions in '56 and again in '68. The 1956 Democratic convention in Chicago was a pretty good one. Happy Chandler was a candidate for the presidential nomination. They finally nominated Adlai Stevenson and almost nominated John Kennedy for Vice-President. Kennedy was in the Stockyard Inn writing his acceptance speech when they decided to go for Coonskin Cap—Kefauver. Anyway, there was Happy Chandler. He was a good, soft touch for one column. There was Governor Clements of Tennessee. He made one of the great cornball keynote addresses of our time, and he was good for another column. Let me see, what else? Oh, yes, Truman came on. He looked like the old champ, trying to make a comeback, like Dempsey. Truman wasn't running for reelection, but he showed up at the convention and made for lively copy. On the whole I just felt loose and easy and free to write what I pleased, and it seemed to come off well.

Over the years people have said to me, "Isn't it dull covering baseball every day?" My answer used to be "It becomes dull only to dull minds." Today's game is always different from yesterday's game. If you have the perception and the interest to see it, and the wit to express it, your story is always different from yesterday's story. I thoroughly enjoyed covering baseball daily.

I still think every game is different, not that some of them aren't dull, but it's a rare person who lives his life without encountering dull spots. It's up to the writer to take a lively interest and see the difference. Of course most of my years I was with a club to which a pennant race was only a rumor—the Philadelphia Athletics. I did ten years with them. They were always last.

I don't agree with him, but yesterday, at Yale, Leonard Koppett said one of the great untrue clichés in sports is that the legs go first. He said that's not true. He insists that the enthusiasm, the desire go first. And he said this is generally true of the athlete and, of course, when the athlete gets above thirty-five or forty he just can't go on. He's physically unable to. The writer can go on, he is able to physically, but Leonard believes writers lose their enthusiasm, too. He thinks very few writers of forty-five have had the enthusiasm of their youth for the job. He said he didn't know how writers of sixty-five felt, and I said, "Neither do I, but I don't think I've lost my enthusiasm." If I did, I'd want to quit.

My enthusiasm is self-generating, self-renewing. My life, the way it's been going now, I see very few baseball games in the summer. I'll start with the opening of the season. I'll see the games then, but things like the Kentucky Derby and Preakness get in the way, and lately we've had a home up in Martha's Vineyard, where I like to spend as much of the summer as I can, working from there. By the time the World Series comes along I may feel that I've had very little baseball for the year. But I find that old enthusiasm renewing itself when I sit there at the playoffs.

I don't enjoy the actual labor of writing. I love my job, but I find one of the disadvantages is the several hours at the typewriter each day. That's how I pay for this nice job. And I pay pretty dearly. I sweat. I bleed. I'm a slow writer. Once, through necessity, I was a fast rewrite man, when I had to be. I had no choice.

But when I began doing a column, which is a much more personal thing, I found it wasn't something that I could rip off the top of my head. I had to do it painstakingly. I'm always unhappy, very unhappy, at anything that takes less than two hours. I can do it in two hours, if I must. But my usual answer to the question "How long does it take to write a column?" is "How much time do I have?" If I have six hours, I take it. I wish I could say that the ones that take six hours turn out better. Not necessarily. But I will say this: I do think that, over three hundred days, effort pays off. If you do the best you can every day, taking as much time as necessary, or as much time as you have, then it's going to be better than if you brushed it off.

It's not very often that I feel gratified with a piece I've just written. Very often I feel, "Well, this one is okay." Or "This one will get by." The next day when I read it in print, clean and in two-column measure, it often looks better. But sometimes I'm disappointed. If I think I've written a clinker, I'm terribly depressed for twenty-four hours. But when you write a good one, you feel set up, the adrenalin is flowing.

Arthur Daley once told me that Paul Gallico asked him, "How many good columns do you strive for?"

Arthur said, "One every day."

And Gallico said, "I'll settle for two a week."

In my later years I have sought to become simpler, straighter, and purer in my handling of the language. I've had many writing heroes, writers who have influenced me. Of the ones still alive, I can think of E. B. White. I certainly admire the pure, crystal stream of his prose. When I was very young as a sportswriter I knowingly and unashamedly imitated others. I had a series of heroes who would delight me for a while and I'd imitate them—Damon Runyon, Westbrook Pegler, Joe Williams. This may surprise you, but at the top of his game I thought Joe Williams was pretty good.

I think you pick up something from this guy and something from that. I know that I deliberately imitated those three guys, one by one, never together. I'd read one daily, faithfully, and be delighted by him and imitate him. Then someone else would catch my fancy. That's a shameful admission. But slowly, by what process I have no idea, your own writing tends to crystallize, to take shape. Yet you have learned some moves from all these guys and they are somehow incorporated into your own style. Pretty soon you're not imitating any longer.

I was a very shy, timid kid. Going to Notre Dame and living for four years with guys—no girls, of course, were around—was good for me. It gave me a feeling of comfort mixing with my peers, a sense of comfort I didn't have in grade school or in high school. But my defense mechanism has been at work so long I still find myself talking too much at parties, things like that. I know this is a defense to cover shyness. I often hear myself babbling on and wish I'd shut up. I know it's because I'm shy. It's a defensive mechanism that has developed and operated over the years.

I'm not a psychologist, but I do know, for example, that a fellow like Howard Cosell is the braggart that he is because of a massive insecurity. He has to be told every couple minutes how great he is because he's so insecure. And if you don't tell him, he tells you. He can't help this.

I was born in Green Bay, Wisconsin. My father, Walter P. Smith, was the third generation in a family business—wholesale produce and retail groceries. My mother was born and grew up in New York. Her name was Ida Richardson. On vacation one time, visiting a friend out in Green Bay, she met my father and they got married. She spent the rest of her life in Green Bay, virtually all of it. My great-grandfather had come out from New Jersey and cleared a cedar swamp and started truck gardens. They raised garden truck and bought from farmers around there and shipped to northern Wisconsin and the northern peninsula of Michigan. They supplied hotels, restaurants, and grocery stores and they ran a grocery store in Green Bay. They went broke during the Depression.

There were three kids. I was the second son. My brother, Art, is still alive. He lives in the Bronx, and I guess he is retired. My brother never went to college. He had fun in high school, dating the French teacher and that sort of thing, and didn't bother reading any books. So eventually, well, my father said, "Look, for gosh sakes, either you do something or you go to work." So Art went to work on the hometown newspaper. He was a newspaperman all of his life. He was essentially a rewrite man and worked all the papers—Chicago, Milwaukee, Detroit, St. Louis, and New York. In New York he did rod and gun for the *Daily News* and for the *Herald Tribune*. That was his last newspaper job. He is a bit more than a year older than I am. We had a little sister, Catherine. She died of tuberculosis at about nineteen, while I was in college.

My parents read all the time. They weren't scholars or anything, but they were literate and there were books in the house. I remember bookcases with the glass doors in front. I read everything in the house. Corny 1910 romances entitled *The Long Straight Road*, and *When Knighthood Was in Flower*. Everything that was there, I read.

I was a real dedicated small-boy baseball fan up to World War I. Let's see, I was nine when World War I started and the Wisconsin-Illinois League folded about that time. For years I tried never to miss a game when the Green Bay team played at home. Casey Stengel won the batting championship that year. He played for Aurora, Illinois. I don't remember Stengel, but I can still almost recite the lineup of the Green Bay team of 1912 or 1914, whatever year Casey won the championship. I remember George Mollwitz, the Green Bay first baseman. I met him many years later in Bradenton, Florida. Somehow, all old ball players go to Bradenton. Mollwitz had a cup of coffee with the Cincinnati Reds, so he'd be in the record books.

And, of course, I played all sports. Everybody did. We played football and baseball on our lawn and we tried to take a clothes pole and vault, the way all kids do. But I never had any proficiency in sports. I learned to swim and loved it. Pretty early in life I learned to enjoy fishing, which is still my dodge. If I'm a participant in any recreation, it's fishing.

I was always out in the woods, just a kid playing along the creek. I remember meeting a young man who was fly-casting. I had never seen a fly rod before, or anyone casting flies. He was about five years older and turned out to be a very amiable guy. He taught me how to cut a willow branch and make a very poor fly rod out of it and cast for chubs and minnows in the stream. He became a hero of mine. His name was Vince Engel. He was going to Notre Dame, studying journalism, and therefore I felt it was necessary for me to do the same. That was great. I'd be like him. And of course, later I realized that sitting on my duff pounding a typewriter was a pretty easy way to make a living. It seemed very attractive, a lot better than lifting things.

I remember one day in high school I had a Notre Dame catalogue which I was studying, and a senior who was going to go to

Notre Dame borrowed it from me. This was Jimmy Crowley, the left halfback on the Four Horsemen. He was a year ahead of me and a big football star, and I remember him borrowing it. He didn't need a catalogue because some old Notre Damer was sending him to Rockne. But he was interested in looking at it.

I stayed out of school for one year—between high school and college—simply to get a few hundred bucks because we had no money. I was an order clerk, filled orders for the Morley-Murphy-Olfell Hardware Company in Green Bay, not a very responsible job. I scuffled my way through Notre Dame. I got a job waiting on tables in a restaurant in South Bend. I borrowed money from a cousin. I contrived this and that. I got involved in class politics and, by chance, belonged to the winning party which elected the class president, and so on. As a reward for my political activities I got elected editor of the *Dome* and that was worth five hundred bucks.

I took a general arts course with a major in journalism. The journalism school consisted of one man, a darling old guy, Dr. John Cooney. I hadn't written very much. I did write an essay in high school, when I was a senior, that was published in the annual, some silly little thing. If I remember correctly, and I do, it was about the debating team. It was supposed to be a humorous sketch. God, I'd hate to read that today. Then I worked a little bit on what they called the Notre Dame *Daily,* which came out two or three times a week. I probably did fragments of news. But I didn't work there very long, because it was a dull operation.

I knew Rockne, of course, but whether he knew me I don't know. I tried to run on his track team. He was the track coach as well as the football coach. He coached pretty near everything when I was at Notre Dame.

In order to graduate we were supposed to have one credit in physical education, which really meant that once or twice a week you went to gym class and took calisthenics unless you did something else. And that something else could be participation in any sport. You were excused from gym class for the season of your sport, if you participated.

I loathed this gym class and didn't like the instructor. He was a senior trackman who just said, "Up, down! Up, down! C'mon there, Smith, get the lead out!" and so I signed up for freshman track. I don't think I had any misconceptions about my speed. I tried to run the mile because I knew I couldn't run very fast. I thought maybe I could run long. But I was mistaken about that, too. For just a few weeks I trained with the track team. I remember the freshman-varsity handicap meet came along, starting the indoor season, and I finished last in the mile, that's last among many. Paul Kennedy, who was an upperclassman and the star miler, went in 4:21, which sounds slow, but this was a dirt track, twelve laps to the mile, and 4:21 was a fast mile in that day, on that track. I was many laps behind. I never did any sportswriting at Notre Dame, not even in the annual where you sum up the football season and so on.

When I finished at Notre Dame I wrote about—now I say a hundred—but maybe it was only fifty letters to newspapers I got out of the Ayers Directory. I got my first job on the Milwaukee *Sentinel*. That was in the summer of '27. I was a cub reporter, chasing fire engines. I didn't do much. I was mostly being used to cover conventions, speeches, luncheons, and dinners. Every once in a while I'd be the ninth guy covering a murder investigation and it was pretty exciting. It was a morning paper and I'd be up all night. I didn't get off until midnight. These were Prohibition times, and I'd go down into the Italian ward where they had speakeasies and nightclubs with three-piece combos and canaries. Those were the people I knew. And I thought it was the most exciting thing in the world.

I was being promised raises but still getting twenty-four dollars a week, and then I moved to St. Louis. A guy who had been on the *Sentinel* had gone to the St. Louis *Star,* and he wrote a letter back to the makeup editor at the *Sentinel* which said, "Come on down, they're looking for people." He was really looking for friends to join him. The makeup editor had a divorce case coming up and couldn't leave the state, so he showed me the letter. And I wired the *Star,* faking it, advertising myself as an all-around newspaperman with complete experience—and got an offer of forty dollars a week on the copy desk. I was terrified but I took it.

That fall the managing editor, a man named Frank Taylor, fired two guys in the sports department, and he came over to me on the copy desk and he said, "Did you ever work in sports?"

And I said, "No."

"Do you know anything about sports?"

And I said, "Just what the average fan knows."

"They tell me you're very good on football."

"Well, if you say so."

And he said, "Are you honest? If a fight promoter offered you ten dollars would you take it?"

I said, "Ten dollars is a lot of money."

And he said, "Report to the sports editor Monday."

I stayed in sports about four years. Then I moved back to the local side, doing rewrite and general reporting. This was an exciting time. A lot of things were happening in St. Louis. Roosevelt had been elected and in his first message to Congress he said, "Bring back beer" and they brought it back, in about June. For months I wrote nothing but beer. It was a running story.

Beer was one of the big industries in St. Louis. I was always interviewing Gus Busch and Alvin Griesedick. I lived in the breweries in those days, doing stories such as should the alcohol content of beer be 3.2 by volume or by weight? Anheuser-Busch is almost a city by itself down in South St. Louis. The night beer came back—you wouldn't believe it. Several hundred guests were invited to the bottling plant which had a big bar, a rathskeller sort of place. Thousands of St. Louisans jammed the streets, dancing and singing and celebrating the end of Prohibition. At 12:01 the first bottle came down the conveyor and everybody got Gussie Busch to autograph the label.

I had been Walter W. Smith in the sports department, but I was anonymous ninety-nine percent of the time on the news side. Everybody was, except Harry T. Brundage, our star reporter. He was the crime chaser and glamor boy. If Frank Taylor, the managing editor, felt very indulgent he might give you an occasional by-line. I remember seeing a note he wrote to the city desk, advising that I be sent to interview George M. Cohan, and it said, "If he writes a good story give him a by-line."

One time Taylor called me over and said, "I want you to go out in the sticks and get some old lady, some old doll who has never been to a city, who has never seen an electric light. Bring her to town as our guest. Get an old guy if you have to, but preferably get a woman."

I had just read a story about a strike of tiffminers in a place called Old Mines, Missouri, in the foothills of the Ozarks. This was an area settled by the French at about the same time the fur traders were coming up from New Orleans and settling St. Louis. These tiffminers were completely isolated—only I had read a travel piece about how the hard road had just come into Old Mines.

My wife and I drove to Old Mines. It wasn't more than seventy-five miles out of St. Louis. I went to strike headquarters there and told the guys what I wanted, and they said I should go see old Lady Tygert, in Callico Creek Hollow. Susan Tygert. I found this old lady smoking a corncob pipe and wearing a black sunbonnet and living in a one-room shack with her husband, John. She was seventy-nine or eighty, at the least, and had never been out of Callico Creek Hollow. She had never ridden in an automobile, never turned on an electric light, had never used the telephone.

I had a hell of a time getting her to come to St. Louis. She liked my wife, and besides, I promised she could ride on a Mississippi riverboat. She wasn't in St. Louis more than four or five days, and every day I wrote a story about her. I took her to the zoo and to places like the Statler Roof, where there was dancing and a show. She was charming and colorful, smoking that corncob pipe and wearing that black sunbonnet. Everybody was daffy about her. The stories got a warm response.

But O. K. Bovard, who was the managing editor of the St. Louis *Post-Dispatch*—the rival paper—read them and said, "It's a movie scenario." Bovard simply decided I was a faker, had faked the whole thing.

A little while after that Ed Wray, the sports editor of the *Post-Dispatch,* made me an offer. But first I had to go see Bovard and he wouldn't see me. I could have gone to work there, anyway, but I decided even if I could beat down his resistance it would be unwise to be working for a managing editor who was convinced I was a faker.

I went to the Philadelphia *Record* instead and stayed there ten years, all in sports, covering the Phillies and Connie Mack's A's.

In those days New York dominated the newspaper business, far more than it does today. The big papers were all here, the headquarters of the syndicates, the magazines, the book publishers, everybody so far as paper and ink was concerned. I had to take my shot at it. It was the pure ham in me, I guess. It was like playing the Palace.

I got my shot on V-J Day. I had heard Stanley Woodward was after me—he was the sports editor of the New York *Herald Tribune.* Early in 1945, during the first few weeks of the baseball season, an old friend of mine, Garry Schumacher, a New York baseball writer, said to me, "Have you heard from Stanley Woodward?"

I said he had called the other day, but I was out and when I called back he was out. I thought he wanted to know how old Connie Mack was, or something, you know, for a story. And Garry said, "Well, get plenty. He's coming after you."

I waited all summer and I never heard a sound out of Stanley, and I was dying. Finally, the morning after V-J Day, he called. We dickered and then we made a deal. It wasn't to write a column. He just hired me to work in the sports department, to take assignments, but he told me later he hoped I would wind up doing a column. I came over on September 24, 1945, one day before my fortieth birthday. Stanley lied to the *Tribune* about my age. He told them I was in my early thirties.

When I first knew Stanley as a casual press box acquaintance, I guess I resented him a little bit. He was an iconoclast. He was never one to accept the handout. He wanted to know himself. Also, during the war he was dead against sports. He felt games were nonessential and that we all should be fighting the war, that there shouldn't be a sports page, no baseball or horse racing, not even football—and he loved football. Well, of course, there shouldn't be necktie salesmen or florists or any of the nonessential industries, if you're fighting an all-out, one hundred percent war. I disagreed with him. I felt there was some morale value to games.

He was perhaps the most thoroughly competent, all-around newspaperman I've known, a fine reporter, a great editor, a man who could do anything on the paper. He would have been a great managing editor. But he was impolitic and absolutely refused to compromise. He got fired for telling Mrs. Reid that she didn't know anything about running a newspaper.

Soon after he hired me there was an economy wave on the paper and he was ordered to cut two people from his staff, two older men who were near retirement. He said, "Give me some time and I'll arrange their retirement and we won't fire anybody."

But they said, "No, you've got to do it right now."

He refused. He lost his temper and said, "All right then, fire Smith and Woodward."

In those days they had all sorts of forms for the personnel department—added to payroll, substratcted from payroll, and so on. He got one of these payroll forms, for dismissal, listing reasons from one to ten and he wrote "Incompetence" and sent it through and that night, down in the office saloon, he told me, with great glee, what he had done.

The last straw was the silliest thing in the world. *The New York Times,* which in those days had an awful lot of space, had a banner on one of the inside pages on a women's golf tournament in Westchester. It wasn't of interest to anybody but the players, but some of Mrs. Reid's Westchester friends were offended because the *Tribune* didn't carry anything about the tournament, and she raised cain.

So Stanley investigated, found it was a weekly tournament and would require so much space to publish the results. He wrote a very snotty memo to this effect to Mrs. Reid and said if she insisted on him wasting space and effort on this tripe he wanted two additional columns of space for the sports section. He also told her he wouldn't insult one of his staff members by sending him on such an assignment. He would send a copyboy. She lost her temper and had him fired.

Stanley was a great man, and a great newspaperman and was always trying to put out the best section possible. Once, after he had left the paper, I tried to explain this to Mrs. Reid. I told her, "Didn't you understand, he was fighting with you to help improve your paper?"

But she simply fluttered. She just said something fluttery. I didn't know what the hell she was talking about.

Unlike the normal pattern, I know I have grown more liberal as I've grown older. I have become more convinced that there is room for improvement in the world. I seem to be finding this a much less pretty world than it seemed when I was younger, and I feel things should be done about it and that sports are part of this world. Maybe I'm sounding too damn profound or maybe I'm taking bows when I shouldn't. I truly don't know. But I do know I am more liberal and probably one of the reasons is that I married not only Phyllis, who is younger and more of today than I was, but I married five stepchildren who are very much of the current generation. They are very good friends and very articulate, and I think that this association has helped me to have a younger and fresher view.

My sympathies almost always have been on the side of the underdog, or the guy I think is the underdog. There was a time when I was more inclined to go along with the establishment. It may be because I'm no longer traveling with a baseball club and no longer exposed to the establishment day in and day out. I supported the players this past season when they went on that historic thirteen-day strike. Now that I do a column, I can stand there, a little removed, and look at what the Charlie Finleys and Bowie Kuhns are doing.

When I first heard about Marvin Miller—the players' man—I didn't hear anything favorable. I heard complaints from owners and club executives about how these ball players were putting themselves into the hands of a bloody labor organizer, a steel mill guy. I remember hearing one player, Dick Groat, saying he was in Pittsburgh and how he saw some of the results of union operations and that he wasn't in favor of it. He voted against employing Miller, as some other ball players did.

Then I began to hear that Miller is a pretty smart guy, seems like a very nice guy. The owners and the hierarchy, like the league presidents and such, were beginning to be very discreet in their remarks about Marvin. I had never met him until the winter baseball meetings in Mexico City, in 1968. I introduced myself. Since then, when there has been a newsworthy dispute in baseball—and there have been a lot of them—I have found I get straighter answers from Marvin than from anyone else I know in baseball. I have yet to find any trace of evidence that he's ever told me an untruth.

There have been times when he has said, "I think I had better not talk about that now," which is understandable. I don't doubt for a moment that he knows he's talking for publication and he's going to tell me what he thinks will look good on his side of the argument. But as far as I know, it's the absolute truth. More honest than most. Sports promoters find lying to the press is part of their business. They have no hesitation at all about it.

This generally applies across the board. I was going to say it also includes league presidents, but I would hate to think of Chub

Feeney lying. I think Joe Cronin would avoid a fact now and then, or evade one. As for the present commissioner, Bowie Kuhn, he doesn't tell you anything so I don't know whether he lies or not. But the sportswriter learns to adjust, to make allowances. When you're listening to these people, who are serving special interests, you simply adjust by taking a little off the top.

Over the years, of course, all sportswriters, especially those assigned to and traveling with ball clubs, have difficulties with a ball player, or ball players. I never had anything as crucial as an actual fist fight, but I did have some differences with Bill Werber. This was when I was in Philadelphia and when he was traded or sold. The A's sent him to the Cincinnati Reds, and when the deal was announced I think I probably wrote something to the general effect of "Good riddance." I'm not sure. I didn't care deeply for Bill. I thought he paraded his formal education. He was out of Duke, you know, and he used to correct the grammar of other ball players. There were things about Bill that didn't enchant me.

In 1939 the Reds were in the World Series—that was the year the Yankees won in four straight and when big Ernie Lombardi wound up sprawled out at the plate. When we got to Cincinnati for the third game I went down to the bench before the game, and my old friend Paul Derringer said, "Hello, Red, you know Bill Werber, don't you?"

And Werber said, "Yes, I know the sonofabitch."

It went on, a tiny few exchanges like that, and then he said, "Get off this bench! Get out of the dugout!"

I said, "No, I'm a guest here."

And he got up and shouldered me out of the dugout, just kind of strongarmed me out. I had my portable and I was strongly tempted to let him have it—with the typewriter. But I somehow didn't feel like doing that on the field before the first World Series game in Cincinnati and so I left.

I remember Charlie Dexter coming along behind me and he said, "What are you going to do? Are you going to protest to the Baseball Writers Association?"

And I said, "No, Charlie, the player doesn't like me."

I didn't speak to him again. And then one day I was in Washington, in the National Press Building. I was on the elevator going to the Press Club and a most successful-looking insurance salesman carrying a briefcase, well dressed, got aboard and said, "Hello, Susie," to the elevator operator.

And I said, "Hello, Bill," and we shook hands. It had been at least ten years.

When Curt Flood sued baseball, Bill wrote me a letter. He was absolutely against Flood's suit and wrote disagreeing with something I had written in a column. Bill said that Curt Flood, with his limited education, was doing better than he had any right to expect.

I wrote back one letter saying that Flood had more ability and character than a great many educated men. I was trying to put Bill down. But he quickly responded with further argument which I didn't bother to answer. I didn't want to become his pen pal.

I won't deny that the heavy majority of sportswriters, myself included, have been and still are guilty of puffing up the people they write about. I remember one time when Stanley Woodward, my beloved leader, was on the point of sending me a wire during spring training, saying, "Will you stop Godding up those ball players?" I didn't realize what I had been doing. I thought I had been writing pleasant little spring training columns about ball players.

If we've made heroes out of them, and we have, then we must also lay a whole set of false values at the doorsteps of historians and biographers. Not only has the athlete been blown up larger than life, but so have the politicians and celebrities in all fields, including rock singers and movie stars.

When you go through Westminster Abbey you'll find that excepting for that little Poets' Corner almost all of the statues and memorials are to killers. To generals and admirals who won battles, whose specialty was human slaughter. I don't think they're such glorious heroes.

I've tried not to exaggerate the glory of athletes. I'd rather, if I could, preserve a sense of proportion, to write about them as excellent ball players, first-rate players. But I'm sure I have contributed to false values—as Stanley Woodward said, "Godding up those ball players."

John R. Tunis

John Robert Tunis, who died in 1975 at the age of eighty-five, was America's most misunderstood sportswriter. The assumption was that his books were juveniles, harmless fluff in the manner of Frank Merriwell. The opposite was true. The heroes in the vast Tunis library are not the winners, but the losers. Mr. Tunis repeatedly emphasized that the outcome of a football game, or a track meet, was of secondary and brief significance. Sports are and should be fun, he insisted, but nothing more. Only a fool swallows the guff that football coaches mold character or that the Battle of Waterloo was won on the playing fields of Eton.

Mr. Tunis's father was an Episcopalian-Unitarian minister. His mother, widowed early, was a woman of rare energy and stern resolve who taught in the Boston public schools by day and gave John and his younger brother, Robert, Latin lessons at night. From the beginning, Mr. Tunis warned against the rise of professionalism in sports, insisting that monetary rewards would weaken and eventually deaden the joy of amateur participation. He often strayed from sports, attacking pomposity, prejudice, and other symptoms of social corruption. Was College Worthwhile?, *a searing assault on Harvard traditions published in 1936, was a best-seller.*

A tireless freelance, Mr. Tunis's only major newspaper connection was with the New York Post. *He covered court games for* The New Yorker, *and wrote hundreds of magazine stories and forty-one books, up to* Grand National, *published in 1973. Tall and tweedy, Mr. Tunis played tennis until eighty, when he won the men's doubles championship at the Old Lyme Country Club. He lived on an acre in Essex, Connecticut, with his wife of fifty years. He expressed delight that 86 percent of the Harvard class of 1972 graduated with honors. "I'd rather see that," he said, "than a winning football team."*

Sports is the great opium of the people. It has become an addiction. It has made them forget more important things. Politics, for one thing. Look at how 47 million people voted for Nixon, but only 27 million for McGovern. Well, that's all you need to say. People should think more. People are more concerned with sports than politics, and this is just the reverse of what it should be.

Losing is the great American sin. Nobody likes to lose. Certainly, I never saw anybody who likes to lose. But the American athletes hate to lose more than anybody, especially those in the Olympic Games. My heroes are the losers. All my books have been in that vein. Every book I've ever written.

I'm writing a story now for *Boys' Life* which is going to be called "When They Separate the Men from the Boys." It's about a football team, a very strong team, a great team from this academy. They haven't lost a game in three or four years, and they play this small high school team and expect to win easily.

But this raggedy high school team comes up and beats the life out of them. It isn't the customary thing, is it? The academy players come into the locker room all discouraged and beaten. You know how it is when a team is beaten. And while they're in the locker room a fire starts at the bottom of the building, sweeps up a stairwell. And that's when this kid who has fumbled a punt, that's when he makes good—during the fire. He leads everybody to safety. He was a loser on the football field, wasn't he? But actually he's a winner. Football isn't life. It's a game.

I've always believed Little League is harmful to the extreme. It's for the parents, and that's what I object to. The adults take over. I don't like the idea of having little boys playing in front of their parents and friends. Little boys should be playing their sports by themselves. But we dress them up in football and baseball uniforms. Now I understand it's spread to hockey and basketball. They're professionals in miniature, at the age of ten.

These boys can't grow up and understand the enjoyment of simply playing. When a boy is told, by his coach or his parent, that it's important for him to scoot for a touchdown, or to score a run, can he get anything out of the game? It takes the sport out of it. There's too much pressure on them to succeed. The Little League coaches are also prisoners. They feel they have to win.

There's too damn much organization. I think it's pretty well true in everything. We're overorganized in this country. I'm glad I grew up when I did. Damn right. When I was a boy we played in the backyard. I never felt any pressure. I never had a uniform, not of any kind.

I wrote a book about this once, thirty years ago. Never heard a word from anybody. I could see what was coming.

Sports can be derogatory, hurt a boy a great deal. This training, this competition. The competition is bad for most boys, especially for the boys who don't win. Some boys never get over their failures at athletics. It's a rather sad thing.

I never dropped a punt, as a boy. Well, I suppose I did, but it left no scar, or things of that sort. I just understood the loser is the same as the winner, except that he's the unlucky one. The loser is just as talented as the winner. There is such a thin line between winning and losing. Yet the laurels only go to the winner. The rush is always to the champion.

Sports was more beneficial years ago. There weren't so many rewards, so many prizes. The athlete was in it more for the love of the game, and you got a reward for participating. Sports has changed more than most things in this country. There never were monetary rewards in many cases where there are now.

We read about ball players getting salaries of $100,000 and $200,000 a year. It's wasted on them. I don't know who should get the money, but I know they shouldn't. I'd rather see it go to some schoolteacher, some librarian, or somebody who isn't known to everybody, somebody who isn't in the mainstream. I know many, many teachers who deserve it more than the athletes.

I've always felt this way. In a sense, an extremely small sense, I've tried to fight this thing, to go against the so-called American grain of winning at all costs. But you can't reverse the trend. Certainly, I didn't.

The whole damn society is too competitive. I've been a winner myself. I've got a box full of nice stocks and bonds and all that sort of thing to prove it. I've always felt somewhat guilty about it, that you have to beat the other fellow. But age has blunted my competitive desire. Nature took care of that at the age of seventy. At eighty you're out of the picture.

I have written forty books. I'm now finishing my forty-first book. I suppose you can say, with all these books, I've tried to teach. But like most teachers nobody listens to what you say. Damn few.

A good many years ago Horace Taft called me up and said, "John, c'mon down and have lunch with us."

I said, "All right, Uncle Horace," and we made a date.

He was the head of the Taft School, in Watertown, and I went up there and he said, "John, tell me, you've been fighting this professionalism now for a long while. You said the players were all professionals and the colleges have been bribing them to play. Tell me the truth. Has it ever done any good?"

I said, "No, not the slightest good in the world. Hasn't had any effect at all."

He was surprised.

But once in a while I do get a letter from somebody who sees through it. But very rarely. They'll write, "Yes, I understand."

I receive about a hundred letters a year, mostly from young

people. This has been a sufficient reward. The first thing I do every morning is to sit down and answer my correspondence. I've corresponded with some people longer than twenty years.

Here, this letter came last week:

Dear Mr. Tunis:

I am sixteen years old and perhaps not a very good judge of literature. But again I may be as good as anyone else I know. I read one of your books the other night, *His Enemy, His Friend,* and I thought it was damn good. I just want to thank you for an evening of enjoyable reading.

He wrote that from his heart, you know.

Here are some others:

Dear Mr. Tunis:

I love your books. I've read nine of your books. All of them are very exciting. I am now reading *His Enemy, His Friend.* All of them are realistic and fun to read.

Yours truly. May I have an autographed picture of you?

Dear Mr. Tunis:

I like your book *The Kid Comes Back.* How did you get the idea of writing about Roy Tucker? I also liked Scott, Jim, John, and Erroll. Were they true characters? The most interesting part was the scene when Roy caught the pennant for his team. I enjoyed the book because it was about a real person.

From kids. I've been getting letters like that for years.

I've never been interviewed before. No, that's not true. A year ago a kid from Austin, Texas, called me on the telephone. His mother was on the telephone with him. I couldn't understand her very well but finally I gathered that she wanted him to interview me. So I said, "Sure."

She gave the kid the phone and he came on and, of course, asked some stupid questions. "Who's your favorite player? Who do you like the best?" The whole thing lasted about ten minutes. He was going to do a story on this interview for some high school magazine. I asked him if he would send me a copy of this thing when the story came out. He said he would. He promised. But he never did.

John F. Kennedy read my stories, as a boy. I remember once I was in his home. His father, Joe Kennedy, had roomed across the hall from me at Harvard. Joe was in the class of 1912. Nice fellow. He roomed with Bob Fisher, captain of the football team. Joe wasn't good enough to make the football team, but he did play on the baseball team. He was a left-handed first baseman.

Joe invited us to dinner one night, down at the Cape. I don't remember the occasion. Joe was his expansive self. He and Rose, Mrs. Kennedy, were very hospitable and that sort of thing. Johnny was maybe five or six years old, about this high. He was reading then, a precocious kid. He had been naughty and his father was angry, about to punish him. And Joe said, "You do that again, Johnny, and I won't allow you to read any more of Mr. Tunis's books." And Johnny ran upstairs, crying.

Joe Kennedy was a wonderful man. Of course, Joe was a winner but I liked him anyway. He was nice to me and a personal friend. If he hadn't been I don't suppose I would have admired him. I owe Joe a great deal. I was trying to do an announcing job for NBC, on some tennis matches, the Davis Cup, Wimbledon. I had to see John Royal, who was then the general manager, but I couldn't get in to see him. He was always busy.

I happened to run into Joe somewhere and asked him a favor, if he'd call up and arrange things. I've never told this story before. Joe picks up the phone and calls John Royal and says, "Won't you see John Tunis?" and Royal says "Why not?"

About a year ago I saw Teddy Kennedy, the youngest. This was at a woman's house near here, at a rally. I was introduced to him and I said, "I roomed across the hall from your father at Harvard."

And he said, "Oh, did you?"

And I said, "Yes."

That's all there was to it.

There was a time when I was Public Enemy Number One at Harvard. It was when I wrote a book called *Was College Worthwhile?* It wasn't a sports book. Many of my books were not on sports. Anyway, when the book came out all the people at Harvard, my so-called friends, told me I was a no-good sonofabitch.

The book showed that the fellows who went to Harvard didn't necessarily know anything, do anything, or think anything. I said

Harvard was a lousy place. You never get an education there. Things like that. I said the Harvard students had three ambitions—to break 80 at golf, to vote the Republican ticket, and to get a Harvard degree.

The year before the book was published, in 1936, was the twenty-fifth reunion of my class. I was at a class meeting that year, one of those Harvard Club dinners in Boston, and one of my classmates made some rather vicious remarks about Franklin Delano Roosevelt. During this speech—they were God-damning him, the whole bunch, and I stood up and called out "Hooray for Roosevelt!" They didn't like it very well. They shouted me down, all except one fellow who did agree with me. But he was so frightened he didn't say anything. Poor fellow.

They were convinced, of course, that Roosevelt was a traitor. But it depends how you look at him. He was our greatest President. He saved the capitalistic system. The very people he saved were his greatest enemies.

When my book came out I wrote a little note to Roosevelt. I said, "You may be interested in knowing you were the most hated man by the class of 1911, but you have been pushed out of first place by yours truly." And I enclosed a copy of the book and said, "This will give you a good laugh."

And he wrote and said, "It not only gave me a good laugh but a horse laugh."

I still have the letter. It's up there on the wall.

When I was a boy Roosevelt stayed at our house. My mother kept a boarding house in Boston. She was a remarkable woman, great determination and courage. I wrote a whole book about her. She was left a widow with two children, ages six and seven. She taught for thirty-five years in the public schools in Boston. I do think that's quite a feat. The public schools in Boston were very rough.

She kept a boarding house for Harvard students for a year or two. Roosevelt was among them. I have no recollection of him, and my mother didn't say much about him except that she disliked him. He was one of those rich boys. He boarded with us when he was a freshman. He complained that we were too far from the campus, that it was too long a walk for the students. He actively led the other students out of our house, a minor rebellion of a sort, I guess. When the students decided to go somewhere else, my mother was through running a boarding house.

I don't know why, really, but I have always had this feeling the world is unfairly situated in regard to individuals. Often, if a person has got a nice smile, or a nice dimple, or a nice this or that, that fellow will get ahead where someone else won't. But I think the fellow with the nice smile and so forth is really very much handicapped, like a rich man's son is handicapped. The percentage of rich men's sons who succeed is comparatively small. They have to become competitive.

I've always admired a rich man's son who gets ahead. They go to good schools, have the best of education, the best of health, everything, and they're competing with you fellows. As a rule the fellows without these gifts, if you want to call them that, make the bigger gains.

My father was a poor minister. He came from a wealthy family, lived in a big house on Twentieth Street in New York, but his father cut him off without a nickle. His family, particularly his father, raised holy hell when he married my mother. They were against the marriage because my mother had come from a family with no social standing. Her father was a waiter. My grandfather—that is, my paternal grandfather—didn't want his son marrying the daughter of a waiter. My father was disowned. It wasn't until I was ten years old, or so, that I met anybody from my father's family.

I had a happy boyhood. I was born in Cambridge, Massachusetts, on Pearl Harbor Day, 1891. No, I'm cheating on two years. It was 1889. This was in the period before Americans had forgotten to use their legs. We were very much governed by the fact we didn't have a car. Nobody had a car. Only rich people.

I went to the Cambridge Latin School and then to Harvard. My mother, being the widow of a minister, did have some connections, and I'm sure she got me in at a cut rate. We always seemed to get a cut rate. Recently, somebody asked me what I majored in at Harvard. I had to laugh. You didn't major in anything in those days. I told him, "My dear boy, I had no intentions. No intentions at all. You just got through."

I didn't play on any of the teams at Harvard. I wasn't good enough, but I did come close. Well, I ran a little on the track team and played some tennis, but this wasn't at the varsity level. I ran the two-mile. There wasn't much competition at the distance. My best time was 10:58.

After graduation I did some work in a cotton mill in Newburyport, the home of John Marquand. I tended a yarn machine. Worked there for several years, and then I went off into the service. I was in France, in a field artillery outfit, but I didn't do anything, really. I was an officer but not a very good one. I wasn't one of the spit-and-polish boys.

I wrote letters home to my mother every day and I suppose this was the start of me as a writer. My mother took one of my letters, about an air raid in Paris, and brought it to the Boston *Transcript* and it was published. It ran a whole column. I was delighted.

I returned home after the war and did nothing, really. Then my wife, Lucy, and I decided we should go back to Europe. I had an aunt who had left me eight hundred dollars, and we decided we'd stay as long as we could. By this time I had written a few stories for the *Lawn Tennis Magazine*. I called them before we left and they indicated they might publish some stories on European tennis but offered no guarantee.

Only a fool would have gone over there the way I did. But Lucy and I had a wonderful time. We spent the summer on the Riviera, and being a tennis player of sorts, I would enter a few of the local tournaments. Every week there was a different tournament. I wasn't that good, but there were times when I survived the first or second round.

Once, in the finals of a doubles tournament, I played against King Gustaf V of Sweden, who at that time was about seventy years old. He played on a dime, hugged the net, and usually had the best possible partner. On another occasion I even had the good fortune of playing Madame Suzanne Lenglen in a doubles match, in a tournament at Beaulieu. She was then the champion of France and had won several All-England titles at Wimbledon.

This was in the summer of 1921 and that winter I returned to Boston, and, as usual, was short of cash. For years I was short of cash. I went to the office of the Boston *Globe* to see Lawrence Winship, who had just been promoted to Sunday editor. Winship and I had been classmates at Harvard, and he had bought a few pieces from me.

We sat and visited. I mentioned that I had played Madame Lenglen. He was startled.

"You mean you played her?"

"Yes."

"Sit down and give us a piece."

"Now?"

"Of course, now. Why wait?"

I don't believe I ever knew such panic. I had never written under the pressure of a deadline before. For the first half-hour I didn't know what to do. I thought everyone in the office was watching. Then, I went out on the fire escape, leaned over the railing, and threw up. I'll never forget it. I wiped my face with my copy paper. But I did the story.

I was a great admirer of Madame Lenglen. She was a woman of great integrity and the best woman tennis player I ever saw. By all odds. She was not just a tennis player, any more than Picasso is just a painter. I saw many great women tennis players, but there was only one Suzanne. She wasn't a beautiful woman, not in the usual sense by which we seem to measure beauty. But I once saw her enter a Riviera drawing room full of exquisitely dressed women, and suddenly they all became commonplace and dowdy.

I always thought it was just as well not to make friends with the players. When you become friendly you inevitably tend to write something favorable about them. I knocked almost everybody I became friendly with—Bill Tilden, Helen Wills Moody, Lenglen, all of them. I can't recall why. I don't have my scrapbooks. I'm sure they would tell me. I had to send all my scrapbooks to Boston University. It was the only place that would take them.

And of course, when you criticize an athlete, or write anything they don't regard as totally complimentary, they don't like it. This can rather strain friendship. Oh, I've had two or three of these athletes threaten to punch me in the nose. They always threaten. Don't you find that? But they never do. Nobody came close.

Bill Tilden was arrogant as hell. That's what I didn't like about him, his general deportment. He could be very nice to people, if he wanted to be. He knew who I was, of course, but he didn't take much notice of me. He was busy going his way, you know. But I remember one crossing to England, on the *Olympic*. We sat down in the grand salon and he talked, quite friendly. We had a nice two-hour conversation. He unburdened himself. He talked with the greatest of freedom. He was extremely pleasant.

Eventually I became a full-time freelancer and began selling to magazines. In those days it wasn't as difficult as it is today. There were dozens of magazines that would buy your stuff. I got to know Harold Ross when he was the editor of the *American Legion Monthly.* When he started *The New Yorker* I went around to see him and asked if there was anything I could do. "Sure," he said. He was bringing fellows in, and he hired me to do a weekly sports column, but I did more than that. I did profiles, reporter-at-large, that sort of thing.

This was in the middle twenties when *The New Yorker* was just starting. One day I didn't get my check and I went in to see Ross. I was getting fifty dollars a week for the sports column. Ross said the magazine didn't have much money and told me he would pay me in stock. I went over to the Harvard Club for lunch and ran into Frank Crowninshield. We had been bunkmates in the army. He was then editor of *Vanity Fair.*

Frank put his arm around me and said, "My boy, if you take stock from *The New Yorker,* you'll be very, very wrong. They haven't got the money to last."

I said, "Is that so?"

And he said, "Yes, that's so."

I didn't really need the money but I went back and told Ross I wouldn't take the stock. So he gave me a check. It was the biggest financial mistake of my life. If I had taken stock for the next year or two, I'd now have over a thousand shares, after splits and everything. Would have been a millionaire. That's why I never give advice to anybody, even those who seek it. I never tell anybody what or what not to buy.

I was writing feverishly, working ten to twelve hours a day, six days a week. Then one day—it must have been in '27—I got a call from the sports editor of the New York *Post.* He liked some stories I had written and hired me to do three stories a week on anything I wanted, but usually they were about tennis. On the day I was interviewed I said, "Is Mr. Julian Mason in?"

And, my God, Mason was the great king of everything. He was

the big editor of the *Post* and a Yale man. I've always believed in meeting the top man, going right to the top.

The sports editor said, "Yes, he's in. Do you want to see him?"

I said, "Yes."

He must have thought I was crazy or something. Apparently nobody ever asked to see Mason. But I went up and saw him, and he was very nice and I was very nice. When I came back to the sports department the sports editor hired me at seventy dollars a week, which was a lot of money in those days. I don't think he intended to give me that much. I think I frightened him.

I worked for the *Post* for about fifteen years. Every summer I'd go to Europe and cover the big tennis matches. I've made eighty Atlantic crossings in all. But then the *Post* was sold and they started cutting at the top. I quit and once again put all my time in magazine work.

That's when I was doing my solid dog work, producing an average of two books a year, and in addition I was doing a hell of a lot of magazine writing. I'd write two thousand words a day, sometimes more. I took Sundays off. Played tennis on Sundays. Otherwise I was at the typewriter. I was selling the top markets. I sold the *Saturday Evening Post* dozens of nonfiction stories at the same time I was doing fiction for *Collier's*.

I did my first book between magazine assignments. It was the story of a boy from the Midwest, a scholar-athlete who comes east and gets lost and encounters prejudice in the Harvard social whirl. As I said, I've always been a firm believer in going to the top. I sent the book to Mr. Alfred Harcourt, the founder of Harcourt, Brace. Two weeks later I got a letter from him asking me to come in. He said he liked the book and wanted it to be published as a juvenile, as a book for boys.

I was shocked and disappointed. I didn't know what a juvenile was. But I signed a contract and that book, *The Iron Duke,* won a prize as the best juvenile. And my career took a new direction. I continued writing these so-called boys' books, but I've never considered them that. They can be read by adults. Oh, well, they sold. Harcourt, Brace was surprised as hell and so was I. I've written about twenty of them, and fifteen are still in print. People tell me that the *Kid from Tompkinsville* was the best book. It's still selling. But my best book is *His Enemy, His Friend*. It's not a sports book. It's a war book, about a German soldier in a French town. It has a sports background. But I regard it as more than a sports story.

I've written what I wanted to and tried to explain there is more to life than throwing a football around. You can say that my books have been read, but only by kids, really. Nobody has paid attention. They read, but they don't know what's in it. Still, my books are important to me. They're the most important thing I did. Damn right. There was a time when I expected to do some good. But that was a long while ago.

Jimmy Cannon is probably the best sportswriter this country has ever seen. He's more for the underdog than most people. But most sportswriters are dopes. They get their egos hepped up. They are guilty of overblowing everything. Absolutely. Every game is the most important, most vital, most exciting, most dazzling, most beautiful they've ever seen.

Some of them say this through necessity. If they admit many of the games and the athletes are dull, they're fearful of losing their jobs. But they're wrong. They should write what they feel, what they know. But I suppose the spectators, the fans, don't want to be told, either. They may not like it if you tell them sports is unimportant. I understand some sportswriters are trying to do this, that this is the new trend. Good. But it's taken a hell of a long time.

I just sent the proofs back this morning on my latest book, *The Grand National*. I don't know why, but I just wanted to write it. I think it's my forty-first book. I doubt I'll do another one. I don't have the yen to write at the present. Maybe a year from now it will be different. I'll be eighty-four in December. I've always been busy, and this is the first time I haven't another book to begin. Now I may have time to read Flaubert.

○ ○ ○ ○
○ ○ ○ ○
○ ○ ○ ○

Jimmy Cannon

Jimmy Cannon, who died on December 5, 1973, at the age of sixty-three, was the most distinctive sportswriter of his time, as his big-brother friend Damon Runyon had been in the previous generation. But Mr. Cannon, unlike Runyon, never wrote fiction. He was an essayist, a master of the epigram and the memorable phrase. Though he generally viewed the sporting scene as entertainment, an extension of show business, he was also a vigorous curmudgeon, alert and eager to strike at hypocrisy and social injustice. Only Westbrook Pegler could be said to have had a more penetrating and vivid vocabulary.

A lifelong New Yorker with a passion for Broadway and the big city, Mr. Cannon was born on the Lower West Side, one of three children of a Tammany politician. With no formal education, he was a working reporter, at the Daily News, *at the age of sixteen. He gained a genuine cult of readers, particularly during the twenty-year period from 1940 to 1960 when he was writing syndicated columns for the New York Post and subsequently the Journal-American. He occasionally strayed from sports and covered murder trials, presidential inaugurations, and national political conventions; during most of World War II, he was a correspondent for Stars and Stripes. There are two collections of his work, Nobody Asked Me, But and Who Struck John?*

Mr. Cannon suffered a stroke in May 1971, as he was packing to go to the Kentucky Derby. His left side was paralyzed and he lived his remaining days in a wheelchair, seldom leaving his Fifty-sixth Street apartment, with its floor-to-ceiling bookshelves that included literary classics as well as the Baseball Register and the Ring Record Book. In the year prior to his death there seemed to be a modest Jimmy Cannon revival, sponsored by practitioners of the so-called New Journalism, some of whom insisted they were his progeny. At the conclusion of my interview I asked Mr. Cannon how he would prefer to be remembered. His reply: "He gave us a few laughs."

Today was a big day for me. For the first time I took a leak standing up. Maybe I shouldn't say that. People will think I'm feeling sorry for myself, playing for sympathy. But it was a big day. There are things that happen to you that make you realize that life is not a series of glorious experiences but a chain of small happenings.

Like today. It was the first time since I've been in bed, or in a wheelchair, that I've been out. I have a wonderful man who is taking care of me, named Charles Ford. He took me shopping, to Bloomingdale's. We looked around the town, and then he pushed me in my wheelchair over to Toots Shor's new restaurant. A couple of us sat around and cut up touches, and I was able to go to the men's room and stand and take a leak. And this was a moment of triumph for me, an elation.

You know what's a very important thing in your life but you don't realize it? Posture. I try to sit up straight, but you can't get comfortable in a wheelchair. You keep slipping down, and when you sit in one with your clothes on your fly tightens up. It's just one of those God damned uncomfortable things.

I'll tell you how I found out I was getting old. Or I was old. I was on the train one day with Mickey Mantle and Whitey Ford. I was telling some Lefty Gomez stories, and Mantle looked at me with amazement. It was his first year. He was about eighteen or nineteen, and he says, "Did you see Gomez pitch?"

"Did I see Gomez pitch? I traveled with the ball club when he was pitching. He was my running mate on the road."

Mantle looked at me with great astonishment, and the thing that hit me was that Gomez was about the same age as I am. And I realized he was being regarded by Mantle as I used to listen to Damon Runyon and Warren Brown talk about guys like Moose McCormick and Amos Rusie. They were some guys lost in the fog of time.

Time is a vandal and the young ball players should enjoy what's happening to them today, because a lot of times famous men quit baseball and it's like they fell off the rim of the world into some sort of obscurity.

When I was in the hospital, the greatest pitcher who ever lived came to see me, Waite Hoyt of the Yankees. He was big in New York, like Tom Seaver is today, except that he was pitching on the Babe Ruth ball clubs. And he came to see me in the hospital, still handsome and looking very young, and the only people who recognized his name were guys around seventy years old. And this guy was a legend, not only in New York, but all over the league. He was about sixteen years old when he broke in. He was called the Brooklyn Schoolboy.

I saw Carl Furillo come to Brooklyn. Until Clemente, I didn't know a better right fielder. He was very hard, a very tough guy. He was the working stiff in sports. He played baseball like guys who go to work on a job with a pick and shovel. But he did everything. I watched his career, saw him at the finish, and now Carl Furillo is considered an ancient by most of the young ball writers. Incredible!

Joe Louis was the greatest heavyweight I ever saw, and Ray Robinson the best all-around fighter. Most of the kids reading sports pages today never saw them fight. A sportswriter doesn't realize this. We have a tendency to write about the past, to let time telescope on us. We live through so many generations of ball players, they all get mixed up in our minds. We do not judge time at all. A sportswriter is entombed in a prolonged boyhood.

We were talking about cheering in the press box. It goes on all around the league. It's one of the great boasts of all journalists, and especially baseball writers, that they are not influenced by their relationships with people off the field. This is an absolute myth. I always considered myself a fair and neutral man, and yet how could I not be for Joe DiMaggio, who lived in the same hotel with me? We went on vacations together. We were great friends.

But I never cheered out loud. I've heard guys cheering. Most of them do. They're in every town. Most of the guys traveling with ball clubs are more publicists than reporters. A guy might be traveling with the Cincinnati Reds, though it could be any team, and he refers to the ball club as "we." I've seen sportswriters with World Series rings, and they wear them as though they had something to do with the winning of the World Series. Maybe they're entitled to them. Maybe their biased cheerfulness helped the club. I wouldn't know. I would not wear a World Series ring.

Sportswriting has survived because of the guys who don't cheer. They're the truth-tellers. Lies die. Go into any town where they have placid baseball writing, where they're all for the home team, and you'll find out that in that town baseball is not considered an exciting game. Telling the truth—and writing it with vigor and clarity—that's what makes it exciting.

A guy shouldn't hang out strictly with baseball writers. It gets incestuous. Baseball, that's all you talk about. You close the world out, and the world must be let in. The thing I try to do is get the world in over the bleacher walls. That was my whole idea in sportswriting.

The worst thing a sportswriter can be is a fan. I was never a fan, not since I was in short pants. My great hero in sports, when I was a kid, was Pie Traynor. He played a wonderful third base for the Pittsburgh Pirates and was particularly good against the Giants. I think the name fascinated me. I never heard of a guy called Pie before, except there was a homely girl in our neighborhood who we called Pie-face.

I don't want sportswriters being fans. I want them to be the guys who neither love nor hate the sport and whose life is not wrapped up in the sport and who remember they are working newspapermen and not baseball people. No more than a police reporter is a cop. You hear these guys in press boxes arguing whether it's good for baseball, or bad for baseball, as if they owned the thing. What I care about, what I hope I care about, is, "Is it good for the paper? Is it a good piece?"

We're not like police reporters because the police reporter has to scuffle. Every time a police reporter goes out on a story, it's a new deal. It's a new precinct, new detectives, certainly new criminals. There is no schedule on crime. A guy is hit in the head. There is no spring training for murderers. They don't go south with the club. The muggers don't take infield practice.

The sportswriter is given a reserved seat in the press box, and the ball clubs work to make it easy for him and it gets easier year by year. But as you grow a year older it doesn't seem easier. It gets tougher as you age.

A baseball writer's relationship with a ball player is a cop-and-crook relationship. You're not there as his buddy, as his fan, as his teammate. It's an adversary relationship. A lot of writers think that ball players love them. But ball players are amused by writers and consider them necessary evils. One thing I know about ball players: They never thank you for the praise. But they really complain if you rip them. They think they are entitled to good notices.

I don't agree with the delusion that a baseball writer is similar to the drama critic. The guys who cover the theater don't live with the actors and the actresses. They don't travel with them on the same trains and the same planes and stay in the same hotels. They're not on the road with their subjects. I know some guys, career baseball writers, say they've spent more time with ball players than their own kids.

The drama critic sits back and watches, like we do, but he never goes backstage, or very rarely, and says, "Why did you give a bad performance tonight?" The baseball writer goes to the losers after every game and demands that the athletes discuss their flaws. The baseball writer has it tough. He is many things: part psychiatrist, part stool pigeon, part house detective, part doctor, certainly part friend and enemy. And he is forced to take a game seriously, and you must take it seriously when you realize how much it affects the lives of the guys who are playing it. And it's not, as I've heard said, a children's game. Children play for fun and out of gladness. Professional ball players play for money and for fame. It's a tough hustle at the major league level.

I have never felt any envy toward the ball player. I had a normal childhood of baseball and football, a little basketball. But I never felt bad about not being a good athlete. I would much rather have been Ernest Hemingway than Babe Ruth or Red Grange. Anyway, I've never been a good team man. I don't like partners. I've gone my way by myself, and that's how it figures. The games I was best at were casino and five-card stud.

I remember when Louie Effrat, who is on the *Times,* a good sportswriter, was being interviewed on one of the talk shows here and he said what a great life he'd led and how fortunate he was that he had met all the great athletes of his time. I think the great athletes are fortunate that they met me.

I love the newspaper business. I can't imagine myself doing anything else. I love the pace. It's right now, the immediacy of it. You do it and it's out. You don't have to wait a long time to find out how it hangs together.

I once tried the advertising business. I was a copy writer for a couple of years. After a while I hated the work. I went back to the papers for less money because that was the kind of life I wanted. This was in the thirties, for Lord and Thomas. No, for Arthur Kudner, I think it's folded. I guess I contributed to the folding of it. I did signed ads. They sent me out with a detective to find a brand of car, where it was parked, who owned it. It was like covering a story, or pretending to. It was an advertisement for the sale of a car. I don't remember what car.

Writing is work for me. I hate it. I always hated it. It's a struggle. But I have stretches. Sometimes I'm going good and it flows easily, and sometimes there's a big block there. I can get a column done in two, two and a half hours, but I've labored eight hours on a column, too. Time doesn't seem to improve it, or disfigure it. I can write a story under the gun that is just as good as when I take a long time.

I like writing at home best, but I've written most of my stuff in press boxes. Even though I can ignore them, there are always more distractions in the press box. At home you can shut it all out. I like writing for a deadline, when the press box is good, and when I've got my own typewriter and the distractions aren't great. I like the feel I've got on my own typewriter. I think that the speed at which I write influences the quality, even the thought. The feel of a typewriter is important. A bad typewriter has given me many a bad story. I'll tell what can give me a bad story—stuck keys. It breaks your whole rhythm, your whole chain of thought.

I think the three greatest writers I ever read in newspapers were Ben Hecht, when he was doing a column in Chicago, Westbrook Pegler, and Damon Runyon. Maybe Percy Hammond, too. I didn't know his stuff when he was in Chicago, but I knew it when he was the drama critic on the old *Tribune*. The *Herald Tribune*.

Rebecca West was once quoted by ship-news reporters as saying that I was one of the writers in America she wanted to meet. She is a charming and graceful woman, as interesting as she is a writer. And incidentally, Truman Capote came out with *In Cold Blood* and announced that this was a new form of literature. Rebecca West had been doing that for years. Did you read her piece on Lord Haw Haw? When I named the people I thought wrote very well for newspapers I neglected Miss West because she wrote for English papers and I was talking about American papers. No one in the history of the world ever wrote better than Rebecca West. I'm always burned up at people who say, "That's too good for a newspaper." Nothing is too good for a newspaper.

I've tried. There was a piece the other day written by Jack Newfield. It was a serious piece in which he said that the New Journalism that all these guys are now claiming as their own was started by me thirty years ago. I'm perfectly willing to take the bow. But I've got to add something else—the so-called New Journalism was the iceberg that sank the *Herald Tribune*.

And if the New Journalists are my bastard children, I want to disown them. I prefer them not to bear my name. My main objection to some of them is that they make up quotes. They invent action. When I was a kid we used to call it faking and piping, smoking the pipe, opium smoking.

The Newfield piece and a lot of other pieces claim Jimmy Breslin is a pup out of me. I think Breslin is capable of writing good, authentic copy, but it's not enough for him.

I'm paid and so is he to report an event the way it is. But he writes the way he thinks it should be. He fakes it until it becomes fantasy. Then it stops being journalism with me. It's a betrayal of your readers.

We covered a fight together one night in Philadelphia, a Ray Robinson fight. Breslin was sitting alongside of me. We asked John Condon, who works for Madison Square Garden, to go back to the dressing room after the fight was over and Condon came out with a very, very shallow quote from one of the fighters. I followed the quote carefully, wrote it just the way Condon reported it to us.

But Breslin stretched it into a long, long quote. He also had a description of Robinson and his handlers as they got into the car that picked them up outside and how the night looked as they left the arena. And he wrote this while he was still sitting at ringside. Anyway, I don't want to savage him. He and I are not very friendly. We don't go to the same places, or hang out with the same people.

Most of the new guys on the baseball beat aren't so bad. I gave 'em their name—Chipmunks. You know how that happened? I was trying to write a piece in the Yankee Stadium press box and four guys are sitting next to me, jabbering away. I said, "You sound like small, furry animals. You're making that kind of noise." I said, "You sound like a God damn lot of chipmunks."

And the name hung on 'em. Some of them are now going bald, and have gray hair, but they're still known as Chipmunks. My definition of a Chipmunk is a guy who wears a corduroy jacket and stands in press boxes with other guys wearing corduroy jackets and they only discuss what they've written. They don't watch the game. They hate baseball. They hate the players. Except those ball players who fawn on them, who insult them. Like Bob Gibson. He's hostile, so they love him. They loved Bouton, too. They'd rather have Bouton than Mickey Mantle because Mantle has some class. The Chipmunks love the big-word guys, the guys with the small batting averages but who have the big vocabularies.

The Chipmunks refuse to follow the techniques of the interview. They go up and challenge guys with rude questions. They think they're very big if they walk up to an athlete and insult him with a question. They regard this as a sort of bravery. They risk the chance of ending interviews in the first few minutes.

The trick of interviewing is to start with the easy question. I usually start with a little small talk. You warm up slowly. Then you drop the bomb, and if the guy doesn't answer, the interview will be almost completed. I save the tough questions for last because I don't want an empty notebook.

Let's face it, the ball player, or the average ball player, considers the writer a spy. None of us like to have our skin peeled back. That's why the ball player would rather be interviewed on television or radio. It's a pleasant sit-down routine with the radio and television guys, who are usually shills for the club, asking routine questions that will make the ball player look good.

There isn't much left of the newspaper business in New York today, only three papers. They don't hire guys without college educations. I guess that's the way it is everywhere. Sometimes I wonder if Thomas Edison could get a job at IBM today.

These kids keep coming out of the journalism schools, and I say they should escape the schools of journalism. The people that come out of them all write like they were writing for the AP or *The New York Times* or the Washington *Post*. Originality of style—that's what's important. It's not encouraged by the journalism professors. Still, I think sportswriting today, as a general rule, is better than it was in my generation. At the top, maybe, we were better. But the general sportswriter is up. There are better sportswriters today. But we had a couple of flashier guys.

I grew up on the Lower West Side. My father's name, naturally, was Cannon. He's dead. My mother's name was Monahan. So, I'm an FBI—full blooded Irish. I had a Catholic education. I went to St. Anthony's down in the unfreaky part of Greenwich Village. Then I went to Regis Prep School, run by the Jesuits. I went there a year. I don't have what is considered a formal education.

Reading interested me. As long as I can remember I was reading books. My family didn't encourage me. It was my own idea. Some of the people in my family were worried I would ruin my eyes. I used to go to the public library on Leroy Street, in Manhattan. I read the usual things that everybody read in those days—Frank Merriwell, Horatio Alger, *Boys' Life*.

We lived in a cold-water flat, near the docks. My old man always had a good job, for that place. He worked for the city as a clerk. He was a Tammany politician, a minor one. He believed in what he did.

He thought it was disgraceful to take money from a neighbor for doing them a favor. And he spent his whole life doing small favors for people in the neighborhood. He wound up without any money but there was enough insurance to take care of his family. He liked all of his kids. He was a very decent man.

I was about fourteen when I started as an office boy on the *Daily News*. I worked the lobster trick—from midnight to eight in the morning. One night, after I'd been there for about two years, there was a shortage of rewrite men. The whiskey must have been flowing pretty well, and for some reason a guy on the desk gave me a short story to write, about three hundred words. It was on Decoration Day, about a kid who ran away from a summer resort and came to Manhattan.

Harvey Duell, who was one of the great newspapermen, was the city editor of the *Daily News*. He read the story, and the next day there was a note in my box: "See Mr. Duell." Well, us boys didn't see the city editor unless we were in trouble. I thought I was in trouble. When I went to see him, he was very kind and said, "I understand you wrote this, young man."

He asked me where I learned to write. I said, "I don't know if I can write at all."

Then he told me, "This is the second thing you've done that's impressed me."

"What's the first?"

"I sent you out for coffee one night and you refused a tip."

I said, "I don't remember. I must have been crazy that night."

That's how I became a city-side reporter.

I covered the Lindbergh kidnapping trial. That's when I first met Damon Runyon. It's been written, many times, that I was his protégé. I suppose you could say that. I was about twenty-four or twenty-five then, and Damon came to me and said, "You shouldn't be doing this. You have a natural style. You should be a sportswriter." I was working then for the *Journal*, the Hearst afternoon paper, and Runyon was with the *American*. So he got me on the *American*.

Maybe subconsciously you could say Damon inflenced my writing. But I'm not sure if that's true. I'm not being pompous when I say this, but my style just developed. It's the way I write. Damon never acted as an editor with me. He treated me like a kid brother. He was thirty years older than I was. I went out with him a lot. He took me to all the places. He was great for guys like me. He was a great listener. He'd put you on, get you to talk. He liked to listen. He listened to just about everybody, and he always picked up the tab with newspapermen but never with anyone else. I think he thought newspaper guys were entitled to a little freeloading. I don't think Damon was a champion freeloader, but I think he did his share.

The greatest freeloader I ever heard of is a guy who is now a boxing press agent. One time he was a boxing writer. One night, in a blizzard, he went from his home in Brooklyn to a party in Yonkers for a Swedish heavyweight, for a smorgasbord. This was back in Joe Louis's time. When you go through a blizzard for a meatball, you're a pretty good freeloader.

Runyon used to cover fights and did something you rarely see. He did the running on a fight on a typewriter. He wouldn't take notes and write after the round. He had an operator named Levitt, a postal telegraph guy who read over his shoulder all the time. And the big thing about Runyon in those days, he used to cover all the big murder trials that would bring the stars out. They would all use legmen. But he didn't. He did all his own work.

He covered the Judd Gray–Mrs. Snyder murder trial. A man and a woman beat up the woman's husband, killed him with a sashweight. The guy was supposed to have used the sashweight. And Runyon, in describing the scene as the guy reenacted it in the courtroom, said, "When he picked the sashweight up, his batting stance reminded me of Paul Waner."

Runyon loved heavyweights. I think he would rather have managed the heavyweight champion of the world than anything else. His walk was boxing, beyond all other things, though he did own horses. His favorite athlete, I've always thought, was Dempsey, in a dead heat with Christy Mathewson. He thought Mathewson was a great pitcher, an intelligent guy, and a great card player. They played cards together a lot. Damon wasn't particularly a great card player. He was a gin rummy player, and once I complimented him on playing a good gin rummy. He said, "You can teach a monkey to play gin rummy."

A lot of people talk of Damon as a cold, remote man. But he

was kind and generous to me. I lived in his house in Miami every winter. He'd spend a lot of time talking to me about writing. And one of the odd things about Damon was that he was a very cultured man. He pretended he wasn't. He concealed his culture and much of his knowledge. I have no idea why—but I think Damon wanted to get as close to the people he wanted to write about as he could. He wrote about mugs because they were interesting people.

Damon did things that were extraordinary for those times, and for these times. They talk about guys doing daring things. Well, Runyon's heroes were pimps and prostitutes and murderers. He treated them as human beings. This is now the style. He was one of the forerunners.

He'd take a stickup guy—that was the guy's business—and he'd write about the stickup guy as writers and novelists write about clergymen. I remember one of his lines. He mentioned a certain guy and he said, "He's out hustling, doing the best he can. It's a very over-crowded profession today." A hustler is a knock-around guy who'll take a piece of an illegitimate proposition.

He disguised most of the people he wrote about, but I can pick them out. I knew most of them. Some of them knew they were being written about, I guess. I never heard one complain. But they never knew how sophisticated Damon really was. Most of all, he was a fairy-tale teller. He liked writing the stuff he did. It was his choice and I think he made it early. That was his style. He made that choice be-cause he was a sportswriter. Let's face it—sportswriters, well, we're not hanging around with brain surgeons.

Damon was a night guy. He was married, and once in a while his wife would go out with him. But mostly he was a single duke. He was a Western guy. His father was a tramp printer, out of the mining towns of the old West. Damon was closer to the frontier than most people realize. He worked in Denver, Trinidad—towns like that.

He had three flowers delivered to himself every day. Carnations —red, white, and blue, in a water glass on his dresser. He had special closets built for his suits. He had more suits than any man I've ever known. And he dressed Broadway style. He looked like a guy who might have managed a good shoe store, or had a very good job in a bank. When he'd go out in his Broadway clothes, and he knew how to wear them, he always suggested to me a city pigeon disguised as a peacock. And he was aware of everything about himself. He was one of the big celebrities in the country.

Damon was a cynical humorist. He was like Ring Lardner. I didn't think he thought very much of the human race. We've had three great original writers—Lardner, Mark Twain, and Ernest Hemingway. And I think Lardner has to be classified among the ten greatest serious writers produced by this country. He was ferociously accurate. He just didn't think much of people. I don't think he masked his humor. This was the way he saw life, and that was the way it came out. There was a bias against Lardner because he was a sportswriter. The critics thought he was a guy who just wrote funny little stories about ball players.

Hemingway was a sportswriter. Read him and you'll find out that he was concerned with losers—from Robert Jordan lying under a tree to die, to his bullfighters. They all lost. He was the only guy who could make fishing sound interesting to me. Fishing, with me, has always been an excuse to drink in the daytime.

I once wrote a piece saying he was a sportswriter, and he sent me a letter, thanking me for it. Ernest and I were very good friends. I liked him very much. But he could be very cruel. He was a tough, blustering guy, but I think as a novelist he is the greatest artist we've ever produced. He didn't dissipate his talent. He never let any of it trickle away into small jobs like other guys did. He never took a job in Hollywood to make a quick touch. He did his trade. I don't think he ever wrote a bad sentence.

Ernest was very physical, very proud of his strength. He might have been the heavyweight champion if he had gone up as a kid, through the amateurs, and decided to become a professional fighter. He boxed very well and he boxed all the time, in George Brown's gym here, and he could hold his own with a lot of tough guys, ex-fighters. He was still boxing when he was fifty.

I remember one night in the Stork Club. We were loaded. He was much younger then, and he invited me to come to watch him box at nine o'clock in the morning. It was then four o'clock. I never showed up. I just paid no attention—at four o'clock in the morning a drunken guy is saying he's going to box at nine o'clock. But he did.

And he called me up the next day, very indignant, and said, "We had a date this morning."

Incidentally, the most neglected writer in this country lives in Chicago. Nelson Algren. I've met him and I like him. I hope he reads this because I want him to know he's not the first guy who was born in a slum. He acts like he discovered poverty, put a flag on it, and claimed it for himself. But I thought *The Man with the Golden Arm* was one of the great novels of America. His descriptions of that neighborhood, that saloon, and those people. He wrote better about Chicago than anybody—including Carl Sandburg. What happened to Algren? Did he just get tired and peter out? I knew Ben Hecht, too. But he was a fiction writer.

Of all writers maybe I revere Mencken the most. He influenced my generation more than anybody influenced any generation since I've been alive. Mencken taught a whole generation how to think, and one of the reasons I adored him was because he was a newspaperman. He was like Runyon. No matter how well they did outside the newspaper business, they were still newspaper people. Mencken wrote awfully good stuff, and his best was in the Baltimore *Sun*. Newspaper people are special to me, probably because I'm a newspaperman. Maybe if I was a plumber I'd talk about plumbers.

I've covered everything there is to cover on a newspaper, but I like sports the best. To begin with, it's a better life. It's an easier life. In sports everything happens in front of you. The thing about politics is that it's happening in rooms. People don't see murders. They go to murder trials and hear people talk about it. But I write best about action, that's why they made me a war correspondent.

When I was a young guy they sent me to Washington to cover the White House. I did it for a while, but the town bored me and I left. I can't stand politicians. They lie more than football coaches. I had to be transferred out of there. I did a radio column, too, but I didn't like it. It was the loneliest kind of life. Sportswriting is best and that's what I am—a sportswriter. I can't think of myself as being anything else.

Some of the best and some of the worst writing in newspapers can be found on the sports page. And when sportswriting is bad, it's the worst in the paper. When it's good, it's the best. You always know when it's bad. You can feel the clink.

I've been the luckiest guy on earth. I've had a great life. I sat, most of my life, at glad events, as a sportswriter, amid friendly multitudes, gathered for the purpose of pleasure. And I've liked some of the people. My two favorite people in sports—and it's a dead heat— were Joe Louis and Joe DiMaggio. They were my friends, and I think explaining friendship is like explaining pain. It's impossible after it's subsided. I have terrible pain right now.

Al Abrams

Al Edward Abrams was Mr. Pittsburgh, its most honored and recognizable personality. Born and raised in the Lower Hills of Pittsburgh, he lived his entire adult life downtown, mostly at the Carlton House. On the several occasions when I was with him away from the ballpark, he was constantly greeted by well-wishers, many of whom he didn't know. "Sure, I enjoy it," he said. "It's nice to be known in your hometown."

Gregarious but nonetheless quiet in manner, he seldom raised his voice or changed his expression. His Dapper Dan promotions earned him national celebrity but he was essentially a working sportswriter—fifty-one years in the newspaper business, all with the Post-Gazette. *From 1934 through 1974, he wrote a column six days a week, "Sidelights on Sports."*

He was a man of considerable thoughtfulness. Typically, when Jack Hernon, the baseball writer for the Post-Gazette, *became ill with cancer and unable to perform daily, Mr. Abrams, then the sports editor, purposely rotated the baseball assignment among three writers to assure Hernon that he was not being replaced. Mr. Abrams was a Leap Year baby, born on February 29, 1904. He died at the age of seventy-three.*

Paul Waner was the big drinker, not his brother. Lloyd just drank his glass of beer. One night, in New York, a Saturday night during Prohibition, Paul and I went out together. You couldn't stop Paul from getting two or three bottles of whiskey. He had a couple of Follies girls with him. As the night wore on, I was getting worried. I knew I'd have to pull him together. We got back to the hotel at five in the morning.

The Pirates had a Sunday doubleheader. Paul got a home run, two doubles and a single in the first game and a home run, a triple and a single in the second game: 7 for 9. Now how can you fault a guy like that for his drinking?

Of course, I didn't write about it. I covered the game. Today, if the writers got hold of that, all they'd write about was his boozing. Maybe not all, but a lot of them. They don't write about the game anymore. They're interested only in a ball player's personal life, what he does off the field. Some of our greatest athletes were drinkers, big drinkers: Babe Ruth, Jim Thorpe, Grover Cleveland Alexander, Walter Hagen. Give me ten minutes and I could add a dozen more to the list.

The WCTU wouldn't like to hear this but drinking might have helped Paul. It certainly didn't hurt. He was the sixth player to get three thousand hits, the first here since Honus Wagner. Led the league three times. Twelve years in a row over .300. In 1927, he hit .380; twelve more hits and he and he would have hit .400. He and Lloyd helped the Pirates win the pennant that year. Between them they got 460 hits—237 by Paul, 223 by Lloyd. Talk about a brother act.

I read *Ball Four* out of curiosity. I thought it was interesting but I don't believe Bouton should hurt his friends that way. In some cases what he wrote probably wasn't the truth. And even if it was the truth what they did on their time didn't have anything to do with their baseball careers.

A friend of mine is always telling me, "Al, you're a piece of cake. You're too nice a guy." He's wrong. A newspaperman can't be a nice guy. Things come up. You can't go along just being a nice guy. But I'm never going to give anybody the worst of it, pick on anyone and try to chase them out of town.

I didn't talk to Roberto Clemente for a full year because of something I wrote. It happened in Chicago. A Chicago baseball writer, a friend of mine, put me in the middle of this thing.

I didn't actually hear Roberto make the statement but he approached this newspaperman and told him to put it in his paper that he wanted the Pirates to trade him. After the game I began checking it out. Jim Woods, the announcer, heard it. So did Don Hoak. I tried to get the newspaperman. He was out to dinner. I tried to get Clemente. He was out to dinner.

I didn't want to miss my deadline. It was a major story. So I wrote it. And as I expected, he denied it the next morning. He said, "I don't want to call that fellow a liar but I didn't say that."

It really burned me up. I went to to him and told him, "Nobody calls me a liar."

He said, "Well, I didn't say it that way."

A year later Roberto came to one of our Dapper Dan dinners. He was invited along with the other award winners. He called me and said he wanted to see me. Alone. And he said, "If you think I'm wrong, I apologize." He put his hand out. We've been friends ever since.

I had my disagreements with Joe Brown, when he was running the Pirates. Nothing serious but he didn't like everything I wrote. I did a series of six articles on Branch Rickey. Some people said I forced that great man to leave the city.

All I did was recite the facts. I pointed out everything that had happened since Rickey came to Pittsburgh. The Pirates lost almost $3 million and finished last four years in a row, tied for last place the fifth year. All my figures were right. I got them before I printed anything.

Mr. Rickey told me himself, "I don't know where you got your figures but they're right."

I was on the inside of the fight game. I knew what was going on. Covered fights for many years. A fight manager, who was well-known in the East, was really angry with me. He had some good fighters. Before a fight, it was in New York, I wrote that it was a fake. Now you know what that means. If it isn't true, it's libelous. The next time he came to Pittsburgh he called a shot on me. I stood my ground.

I said, "Why don't you sue the paper? Why don't you sue me? It was a fake and it's still a fake."

A year or two later everyone had the story. It was a fake. I'm not going to mention his name. After that he became a friend of mine. We're still friends.

The most recent difficulty I had was with a nice guy, Chuck Noll, the Steelers' coach. This was two years ago. We were down in Miami. The Steelers had a 21–3 or 21–0 lead at halftime. Miami came back to win 24–21. It was a tough loss for a coach and the players. I was busy writing after the game so I didn't talk to anybody.

We got on the plane, had dinner, and a half hour later I walked up to where Chuck Noll was sitting and asked him four questions. To every question he said, very curtly, "I don't know." Meaning he didn't want to talk to me. Now this is four, five hours after the game, not five minutes or fifteen minutes. So I told him to his face, "Chuck, I guess you don't know anything." I walked away and wrote the story that way. He's been nice ever since.

There are times when I look back and wonder why I didn't go into something else where I could have made a lot of money. I think I had the ability, no matter what the game was, to make fifty thousand dollars a year. Or a hundred thousand dollars. Then I see some big-money people, millionaires, who are unhappy. They'd rather be sportswriters. The president of one of the biggest banks in Pittsburgh told me he wanted to change jobs with me. This was twenty-five years ago. I said, "Let's do it." He backed away.

President Nixon has said he would rather be a sportswriter than be President. I can't understand that. I've been with him three or four times, here at banquets, and during the 1969 All-Star game when he had four hundred sportswriters in the East Room at the White House.

That may have been Bowie Kuhn's greatest moment. The next day Pete Rozelle, the football commissioner, and Walter Kennedy, the basketball commissioner, called Bowie with their congratulations. They wanted to know how he was able to arrange it.

The first time I met Nixon was when he came to one of our dinners. He was vice president. After the banquet he went down to the Pittsburgh Room at the William Penn Hotel. Took his coat off. Sat there for two hours and talked with sportswriters. He knew sports. Harmon Killebrew was his favorite player. He rattled off figures about

Killebrew. A lot of people talk about Nixon being phony, tricky, all that stuff. Nobody could tell me was phony that night, that he had been briefed. He wasn't trying to get votes. He just enjoyed the company.

I came close to quitting twice. The first time I asked for a five-dollar raise. I didn't get it. I was ready to quit. I was talked out of it.

The second time was after I had promoted five or six fights. Art Rooney and Barney McGinley were the co-promoters. The first fight was Billy Conn against Buddy Knox of Ohio. This was in 1941. Billy was to fight Joe Louis three weeks later in New York.

I anticipated there would be a lot of interest in Billy, a local boy who was going to fight the greatest fighter in the country at the time. Anything can happen in a fight. He could trip or get hurt, get his eye cut. Mike Jacobs screamed in New York because we were using Billy. Billy's manager told him where he could get off. Billy wanted to fight. We drew twenty-nine thousand, a seventy-thousand-dollar gate, big money for that time.

After the fight we were sitting around talking. Art Rooney said, "You might have helped a little bit. But Billy Conn drew the people."

So I said, "Okay, Art, let's try another fight." I put on five ten-rounders. Jake Mintz was the matchmaker for Rooney-McGinley. He made the fights. We drew 28,800-something at Forbes Field at five dollars a copy, a few hundred short of the Conn-Knox fight.

That impressed Art very much and he asked me, "Would you like to work for me? As a part-promoter."

I wanted to know what he meant by part-promoter.

"We'll give you twenty-five percent of the profits of any show we promote. You won't be responsible for any losses. And whatever you make at the paper I'll guarantee you five thousand dollars a year more."

Fighting was a booming business then. That interested me very much. I said "Okay, Art, but I've got to quit my job at the paper. I can't hold both jobs." I gave the paper notice. Cleaned out my desk. The last day the managing editor came over, stood at my desk, and called me every name in the book.

He said, "I don't want you to quit. I want you to stay. You can take the other job but just be careful not overdoing the publicity." I was writing boxing at the time. I assured him I would never give a fight any more space then it deserved. We had two big years together.

What I really wanted to get into was pro football. I could foresee it was going to get big. I was one of the few who had the foresight to see it would grow. Art Rooney was the principal owner of the Steelers, just as he is today. This was in the early forties when Art was having a hard time.

Bert Bell, who later became the commissioner of the National Football League, was Art's partner. Bert wanted to sell his end. He was asking $60,000. I was married to a wealthy woman at the time. Her father wanted me to step into that. I thought I'd become rich. When we were ready to close the deal, a fellow from Philadelphia, Alexis Thompson, came in and gave Bert $180,000. Knocked me out of the box.

Before I began writing a column, the fight game was my main beat. I loved boxing. I don't think it's a cruel sport. When you put one man against another, they're supposed to know how to defend themselves. That's what I liked about it. It teaches you how to handle yourself, to protect yourself. Certainly, there have been fighters who have been beaten up. But boxing isn't any more cruel than hockey. I think hockey is the toughest sport in the world as far as maiming, hurting people.

There was a period, in the early forties, when there were eight weight classes and five of the eight champions were from the Pittsburgh area: Billy Conn, light heavyweight; Billy Soose, middleweight; Fritzie Zivic, welterweight; Sammy Angott, lightweight, and Jackie Wilson, featherweight. It's a great number to have from one area. Pittsburgh was the biggest fight town in the country. We had a lot of small clubs.

There is no question about the best fighter. The best I ever saw was Sugar Ray Robinson. He could take you out with one punch. He could box, move around. He could give just about anybody a pretty good beating. And in those days there were a lot of strong middleweights. He was the ideal fighter.

I didn't like the way his career ended, making so many comebacks. There was a fight program up in Johnstown about eight years ago. Two main events, Sugar Ray fighting somebody nobody knew, and Willie Pep fighting somebody nobody knew. Now here were two of the greatest fighters of all time in their classes being degraded; 250 people in the crowd. They were fighting for a two-hundred- three-hundred-dollar purse. One comeback is okay. Maybe two. Not four or five.

Joe Louis was probably the best heavyweight I saw. Rocky Marciano was more exciting but didn't have the boxing class. Early in his career, he'd just come at you, swinging, just whaling away with both hands. When I called him a crude fighter I was bombarded with letters from every Italian-American in the area. It was just an honest opinion. He was a crude fighter. Then, as he went along he learned how to protect himself, how to hold his hands up, how to move.

Of all the heavyweights I saw Marciano was the toughest. He had the greatest heart. His fight with Jersey Joe Walcott in Philadelphia was the best championship fight I ever saw. Joe was giving him a terrible beating. I had Joe winning nine rounds to two when Marciano hit him with that left hook and knocked him out.

Back in Marciano's time we had a heavyweight prospect here by the name of Bob Baker. He was very good, had possibilities. But he broke his hand, both his hands, against a fighter named Henry in New York. Baker ate himself out of the ring. He would run five miles in the morning, come back and eat five pies to make up for it.

I've known Fritzie Zivic since he was a young fighter, when he was starting out. He's one of the funniest men I've ever known in the boxing game. Without knocking Rocky Graziano, Fritzie, not Rocky, should have been the one doing all those television commercials. But Fritzie liked it here. He wouldn't go to New York. He's still here, working in the steelworks.

Billy Conn, I first saw him when he was fourteen years old. Billy would have beaten Joe Louis in their first fight if he hadn't lost his Irish head. He was ahead on points and then made the mistake, awful mistake, of trying to slug it out. It was the turning point, a big break for Joe. Joe floored him. Put him to sleep. That was the end of Billy.

The boxing game, to me, has gone down ever since Cassius Clay—that's his real name, not Muhammad Ali—came on the scene. It shouldn't be because he is probably the greatest gate attraction since Jack Dempsey. Whether I like him or not probably isn't important. He can come here tomorrow with some ham-and-egger and fill the house. He gained a lot of his popularity with his mouth. I've never known anyone so full of braggadocio.

I don't know how good a fighter he is but I respect some of his opponents. And I don't like it when he taunts them. I like fighters who are fully equipped, who can do everything. I don't think he's a great fighter because he can't punch. He's quick, can dance around, move, good on his feet. I've never been impressed by the fancy stuff. Maybe, with time, he'll improve. But nobody can teach you how to punch.

Pittsburgh's my hometown. I love it. We've got the best sports fans. There are drawbacks. A lot of athletes say if they're not in New York, where the wire services are, or in a big city like Chicago or Los Angeles, nobody knows who they are.

Roberto Clemente used to argue with me about it. We gave Roberto plenty of publicity here. He always felt he should have had a bigger national reputation. The New York writers make superstars out of .240 hitters. Billy Martin is an example. Here, the athlete has to prove himself first before he becomes a superstar. I think that's the way it should be.

Everyone knew Clemente was a great right fielder with a rifle arm. I'm convinced the reason he wasn't written about more was because he didn't hit the home run and drive in a lot of runs. He played eighteen years, a .317 career average, but had only two seasons when he drove in more than a hundred runs. He was a line drive hitter, a great opposite field hitter.

He always said, "I can hit home runs with the best of them." He was right. In 1966, when Harry Walker was the manager, Roberto went after the home run. He hit twenty-nine that year but his average dropped and he went back to his natural swing. The next season he hit .357. That was the year he won his fourth batting championship.

I'd like to write a book about Clemente as a human being. I knew him when he started out with the Pirates, a scared kid. He had great determination. The first five, six years he wasn't making too much money. We used to go to drive-ins, restaurants up on the hill.

Clemente had great compassion for his fellow human beings. I saw that part of him early, long before he was killed in an airplane crash on a mercy mission. When an earthquake hit in Managua, Nicaragua, he helped raise funds and supplies for the victims. The plane fell into the water. It was on New Year's Eve. A terrible loss.

But he also had the human frailties. He was outspoken. If something bothered him, he never let it ride. And he had to be number one in everything. In an athlete it's not a fault. You have to believe you're the best, certainly one of the best. But it turned some of his teammates away from him.

When I was young I never thought about anything except sports. I grew up in the Lower Hills of Pittsburgh. My mother and father were immigrants from Syria. I'm a first-born Lebanese of American or Syrian descent, whatever they call it. They cut the country in half in 1948. Now they call the rich people from that part of the world Lebanese and the poor people Syrians. I picked out a job that kept me poor. So I'm still a Syrian.

They tell me I was a pretty good athlete. Strange enough, for my height, I'm only five-seven, I played a lot of basketball. Playing basketball got me into the newspaper business. I brought the box scores to the old Pittsburgh *Sun* and one day Reggie Welsh, the sports editor of the paper, asked me if I would cover a tournament for him on the South Side. I would be paid fifty cents a box score. The first night there were four or six box scores. I don't recall. And then he said, "Do you know to use a typewriter?"

I said yes, and he told me, "Write what you saw at the game." At the end of the week I was paid twenty-eight dollars for all the box scores and the writing. Then he offered me a full-time job. This was in 1926. I was twenty-two years old.

I'd been working since I was a boy. I sold newspapers, carried baggage at the Pennsylvania Railroad station, and had worked for my dad about a year. He had a wholesale dry goods house and in those days he and his brothers were affluent. They had built themselves up from carrying packs on their back.

Growing up in the Lower Hills of Pittsburgh, we had our gangs, our ethnic groups that sided together. It was a pretty rough life but my mother and father were great people. They believed in decency, in raising their children to become good citizens. Some of the greatest citizens in Pittsburgh and some of the worst were raised in the Lower Hills.

We were Greek Orthodox. My mother was Catholic, my father Greek Orthodox. After he was here for about ten years he became friendly with a Presbyterian minister and changed over to the Protestant religion. I went to church every Sunday when I was young but I got away from it. For the last twenty, twenty-five years, I've been going to church three times a year. To the Protestant church, the Catholic church, and the Jewish synagogue. I want to show my respect for all faiths.

Many people here thought I was Jewish. Some still do. This is a funny story. I was at a banquet a few years ago and Bob Prince, who was the master of ceremonies, called me a "Lebanese Lancer." At the end of the party a beautiful girl comes up to the head table for autographs and she said, "Do you know something, Mr. Abrams. I always thought you were Jewish. I didn't know you were a lesbian."

I started at the paper for twenty-five dollars a week, half what I was getting from my father. My first two years at the paper, I went to Duquesne. Maybe I should have gone for the full four years but I thought I had enough. I wrote high school sports and after a few years moved up to the desk, copyreading, and from then on just branched out.

I started writing a column in 1936—a small column. Notes. Every day, five times a week, I'd pick out two of the best-dressed men in Pittsburgh and put their name in the column. The main idea was to see if anyone was reading the column. I thought it would attract attention and help create local interest.

The thing snowballed. Before I knew it I had a list of about four hundred people. At that time I used to have lunch across the street from the William Penn Hotel, a group of newspapermen and friends of mine. Someone suggested that I hold a banquet and form a club, a Dapper Dan club.

We sold 430 tickets at five dollars apiece. The club wasn't chartered until three years later. We didn't have three cents in the treasury but I had the gall to go to Philadelphia for the National Open golf tournament to see if I could bring it to Pittsburgh as a Dapper Dan promotion. I came back and told the crowd they wanted a ten-thousand-dollar guarantee. I said, "Let's do it."

We brought in all the big names of the time. Sammy Snead. Ben Hogan. Byron Nelson. Gene Sarazen. We made a two-thousand-dollar profit. It was so successful we decided to try it again. But the dates didn't mix with our schedule and so we had to wait until 1948 to repeat it and then we put it on three years in a row.

We went after the PGA tournament in 1951. Fred Corcoran, who ran the PGA, was a friend of mine and helped me out on it. They asked for a $45,000 guarantee. We still didn't have too much money in the bank. We borrowed the $45,000 not knowing whether the tourna ment would go over. As soon as we announced the tournament, we sold

$50,000 worth of tickets. Within a month everyone got their money back.

We held it at the Oakmont Country Club which has one of the greatest courses in the world. It was match play, a seven-day tournament. We had six days of rain. One day was postponed altogether. But we wound up with a profit. A month later we brought in the Jersey Joe Walcott–Ezzard Charles championship fight and drew $294,000 and another $100,000 from television. We made $29,000 on our end.

Last year we had our thirty-seventh Dapper Dan banquet. It's strictly a male affair, a sports banquet. It's always a sellout. We drew 2,354 at twenty dollars each at the Hilton Hotel. We bring in the big sports stars, as many as we can get, and we don't have trouble getting them. We had ninety people on the dais. It scares the devil out of you if you've never been to one before. You wonder if you're ever going to get out. It used to go on past midnight. Now we have a ten o'clock rule.

According to the latest figures we've raised more than $700,000 for charity, from everything, not just the banquets. We now have seventy-eight affiliated chapters throughout the country. People in small towns and some fairly good-sized towns saw what we were doing and asked if they could become part of the organization, if they could have a charter. I'm the national chairman.

I believe in helping people. But it's not strictly goodness of heart. I don't think anyone else would do it. It's a lot of work. But I had a good thing going and it built Al Abrams's name up. It helped put my name across the country. Maybe I've had a little selfish attitude, too.

The beauty of it is that the auxiliary chapters are self-sustaining. Over the years, altogether, we've probably given $5 million to charity. It's been one of the greatest pleasures I've ever had, to see it so successful. I had no idea it would develop the way it did.

I'm proud of the fact that I've been appreciated by the newspaper and accepted by the people of Pittsburgh. One thing I can say about myself, I have never been envious. I root for everyone, whether they're doctors or lawyers or in sports or business.

I know some people think we led the league in so-called robber barons, the Mellon family, Andrew Carnegie, Henry Clay Frick, Charles Schwab. I don't look at it that way. I'm proud of them. They helped build this city. Why not look up to them? Why knock them?

About thirty years ago at four o'clock in the afternoon it was so dark downtown, from the smog, from the thick smoke you couldn't walk around. They cleaned it up. Look at the Golden Triangle. They put up all those big buildings, rebuilt the downtown where the slums used to be. I don't know if they're robber barons or not. I never knew anybody like that. And if there had been robber barons among them, that's their hard luck.

I remember reading about Charles Schwab. Someone went to his office and told him he shouldn't have all that wealth, all that money. He should divide it among the people in the world. Schwab made some quick calculations and said "I think you're right. Here's fourteen cents. That's your share."

◐ ◐ ◐ ◐
◐ ◐ ◐ ◐
◐ ◐ ◐ ◐

Fred Russell

Fred McFerrin Russell was born on August 27, 1906, and is in his eighth decade as a sportswriter. To say he is respected and admired is not sufficient; he is revered. *His wife of almost seventy years, the former Kaye Early of Nashville, said it best: "He is honest, loving, and he's a good man."*

All of which is revealed in his writing. I doubt he has ever written an unkind paragraph. In 1955, after he had been at the Nashville Banner *for more than a quarter century, James B. Stahlman, who owned the paper, told him "Fred, you have done so much for us, we want you to become a vice president of the* Banner.*"*

The most highly regarded sportswriter in the South, Mr. Russell won national attention as a regular contributor to the Saturday Evening Post. *He has been weighted with honors. He wrote his memoir,* Bury Me in an Old Press Box, *in 1957, with the apparent belief he was approaching retirement but is still writing a weekly column at the age of eighty-six. In a 1992 interview with the* Wall Street Journal *he said, "Heaven is a column that's been written." He should know. He's written approximately twelve thousand columns.*

I was with the Nashville ball club in spring training, in Sanford, Florida, 1940, when Red Sanders was named the head football coach at Vanderbilt University. Red and I had been schoolboys together, in the same class. I called him with my congratulations, to tell him how pleased I was we would be back together again.

During the course of the conversation I said I was sure he had given some thought to his staff, but if he had an opening there was a young fellow at Alabama who had impressed me so much. A line coach. That's when I recommended Bear Bryant.

Red was going to try and get Murray Warmath, the line coach at Mississippi State. He wanted Murray because he knew the single wing. Red didn't know Bear.

The next night, about ten o'clock, Red called me at the Mayfair Hotel in Sanford, and said, "I want you to say hello to my line coach."

"Hello, Murray, I'm sure glad you're going to be in Nashville."

And he said, "This ain't Murray. This is Bear!"

I had gone to the Rose Bowl with Alabama in thirty-seven. Bear was then the youngest coach on Frank Thomas's staff. He had played three years at Alabama. Finished up in thirty-five. Back then it was four and a half days on the train going, four and a half days coming back. On a trip like that you get to know people. I could see there was something special about him. He had a forcefulness in a warm sort of way. Even then he radiated a quality that the boys liked.

Bear got his name when he was in high school, at Fordyce, Arkansas. A traveling show came to town, offering three dollars a minute to anybody who would wrestle a trained bear. Bryant's friends pushed him into it. The morning of the show there was a parade down the main street. And there was a sign hung around the neck of the bear: "I will wrestle Paul Bryant at the New Lyric tonight."

In the course of the show, when Bryant was flat on his back, the bear's muzzle came off. The bear leaned over and put his snout against Bryant's cheek. The keeper finally pulled the bear away. Bryant was so scared he ran out of the ring without even trying to collect his money.

Since then Bear has coached here at Vanderbilt, at Maryland, Kentucky, Texas A & M, and, of course, he went back to Alabama and had such great success. I don't like to say this fellow or that fellow was the best ever. Sometimes it's unfair to compare because of the changing times. But Bear was the best.

I really don't know of anything more worthwhile than being a sportswriter. I may be a square and outdated and I hope I'm not kidding myself. But over the years I've come to realize the value, the importance of sports. The standards in sports have had a beneficial influence on many and many a person, on what counts in life and the principles that you try to live by. You get out what you put into it.

The writings of a sportswriter can have a tremendous effect on younger people. We try to approach it that way on our paper, the Nashville *Banner*. The effort is there every day, to motivate, to inspire. We are reaching boys at fifteen, sixteen, eighteen, at a very impressionable age.

Each December the *Banner* has an awards dinner for about eight or nine hundred high school champions, members of the championship teams and it's tied to this theme. I realize there are outstanding people on all the teams. But we've had to limit attendance. The losers aren't there. I like to think this dinner inspires them to try harder. I believe that and I've seen it working.

I'm always disappointed when a star athlete, any athlete, fails to show his gratitude, when they express a lack of respect for sports. Had it not been for sports they could never have attained the recognition they gained. They should be grateful for the wonderful privilege of living and being alive in America and the combination of luck and physical ability that allowed them to excel beyond the ordinary.

That's among the reasons, not the only reason, of course, why I admired Grantland Rice. Admired may not be the right word. He was my idol. There was a gentleness and kindness about him. And along with that, to have the great talent he had, a grace of writing and a wonderful feeling, both as a writer and as a person. I'd have to say he had the most influence on me of any one person as far as writing.

The toughest thing for a sportswriter is not only to create a following but to hold it. To be able to entertain and be read without being controversial. Certainly, the easiest way to gain any attention is to be negative and sensational, approaching things in a highly controversial sort of way.

Grant never traveled that path. There was an inherent goodness about him. He had a great respect for the written word and of the responsibiity of the writer. I believe he wrote about people the way he would have liked to have been treated if he was the subject of an article or a column that the other fellow was writing. That's not done too much today.

Grant was born in Nashville, worked on the *Banner*, and because of that some people thought I was his protégé. We were friends and, of course, I knew him fairly well but I wasn't around him nearly as often as Henry McLemore or Red Smith or Frank Graham. I just got to see him on rare occasions.

By the time I came around, in the late 1930s, the racetrack had the greatest hold on him. No question. He'd rather be at the track than anywhere. He was a good bettor, the kind of guy who had twenty or thirty doubles going. He loved Sunshine Park in Tampa. Sometimes, when I was in Florida, covering the baseball spring training camps, I'd pick him up in front of the Vanoy Park Hotel in St. Petersburg. We'd go to the track together.

He had a side to him that a lot of people didn't know about. We'd be coming back from the track, driving across the Gandy Bridge. You'd think he'd be sleeping and suddenly, he'd sing out, "Give me a Handy Guy like Gandy, building a bridge like this." Taking off on Damon Runyon's Kentucky Derby lead on Earl Sande.

Once I asked him for advice. I was twenty-seven or twenty-eight and thinking how wonderful it would be if I applied in New York or Philadelphia, any of the big cities, and became a baseball writer. To me, a baseball writer traveling with a big league club was heaven, the best possible assignment.

And Grant said,

> Time, that ancient nurse,
> Rock me to patience.

The only application was don't be overly ambitious, that I should take things in stride. A few years later, night baseball began coming in and, in my view, that killed the baseball job. And, of course, I later became aware I already had the best job. The best possible assignment for me was right here in Nashville, writing the sports column for the *Banner*.

Grant had a very special affection for sportswriting. One of his poems went like this:

> If somebody whispered to me—"You can have your
>   pick,"
> If kind fortune came to woo me, where the gold was
>   thick,
> I would still, by hill and hollow, round the world away.
> Stirring deeds of contest follow, till I'm bent and gray.

After he died a group in New York set up a Grantland Rice Award for the writer in America, who, as they worded it, was projecting and carrying on in the Rice tradition. I was the first winner of that. Nothing could have brought me more joy.

Herbert Bayward Swope offered the most simple and eloquent testimony in behalf of Grant. A year or so after Granny's death, his old friends and associates got together to ring the bells for Granny, to wring some joy out of the old memories.

Swope's turn came and he reminisced about his early newspaper days when he and Rice were young sportswriters and had great times going to the games and the races together. As he ended his reminiscing, Swope said that because he had left sportswriting and gone over to the news side, they weren't together much in their middle and late years. Swope insisted that Granny, in remaining in sports, had made the better choice.

And then Swope said, "Grant Rice stayed with happiness."

It would be naive for me to say this has been a constant joy, that there aren't unpleasant moments. The litigation of Wally Butts and Bear Bryant against the *Saturday Evening Post* was one of the most dramatic and moving experiences of my professional life. But I found it also very upsetting. I covered every minute of that trial, in Atlanta. It went on for three weeks.

I was close to both of them, much closer to Bryant than to Butts. The *Post* compared this supposed conspiracy to the Black Sox scandal. I read the story three times and in my own belief there was no way they were guilty. I didn't doubt that they had talked on the phone but for them to conspire and to fix a game, I just couldn't believe that. And, of course, they were absolved. Butts got a settlement of about $400,000. I think Bear got $350,000.

According to the *Post*, Butts had revealed to Bryant some of the practice secrets, tipping him off on the Georgia plays. Butts had been sort of busted as the Georgia coach and had been made athletic director. Georgia and Alabama were opening the season against each other. There was no question there had been telephone conversations. The attorneys for the *Post* had all the telephone company records.

Here was Butts, the athletic director, with nothing to do, time on his hands. A lonesome guy. He'd call me to talk about things. He called a lot of people. And Bear isn't the kind of man who would say, "Wally, I just don't have time. I can't talk to you."

It was journalism at its worst, a sensational story without foundation, an attempt to damage two outstanding men. There was great emotion in the trial. Bryant proved to be a tremendous witness. There was not one tiny bit of evidence of any kind that was put forth to prove that Alabama had received any information helpful to them in beating Georgia pretty badly. And I'm proud to say my personal involvement did not affect my coverage.

Up to that time, in the previous twenty, maybe thirty years, I had been a *Post* regular. I did about thirty-odd stories for them. My first piece, in the late thirties, was on General Bob Neyland, the football coach at the University of Tennessee. I'll never forget opening the envelope and the fear of a rejection slip, and a check for four hundred dollars fell out.

I did mostly profiles but in forty-nine they decided to run a Pigskin Preview every September and I did that for about fifteen years. I had to pick the top twenty teams, preseason All-Americans. It was a lot of work. Took me all summer. By then I was up to $5,000 a story. Later, it was $7,500. A lot of money in those days. It really helped out.

The *Saturday Evening Post*, without question, had been for many, many years the leading magazine in the country. Wholesome, very Americana. The Butts story ran in 1963, a year after the *Post* had changed hands. By then, all my editors, the people I had worked with, were gone. I never did another story for them. I was never asked. If I had been asked, I would not have accepted.

It was an unfortunate episode, the unseemly, unappealing side of sports. I still don't like to read about much of the so-called news of the day: player strikes and holdouts; pension disputes; legal hassles and the reserves clause. Let's take the most recent example: the sale of the Yankees to CBS. It's a financial story and belongs in the financial section.

I think we've been overdoing it. Those stories get far too much coverage. Certainly, there's more strife today, more litigation. I know many sportswriters wouldn't agree but I've spoken to a lot of people about it and I'm convinced they prefer to read about what happens on the field, not what's going on in a courtroom. It bores the hell out of them.

There's something else worth noting. The word sport is an abbreviation of disport, which means to divert, to amuse, to make merry. Let me confess: those things appeal to me.

There is so much of the good part in sports. That's always been my pitch. Sports was in the front, led the way in breaking down segregation. I think integration would have evolved naturally, not only in sports but in every way of life. It was a cinch. It was inevitable. It came easier than I thought it would. It was never a problem for me.

Nashville, for its size, had more black colleges than any city in the country. Three universities—Fisk, Meharry, and Tennessee A & I. Sure, we had some people who resented the forced integration but there were lots of other people who didn't feel that way. I always felt the Northern writers didn't convey the true picture of the South. Of course, there were redneck Southerners but for them to be put forward as characteristic of the times sickened you because it was not a true cross section.

I've always wished I had had more exposure, more experiences with Jackie Robinson when he was breaking the color line. It was something that a Southern sportswriter did not get a very good shot at. The only time we saw big league ballplayers was when they came through, one afternoon, one exhibition game, when they were heading North from spring training.

I remember Babe Ruth and the Yankees coming through. The Babe had a lot of little boy in him. That's what I remember the most, in little ways of letting a ball purposely go through his legs or get by him so it would go into the overflow crowd. And I'm sure he did the same in Birmingham and Chattanooga.

Ruth had a strange kindness about him that he didn't want to show. He didn't want to be thought of that way. But he had great consideration for the minor league writers. Jack Dempsey was even greater than Ruth in that way. They seldom knew the local writers but they went out of their way to talk to you, to give you a story. There was a stretch of years when I felt I was just lucky to be around.

From the beginning I was a hero-worshipper of the major league baseball writers, especially the New York writers. To me, being with them on the field and sitting alongside of them in the press box was always a memorable experience. I've never forgotten Tom Meany and Gary Schumacher. They were so thoughtful and generous of their time. I thought the greatest job in the world was a morning-paper baseball writer traveling with a big league club.

You would get to the ballpark about noon, spend an an hour or so around the bench, which I loved to do, then go upstairs and write six or eight notes. Then the game would unfold. You would do your story and be through forty-five minutes after the game was over. Nothing could be better. When night baseball came along the pace changed. The writers were constantly fighting deadlines. It was no longer a pleasant and leisurely assignment.

Baseball is the easiest sport to cover. The greatest invention that ever came along is the box score. You can look in that little space of three or four inches and you know what happened. You can tell what each player did or didn't do, whether he's a pitcher, infielder, or catcher.

In football there is no way in the world to know through the newspapers. Certainly, it's a drawback. The way football is played, college and pro, an offensive guard or center can go through an entire season and never be mentioned. To some extent television, with its replays, has helped show what the linemen do but I think the only way you could cover a game fairly would be if you assigned twenty-two reporters, one for each defensive and offensive position.

Big league baseball was the only sport I had a yearning for. But other than those summer months there were many compensations. College football was just about as good. And, of course, all those years

I was covering the Vanderbilt football team which played a major intersectional schedule.

This was beyond belief but in 1929, my second year on the paper, I drew the Vanderbilt assignment. I had the good fortune of coming in with Dan McGugin, an extraordinary man. Grantland Rice always insisted McGugin was the greatest football coach of his time.

McGugin had been coaching at Vanderbilt since 1904, had the greatest teams in the South and some of the greatest teams in the country. I can still remember the thrill of going to Minnesota in 1930. Vanderbilt was a fourteen to twenty point underdog that day and beat Minnesota 33–7. But McGugin was in his last years. He had played under Yost at Michigan. He and Yost married sisters.

Ray Morrison succeeded McGugin. Then Ray suddenly left. He went to Temple University. And Ray Sanders, who had been the backfield coach at LSU, took over. It was one of those things you figure could never happen. Ray Sanders and I had been classmates at the Duncan Preparatory School, a prep school for Vanderbilt.

When I was thirteen we moved from Warpace, a little town of eight hundred. My parents decided my brother and I should get better schooling. We moved to Nashville about fifty miles away. I was so scared about going to a new school I didn't sleep for two or three nights. I didn't know a soul, not a soul. They had these old-time school desks and the person seated behind me who, of course, I had never seen before, was Red Sanders.

From that day on we became the closest friends, classmates at Vanderbilt, teammates on the baseball team. He played shortstop, I played second base. Well, here we are twenty years later, reunited. Who could have figured it? It was a million-to-one shot. Red was not only an old friend but he was great copy. He had an uncanny grasp of the newspaper business. He never sent a reporter away empty-handed.

Larry Gilbert was like that, too. Larry was the number one baseball man in town, for many years the manager of the Nashville Vols in the Southern Association. He had championship teams year after year. In my opinion, the 1940 and 1941 Nashville teams would not finish last in the major leagues today.

Larry had four or five opportunities to manage in the big leagues. Turned all of them down. He was just more comfortable in Nashville. I am convinced this was also true with some of the star minor league players at that time. The money didn't mean as much then as it does now. So there was no great urgency for them to move on.

Nick Cullop was one of the players who could have had a big career in the major leagues but didn't. He was an a outfielder, one of the most powerful minor league hitters who ever played in the South. Maybe he had some sort of complex; in his own mind he wasn't a major league player. He had four or five trials in the big leagues. He hit 420 home runs in the minors but only eleven in the big leagues.

Larry sent seventy players to the big leagues. He made the Boston Braves take pitcher Johnny Sain. The Braves didn't have any money and Larry told them it was all right, they could pay him later. Larry discovered Dusty Rhodes. I can go on and on.

He had come up the hard way and knew how to handle players. He had a photographic memory. Remembered everything. This is something you may not know. He was the center fielder with the 1914 Miracle Braves who were in last place on July 4 and came on to win the National League pennant. And they just didn't flash across the finish line. They won by ten and a half games.

Through the years I may have wearied of minor league baseball. The Southern Association wasn't in the top minors. The American Association, the International League, and the Pacific Coast League were a rung above us. But I always enjoyed spring training. I'd move from club to club, interviewing the big league managers and star players. It was something I would dream about as a boy. It never occurred to me it would become a reality.

I had what you could say was an idyllic boyhood. My father, John Russell, was a drummer. In those days they were never called traveling salesman. It was horse and buggy. He covered the area selling groceries. He would have a specialty man travel with him, candy or canned goods.

Drummers were prosperous. It was a good life. We wanted for nothing. I have so many wonderful memories of Christmas. Golly, bicycles and everything. My father was a big gagster, a jokeman. Christmastime, he'd take a few bricks out of the chimney to make room for Santa Claus. One year he bought us a roller coaster that started up high, near the ceiling, and ran all the way through the house, right out the kitchen door.

I have never known a more avid reader of newspapers, morning and afternoon, than my father. That's how I learned to read. I was always a tremendous sports fan. When I was five, six years old I knew all the batting averages of the players on the Nashville team.

I can remember when Swanee, the University of the South, upset Vanderbilt. They always played on Thanksgiving Day, a big event. Morgan Blakely, who was then the sports editor of the *Banner*, did a poem, six or eight little quatrains or verses. The hero of the game was a Swanee player, Lee Tolley. Vanderbilt's hero was Rabbit Curry, a great player from Marlin, Texas.

Blakely wrote:

> "Who tackled Tolley?"
> "Not I," said Curry.
> "He was in too big a hurry."

I had an eccentric grandmother, Tennessee McFerrin. She was a music teacher, taught the mandolin and guitar and all that. She fancied herself as a writer. I doubt much of her stuff got published but when I was ten years old she began writing me letters. She always addressed her letters, "Dear Attorney Fred."

She was a woman of great influence. Also prophetic, to a point. I passed the state bar exam and the day I got out of the Vanderbilt Law School, that same day, I went to work for a law firm. It was the dullest kind of work: titles, deeds, mortgages, loans. I hadn't been there three months when I knew I had to escape, to get out of this thing.

I didn't want to hurt the feelings of Manning Kirby, the man who had given me the job. After I had been there two years he had some bad times, had to merge the firm. It just knocked the props out of everybody. But I wasn't too sad about it. It solved my problem. Manning Kirby knew James B. Stahlman, the publisher of the *Banner*, a wonderful man. Stahlman told him to have me come in. He gave me two choices: selling advertising for twelve dollars a week, or cub reporter, four dollars a week. I took the cub reporter job.

After the first day I knew that's where I belonged. Someone, maybe it was Thomas Carlyle, said, "Blessed is he who has found his work and let him ask for no other blessing."

I've been truly blessed, working as a sportswriter and living in America. Admittedly, I'm a square. I don't want to say I'm a patriot or anything like that but I have a great feel for the things I think made this country great. I get a tingle out of bands and flags coming down the street, watching the West Point cadets parade.

If that's old-fashioned, that's it. It's part of my inner feelings. I've been to the last three Olympics and I'm all for that presentation up on the stand and the playing of the music of the country. I can't see anything wrong with that. And personally I can't see anything wrong with the playing of Dixie. I can't understand how that's become so objectionable, a song that is the stirring tune that it is. I have never read anything else into it.

Maybe I don't have the full grasp of it but I don't understand how that offends anyone. I used to have great arguments with Ralph McGill. He was against it, said it was an affront to certain people. He was a great liberal, a wonderful man. Tremendous writer, a man of great courage. I always had a lot of respect for him. We just disagreed on that point.

I'm sure some of my own children regard me as a square. I'm not able to accept the permissiveness that has developed. I don't understand the necessity for the change in customs. At Vanderbilt, for example, the lack of rules in certain disciplines, where the girls and boys can room on the same floor.

I guess that's just a part of being old. I'm not amenable to change. It's too late in the game. I know that someone like Red Smith could put up a pretty convincing argument for the other side.

◎ ◎ ◎
◎ ◎ ◎
◎ ◎ ◎

Wendell Smith

Unlike most sportswriters, John Wendell Smith was an outstanding athlete. He was an all-city high school basketball and baseball player in Detroit and also starred and was the team captain in both sports at West Virginia State College, which he attended on an athletic scholarship. He began writing sports in 1937 after his college graduation. He worked for two papers, the Pittsburgh Courier *and the Chicago* American *which he joined in 1947.*

He was the first black member of the Baseball Writers Association of America. In the early 1960s, when he was covering the White Sox, he was instrumental in integrating spring training facilities in Florida. He wrote the first Jackie Robinson biography and was among the most literate and able sportswriters of his time.

Mr. Smith and Jackie Robinson went to the grave together. Mr. Smith died at the age of fifty-eight in 1972, a month after Robinson's death. More than a thousand mourners attended Mr. Smith's fu-

neral, including many of Chicago's civic leaders. Awards at Notre Dame and by the Chicago baseball writers are presented annually in his memory. A Chicago elementary school was named in his honor in 1973.

I was working in Pittsburgh, for the Pittsburgh *Courier*, at that time the largest Negro weekly newspaper in the country, and was in weekly contact with Branch Rickey. I knew it was a big story and was tempted to write it, that the Brooklyn Dodgers were tailing him. But it would have killed it. I was sworn to secrecy. When we talked on the telephone we never used Jackie Robinson's name. It was always the "Young Man from the West."

I had sent him the schedules of the various teams so he knew every minute, practically every minute, where we were staying. He knew everything about Jackie.

For example, in one game, Jackie had a dispute with an umpire. In this situation, playing in these small towns, there were seldom any black umpires. There weren't many black umpires. I'm sure this was a white umpire. It wasn't a racial thing. Two black teams playing each other. It was just an argument between a ballplayer and an umpire. Jackie threatened, or appeared to threaten, to punch the umpire.

Mr. Rickey had assigned Clyde Sukeforth, one of his top scouts, to follow Jackie, to see him in as many games as possible. In comparing ballplayers, Sukeforth asked, "What do you think about Robinson?"

It was just conversation with one of his white baseball colleagues. This guy may have been a scout, or maybe he owned one of those minor league ballparks where they played. As Sukeforth went around he ran into a lot of baseball people he knew. This guy gave Sukeforth a description of this incident. He gave Jackie a bad rap.

Sukeforth called Mr. Rickey and Mr. Rickey was very, very concerned. Mr. Rickey called me and asked if Jackie was a belligerent type of individual. I knew he was belligerent. To survive, he had to be. He couldn't be a Mickey Mouse. I knew he was going to encounter things worse than having an argument with an umpire over balls and strikes.

I assured Mr. Rickey that Jackie wasn't belligerent and that it probably was just a routine argument with an umpire. I didn't want to tell Mr. Rickey, "Yes, he's tough to get along with." A lot of us knew that. When he was aroused, Jackie had a sizable temper. Then I told

Jackie to watch himself, to watch his conduct. Everything he did, on and off the field, would get back to Mr. Rickey.

There has been a great discrepancy in some of the books I have read of the history of this thing. Tom Greenwade has often claimed he was the scout who trailed Jackie. Greenwade has taken credit for discovering Jackie. But that's not true. Sukeforth was the man who started following Jackie from town to town.

It all began in 1938, after I had been named sports editor of the Pittsburgh *Courier*. I had been working there for about a year for seventeen dollars a week, which at that time, I'd guess, was the average starting salary. I did a little bit of everything. I wrote fillers and high school sports. I didn't cover anything big but I learned the mechanics of the business: makeup, how to write captions, a basic journalism education. When the sports editor was promoted, he was made the business manager, I succeeded him.

The *Courier* always had some kind of a program going, a crusade for something of consequence. I suggested a campaign for the admittance, the inclusion of Negro ballplayers in the big leagues. The paper picked up on it. Everyone seemed to think it was a very good idea and so I began interviewing big league ballplayers and asking them whether or not they would welcome a Negro player as a teammate. Some were for it and, naturally, some were against it.

I was in Pittsburgh, a National League town. I interviewed all eight National League managers and about forty players: Dizzy Dean, Paul Dean, Pepper Martin, Gabby Hartnett, Carl Hubbell, the big stars. Leo Durocher, he was managing the Brooklyn Dodgers, said, "Hell, if they can play ball I have absolutely no objection."

Bill Terry, he was managing the Giants, didn't have any objections but said it wouldn't work. Most of the ballplayers said if a Negro had the skills to play in the big leagues it was okay with them. The voting was 75 percent for, let's say 20 percent against. About 5 percent had no reaction either way. Some guys were very guarded. But just about all of them were very courteous.

I usually started off the interview by asking "Have you seen any Negro ballplayers who you think could play in the major leagues?" Ninety percent had played against Negro players after the season, in exhibition all-star games. They don't do it now, stopped it many years ago, but in those days, after the World Series, a group of major leaguers would barnstorm around the country. And they'd play Negro teams, the Pittsburgh Crawfords, the Homestead Grays, the Kansas City Monarchs, Cleveland Buckeyes, the best Negro teams.

Pittsburgh was a hotbed of Negro baseball. We had two teams, the Crawfords and the Homestead Grays. It was one of the few towns where the attendance was so good, the Crawfords built their own ballpark, Greenlee Field, named after Gus Greenlee, the owner. It was similar to a Class C or a Class B minor league park: five thousand seats. They played at night, almost always to capacity crowds. Satchel Paige and Josh Gibson played on those teams, on both teams. At one time they were together as a battery. During the week they traveled around, but there were always games in Pittsburgh every weekend, Friday night and doubleheaders on Saturday and Sunday.

Josh Gibson was one of the best hitters I ever saw. They talk about Josh hitting a ball so far it never came down. That was folklore. But he was the most powerful hitter in the Negro leagues. He was, in my opinion, comparable to Babe Ruth. And, of course, Paige was a star pitcher for many years. Amazing control. He could hit a gum wrapper nine times out of ten.

I couldn't get a baseball writers' card so I wasn't always particularly welcome at Forbes Field, which is where the Pirates played. So I would go to the Schenley Hotel where the visiting clubs stayed. The ballplayers were sitting around, you know how ballplayers sit around in the lobby. That's where I did most of my interviewing.

The paper was elated. The managing editor was very enthusiastic. I got raises. It really got me on my way, got me going, helped me get a name in the sportswriting business. My stories were a revelation because the baseball owners had been constantly saying that the major league ballplayers would not play with Negro ballplayers.

A lot of my stories were picked up. They ran in *The Sporting News* and the Pittsburgh *Post-Gazette* and the *Sun Telegram*. From time to time other papers around the country picked them up, and naturally, they would always give the *Courier* credit. The reaction was very favorable.

Ira Lewis, the publisher of the *Courier*, and Paul Robeson, the famous singer, accompanied me to an owners' meeting at the Roosevelt Hotel in New York. I should say I accompanied them. This was in 1939. Judge Landis was the commissioner. We had written a letter asking if we could make an appearance, if we could make an appeal on behalf of the Negro ballplayers. Robeson, at that time, had a good name. Later, he became controversial. Paul Robeson and Ira Lewis spoke, for twenty minutes to a half hour.

They said, "Gentlemen, there is a wealth of baseball talent out there and contrary to what many people say, we believe these men can play major league baseball and that the majority of the players would tolerate them on their teams."

The reaction, frankly, it was silence. We went in, made the presentation, came out and the meeting continued. Later, a letter was written to Landis thanking him for the privilege. There was no reply. But I do recall that the man who seemed the most interested was Branch Rickey. Mr. Rickey didn't say anything during the meeting but he was very gracious. He was then the general manager of the St. Louis Cardinals.

Early during the next season I approached Bill Benswanger. He owned the Pittsburgh Pirates. I got him to say he would have his scouts take a look at some of the Negro ballplayers. But he got cold feet and got out of it. He never gave us an explanation. Maybe some of the other owners got to him. I don't know. We didn't give up. I continued writing stories.

In 1944–1945, the country was turning fairly liberal. We were winning the war. The war was ending. Joe Louis was at his peak. There was a definite liberal trend. People were becoming very conscious of this question. The public, the general public, was on our side. And baseball was beginning to find itself mildly on the defensive. The owners began making excuses.

From time to time, reporters, white reporters, approached some of the top baseball executives. Jimmy Powers of the New York *Daily News* began campaigning on our behalf. And Dan Parker of the New York *Daily Mirror*. And Warren Brown, the dean of the Chicago press corps. It would seem that every time there was a lull in baseball news these men, in particular, would bring up the issue, three or four times during the off-season. Hot stove stuff.

I've still got the clipping of a column written by Dave Egan of the Boston *Record*. Egan wasn't very popular with many of his fellow writers. They called him Dave Ego. This is what Egan wrote:

"We are fighting, as I understand it, for the rights of underprivileged people everywhere. We weep for the teeming masses of India. Down the years we have contributed millions of dollars to the suffering Armenians. We have room in our souls to pity the Chinese and the Arabs and the brave Greeks. Could we, by chance, spare a thought for the Negro in the United States? Do we, by any chance, feel disgust at the thought that Negro players, solely because of their color, are barred from playing baseball?"

Shirley Povich of the Washington *Post* was another who was very forthright. Shirley was exposed to Negro baseball. The Negro population in Washington was very large and the Negro teams always appeared at Griffith Stadium. I recall once when Shirley, commenting on the barrier, said that the Washington Senators had a lot of Cubans on their club but no Negroes as such, some of whom were suspect. He wrote that everyone in the ballpark should sing the "Star Spangled Banner" except the Washington squad.

The baseball writers, at that time, were very conservative. Individually, a lot of them were wonderful. But as a group they never have been known to be overly liberal. As an organization they didn't do much to advance our cause. When I applied for membership I was turned down. They said I wasn't eligible because I wasn't covering day to day, that it wasn't my daily assignment. I made my appeal on the basis that if the sports editor for the *Daily Worker*, a Communist paper, was qualified, so was I. I finally got a card in 1948 after I came to Chicago and was covering the White Sox for the Chicago *American*.

The press always portrayed Branch Rickey as a skinflint, tight with the dollar. Some of the New York writers called him "El Cheapo." I'll never criticize Mr. Rickey. He was a great man. He never admitted it but in the very beginning his interest may have been prompted by economics.

During the war years the Negro teams, on Sundays, were drawing crowds of twenty to thirty thousand at Yankee Stadium and the Polo Grounds. In Chicago, this was in the days when there wasn't much interest in the Cubs, they played on the South Side, at Comiskey Park, and were outdrawing the Cubs. In Washington, it was said that the Negro teams, by renting Griffith Stadium, were saving the Senators from bankruptcy.

Mr. Rickey had Ebbets Field and when the Dodgers were on the road, he had an empty ballpark. Rickey wanted to get some of this extra revenue and decided he was going to form a third Negro league. There were then two Negro leagues, the Negro American League and the Negro National League. Mr. Rickey said his league would have a team in his third league known as the Brooklyn Brown Dodgers.

In February 1945, maybe it was early March, I contacted a Boston councilman by the name of Isadore Muchnick. He was white, in his forties. I saw this little piece in the paper where he was running for reelection in a predominantly Negro area and was having quite a time getting reelected. I called him and told him he should include in his platform a program, or a threat, that he would protest Sunday baseball in Boston if the Braves and the Red Sox didn't express interest in our campaign. The churches in Boston frowned on Sunday baseball. The Braves and Red Sox needed a unanimous vote from the City Council.

I telephoned him from Pittsburgh and told him, "If you want some Negro votes why don't you stand up in the City Council and threaten to vote against Sunday baseball?" It hit home with him. He said he would. And he did. Now, of course, the reaction of the Braves and Red Sox was "Oh, yes, we have nothing against signing Negro ballplayers."

So I called him back and said I was prepared to bring some Negro ballplayers for a tryout: "The Braves and Red Sox said they will give them tryouts. Will you make the arrangements?" And he did, with both Boston clubs. He told them I would be bringing some ballplayers to Boston—under his sponsorship. Then I picked three players, on my own.

I picked Jackie Robinson, Marvin Williams who was a second baseman for the Philadelphia Stars, and Sam Jethroe of the Cleveland Buckeyes. Jethroe was an outstanding outfielder, great speed, a good hitter. He wasn't a power hitter. He was more of slap hitter. In the Negro leagues he was a .350 hitter. Williams was what I could call a steady, dependable hitter.

I picked Jackie because he had played on integrated teams. He was a college man, UCLA, great collegiate athlete, a natural. He played all the major sports—football, basketball, and baseball. He had just come out of the Army and had signed with the Kansas City Monarchs. He wasn't necessarily the best player but he was the best player at that time for this particular situation.

Many people have asked me why I didn't pick the big-name players, Satchel Paige and Josh Gibson. Number one, I knew that if a guy got on a major league club he would have to be able to play every day. Number two, I thought Satchel was too old. He was about forty. I was wrong about that. Satchel had plenty left. He could have played. I just ruled him out.

I didn't approach anyone about Paige. But I approached the owners of the Homestead Grays on Josh Gibson. They were opposed. The Homestead Grays were owned by two black men, Rufus (Sonnyman) Jackson and Cumberland Posey. They wouldn't let Josh Gibson go because he was their ace drawing card. Eddie Gottlieb, a white man, well-known in basketball, owned the Philadelphia Stars. When I asked if I could take Marvin Williams to the Boston tryout, Eddie said, "Sure. Good luck."

I had several other black players in mind but I didn't want to take a whole gang. I figured if I took as many as five or six the reaction would be negative. Once I knew I couldn't get Gibson I didn't try to get anybody else beyond Robinson, Williams, and Jethroe.

Ten days elapsed from the time I contacted them before the tryout. The players were skeptical. I'm sure they were excited. It was something different and all their expenses were being paid. They had nothing to lose. Outwardly, they took the attitude, "It probably doesn't mean a thing but we'll go through [with] it."

They never did try out with the Braves. This was in mid-April. The Braves were on their way home from spring training. The Red Sox were in Boston on that particular day but they didn't work out. They were getting ready to catch a train to New York. They opened the season against the Yankees the next day.

The Red Sox had about a dozen young recruits, high school players they wanted to check out and a few players in their system, from the low minors, prospects they were getting ready to ship out to the Class C and D leagues. It was demeaning to put these black stars with a bunch of kids. It would be difficult to call it a tryout because they had these kid pitchers throwing. It wasn't any kind of a real test hitting in Fenway Park against these kids. They just rattled that tin left-field fence.

The tryout was held on April 16, 1945, at noon, and lasted an hour. Duffy Lewis, who at that time was the Red Sox traveling secretary, ran the tryout. Lewis had been a famous Red Sox player. He was probably in his sixties. He had a handful of cards, index cards, you know, "Can the guy hit? Can he throw?" He marked them, just like he marked the cards on the white kids.

Joe Cronin was not available. He had broken his leg or something. He was then the Red Sox manager. Eddie Collins, the general manager, stood by himself, high up in the stands. Tom Yawkey, who owned the club, was said to be there but I was never able to confirm it. A few sportswriters were there.

I envisioned quite a big play in the papers the next day. But the papers didn't take it very seriously. The publicity would have helped. President Roosevelt had died a few days before and, of course, that was the big story. After the tryout, I called Dave Egan but he only wrote what happened, a few paragraphs. Had he been there himself, I'm sure he would have stretched it into a column.

When it was over Duffy Lewis said, "They look like pretty good ballplayers." He thanked me for bringing them and said, "You'll hear from us." I took it as a courtesy. I should say the reception was fine. They did what they said they would. But I was disappointed in the reaction. We never heard from them again.

In the meantime, Branch Rickey was still tiptoeing around in the background, threatening to start this third Negro league. I called Mr. Rickey and told him the story, just like I've been telling you. He said he wanted to see me the first thing tomorrow morning. The ballplayers went back to their respective teams but on the way back to Pittsburgh I went to Brooklyn, to see him at his Ebbets Field office.

I told him what had happened and when I said, "Jackie Robinson," he raised his bushy eyebrows and he said, "Jackie Robinson! I knew he was an All-American football player and an All-American basketball player. But I didn't know he played baseball."

I said, "He's quite a baseball player, Mr. Rickey. He's a shortstop."

We talked for a long time about the merits of the three ballplayers I had taken to Boston. Then he said, "You will hear from me."

He called a week later. He was basically interested in Jackie, probably because he had been a famous college athlete. And Jackie's older brother, Mack, had been an Olympic track man. He was intrigued by all that. And that's when he told me he was sending Clyde Sukeforth to look at the "Young Man from the West."

Rickey told me in a roundabout way, "This may be more extensive than you visualize. I don't know exactly how this is going to turn out."

I asked him outright, "Mr, Rickey, is there any chance of this ballplayer ever becoming part of the Brooklyn ball club?" He was evasive. He didn't say yes and he didn't say no. But I had the definite impression there was more behind it than the Brown Dodgers. But he never came out and said so until he signed Jackie for the Montreal Royals.

I saw Jackie a week or two later. I told him, "Jackie, the Dodgers are trailing you." I mentioned Mr. Rickey's idea for this alleged third Negro league. Everybody, Sukeforth, too, thought it was for the Brown Dodgers. In the beginning, I think Mr. Rickey really wanted to organize a third league but as I say liberalism was creeping in. Now I was aware Mr. Rickey had a greater purpose in mind. I just told Jackie, "They're looking at you for the Brown Dodgers." I didn't tell him the truth because I didn't want him to tighten up. But I was convinced of what was happening.

Sukeforth followed him through the summer of forty-five. That fall, after the season, Mr. Rickey signed Jackie to a Montreal contract. Montreal was the Dodgers' top farm club. Mr. Rickey announced Jackie would be going to Sanford, Florida, where the Dodgers had a baseball complex, the first one, I think, in the major leagues. With the exception of the Montreal club, all the minor league ballplayers from within the Dodger organization, as many as two hundred, reported to Sanford, Florida.

Mr. Rickey asked if me if I would live with Jackie, be his companion on the road. That's when he put me on the Brooklyn payroll, fifty dollars a week, about the same amount I was getting as sports editor of the *Courier*. He hired me as a scout, to scout Negro ballplayers. I had been a ballplayer, an all-city high school pitcher in Detroit but I knew nothing of scouting. I was getting paid to help Jackie jump the hurdles.

Mr. Rickey was very respectful. He asked my opinion on John Wright. Wright had pitched for the Homestead Grays and had just come out of the Navy. I said, "He's a pretty good pitcher," and Mr. Rickey said he was going to send Wright to Sanford. It was Sukeforth who had recommended Wright.

Sanford was segregated. I had to figure out a place where we could stay. Lady luck came to the rescue. It so happened I knew a girl, a college classmate who lived in Sanford. This is ten years later. We knew each other as college freshmen.

I had to tell her what was happening and I said, "Can we stay with your family?" And, of course, she said yes. They were well-to-do, had a beautiful home, a mansion. If Mr. Rickey had known he might not have approved but her father was a numbers man, a policy operator.

We couldn't eat with the other ballplayers. There was a noon break for lunch and so we went back to the house. The girl's mother prepared our meals. On the second or third day, while Jackie and John Wright were in the house, a white man approached me. I was on the porch.

He said, "You are with Robinson, you're chaperoning Robinson?" I said, "That's right." And he told me, "You better get out of town." He said he was from Ohio and indicated he didn't approve. He had just come from a meeting of approximately one hundred businessmen in the town hall and was advising me, on their behalf, to be out of town by nightfall.

I called Mr. Rickey. He said we should go to Daytona Beach, about fifty miles north, where the Dodgers and their Montreal farm club were training. We piled in Johnny Rowe's car. Johnny Rowe was a photographer with the *Courier*. He did the driving. The ballplayers didn't know why we were leaving. We didn't want to upset them. Once we were on the highway, out of town, I told them we had been ordered to get out: "They won't stand for Negro ballplayers on the same field with whites."

The next day they were working out with the Dodgers' B club but were wearing Montreal uniforms. On that B squad were guys who became great ballplayers. Carl Furillo and Duke Snider. Gil Hodges was the catcher. It was a totally different atmosphere. In Sanford, they told me I couldn't sit in the press box. In Daytona, I was welcome. Almost all of the New York writers who were covering the Dodgers introduced themselves.

Dick Young of the *Daily News* and Gus Steiger of the *Mirror* always seemed to be at my side. They knew history was being made. They didn't express their personal opinions but they never said anything negative. They were constantly querying me. You know how it is in spring training, the ballplayers aren't always available. They're on the field. So every day they'd talk to me. After all, I was living with Jackie and he was the big story, not the Brooklyn club.

I never socialized with the writers. In the South it was forbidden. If they wanted me to go to dinner with them, it was against the law. I'm sure they would have liked to have me join them. They didn't ask because they knew it was impossible. But I considered myself part of the press corps. I was writing daily stories. I was Jackie's Boswell.

We played it close to the vest. I always tried to keep it from becoming flamboyant or highly militant. There were people who wanted to become part of it, to push it faster. Fortunately, I managed to keep them away. If more people had been involved, it would have done more harm than good. That's one of the reasons we succeeded. We always tried to play it in low-key.

Everything was looking good and so I began recommending other Negro ballplayers to Mr. Rickey: Monte Irvin and Larry Doby. But Mr. Rickey said, "Let's leave them alone. I want some of the other ball clubs to take them."

That's why Larry Doby and Monte Irvin missed the Dodgers. Bill Veeck, he then owned Cleveland, signed Doby, the first black player to play in the American League. The Giants signed Monte. But Mr. Rickey couldn't resist. He signed Roy Campanella because he was such a great catcher. He just couldn't let that kind of talent get away.

When I think back, it was absolutely fantastic, all the things we went through. I still think about it; it's hard to conceive. Going into a town and finding a decent place to stay was not easy in those days. Eating in the places we ate, second and third rate. Always having this stigma hanging over your head. But I knew Jackie would make it. And I knew if he made it things had to open up.

I first ran into prejudice when I was playing American Legion baseball. I was a pitcher. Mike Tresh was my catcher. Mike played in the big leagues sixteen years. We were in a playoff game and I beat the opposing pitcher 1–0. Wish Egan, the great scout for the Detroit Tigers, was in the stands. He was the scout who came up with Charlie Gehringer and a lot of other big players. He signed Mike Tresh and the pitcher I beat and he said, "I wish I could sign you, too, kid. But I can't."

That broke me up. It was then that I made the vow that I would dedicate myself and do something on behalf of the Negro ballplayers. That was one of the reasons I became a sportswriter.

Wendell Smith   323

I grew up in Detroit, in an all-white neighborhood. I went to Southeastern High School. I was the only Negro there. Everybody was great to me. Of course, once in a while you would run across some jerks but that never disturbed me. I played all sports and always had the feeling if I had any problems the guys on the team were with me. Also, I was the only one there. There was no feeling among the whites of being overcrowded. In neighborhoods where they are very few Negroes the relationship is usually much better than in the areas where the mixed population is heavy.

My father was Canadian, born in Dresden, Ontario, about seventy miles from Detroit. He was raised on a farm. When he was a young man he worked on the boats, running from Detroit to Buffalo. He started out as a dishwasher and moved up. Eventually, he became associated with Henry Ford, got a job as Mr. Ford's chef.

When I was a kid, probably ten or eleven, he started taking me to the Ford mansion with him. It was like a castle. In the summers I was there once a week. I knew the kids, Edsel, Benson, and Henry. We played ball together.

The first time I met Henry Ford, my father said, "Mr. Ford, this is my son, Wendell." Mr. Ford shook my hand, patted me on the back and said, "He's a fine-looking boy, John. What does he want to be when he grows up?"

o o o o
o o o o
o o o o

Gene Kessler

Eugene Kessler was born on May 18, 1898, in Lawrenceville, Illinois. During the interview he several times said, "I didn't have much of a boyhood." He was from a poor family and recalled going hungry as a boy. He attended public schools in Indiana, in Vincennes and Indianapolis, and began working full-time as a newspaperman when he was a freshman at Wabash College.

Mr. Kessler's career as a sportswriter spanned five decades. He worked for the Crawfordsville Review, *the South Bend* Tribune, Washington (D.C.) News, The Sporting News *in St. Louis, the St. Louis* Star-Times, *the Chicago* Journal, *which was the forerunner of the Chicago* Daily Times, *and was sports editor and columnist in 1948 when it merged with the Chicago* Sun. *He was kindly and soft-spoken, impeccable in his dress.*

Mr. Kessler covered all the major sports. Boxing was his forte. He had a national reputation as a fight writer. In his middle and later years he was a man of means, living comfortably in an early retirement. During the last twenty years of his life he raised the flag every day. "There is so much to be thankful for," he said. When I interviewed him his flag was at half mast in tribute to the death of President Lyndon Johnson. Mr. Kessler died at the age of eighty-three.

I went on the field and introduced myself to Knute Rockne. It was his second game as the head coach at Notre Dame. It was a cold, zero cold day. I said, "Coach, I know the Wabash players. Could you have someone give me the names of your players?"

He said, "Just keep up with me. I'll give you all the dope."

Rockne ran up and down the field on every play. And all through the game he kept telling me, "Don't write about those fellows carrying the ball. Write about the linemen. The linemen are making those holes. See those holes. I could run through there with my overcoat on."

Notre Dame beat Wabash 67–7. I went back to the office and wrote the story about covering the game with Coach Rockne at my side. I quoted him all the way through. The Indianapolis *Star* played it with a streamer and put my byline on it. I was just a stringer. They paid five dollars for a full column of type. Steve Hannegan, who later became Postmaster General, was at Purdue. He was the correspondent up in Lafayette.

This was in 1918. I was in my second year at Wabash. I needed money to stay in school and was working full-time. I was the city editor of the Crawfordsville *Review*.

I got a call near the end of the season from the managing editor of the South Bend *Tribune*, a fellow named Rudy Hoerst. He told me, "Knute Rockne has recommended you to become our sports editor." Rockne liked the story I wrote. Even in those days Rockne was a big man in South Bend. The *Tribune* catered to him.

I was making fifteen dollars a week at the *Review*. I asked him, "How much do they pay?"

He offered twenty dollars. I quit school and went to work at the South Bend *Tribune*. I was there seven years. Then, I went to Washington, D.C., and was the sports editor of the Washington *News*, which was just starting up. Ernie Pyle went to work at the paper at the same time.

I was very friendly with George Gipp. We made trips together. He went to Indianapolis with me. Helped me cover the races. I was with him in the hospital a week before he died.

Gipp was from Laurium, Michigan, a small town along the Canadian border. Some people said he didn't play football in high school. But he did. He was a natural athlete. In those days drop-kicking was the big thing. The football was smaller. Gipp was a great passer and, of course, he was a great runner. But he was a fiend at drop-kicking.

He didn't go to college right away. When he got to Notre Dame he was two, three years older than his classmates. He was a loner. If it wasn't for football, he'd be what you'd call a misfit. He didn't mix much with the other players. He was a pool shark and a good poker player. Loved to gamble. And he had other interests but I'm not going to go into that.

He drove a taxicab in Ypsilanti after he got out of high school. His father was a minister, but they were very poor. In the summer Gipp played baseball on a semipro team. Back then all the towns had semipro teams. He always said he was a better baseball player than a football player. A lot of people said that.

The fellow who discovered him was a scout for the White Sox, Dolly Gray. Gray was a Notre Dame alumnus. He had played on the Notre Dame baseball team. Later, he played some pro ball. He was a catcher in the White Sox organization, when the White Sox had Ray Schalk.

Once Dolly Gray saw Gipp on the baseball field he decided he couldn't miss as a ballplayer. He could do everything in baseball. He was an outfielder. He could hit. He could run. He could throw a strike to the plate. It was Gray who got him a baseball scholarship to Notre Dame. Gray told him, "Don't make the mistake and go out for the football team down there. They're too good for you."

Gipp was with his Hall baseball team, in the yard at Corby Hall. A football got loose and bounced to where he was standing. Gipp just picked it up and drop-kicked it back to where the freshman football team was practicing. Rockne ran over to him and said, "Why aren't you out for football?"

"Oh," he said, "I'm a baseball player. I'm not supposed to go out for football."

Rockne walked him over to the football field and said, "I want you to try out for football. Would you do that?"

From then on Gipp was a football player. He was terrific as a football player. The quickest thinker on a football field I ever saw and I've seen a lot of them. One game stands out: a freshman game against Western Michigan on an icy field. Neither team had scored. There were a few minutes left. Notre Dame had the ball and was going to punt. This was in 1916. Rockne was coaching the freshman team.

Gipp called time and went over to the sideline and told Rockne, "I can win this game for you. Just let them pass me the ball and I'll drop-kick it." And he kicked the ball right through the uprights, sixty-three yards, a record. Or I should say it was a record.

Gipp didn't finish his freshman year. He went home for the Christmas break and didn't come back until the following fall, seven or eight months later, just in time for football practice. When they began assembling his records, the 1916 season wasn't included, as if he wasn't there.

He played four years of varsity ball, from 1917 through 1920. Every year he led the team in everything—kicking, passing, running. He could throw a football just like he threw a baseball. He was a great runner. Once he broke into the open he was gone.

He was the left halfback. In those days the left halfback was the passer. In his junior and senior years Notre Dame was undefeated. His biggest games, the games that got him the most publicity, were against Army. They were two of the greatest games of the time. Both times Notre Dame came from behind. Gipp was the hero in both games.

After the first Army game Ring Lardner—he was then in New York—wrote me a letter and said, "Notre Dame has the greatest system I ever saw. All they do is give Gipp the ball and let him do whatever he wants." I still have that letter. It's here somewhere.

Now I'll give you the story of the injury. That's what led to his death. It was against Indiana in the next to last game of the 1920 season. I was with Gipp the evening before the game, in Indianapolis at the Claypool Hotel. He was with some friends. Gipp wouldn't bet. People would bet for him.

I said to his friends, "The only bet you can make is that George will score more points than the Indiana team." George smiled when I said that. He kind of liked the idea.

The Indiana players were set for Gipp. One or two of the Indiana players were from South Bend. They knew the Notre Dame formations, all the plays. They were right on top of Gipp in the first series, gang-tackled him and injured his neck. He had to leave the game.

Finally, Rockne realized what was happening. He started using some old formations. Norm Barry, who was a very smart player, was on that team. With Barry in charge, Notre Dame began moving the ball. Barry carried to within scoring distance but then he got hurt.

Gipp got up from the bench and took off his robe and said, "I'm going in." And he ran for the winning touchdown. Injury and all, he scored nine points, one point less than the Indiana team. Notre Dame won 13–10.

The final game was against Northwestern. They played in Evanston, just outside of Chicago. Notre Dame always had its biggest following in Chicago. By this time Gipp was a big hero all over the country. Rockne wasn't going to use him because of his neck injury. In the fourth quarter, the fans set up the chant "We Want Gipp! We Want Gipp!"

Gipp pleaded with Rockne. "I can go out there and throw a pass."

Rockne shouldn't have done it. It was the regret of his life. Gipp played ten minutes. He threw two touchdown passes. I think the first pass was to Norm Barry, the second to Roger Kiley, both from Chicago. Gipp didn't come out of the game until he reinjured his neck.

But that isn't what killed him, although it led to it. It weakened him. He caught a cold and got a sore throat, a strep throat. Streptococci. In those days there was no cure for streptococci. He thought he'd be in the hospital about a week. He never came out. He died in mid-December, on the day of the first winter snow.

Notre Dame had had a lot of great players but Gipp was the first Notre Dame man to make Walter Camp's All-American team. As soon as Walter Camp's team came over the wire I left the office and brought it to the hospital. Gipp was very sick, very low. He was as thin as your arm.

I took it to his bed. He smiled. He was very pleased. Rockne and a priest were there. He looked up at Rockne and saw that Rockne was broken up. He told Rockne, "Don't worry about me. I'm real happy now. I'm ready to go."

Then he said, "When the going gets tough out there, Rock, do me a favor and tell the boys to win one for the Gipper."

Gene Kessler   329

That was one of the big scenes in the movie. But in the movie they have Rockne telling him he made Walter Camp's team.

Rockne was the greatest coach of the time. He was a disciple of Fielding Yost of Michigan. Yost used to win from everybody. When he took Michigan to the Rose Bowl, Rockne noticed that Yost had the fastest players. They got the jump on everybody. Rockne picked up on it. He was always looking for fast men. He built his teams on speed.

That's why Rockne devised the Notre Dame shift: 1-2-3 hip. His backfield men were fast and had perfect timing. They would come down on their feet with the snap of the ball and were off and gone. Rockne always claimed the little man won football games. It's not true today but it was true then.

Rockne had a way of bawling out people and making them like it. I never knew anybody who didn't like him. He was a perfectionist. He emphasized the importance of practice. He ate and slept football. Once, when we were returning from a game his wife met the train. He was so engrossed he walked right past her.

Rockne was very loyal. Very sincere. He was a brilliant man. Later, he became a good storyteller and inspirational speaker. He worked on that. He was in great demand as a speaker. He could motivate a mouse. He died in a plane crash, coming home after he had given a speech in Wichita.

During those years in South Bend I put on a couple of charity fights. They didn't draw. None made money. I didn't know too much about fights. But I became a so-called boxing expert overnight because of my friendship with a promoter in Benton Harbor, a fellow named Floyd Fitzsimmons.

It was Fitzsimmons who gave Jack Dempsey his big break. Dempsey was on the Pacific Coast fighting four-rounders, getting nowhere. Dempsey was knocked out once, in some small town in Utah. Jack Kearns took him over, taught him how to bob and weave, how to crouch. Dempsey learned that a punch is more effective if you hit your opponent when he is boring in, coming toward you. By pivoting from the waist, he punched hard at close range, in the clinches.

They came to Chicago expecting to get fights right off. No one would give Dempsey a fight. The fighters were afraid of him. In those days Dempsey didn't have that good a name. He wasn't a drawing card. He was Kid Blackie. He was known only in northern California, in the Bay area.

He and Kearns took a room at the Morrison Hotel. They didn't have enough money to pay the bill. Broke or not, Kearns was a genius at getting publicity. He told the Chicago boxing writers and, of course, they wrote about it, he would bet ten thousand dollars Dempsey could beat any two fighters, *simultaneously*.

Nothing happened until Fitzsimmons came in from Benton Harbor. He saw Dempsey working out in Kid Howard's gymnasium. Fitzsimmons had a fighter, Homer Smith, a big hulking fellow, six-foot-four, a half foot taller than Dempsey. Homer Smith was a contender for Jess Willard's title and was booked in Racine, Wisconsin. The promoter in Racine, John Wagner, told Fitzsimmons "I'll let you pick your opponent."

Fitzsimmons had taken a liking to Dempsey and Kearns. He felt sorry for them. He told Dempsey: "I can put you into a fight. You might knock off my contender. But I'll take that chance."

Dempsey came out swinging. He knocked out Homer Smith in the first round.

Kearns took Dempsey East. Within a few months he was "Jack the Giant Killer." Still, it wasn't until eighteen months after he had knocked out Homer Smith he got the title match with Willard in Toledo. It became a famous date in boxing history, July 4, 1919.

Fitzsimmons kept telling me Dempsey would destroy Willard. Not too many people believed that. Willard was six-six, outweighed Dempsey by sixty-five pounds. Fitzsimmons sold me a bill of goods. I was one of the few sportswriters to pick Dempsey.

Dempsey knocked Willard down seven times in the first round. Willard took a terrible beating. Dempsey broke his jaw. Broke his nose. Split his cheekbone. Cracked at least one rib. Willard's body was covered with red welts.

Dempsey had thrown so many punches he had sapped his strength. There wasn't much action in the second and third rounds. Willard couldn't come out for the fourth round. It was a big victory for Dempsey. For me, too. That fight made me a boxing expert.

Dempsey turned around and told Fitzsimmons, "Now I want to repay you. I'll fight my first title defense for you and give you a chance to make some money."

It was Dempsey against Billy Miske in Benton Harbor. Dempsey picked Miske for old times' sake, to give him a payday. He liked Miske. He had beaten him twice before. By this time Miske was washed up. Dempsey knocked him out in the third round. It was Miske's last fight. For the next thirty years I covered every heavyweight title fight.

Six months later, in the summer of 1920, Fitzsimmons put on another big show in Benton Harbor, Benny Leonard and Charlie White. Benny Leonard was one of the greatest lightweights who ever lived. One of the greatest I ever saw. Charlie White was a hard-luck fighter. He was "Hard Luck Charlie." White had floored and almost won the title from two or three lightweights.

In the fifth or sixth round White connected with a left hook. He had a great left hook. He knocked Leonard out of the ring. I was in the first row, under the canvas. Leonard landed right in front of me, almost in my lap. Benny Leonard's brother pushed him back in the ring. Leonard knocked Charlie White out in the ninth round. Like there was nothing to it.

Later, when I was the sports editor in Washington, D.C., I went to New York for the Dempsey-Firpo fight. The New York writers had the front row. I was behind Jack Lawrence of the New York *American*. Firpo was a terrific puncher, a tremendously powerful man and a pretty good fighter. He was a great deal like Marciano except he was about twice as big and just about as fast.

Jimmy De Forest was Firpo's trainer. But Firpo fired De Forest. He got Leo Friend to train him. Friend was a smart guy. He set up a surprise punch for Firpo. He told Firpo, "Now when you come out to shake hands, instead of shaking hands, start a right uppercut to the chin." I had the inside story on that.

Firpo knocked Dempsey to his knees. Before Dempsey could get his hands up Firpo knocked him out of the ring. Almost knocked him out. Dempsey fell on Jack Lawrence's typewriter. So two of the greatest fighters who ever lived were knocked out of the ring, right in front of me.

Dempsey said he didn't remember anything about the first round, that he fought the entire round in a daze. It shows you the kind of fighter Dempsey was. It was the greatest round in boxing history. Seven knockdowns. Firpo was down five times, Dempsey twice. Dempsey knocked him down two more times. Firpo lasted fifty-seven seconds into the second round. Nine knockdowns in less than four minutes.

I saw Joe Louis for the first time about eight or nine years later, in the early 1930s when he was an amateur, in the Golden Gloves. I could see he had ability but I waited. I wanted to see what he could do when they got him in with a tough heavyweight.

Louis turned pro in 1934, right in my front yard. I was in Chicago, assistant sports editor of the *Daily Times*. They wanted me to write fights. Eight of Louis's first eleven fights were in Chicago. I saw five or six them and two or three in Detroit. Between fights I watched him working out at Trafton's Gym.

They matched him with a fellow named Lee Ramage, a good boxer. Very clever. For the first four rounds Louis was outboxed, badly, but he caught up with him and knocked him out in the eighth round. A month later they fought again in Los Angeles. When Louis took him out in two I was convinced.

I used to see Julian Black at Trafton's. Black and John Roxborough were Louis's co-managers. Roxborough had discovered Louis in Detroit. Black was the money man. He was in the numbers game, a big policy man on the South Side. I told Black, "This fellow's going to make you an awful lot of money. If he gets a chance, he can't miss."

Black asked me if I'd be interested in handling the publicity. I was agreeable. I signed a contract, for five years, that gave me exclusive use of Louis's byline. When I began sending out stories, some people said, "You're crazy. The papers aren't going to print that stuff. He's a colored man, a Negro."

I said, "What's the difference? He's a good fighter. He's the best fighter."

I did the first book on him, *Joe Louis, The Brown Bomber*. I knew a fellow named Schlesinger who circulated the Big Little Books in all the dime stores. The book sold for a dime. It was a big seller. Almost a million copies were sold. From the money I made on Louis I was able to build my house in Elmhurst, my first house.

But my big break came when I got in with Fulton Oursler who was the editor of *Liberty* magazine. Oursler called me. He wanted a four-part series. Altogether, I sold *Liberty* sixteen stories, "Joe Louis as told to Gene Kessler." Some were biographical, some were feature stories, usually hooked up with a fight that was coming up.

Louis was the nicest fellow you ever met. He was very polite, very humble. I always got along with him. I understood him when a lot of people didn't. He was from the South and sometimes wasn't too good pronouncing his words.

I'm prejudiced, of course, but Louis did more to help the colored people than any other athlete because he handled himself so well. He was the exact opposite of Jack Johnson. Johnson had an arrogant way about him. Louis was so perfect nobody could complain about him. There was no braggadocio in him like this Muhammad Ali. I'm not criticizing Ali. That's his business.

The guy who gave me a lot of the stuff was Jack Blackburn. Blackburn was Louis's trainer, one of the best trainers of that time. He trained Sammy Mandell and Bud Taylor and quite a few other champions. He was reluctant to take Louis over. He told Julian Black, "I made a lot of money training white boys because they get the big money. A colored boy won't get the big fights."

Julian Black extended my contract for two more years. There were advantages as a boxing writer. After a fight I was usually the first one in the dressing room. When Max Schmeling knocked out Louis, Tom Dewey, the governor of New York, came down to the dressing room and wanted in. They wouldn't let him in, not right away. But I went on through. I got kick out of that.

Once Mike Jacobs took over, he took over everything. He called all the shots. The Garden had its own publicity man. Of course, Mike Jacobs made Louis. He got him his title. But he was responsible for his trouble with the government.

Louis was married to Marva Trotter. He never played around. Then he went into the army and the guy who led him around was Sugar Ray Robinson, his buddy. After that I guess you could say Louis played the field. He didn't have to go looking. They were knocking on his door.

Louis liked Marva and she liked him. But she wanted a divorce and a big settlement. You can't blame her for that. Mike Jacobs came up with an idea. He cut Julian Black out and gave Marva half interest on the managerial end. The managers get 50 percent. Her lawyers advised her to take it. She grabbed it.

They gave her $500,000 up front. Maybe it was $1 million. And she got 25 percent of the money Louis made in the ring. In effect, that was her alimony. Five or six years later the IRS, the income tax people, disallowed the deduction. They leveled the tax at him, claiming it was part of the divorce settlement. That's what put Louis in debt. The interest ran into the millions.

I got into the newspaper game because I didn't want to spend my life working in a furniture factory. My father had a small lumber business. He lost everything in the Depression, the McKinley Depression. He had to go to Indianapolis and went to work in a furniture factory. He was a finisher. I worked there two summers. I was an apprentice upholsterer.

When I was in grammar school I had an English teacher, Miss Foy. Roy Howard was her prize pupil. At that time Roy Howard was in South America working for Scripps and organizing the United Press. He sent Miss Foy postal cards about how he was doing. She read the cards to the class.

Miss Foy told us how Roy Howard had started, how he got books on newspaper reporting from the library. When he graduated from high school, he went to work on the Indianapolis *Star*. I read the books he did and got a job on the Indianapolis *News*. When it was time for me to go to college I switched to the Crawfordsville *Review*.

I followed Roy Howard's career. He was a legend in the newspaper business. He scooped the world on the end of World War I. After I had been at the South Bend *Tribune* for seven years I wrote him a letter and told him about Miss Foy, that we had had the same teacher. He was starting the Washington *News* and expanding the Scripps papers, what later became the Scripps-Howard chain.

Roy Howard recruited quite a few writers from Indiana. He hired me as the sports editor of the Washington *News*. Ernie Pyle was from Dana, Indiana. He grew up on a farm. I knew him when he was working in LaPorte. Roy Howard brought him to Washington, too, at the same time, in 1923. Ernie was a deskman. Nobody knew he would become one of the great American war correspondents.

Ernie Pyle didn't stay in Washington. He went to New York as the aviation editor of Scripps-Howard. He became ill, with tuberculosis. The doctors told him to stay in the open as much as he could. In those days they thought fresh air was the cure for it.

The paper bought him a car and he and his wife began touring the country. Ernie wrote about individuals, ordinary people. He would find an old man in a trailer camp, find out how life had treated him. He caught on. Scripps-Howard began syndicating him. When World

War II began he was sent overseas. He was killed by a sniper's bullet on some small island near Okinawa.

I was surprised when he went over big. Now I realize it was because he wrote in the vein like Fulton Oursler said I did when I wrote for *Liberty*. Fulton Oursler didn't want deep-thinkers. He emphasized simplicity. That's why Ernie Pyle was so well-read. He didn't use big, fancy words or phrases. He wrote in a way everyone could understand.

Scripps-Howard never raised anyone. When I left Washington I was still getting sixty dollars a week and I had been there five years. I took a job as the editor of *The Sporting News* in St. Louis. J. G. Taylor Spink hired me. This was in 1929. I hadn't been there for more than a few weeks when Taylor called me into his office and said, "I want to give you a little history, background on *The Sporting News*."

He told me why his father, Charlie Spink, fired Ring Lardner. Ring had been the editor. He was fired because he refused to violate a release date. In those days, baseball had an agreement with the Associated Press to handle the weekly baseball averages. *The Sporting News* didn't take the AP service. They got the averages early, from a guy name of Harry Barnes, who worked on a paper in Danville, Illinois.

Ring refused to run the averages. He told Charlie Spink he wouldn't break a release date. Ring put the paper to bed without them. The old man fired him. It had been almost twenty years since Ring Lardner had been at *The Sporting News*. What Taylor was really telling me was that he wanted me to know he was running the paper the way his father did, that I was expected to follow orders.

Later, I realized he hired me because he knew I was friendly with Judge Landis. He expected me to heal the wounds. I knew there was enmity between them. Judge Landis hated him.

One day when Landis was in St. Louis, Spink told me: "Landis is at the Coronado Hotel. I want you to go over and see him. Find out if we can become friends."

I saw Landis and, finally after I had been with him a long while, I told him why I was there. And Landis said, "You go back and tell that dirty sonofabitch that as long as you're working for him I won't talk to you, either." It wasn't long after that that Spink let me go. It was the only time in my life I was fired.

○ ○ ○ ○
○ ○ ○ ○
○ ○ ○ ○

Ray Gillespie

In his early years as a baseball writer, Raymond John Gillespie wrote an article defending Ty Cobb who had had an altercation with a fan. Gillespie reported that the fan was at fault; he had instigated the brawl with a blizzard of obscenities. Pleased that someone had written his side, Cobb told Gillespie, "I'll get you out of this hick town and into New York where you belong."

Gillespie had several opportunities to work elsewhere but never left St. Louis. "This is my hometown and this is where I belong," he said at the conclusion of my interview. He worked at the St. Louis Star *and its successor, the* Star-Times, *for the next thirty-two years. His first job was as a dollar-a-day sports department copy boy when he was a high school sophomore.*

After he was graduated he planned to enroll at the University of Missouri, majoring in journalism, but his boss told him, "The best school for a young man is the school of experience.*" Four years later, in 1923, he began his twenty-eight-year career as a baseball writer, alternating between the Browns and Cardinals. His enthusiasm for the newspaper business never waned. When the* Star-Times *folded in 1951, he joined* The Sporting News *and worked there until he died in 1979 at the age of seventy-five.*

He had come to St. Louis to see his brother and sister. They had been having separate romantic affairs in Mexico City, an embarrassment to the family. I got them the apartment that Leo Durocher had given up. Eventually, the girl married the boyfriend, the fellow Jorge Pasquel was trying to keep out of the picture.

Jorge Pasquel was a great baseball fan. He owned the club in Vera Cruz. Actually, he and his brothers owned the Mexican League. I had known him a few years by the time he got to St. Louis. The Cardinals were in town and so I took him to Sportsman's Park. It was early in the season, in forty-five. Marty Marion was holding out. He was Mr. Shortstop of the time. The year before he was the National League's MVP. A dependable hitter. Marvelous in the field.

"Where'd he come from?" Jorge asked. "He didn't play yesterday?"

I told him Marion had been holding out for twelve thousand.

Jorge was surprised: "I'll give him twenty-five thousand to play for me."

I told him he couldn't do that.

"Who says I can't? I'll go down and talk to him."

I did my best to explain. It was against the law. It wasn't allowed. He would be tampering with Organized Baseball.

And he said, "That's a monopoly. Who's that pitching for Pittsburgh?"

It was Al Gerhauser, a left-hander, a run-of-the-mill pitcher. I doubt he ever won more than ten games. He was having a good night.

"How much does he make?"

"Oh, about six or seven thousand."

"Six or seven thousand! I'll give him twenty thousand."

That's when the whole thing was born. Right there, in Sportsman's Park in St. Louis.

He was on his way to Rochester, Minnesota, to the Mayo Clinic. He was a nut on physical culture. He had to know if he was in perfect condition. He had brought his barber with him and his mother but they stayed in St. Louis.

He wanted to stop in Chicago, to go to Comiskey Park and see the White Sox. We stayed at the Stevens Hotel. In those days, during the war, you couldn't get a room. A hotelman in St. Louis got us rooms.

Anytime Jorge saw a good player he wanted him. After Rochester, he went to New York, the penthouse suite at the Waldorf. He told me the trip, the whole sojurn, a matter of a few months, cost him $282,000.

Jorge Pasquel was very wealthy, one of the richest families in Mexico, estimated fortune $70 to $80 million. Even at the ballpark he ate off a silver tray. He always said, "With money I can buy anything. Every man or woman has a price."

Once, we were in a restaurant, a ritzy place. "You see that girl over there?" She was a beautiful cashier. "I guarantee you for a price I will have her tonight. I'll show you money talks. One thousand dollars will pay the price. Any gal will do whatever you want for a thousand dollars."

And the next night he showed up with this gal on his arm.

Jorge wasn't the head of the family. He was number two. Bernardo was older. But Jorge was very aggressive. He ran the show. He had decided they were going to have big league baseball in Mexico. The sky was the limit. Bernardo usually came to New York to participate in the interviewing.

Their first player was Danny Gardella, an outfielder with the Giants. They signed more than a dozen players, some of them very good players: Mickey Owen. Sal Maglie. Max Lanier. Lou Klein. They came close to getting Stan Musial. Not only Musial but the whole Cardinal outfield.

It was an exciting time, particularly for me. The Brooklyn Dodgers took me into federal court. Branch Rickey brought suit against me. It wasn't pleasant. But I had a fantastic run of exclusive stories for my paper, the *Star-Times*. It was "The Midnight Ride of Jorge Pasquel: The Mexican League Raid."

Ban Johnson was one of my good friends. He had been the president of the American League, one of baseball's great pioneers. He made regular stops here to see Phil Ball, who owned the Browns. They were great friends, with common enemies. They hated Judge

Landis. A lot of people probably don't know this but, after the Black Sox scandal, when Landis was elected commissioner, Phil Ball was the only owner who refused to sign the agreement.

Ban Johnson was always talking up Mexico. He went there twice a year. He'd get on the train here, the Missouri Pacific which went all the way to Mexico City. He would tell me how wonderful those people were and that baseball there was in its infancy, but in years to come it had great possibilities.

He got Ed Wray, who was the sports editor of the *Post Dispatch*, to go down there. When Ed Wray came back, he was converted. I was covering the Browns. Wray said to me, "When you get to San Antonio"—that's where the Browns had their spring training—"why don't you go into Mexico?" I think I made my first trip in 1937. I got to know some people in Laredo who took me into Mexico and introduced me to a lot of sports people, baseball people.

On my first trip in I met a man known as Fray Nano. He was the publisher of the daily sports paper in Mexico City, *El Aficionado*, which means the fan. We got to be very close. Through him I met the Pasquel brothers. Jorge was always in front. He was putting a lot of his money into this Mexican League, to make it go. He felt baseball should be their national pastime rather than bullfighting or soccer.

When I began watching his games, he would ask, "How can we improve our baseball?" I told him he could begin by getting rid of his Cuban umpires and bring in American umpires who are firm and honest and above reproach. I lined up five or six American umpires and sent them down, umpires from the minors, the high minors.

In those days the Negro players were banned from the big leagues. They were welcome in Mexico. Satchel Paige and Josh Gibson played in Mexico. I recruited Roy Campanella. Campy was a very young man in those days, out of Philadelphia, and like most of those boys he would say, "I need another hundred dollars." I'd get the hundred dollars for him. I recruited Quincy Trouppe, another very good catcher. He lived here in St. Louis. I did the negotiating for them.

When Jorge began signing big league players I was not involved. Not directly. Because of our friendship, Jorge would call me and tell me who he was signing. Filled me in on everything. And we'd run the exclusive story: "Jorge Pasquel announced today in Mexico City he has signed pitcher Ace Adams of the New York Giants," and so on.

A New York newspaperman would call the Giants and they didn't know anything. I was scooping them on their own activities. I remember one club official saying, "That's funny, he was just here in the clubhouse an hour ago."

The wire services were picking up my stories, the Associated Press, International News, United Press. Naturally, they would quote the *Star-Times*. The heat got a little rough on our opposition, the *Post Dispatch*. I had these scoops on an average of about once a week.

The *Post Dispatch* called me and wanted to know if I was getting my information from Mexico. I said, "Is this confidential?"

"Yes, it is."

"All right, then, if it's in confidence, I'll tell you. I'm getting it from Mexico City. From Jorge Pasquel."

Then they wanted to know if I had been dealing with Mickey Owen. He had jumped from the Brooklyn Dodgers. And in the next edition the *Post Dispatch* came out with a story naming me as an agent for the Mexican League.

The publisher of the *Star-Times* became concerned that the mighty *Post Dispatch* was coming after us. All the big shots at the *Star-Times* ran scared of the *Post Dispatch*. I gave the publisher all the details. I told him I was just reporting the news.

Then, when Branch Rickey, who was one of his church buddies, filed a suit against me, well, that really upset him. Rickey had left the Cardinals two or three years before. He was now with the Dodgers, hooked up with Walter O'Malley. At that time they may have been co-owners.

Down through the years Rickey and I had been good friends. This much of a friend: When I was a young guy breaking in, a young punk of twenty-three or twenty-four, he offered me a job as the general manager of the Danville club in the Three Eye League which was a Cardinal farm.

I talked to my boss about it and he told me, "Mr. Rickey is a very smart man. And if he likes you, you'll go places. Go ahead. Take a shot at it."

When I went to take the job, Charlie Barrett, the Cardinals' chief scout, intercepted me. Mr. Rickey had changed his mind. He had decided I was more valuable to the Cardinals as a newspaperman, that I was a very talented newspaperman.

Rickey sued me on the grounds I had committed an act detrimental to baseball, that I had enticed Mickey Owen to jump his contract. It wasn't just Rickey. It was Walter O'Malley and the Brooklyn Baseball Club: a hundred thousand dollars in damages and an injunction to prevent me from tampering with their players.

It was a federal suit, heard here in St. Louis. The suit wasn't against the *Star-Times*. It was against me. So I had to hire a lawyer which was going to cost me $2,500.

Sam Breadon, who owned the Cardinals, disliked Rickey. They had had a falling out. Rickey had worked for the Cardinals for a lot of years. He was a very smart baseball man. I'll tell you how how smart he was: In forty-two, his last year with the Cardinals, he made eighty thousand dollars.

That was big, big money in those days. He was on salary and got a share of the profits, 20 percent of what the Cardinals made on all player sales. The Cardinals were always selling players. They had a huge farm system. Rickey was the father of chain gang baseball.

The Cardinals had suffered more than the Dodgers. Sam Breadon lost three players to the Mexican League. Breadon and I were good friends. He knew I had nothing to do with it. So he went to bat for me. We had a meeting at the Jefferson Hotel. He said, "Do you have money to pay for a suit?" Of course, I didn't have any money. I didn't have change for a quarter. So he said, "Well, I'll guarantee you this: If your paper doesn't pay for this, in spite of the fact that they got all those exclusive stories, I'll see to it that you don't have to pay. I'll pay for it."

I said, "How can I repay you?"

"You don't have to repay me. We've been friends down through the years. You've done marvelous work. You've been aboveboard about everything. I've heard you talk to people straight from the shoulder. Judge Landis likes you. He's a good friend of yours. You just defend yourself and tell it like it is."

I was involved with the Mickey Owen thing but only in a minor way. Mickey was in the service, in the Navy. I think he was stationed in Rochester, somewhere in the East. He got in touch with Mr. Rickey and said, "On such and such a day I'm going to be discharged. What about my contract?"

Rickey told him he wouldn't get the same salary he got before he went in. Owen reminded him that once he had gone into the service his salary was frozen. And Rickey said, "Maybe I can't cut you but I don't even know if you'll play with the Dodgers. We may send you to the minors."

Mickey got in touch with Jorge Pasquel. Jorge was in New York. Mickey explained he was about to become a civilian and was preparing to rejoin the Dodgers but Mr. Rickey wanted to either cut his salary or release him.

Jorge told him he was leaving for Mexico. When he got there he would dictate a salary contract and send it up to the United States. Jorge asked him where he was going. Mickey was heading for Springfield, Missouri, where he lived. They agreed on the terms. I don't remember if it was for twelve thousand or twenty-five thousand. It's all in the data here.

Jorge said, "On your way to Springfield, stop in St. Louis and call Ray Gillespie. I'll send him the contract." And when Jorge got back to Mexico he called to tell me he was sending me the contract. A day or two later Mickey called. I believe he was in Effingham, Illinois. He was driving.

I had the contract but it was in Spanish. I told him by the time he got here I'd have it translated into English so he would know what he was signing. I would go to the embassy or the consulate and have someone sign the thing on behalf of Jorge. But I couldn't find anybody.

So here's Mickey in the *Star-Times* office, with his wife, ready to sign. If he doesn't sign I lose the story. So I said, "I'll tell you what, I'll sign it. But when you get to the Mexican border make them give you a new contract." That was the only player contract I was involved in.

I beat the great Mr. Rickey in court. And the Newspaper Guild, which was in my corner, forced the *Star-Times* to pay for the suit and all my legal expenses. Which they did—$2,500.

The judge, really a tough judge, Rubey M. Hulen, dismissed the case. Wait, I'll get the judge's ruling:

> Inspired by a zeal for "scoops," Gillespie aggressively pressed his opportunities. He was willing to pay a consideration for information by performing favors for the Pasquels. In doing so he subjected himself to suspicion of being a party to the Pasquels' campaign or conspiracy. Suspicion will not sustain a judgment.

I think the judge also took my testimony into consideration. I said, "Mickey Owen was in the military service and when you're in the service you're not under contract to any ball club. You're under contract only to Uncle Sam."

Anyhow, prior to the trial the cloak and dagger stuff was still going on. The Mexican League was attempting to sign Ted Williams, the great Red Sox hitter, and Phil Rizzuto of the Yankees. Mickey Owen was now representing the Mexican League, helping Jorge get players.

Mickey called me and said he was in St. Louis with Alphonso, one of the Pasquel brothers. They were having lunch at Miss Hulling's, a very fine downtown restaurant. From there they were going to see Stan Musial. After Musial, the next step, was Terry Moore, Enos Slaughter, and Whitey Kurowski. Mickey asked me to call Musial and tell him they were on their way.

I said, "Certainly, I'll send a photographer over and we'll get a picture."

As I learned later they they were supposed to bring $150,000 in cash. But for some unknown reason, when they left Neuvo Laredo, they didn't properly get that amount. They brought something like $62,000 and dumped it in front of Stan, at his home. It was a scene out of a gangster movie. The photographer got his picture and we're going to run it in the next edition. In those days we had sports extras, editions every hour.

The makeup editor, a close friend of mine, called me to the composing room and told me my story and the picture had been killed. What happened was that the managing editor notified the federal government that Mickey Owen and one of the Pasquels were in town and the feds were on their way to pick them up.

It was typical of the *Star-Times*. The editors were frightened. It was a small paper. Going into the trial, they even had me write a confession. If I had been with the *Post Dispatch* everything would have been different. It would have been terrific. They probably would have made a big hero out of me instead of a goat.

The intention of the *Star-Times* was to show they were blameless. Sid Keener, my sports editor, was called in to read my confession. He said, "I can't see anything wrong. He should get a bonus for the good work he's been doing." And Sid Keener, in turn, was censured for being disloyal to the paper.

Later, after the trial, I divorced myself from the whole thing. If the paper wasn't going to back me, I wasn't going to write any more stories or allow the use of my byline. This lasted about a week. The Newspaper Guild warned me that if I refused to work I could be fired for insubordination.

Another call came in from Mexico. Junior Stephens of the Red Sox, a very strong hitter, was jumping. I went to the managing editor and asked what I should do. He told me I should work harder than ever digging up exclusive stories but everything I wrote had to go through him before it was set in type. Junior Stephens went down there, played in two games and jumped back. I got that story, too.

I wanted to repay Sam Breadon. He had supported me. He insisted it wasn't necessary. But I felt it was my duty. Then I thought of something I could do but I told him it wouldn't work. He'd be afraid.

"What won't work? I'm afraid of no man or beast. There's nobody alive I'm afraid of."

I told him about Musial and a couple of other Cardinal players. Jorge Pasquel was still negotiating with them. I suggested to Breadon that he go to Mexico and see the Pasquels. He thought for a while and asked if I could arrange it. I told him Jorge would listen to me. I also said I would tell Jorge that Breadon wasn't a friend of Mr. Rickey or Happy Chandler, who was then commissioner.

I reported back to Breadon and told him, "If can convince Jorge you're still enemies with these people that he hates I'm sure he will welcome you."

At first, Jorge was reluctant to meet anybody connected with "The Great American Baseball Monopoly." I told Jorge that Sam Breadon was a different person. "You'll like this man. He's very honest. And he wants to meet the man who took three of his ballplayers. He thinks you're a better man than he is."

Breadon went to Mexico and they got along fine. At the end of their conversation, Jorge told him, "I know these three players we took from you have a value of at least two-hundred and fifty-thousand dollars." Max Lanier, Fred Martin, and Lou Klein had jumped the Cardinals. "I will send them back. I want you to beat Branch Rickey and the Dodgers."

It was too late. Chandler had expelled the jumpers for five years.

"All right. I'll make a deal with you and we'll shake hands. My negotiations with Musial and your other players are off. There will be no more Cardinals."

All of this was very secret. I didn't write about their meeting. But Gordon Cobbledick, the Cleveland sportswriter, was on vacation in Mexico City. Cobbledick bumped into Danny Gardella and Danny, always trying to be a big shot, told him Sam Breadon was meeting with Jorge Pasquel. Cobbledick broke the story.

Happy Chandler rushed into the act. Chandler fined Breadon five thousand dollars for consorting with the enemy and told him he couldn't attend the next owners' meeting. Breadon insisted he not only wouldn't pay the five thousand dollars but threatened to withhold all five of his players, maybe it was seven, from the All-Star game.

The older heads prevailed, Tom Yawkey of the Red Sox and Larry MacPhail of the Yankees. Breadon went to Boston for the meeting. He didn't pay the fine, either. He wrote a check to Chandler, as the commissioner, and Chandler signed it and gave it back to him.

The older I got the more aware I became of all the hate in baseball and it was all at the top. Chandler was disliked and, of course, so was Branch Rickey. One day, when I was in Chicago, I stopped in to see Judge Landis. I made it a habit to visit with him at least once a year. And his greeting was "How is my old friend, Sam Breadon? And how is that sanctimonious sonofabitch, Branch Rickey?"

And he would always tell me, "If I live to be a hundred, I'll never die until I get rid of that dirty sonofabitch." He hated Rickey. Just despised him.

Judge Landis was wonderful to me. Once, when we were together at his office on Michigan Avenue, I reminded him it was almost game time. I had to get out to Wrigley Field. The judge said, "That's exactly where I'm taking you."

So he called for a limousine and we drove out to the park. They opened the gate and we drove right into Wrigley Field. There was this man who supplied him popcorn and he handed him a great big box and Judge Landis said, "I want two today—one for my friend." He took me into his box and there I sat eating popcorn. The guys in the press box were yelling and trying to attract my attention, trying to tell me that my paper was on the wire. I finally excused myself and went up there.

I never really disliked Rickey. I always surmised one of his grievances was because he was trying to sign Negro ballplayers and I was in there ahead of him, sending them to Mexico. Once it was over he acted as though nothing had happened. I would see him when he came in to visit with the Browns. He was a good friend of the DeWitts, Charley and Bill. He never apologized. He never mentioned it and neither did I.

During the suit, maybe it was a year later, Jorge Pasquel bought the biggest newspaper in Mexico City and offered me the job as as managing editor. Sid Keener pleaded with me to go down there. He said, "It's only a matter of time and you'll be a national hero." It was a Spanish-language paper. I can speak a little Spanish but that's all. Anyway, I never wanted to leave St. Louis. I was born here and I want to die here.

I still have a close relationship with the Mexican baseball people. I go there once a year. Just this year, last June, they made me an honorary citizen of Monterrey. The newspapermen there asked me if I thought I had done a good deed for baseball by writing all these stories about the jumpers. I explained it was a good thing because the salaries had been very low. Today, the salaries are so high the players are going to price themselves out of business.

In those days a lot of the big stars, people like Dizzy Dean, that type, were making $7,500 a year. Dean was a character. But he was a great pitcher. Not a good pitcher, a great pitcher. I always had one saying for him: He never did anything wrong on the field and he never did anything right off the field.

I enjoyed being with the ballplayers, the closeness. When I broke in the pickings were rather lean. The Browns and the Cardinals didn't have a lot of money and the newspapermen roomed with the ballplayers. I had a half-dozen roommates: Baby Doll Jacobson; Wally Gerber; Ray Kolp, for many years; a fellow named Rasty Wright. Some of them would watch me while I was writing. Once a player said, "That's not correct. That's not what the argument was about." So I changed my story.

Urban Shocker, the famous pitcher, was one of my closest friends. We never roomed together but he was a pal. Because of him I got the biggest scoop of my life, except for the Mexican League stories. Shocker was traded from the Browns to the Yankees. I went out to the ballpark early, to see him. I believe it was a Saturday. As I'm going through the pass gate at Sportsman's Park, Babe Ruth was coming out. I asked him, "Babe, where are you going? Aren't you playing today?"

"No, not today. I'm going to New York."

I couldn't understand it. Then he says, "You better ask Hug"—that's Miller Huggins, the Yankee manager.

I made a beeline for the Yankee dugout and there's Shocker. I believe he was going to pitch that day. I told him I had bumped into the Babe and that he was going to New York. Shocker winked at me and took me over to see Huggins. Shocker said, "You know Ray Gillespie?"

Huggins said, "Oh, sure."

And Shocker gives me the big buildup. He tells him I'm a good guy, one of his best friends: "He wants to know about the Babe."

Huggins admitted he had fined the Babe five thousand dollars and sent him home. The fine was for insubordination, for breaking training, being out all night.

I said, "Five thousand?" It was unheard of. "Do you mean five hundred?"

The telegraph operators weren't there yet. There was nobody in the press box. So I ran to the telephone and called the office: "Here's a big story! Babe Ruth has just been fined five thousand dollars."

The managing editor gets on the phone. He wouldn't believe it. He said there was nothing on the wires about it. I explained the New York writers were still at the hotel. They hadn't arrived at the ballpark yet. It was too early. He made me go back and check with Huggins again. It was true, of course. And the managing editor, instead of saying, "Thanks, great scoop," said, "If this is incorrect you're fired."

I began traveling in 1923. That year both the Cardinals and Browns had good ball clubs. The Browns missed winning the pennant by one game. The Cardinals were the big club. They won pennants in twenty-six and in twenty-eight. The writers switched off, usually a half season with each club. Some years we alternated seasons.

George Sisler of the Browns probably was the best all-around player I covered. There was no question who was the best hitter. Rogers Hornsby. He hit over .400 three times and had a .358 career lifetime, second only to Cobb and Cobb was a singles' hitter. Hornsby had power.

Hornsby was a martinet. Tough on everybody, a real disciplinarian. He wouldn't tolerate drinking. I never knew a man who was so blunt. He had absolutely no sense of diplomacy. He called a spade a spade.

He had no respect for college ballplayers. He always called them "That college so-and-so." And he didn't like Californians, even though he had two good players from California on the club, Chick Hafey and Duffy Douthit.

The big thing he was known for, aside from being the best right-handed hitter in the game, was his objections to the movies. He was always telling his players, "Don't go the movies, it'll weaken your eyesight." Just about every story written about Hornsby included his dislike of the movies.

I caught him in his own trap. We were at the Alamac Hotel in New York. The game had been called because of rain. I saw him in the lobby. It was about one o'clock. I said, "Where you going, to the races?" He loved to go to the track. Sometimes I went with him.

"No," he said, "I'm going to the movies." There was a poster in the lobby. I think it was for *Christ as King*, something religious.

"You're going to see that?"

Hornsby didn't know how to fudge. "Let's face it," he said. "I've got a date with a broad and that's where she wants to go, so that's where I'm going."

Jim Schlemmer

James Warren Schlemmer was the Mencken of the sports page. Friend or foe, he blasted everyone and was particularly scornful of know-nothing fans and Pollyana sportswriters. During his fifty-year reign as sports editor, columnist, and beat writer for the Akron Beacon-Journal, which encouraged him to ramble, his output was enormous.

"I didn't write to be popular," he often said. Stories of his off-the-field adventures abound. Asked to speak at a minor league winter baseball convention, he insisted the umpiring had to be improved, unaware that more than fifty umpires were in the audience. They didn't allow him to finish. Routed from the podium, he escaped in a freight elevator.

Although acerbic in print, I always found him friendly and of adequate good cheer. Short and stocky and well-read, he was an expert on the Civil War and also an excellent cook. Boston brown bread was his specialty. When he retired in 1970 he donated his 137 cookbooks to the local library. Born on December 24, 1899, in Punxsutawney, Pennsylvania, his desire to live in three centuries was unfulfilled. He died on May 10, 1977.

The Carnegie Foundation had made a national survey of petting on college campuses. The Ohio State *Journal* came out with the story in the morning, with a big scare headline about the high percentage of petting. I was the editor of the Ohio State *Lantern*, the daily student paper, and gave orders to the staff that we weren't going to touch it. If the story had been localized we would have used it. But we didn't have any figures on Ohio State and I didn't want any surmising.

In the middle of the morning somebody said, "If we were carrying the story what percentage of the girls on this campus pet?"

I said, "Oh, 100 percent."

And a girl named Edna Mae Smith said, "Jimmy Schlemmer, do you really think 100 percent of the girls on this campus pet?"

"Well, it might not be 100 percent. I just haven't met quite all of them yet."

I thought that was the end of the conversation but later, in the afternoon, my wonderful girlfriend, Dora Binckley, who was to become my lifelong companion and whom I had met on my way to my very first class, on my first day at Ohio State, telephoned me at my fraternity house.

And she said, "Have you seen the *Dispatch*?" I hadn't seen the Columbus *Dispatch*. It was the afternoon paper. "Well, get one and read it." Bang! She slammed down the telephone.

I sent a pledge down to the corner. He came back with a half-dozen *Dispatch*es and then I saw it—a six-column headline on Page 1: "100 Percent of Ohio State Coeds Pet," says editor of the student publication, James W. Schlemmer. Oh, brother, I knew I was dead.

First thing early the next morning I went to the journalism office. Dean Joseph Myers was waiting for me. I told him exactly what had happened. He didn't blame me at all. He said, "You did the right thing to keep it out of the *Lantern*."

While we were talking the phone rang and Dean Myers said, "He's here now."

And I knew who it was. It was the Dean of Women, Elizabeth Conrad. "When can you be in my office?"

I told her, "I'll be right over."

"I'm not ready for you yet. I want you at ten o'clock."

So I went over at ten o'clock. In all my life, I have never seen a stacked jury like this one. All the do-gooders in Kingdom Come: Parents-Teachers Association from Franklin County, from Worthington, from North Columbus, from South Columbus, East Columbus, West Columbus. Everyone. I tried to explain in what vein I had said it.

"That doesn't do any good," said Dean Conrad, very stern. "You know the correction never catches up with the original mistake. We are suspending you from the university for conduct detrimental to the welfare of the girls on the Ohio State campus."

I didn't graduate with my class. I spent the summer at the *Lantern*. I graduated in September, with the summer school class. It wasn't of any great concern. I was president of five graduating classes.

As soon as I got out of school, in 1923, I became sports editor of the Akron *Times-Press*, and then sports editor of the *Beacon-Journal* from September 1925 until the first day of January 1970, when I called it quits. I'm just proud enough, egotistical enough, to say that I helped build the *Beacon* to the status it has today. The *Times-Press* was within three thousand of the *Beacon*. Once I went to the *Beacon*, the *Beacon* began pulling away.

If you can end a sportswriting career embracing as many years as mine did, fifty-six years in the business, counting the *Lantern*, and can say you have never been hailed into court or been served with a paper or a threat of being sued for libel or slander or anything like that, that in itself, is a pretty fair tribute. Especially in my case. I've been told many times I was a curmudgeon, that my stuff was acerbic, sometimes nasty.

There are so many social graces and things that I lack. I don't dance. I don't golf. I've never been a party boy. I just don't fit in with a lot of crowds. I don't like to see humdrum newspaper work and I didn't want to fit into a pattern of mediocrity. I didn't try to pose and I never thought it was proper for a newspaperman, no matter how expert, to write expertly on things that the readers couldn't understand.

I wrote a lot of nice things but people don't remember nice things. They don't react to them. I wrote to be good reading. To sell newspapers. The most common thing, when I would be introduced to someone, it would always start with "I don't very often agree with what you write but I certainly find it interesting." Heavens, that was the highest compliment.

It isn't hard to be nasty. If you have to struggle to be nasty, forget it. I had a knack for it. For years and years I did a column, "The Voice from the Grandstand." The column was widely read. I got very much mail. Lots of times I deliberately gave nasty answers to people who expected sweet ones and then reversed, sweet answers to people expecting a nasty answer. I crossed them both up.

Part of it was due to the way the questions were asked. I'll give you two examples:

"Dear Jim:

"Do you know who Dale Mitchell's roommate is on the road?"

My answer: "Yes."

A woman wrote in, turned out to be a very influential woman in West Akron.

"Dear Jim:

"How many Catholics are there on the Cleveland Indians?"

My answer: "Why?"

I always got along with John S. Knight. He owned the *Beacon*. He owned other papers, too. He lived here in Akron. He wasn't pleased that I was never a golf man or a horse-race man. He mentioned a half-dozen times in print how stupid I was not to have had Scotty Reston as one of my assistants.

If you read Gay Talese's history of the *New York Times* you'll read in there that Scotty Reston was never fired. That's incorrect. I fired him. Knight had hired him to be my golf writer. Reston came out of Knight's office and into mine and he started telling me how to do things.

He said he wouldn't be coming into the office. He would telephone everything in.

I said, "Who's going to take the calls?"

"Well, you'll have to get somebody to take the calls."

I told him, "Not me, pal. You'll have to pound out your story in this office and I'll edit your copy from this office. But I'm not going to sit here wondering where you are and when you're going to call and have someone waiting for the odd chance we'll be hearing from you."

Reston had been a champion golfer at the University at Illinois and had done a short stint as the sports publicity man at Ohio State. I had nothing against him. I just knew, from the beginning, it wasn't going to work out. It was a big break for him. Years later he established himself as the brains of the *New York Times*.

Knight was big in horse racing. He had a stable, the Fourth Estate. He thought it was idiotic to simply write a straight story of the results. The six-point type told you that much, who won, finished second, prices, and so on. He sent me to the track and told me to be on the lookout for potential feature stories.

I had been on the paper three weeks. In those first three weeks, I made friends with the placement judges and others at the track. In those days we didn't have anything like a photo finish. The judges operated from a pagoda down at the finish line. As a rule, I would go down there about the fifth or sixth race, talk with them and pick up some tips for stories.

One day, in late September 1925, maybe it was the first week in October, a Sunflower entry ran 1–2 in the featured race. And I looked down the track and there was an old colored swipe bringing the two horses back to the victory circle and one of the judges said, "Jim, that man Z. Cloud is the greatest trainer of horses this track has ever known."

I thought he was pointing to that man, Z. Cloud. So that night, and I admit this was poor journalism, I wrote:

"An old Southern colored gentleman, his hair turned kinky white with the suns of possibly eighty summers, leaned against the rail yesterday afternoon at Northampton and watched his Sunflower entry run 1–2 in the feature race. He is Z. Cloud . . ." And I went on from there.

I had made a slight mistake. It was a swipe, a groom. Z. Cloud, it turned out, was a forty-three-year-old very virile, wild, full-blooded Indian.

I went up to the press box the next day, an hour or two before the first race. In those days we had a special turf edition. It came out about ten in the morning with the scratches, up-to-date entries, jockey changes, handicappers' selections. Everything. Of all our editions, this was the one that was read at the track.

And everyone around the stable area started taunting Z. Cloud: "Hiya, brother! Hey, buddy! See what the paper says."

Z. Cloud began drinking and he simply became insane. When I got to the press box, Harvey Sprowl, who was one of the veteran writers with the *Racing Form*, said, "Jim, get out of here. There's a guy looking for you. He's going to kill you. We don't want to have a murder in the press box. Don't ask any questions. Just get out of here, quick."

Well, when you don't know who's looking for you, you just don't know exactly where to go to hide. I went down to the mutuel plant and gave the signal and they opened the door into the vestibule. It wasn't much bigger than a telephone booth. The door closed automatically. I stood there wondering what this was all about. I was dumbfounded. I couldn't figure what had happened. I hadn't accused anybody of anything I could think of.

All of a sudden, bang! Somebody kicked the door off the latch, splintered the door, and in one movement hit me under the chin with a gun. My glasses went up in the air. I came down sort of half standing, half sitting, half crawling against a stack of programs that were to be sold that afternoon. I couldn't see clearly. He stuck a gun here and a gun there and pulled both triggers at the same time. Both guns misfired.

A little fellow whom I had known for a long time by the name of Al Nale had heard the noise from the door being splintered. He was at a concession stand, not very many feet away, waiting for a hot dog or something. He made a flying tackle around this fellow's legs. And at that moment, Ed Pullman, who was then the mutuel manager, knocked the guns out of his hands.

Now, I'm paralyzed. I could hardly speak.

Pullman shouted, "Cloud, what the hell is the meaning of this?"

Then I began to think. If this man is Cloud, this was not the man I wrote about. I tried to explain but it didn't do any good. Cloud was actually frothing.

They corralled him, locked him up, and sent me back to Akron. Someone told me not to worry, they would call me at the *Beacon* after every race with the results. And they would cool him off, sober him up, and the next day we could get together and straighten it out.

I didn't tell anybody at the office about it. It's time for the first race to be called in. The phone rang. I answered and somebody said, "Jim, for heaven's sake, get out of there and get away fast. Cloud has broken loose. He's headed for Akron. And he's going to kill you and he's going to kill Jack Knight. And he doesn't care which one he kills first."

So I went home. I lived in Cuyahoga Falls, a suburb of Akron. I took a back road, a very circuitous, scenic route. We had just had our first son born on the fourth of July. My wife was surprised to see me. She said, "What are you doing home?"

I told her I just wasn't feeling good. Then came a big knock on the door and I said "Will you go to the door?"

She looked at me so damn funny, as if to say, "Why don't you answer the door?"

She opened the door and there are three men who turned out to be Pinkerton men. They were sent over by the track. Then I had to tell her what had been happening. One Pinkerton kept watch on the front porch, another stationed himself at the back door. The third spent the night in the living room.

At about six o'clock Cloud shows up at the *Beacon*. At that time the *Beacon* was on the corner of East Market and Broadway. The office of the circulation department opened off Broadway. Cloud kicked the door down and went in with a couple of guns and wanted to know where Jack Knight was and where I was.

A fellow we called Ty Cobb, Lester Cowan, was in the office. Later, Cowan became a very influential movie producer in Hollywood. Cowan was counting street sales money. He thought it was a holdup. Cowan said, "What did you say your name was?"

And for the first time Cloud slowed down a little bit. Cowan said he didn't know where I lived but told him how to get to Jack Knight's house.

It was a smart thing to do because Cowan then called the police and the police called the sheriff's office and they threw a big guard around Jack Knight's house out on South Portage Pass. Then a search started at Jack Knight's house and kept narrowing down to the *Beacon* office. At three o'clock the next afternoon they found Cloud. He had collapsed thirty feet from the *Journal* building and somebody dragged him into the Ernst Inn, a rooming house for men.

The police department's ballistics expert, Bill Smith, tested both guns and explained either gun would have fired. But because Cloud pulled both triggers simultaneously, he divided the pull, divided the effort, and neither pull was substantial enough to get a perfect firing. If he had fired one gun it would have saved me a lot of typewriter ribbon and, over the years, would have saved the *Journal* reams of newsprint.

I've had other scrapes. Have you ever heard of a fighter, I imagine you did, a fellow named Kayo Christmer? He came out of the Firestone Pit back in 1928, or about then, a heavyweight who before long was fighting the top of the class, eventually fighting Jack Sharkey in Madison Square Garden to what at that time was the record fight crowd at the Garden.

Christmer fought a fellow in Canton, a heavyweight from Detroit, Jack McAuliffe. The fight was the night before the opening of the Mid-Atlantic baseball season. Akron had a team in the Mid-Atlantic League and was scheduled to open the next day at Fort Wayne. It was a stinkeroo of a fight.

Before I left Canton, Kayo Christmer asked me if I was going to the ball game tomorrow in Fort Wayne. He said, "Have you made any arrangements?" I said, "No." He said, "I'm driving over, why don't you go with me?"

I said, "Fine."

Christmer was driving a Marmon, one of the top sports cars of that era. So we came back to Akron together, I wrote my story of the fight and the next morning we drove to Fort Wayne. The game was rained out and we turned around and drove back. We didn't talk much about the fight. I deliberately didn't mention it because it was such a bad fight, so bad I spelled McAuliffe's name Jack McAwful, all through my story. I had been pretty brazen in what I said about both fighters. I thought the less said about the fight, the better.

We had an enjoyable trip together, over and back. Christmer dropped me off at the *Journal* office and went on home. Then he picked up the paper and read my story. Foolishly, I answered the phone. It was about midnight. Christmer said, "I want to see you. I'll be right down."

And he came down and just mopped up the floor with me. I spent the rest of the night under a table in my office.

There is a sequel to the story. Some years passed and Primo Carnera came through here on an exhibition tour. It was when they were building Carnera up for his fight with Sharkey. And lo and behold one of his three sparring partners turned out to be this Jack McAwful.

After the show everybody in the official entourage was to go down to Bruno's restaurant. The party was to go on until it was time for the Capitol Limited to come through Akron at 1:25 in the morning. I don't know where they were going but they were leaving Akron. When the group gathered outside the Armory there were several cabs waiting to pick everyone up.

There weren't enough cabs and so, me and my big mouth, I said, "For heaven's sake, it's only a block down the hill. What do we have to have cabs for?"

I started down the hill and had gone only a few feet when Jack McAwful fell in step with me. Of course, he didn't know me from Adam. He said, "Do you know a newspaperman in this town by the name of Schemler or something like that?"

I said, "There's a guy on the *Beacon Journal* with a name like that."

"How do you spell it?"

I spelled it for him.

"That's the guy."

"What do you want him for?"

"That no good sonofabitch. I made this trip here especially to see him. If I get my hands on him, I'll kill the guy."

I told him, "You'll have to get in line. There's a lot of people ahead of you."

I'm holding my breath. I'm afraid somebody's going to pass us and call me by name. When we got to Bruno's I waited at the door and made sure he was seated at the head table with Carnera. A lot of people in that Canal region knew me pretty well. Once Jack McAwful sat down, I ran under the bridge and down through the locks of the Ohio Canal in a way that he could never find me. I've never seen Jack McAwful since. I've often wondered whether he's still living.

I wasn't always running. I was in my room at the New Yorker Hotel covering the 1940 NCAA meetings and at the same time shilling for Paul Brown when I got a call to go up to Mr. St. John's suite. Lynn

St. John was then the athletic director at Ohio State and was with J. Lewis Morrill and Daddy French. Morrill was a vice president at Ohio State who later became president of the University of Minnesota. French was the head of the engineering school. He designed and built Ohio Stadium.

Mr. St. John had given Francis Schmidt his walking papers and was looking for a new football coach. I was carrying the torch for Paul. I had covered some of his games when he was at Massillon High School and felt that he was capable of becoming a very good college coach.

For a week, through the NCAA meetings in New York, I ate all my meals with Paul and his wife, Katie. I was protecting Paul. Coming from a small town I was afraid he wouldn't say the right thing to some of the writers. And, of course, I knew Paul's stand against tipping. He never gave more than a ten-cent tip in his life. He said the prices were high enough, that the salary of the waiter was included in the cost. I maneuvered around so I could leave a half buck next to his dime. It required considerable figuring. I had to do it without him noticing.

So I go up to St. John's suite and they put me through the third degree on Paul. Basically, the reason they fired Schmidt was because he had brought some charges against Carl Snavely, who was then coaching at Cornell. Schmidt had not accepted defeat in quite the gentlemanly manner that was expected in the Big Ten.

In questioning me on Paul, St. John finally said, "Well, how do we know your man can lose gracefully?"

And I said, "For God's sake, Mr. St. John, I thought you were looking for a successful winner, not a successful loser. If you're looking for that kind of guy, go downstairs. There's nine hundred of them down there right now. I'm talking about a man who only knows how to win."

And I went out and slammed the door.

I was waiting for the elevator when Jim Renick, he was then the sports information director at Ohio State, came running out and said, "Hold it! Hold it! Go home and write all you can. You have just hired Paul Brown. They were sitting in there looking dumbfounded at each other and Mr. St. John broke out in a big grin and said, 'Why are we looking for a successful loser?'"

So I followed Paul Brown through his career at Ohio State, only three years. I set a record in one respect. I covered fifty-one consecutive Ohio State–Michigan games, the first one on October, 23, 1919, that very first fall I was on the *Lantern*. I was in the band, played trumpet, but took notes and did a piece for the *Lantern*, not the main story but a sidebar.

Then came the tragic day. I was in Chicago and got a call with the news that Paul Brown wasn't coming back to Ohio State. He was going to be the head coach with a team in Cleveland with the All-American Conference. And Paul had great success with the Cleveland Browns. I covered those games with great delight.

I remember having breakfast with commissioner Bert Bell in the Warwick Hotel in Philadelphia on the Sunday morning after the Saturday game in which the Browns had given the Philadelphia Eagles a real shellacking, 38–7. It was in 1951, the Browns' first game after the merger of the All-America Conference and the National Football League.

Bell was astounded. He said "I walked into the dressing room after the game and they were just a bunch of guys changing clothes. There wasn't any cheering or anything like that."

"What did you expect?"

"Well, my God, winning a game like that."

I said, "That's all they've ever done. They take winning in stride."

I was a winning writer. In 1954 I wrote more winning stories than any sportswriter in the business. I covered the Cleveland Indians, the Cleveland Browns, and Ohio State. The Indians won 111 games, an American League record. I wrote every one. I missed the Ohio State game on September 25 because the Indians were still playing. Fortunately, the Giants knocked the Indians off four straight in the World Series. But Ohio State made up for it by winning the Rose Bowl and I made that one. The Browns won nine out of twelve. All told, 129 winning games out of 179 games played. It was a freak.

I don't think you'll see anybody else do that because in the big cities the baseball writers don't switch over to football. They didn't cover the major sports the way I did. I would have had a difficult time if the World Series had gone on as anticipated. It ended on October 2 and I didn't miss any football games after that.

Willie Mays's catch on Vic Wertz changed the whole doggone World Series. Johnny Antonelli would have never survived the first inning of the second game. It was unbelievable. We had beaten the

Giants with some degree of regularity in spring training. There was nothing to indicate the Indians were afraid of the Giants.

Al Lopez was a great manager. His record proves that. The year before I went through almost the entire season without speaking to him. We just had a disagreement. But after that fourth-game loss to the Giants I never felt more sorry for anyone. I've never seen a person look so much like death. You can't describe his color. There wasn't any color.

I never felt it was necessary to make too close friendships with ballplayers. I was an independent. Many players, lots of them, have been angry with me. Ken Keltner, in particular. Some of the things I wrote about him would have given him a very good reason for taking a punch at me. Later, he turned out to be a wonderful friend, a close friend.

There is no animosity at all, not now. But I used him as a focal point in attacks against these money-mad ballplayers. You may recall the year he sued the State of Ohio for unemployment compensation. He claimed he was normally employed by the Cleveland Baseball Club but was unemployed from early October until April. And he sued for public tax money. I gave him hell in the paper. Even while the salaries weren't comparable to what they are today neither was anything else.

In 1948, the pennant year, when he had to go to Boston for the Monday playoff game, Keltner was the drunkest I've seen, ever known. I wrote my story in my roomette but was afraid to walk out. Even if Keltner was sober it woud have been a risk. Somebody would have said, "Hey, there's that no good so-and-so." That could have been enough to take a swing at me.

I finally managed to open the door far enough. I called Steve Gromek over and told him what my problem was. He said, "You're smart not going out there because you can't tell what Keltner or any of the rest of them might do to you." So I gave Steve my copy. I don't think he got it into Western Union's hands until Springfield, Massachusetts, but it got to the paper in time.

I covered the Indians for many years. There was always something new every day. Bill Veeck was the greatest showman in baseball history. But I enjoyed covering a lot of things. For years, from 1933 through 1949, I was the assistant general manager of the All-American Soap Box Derby. It was a *Beacon-Journal* promotion, one of my prize projects, the greatest boys' event of its kind that ever came down the pike.

The thing that put it across, the biggest boost we had, was in 1934. Tom Manning, a Cleveland announcer, and the world-famous Graham McNamee were the broadcasters. We were running on a little hill in East Akron. This was the year before Derby Downs was built. The rules were the same then as they are now: no race can start until the track is absolutely clear.

Before the final championship race Manning and McNamee were standing inside the kickboards. I hurried down from the control bridge and told them we couldn't get the race under way. And McNamee said, "Listen, buddy, I have broadcast from submarines deep in the ocean. I have broadcast from blimps and airplanes high in the sky. I have broadcast from the rear end of a racing automobile in Indianapolis. And I don't think I'm going to be/injured by a kiddie car."

It was an insult. We never used the words "kiddie car." These cars were built by boys. You could run with wheels off a lawnmower or anything like that so long as they weren't bicycle wheels. A boy by the name of Norman Brown from Oklahoma City was one of the finalists. He had expected to run on asphalt and found that our shoulders were paved in brick. He had wheels off a wagon with steel treads, no rubber. He wrapped the tread with tire tape to absorb some of the shock.

Just before he reached terminal velocity—it was a free-wheeling downhill event—about sixty or seventy feet from the finish line the tape wore off. He overcontrolled, cut diagonally across the track, and he smacked into Manning and McNamee. They were off the track behind the kickboard. It couldn't have started with them inside.

They had to be taken to the hospital. And the next morning, newspapers from all over the world, on page one, reported that Graham McNamee, the world's best-known announcer, had been injured by a Soap Box Derby racer. Editors from all over the country called our city editor and asked, "What the hell is a Soap Box Derby?"

A woman ruined it. She sued because her daughter was not allowed in the Soap Box Derby. A year ago there were eight city champions, girls, who came to Akron. But you can't have girls in a boys' event. What happened was that in the cities where boys were beaten out by girls, those boys suffered so much loss of pride they wouldn't think of competing again. The whole thing has dropped from eight hundred cities to fewer than two hundred this year. I stopped going when they allowed the girls to come in.

My three daughters-in-law raise the dickens with me for that kind of an attitude. For years and years, I was one of the leaders of keeping women out of the press box. The press box is one of the last few male preserves. Or it was. Women just don't belong there, any more than I belong at some tea party. They should be home doing the laundry and baking cookies.

About the Author

Jerome Holtzman is the baseball columnist and national baseball writer for the Chicago *Tribune*. He joined the *Tribune* in 1981 after thirty-eight years at the Chicago *Sun-Times* and the *Daily Times*, its predecessor. He started as a sports department copy boy at seventeen. He served two years in the Marine Corps during World War II and upon his return covered high school sports. He was assigned to the baseball beat in 1957 and traveled with the Cubs and White Sox for more than a quarter century. The *Wall Street Journal*, in a 1984 article, described him as "the quintessential baseball writer."

In addition to his newspaper work, Mr. Holtzman has authored three books, more than one hundred magazine stories and the twenty-thousand-word entry on Baseball in the *Encyclopedia Britannica*, to which he still serves as a consultant. For many years he wrote the summary of each season for the *Official Baseball Guide*. His byline appeared in more than a thousand consecutive issues of the weekly *Sporting News*, possibly an "iron-man" record.

Mr. Holtzman has also been the patron saint of the bullpen. Aware that earned run averages and won-loss records were not an accurate index of the effectiveness of relief pitchers, he created the first nationally accepted formula for "saves." Seven years later, in 1966, it was adopted by the Official Rules Committee, the first new major statistic since runs batted in was added in 1920.

A native Chicagoan, he has been married to the former Marilyn Ryan for forty-six years and has four children and four grandchildren. He attended Northwestern University and the University of Chicago and has won three Stick o' Type awards from the Chicago Newspaper Guild. Mr. Holtzman was inducted into the writers' wing of the Baseball Hall of Fame in Cooperstown, New York, in 1990.